How to Use This Book

This guide is made up of data-packed chapters that provide the kind of practical information you need to enjoy the Greater Charleston area. The early chapters of this book are generally focused on tourism, history, and attractions. This information is useful to visitors (and residents alike) who want to know more about the city and the surrounding area. Starting with Relocation, the latter chapters are especially helpful to newcomers who have decided to make the Lowcountry their permanent home.

If you are planning a visit or move to Charleston, surf the chapters to make contacts ahead of time. If you are already here or on your way to the city, flip to the Getting Here, Getting Around section of the Welcome to Greater Charleston chapter to determine the best route to your desired destinations, or flip to our Accommodations chapter for information on lodging. And if you have arrived and are carrying the book around as a reference tool, just zip to a particular chapter to find the best or closest restaurants, entertainment, recreation, shopping, and attractions. The index at the back of the book can help you pinpoint a specific subject or place quickly and easily.

Up front, we've provided area maps to help you get your bearings here in the Lowcountry. We give you brief vital statistics, Insiders' Tips (indicated by

South Carolina state flag

) and sidebars for quick insights, and more lengthy Close-ups with information that is particularly interesting, unusual, and distinctly Charlestonian. You'll also find listings accompanied by the ★ symbol—these are our top picks for attractions, restaurants, accommodations, and everything in between that you shouldn't miss while you're in the area. You want the best this region has to offer? Go with our Insiders' Choice.

The chapter called Kids is offered as a collection of some of our favorite ways to show your children a healthy good time. It is a subjective overview of venues and activities that have afforded us hours of fun with children we know.

You will notice that throughout the guide we refer to four main general areas—downtown Charleston, east of the Cooper (River), west of the Ashley (River), and the western islands. Downtown includes the Peninsula and the area slightly north; east of the Cooper includes Mount Pleasant, Sullivan's Island, and Isle of Palms; west of the Ashley refers to the area just across the Ashley River bridges. The western islands are James, Johns, Folly, Kiawah, and Seabrook.

Within chapters such as Dining, Entertainment, and Accommodations, expect to find geographical subcategories for your convenience. Further, Shopping is organized to benefit two broad categories of readers. We start with a rundown for tourists and visitors who want to explore the major shopping venues downtown. We organize the shopping opportunities by merchandise categories.

Moving to the Charleston area or already live here? Be sure to check out the Living Here appendix that offers sections on relocation, retirement, and media.

Whether you're a visitor to Charleston or you've chosen to live here, we hope this guide proves helpful in many ways.

Doors of Charleston

Welcome to Greater Charleston, where three South Carolina counties—Charleston, Berkeley, and Dorchester—blend together and create the scenic backdrop for a unique and wonderful lifestyle.

This is a land of history, the home of Revolutionary statesmen. This is a city of gallantry, glory, folly, and pain—where democracy was nurtured and secession proclaimed. This is where, very early on, beauty was deemed as important as survival, whatever the cost. Pride was encouraged. Families were sacrosanct, and God was dutifully acknowledged in mind and matter.

The sociopolitical passions and turbulent economies that made Charleston such a fascinating place 200 years ago are still very much with us today. Only now the canvas is larger, the paintbrush wider, and Charleston's colorful story just gets bolder as the years go by.

One of the reasons Charleston seems so timeless has to do with geography. The historic Peninsula (the heart of Charleston's identity) is bound by two rivers, the Ashley and the Cooper. Despite whatever else those rivers have meant to Charleston and its people over time, the waters effectively impounded the 18th-century city. This watery restraint forced all real growth and change northward—pushing it upward, spilling it over onto neighboring lands. Even today, neighborhoods that were built "east Cooper" or "west Ashley" always carry the unspoken phrase "of the Peninsula" and bear indirect witness to the old city's powerful presence.

The natural containment of the Ashley and Cooper Rivers (effectively protecting the Peninsula from change) had an accomplice in the Lowcountry itself. The southeastern third of South Carolina is physically low, close to sea level, prone to swampland, marsh, and innumerable shallow creeks and streams. The land was hostile toward early settlers and planters, and it was costly to railroad builders and almost every other developer. It didn't welcome growth, and it resists change to this day.

In many ways Charleston was isolated and remained something of a cultural island while America pushed westward into its destiny. Charleston and its captive Peninsula effectively stayed behind, surrounded by its many coastal distractions.

As it has for eons, the endless marsh seems to change color every day. Unspoiled beaches can be caught playing tag with a restless (occasionally punishing) sea. Charlestonians know that not far away they can find dark and mysterious swamps that, in certain moonlight, whisper primordial secrets in the native tongue of an ancient higher power.

If this is isolation, then it's splendid isolation. This is the Lowcountry: a place, a people, a unique perspective on the world.

Is it any wonder we love living here?

AREA OVERVIEW

Year after year, Charleston has been recognized in popular tourist magazines as one of the top 10 domestic travel destinations. In 2012 *Conde Nast Traveler* brought international attention naming Charleston as the world's number-one destination. It's also been proclaimed by etiquette guru Marjabelle Young Stewart as the "most mannerly" city in America. We hope that will turn out to be your experience as well.

Here's an overview of Charleston and the surrounding area. This chapter is arranged in the geographical order used throughout this book and offers some information that will provide a peek at what's here now to see and enjoy.

Charleston

Exactly 768 miles from New York City, 590 miles from Miami, and almost 2,500 miles from Los Angeles, Charleston remains an undeniably livable city for those fortunate enough to call it home. It's a city of unhurried grace and distinct Southern charm, blessed with an uncanny number of historic structures, many of which have been transformed into handsome offices, restaurants, stores, and homes.

Charleston is the second-largest city in South Carolina (Greenville takes first place). The city's 2010 Census Bureau count was 120,083. In 2012, that estimate had jumped to 125,583. The city's Standard Metropolitan Statistical Area encompasses three counties: Charleston, Berkeley, and Dorchester. This is sometimes called the "Tri-County Area" or the "Trident Area," and in 2010, the population of this area totaled 664,607. By 2012, the estimated total was 697,439.

Charleston has a warm climate. In January the average temperature is 50 degrees; in July, it's 82. It's prudent to note that summertime temperatures can peak above the 100-degree mark, and the humidity, which is considerable in the Lowcountry during any season, makes the hot seem hotter and the cold colder. Spring in Charleston, however, more than compensates for any discomfort during the other seasons. Many consider it the best time of year in the area; days are warm, nights barely chilled, and the whole world appears to be dripping in wisteria vines and azalea blossoms.

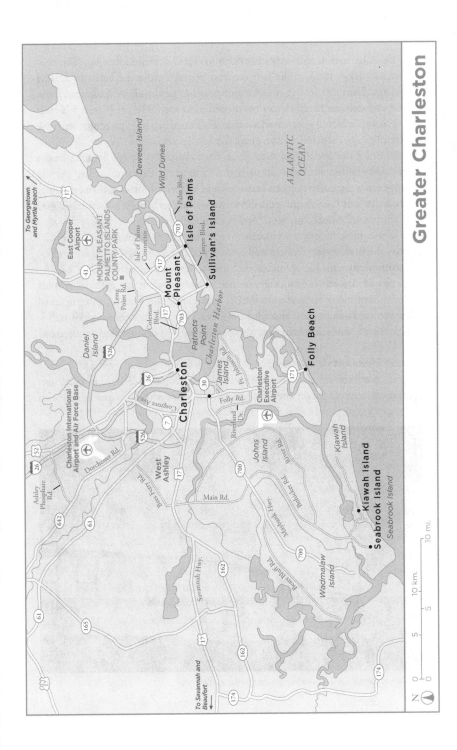

Greater Charleston

The Charleston economy continues to be sound and growing. The economic activity is most evident in the vast, newly connected lands of Daniel Island and Cainhoy. Just to the east and north of peninsular Charleston, these areas were annexed in 1991 to the city of Charleston. Daniel Island, which is 4,500 acres, is now being developed as a planned, environmentally sensitive community. (See the Relocation chapter.)

In 2012 the South Carolina State Ports Authority (SPA) handled more than $63.6 billion in cargo through the Charleston customs facility. As the eighth-largest cargo port in the nation (and still the fourth-largest container port on the East Coast), the port directly and indirectly provides over 260,800 jobs with an economic impact of $45 billion each year.

Throughout its history, Charleston has stood as the cultural capital of the South. The performing arts are well represented here, with a symphony orchestra, community theater groups, and several dance companies. The Gibbes Museum of Art and a growing number of independent art galleries display the city's impressive appreciation for the visual arts. The abundant examples of architectural preservation, showing the city's long-standing heritage of building excellence and craftsmanship, also bear witness to this aesthetic awareness.

Mount Pleasant

Anyone who crosses the Cooper River via the Ravenel Bridge into Mount Pleasant will never forget the journey. Directly across the Cooper River from

Arthur Ravenel Jr. Cooper River Suspension Bridge

Charleston, Mount Pleasant dates its founding to 1680. The original heart of Mount Pleasant is the area known as the Old Village. It is designated a National Register Historic District, with its gracious homes from both the colonial and antebellum periods. Today, the city carefully preserves its rich heritage and small-town appeal. The 2010 Census count for Mount Pleasant was 67,843 (a 42.5 percent jump from the 2000 Census figures). Estimates for 2012 were 71,875.

The population numbers for this thriving community certainly qualify it as a "city." But, as the name implies, the "town" of Mount Pleasant is an apt description for the state of mind and the attitude of the businesses you'll find there. Although it serves as a major bedroom community to the Charleston Peninsula, it's still a viable community unto itself.

The days when Mount Pleasant residents were dependent on the Peninsula for primary shopping, dining, and entertainment venues are gone. Mount Pleasant's $40 million Towne Centre is clear proof of that, with its 15 separate buildings housing about 65 tenants within 425,000 square feet of upscale shopping space.

Patriots Point, the world's largest naval and maritime museum complex, is Mount Pleasant's biggest attraction. It is dominated by the aircraft carrier *Yorktown*, World War II's famous "Fighting Lady." You can also board tour boats at Patriots Point to visit Fort Sumter National Monument, where the Civil War began. (See the Attractions and Tours chapters.)

Adjacent to Patriots Point is Patriots Point Links, one of the area's most popular public golf courses. The 18-hole, par 72 layout provides spectacular views of Charleston Harbor and the Peninsula's skyline. (See the Golf chapter.) The Mount Pleasant Visitor Center at 99 Harry J. Hallman Jr. Blvd. off Coleman Boulevard is a good place to start when exploring Mount Pleasant.

Sullivan's Island

South of Mount Pleasant and across the Intracoastal Waterway, Sullivan's Island is one of Mount Pleasant's three true barrier islands (Isle of Palms and the private island of Dewees are the other two). Access to the island is via the Ben Sawyer Causeway (SR 703) from Mount Pleasant or via the Isle of Palms Connector (SR 517) through the Isle of Palms.

Largely a quiet, residential island of old and new beach houses, the island's estimated population in 2012 was 1,791. There is also a smattering of charming 19th-century "summer homes" that have somehow managed to survive the hurricanes and changing fashions of vacation architecture. The few restaurants and pubs on the island are crowded along Middle Street and create something of a strip for strollers who might want to "pub hop" during the evening hours.

Sullivan's Island is the site of old Fort Moultrie and its accompanying interpretation center, which is operated by the National Park Service. There you can trace the fort's history from the American Revolution through World War II. (See Forts in the Attractions chapter.)

Another interesting by-product of Sullivan's Island's military days is the fine old row of quarters (not far from the lighthouse) that date back to World War I. Still standing at attention along a quiet side street is a handsome line of large frame houses that once served as "officers' row" for the garrison at Fort Moultrie. Now private homes, these former examples of elite military housing speak eloquently of another time from the island's (and our country's) past.

Isle of Palms

Over the years, the Isle of Palms has grown increasingly popular as a resort and residential island. In 2012, the estimated population was 4,133. But when you throw in the seasonal renters and the day visitors, the island can host thousands of additional people on any given summer day. Its proximity to Charleston is one of the reasons; its 6 miles of wide, sparkling beach are another attraction.

Those who are here for the short term can enjoy a wide range of accommodations from one end of the island to the other. The island also has a full complement of shops, restaurants, goods, and services to make life very comfortable.

World-famous Wild Dunes Resort, at the northeast end of the island, offers fine restaurants, conference facilities, a fitness center, multiple tennis courts, and two championship Tom Fazio–designed golf courses. Wild Dunes is a busy destination all year long. (See the Relocation and Accommodations chapters.) The Wild Dunes Yacht Harbor is one of the finest marinas on the Eastern Seaboard. Maybe best of all, Wild Dunes is still only 15 miles from downtown Charleston, offering visitors the chance to enjoy the best of both worlds.

North Charleston

North Charleston, incorporated only in 1972, is geographically the third-largest city in South Carolina, with an estimated population of 97,471. Its reputation as the hub of the Lowcountry is justified; it's clearly the business and transportation center for the lower half of the state. The international airport and the Amtrak station are here. Also, I-26 and the Mark Clark Expressway (I-526) make getting anywhere in the Lowcountry a snap. (See the Getting Here, Getting Around section in this chapter.)

Once known as the location of Charleston's huge naval facility, North Charleston has outgrown that economic dependency. One of the city's main attractions is the Charleston Area Convention Center Complex, which includes the 14,000-seat Coliseum and the 2,250-seat Performing Arts Center. These state-of-the-art venues draw crowds from all over the area and host a wide variety of events ranging from Broadway shows to major rock concerts and ice shows. The Coliseum is also the home of the South Carolina Stingrays, our local ice hockey team.

Not only does the area have more than 6,000 hotel rooms, but the rates are also generally lower than those found elsewhere in the Lowcountry (especially downtown Charleston). This makes North Charleston a favorite haunt for business types and convention travelers. If you're arriving via I-26, you may want to stop at the North Charleston Visitor Center just across from the Coliseum.

Berkeley County

In the 1980s, Berkeley County, just north of Charleston County, was the fastest-growing county in all of South Carolina. The boom came when major new industrial concerns invested more than $1.7 billion in the county economy.

The greatest concentration of population and residential and commercial development has been in the southern portion of the county near Moncks Corner. Berkeley's central town, however, remains Goose Creek. Other county towns include Hanahan and St. Stephen. Total population of these towns is more than 68,000, according to recent estimates.

Currently, industrial development is concentrated along US 52 north of Goose Creek and on the island formed by the Cooper River and the Black River and its tributary branches. The major Berkeley County employers are Naval Weapons Station Charleston and Nucor Steel.

Much of the northern portion of Berkeley County is still productive, cultivated farmland. Most of the eastern portion of the county and large areas of the west remain as beautiful pine forests—one of the county's most distinctive features.

Dorchester County

Dorchester's $127 million in economic development in recent years largely came from the expansion of existing industries. The major employers in Dorchester County include the Robert Bosch Corp. (antilock braking systems) and Showa Denko Carbon, Inc. (graphite electrodes for the steel industry). Although St. George, with its estimated 2012 population of 2,127, is the county seat, the part of Dorchester County currently seeing the greatest amount of economic growth is Summerville. With a 2012 estimated population of 44,719, the town's healthy mix of retail, commercial, and tourist-related businesses, along

Charleston Index

- Population:
  City of Charleston: 120,083 (in 2010)
  Metro Area: 664,607 in 2010
  South Carolina: 4,625,364 in 2010

- Area (square miles):
  City of Charleston: 88.14 square miles
  Business district: 7.6 square miles
  South Carolina: 31,113 square miles

- Nickname/Motto: "The Holy City"

- Translation of Latin motto from the city's official seal:
  Aedes Mora Juraque Curat, "She guards her buildings, her customs, and her laws."

- Average temperatures: Jan: 50°F July: 82°F

- Average rainfall: 51 inches per year

- City/state founded:
  First English colony of Carolina founded: 1670
  Officially separated as Royal Colony of South Carolina: 1729
  Incorporated as City of Charleston: 1783

- South Carolina's major cities: Columbia (state capital), Charleston, Florence, Georgetown, Greenville, Hilton Head, Mount Pleasant, Myrtle Beach, North Charleston, Spartanburg, Sumter

- Major colleges/universities: Charleston Southern University, College of Charleston/University of Charleston, The Citadel, Trident Technical College, Medical University of South Carolina, Charleston School of Law

- Important dates in history:
1670	Founding of Charles Towne colony
1680	Colony moved to safer location on peninsula
1719	Revolt leading to establishment of South Carolina as province of British Crown

1783	Newly liberated city changes name to "Charleston"
1822	Denmark Vesey slave uprising
1861	Outbreak of War between the States
1886	The Great Earthquake
1904	Construction of US Navy Yard
1977	Debut of Spoleto Festival USA
1989	Devastation by Hurricane Hugo

- Major area employers: Medical University of South Carolina, Joint Base Charleston, Charleston County School District, Roper St. Francis Healthcare, Berkeley County School District, JEM Restaurant Group, Trident Health System, Dorchester County School District II, Boeing South Carolina, Walmart

- Major airports/interstates: Charleston International Airport; I-26; I-526; Public transportation: CARTA (bus system); DASH (downtown area shuttle)

- Military bases: Charleston Air Force Base (437th Airlift Wing) and 315th Airlift Wing (Reserves); US Coast Guard Group Charleston Station; Naval Weapons Station Charleston

- Driving laws: Right turn on red permitted; seatbelts must be worn at all times in moving vehicle; headlights must be on when wipers are used; speed limit on state highways is 55 mph; speed limit on interstates is 70 mph in designated limited-access areas.

- Alcohol laws: Legal drinking age is 21 years; blood-alcohol content of .08 percent or higher is DUI in South Carolina, but lower percentages can also be designated DUI at arresting officer's discretion.

- Daily newspaper: *The Post and Courier;* daily circulation, 85,037; Sunday, 93,577

- Sales tax: 8.5 percent city/state sales tax (1 percent sales tax discount for citizens age 85 and over), 14.5 percent city/state accommodations tax with light manufacturing concerns, seems to be attracting both newcomers and business investors.

West Ashley

The City of Charleston annexed its first West Ashley tract in 1960, and the area has been growing ever since. The population figure for this area is more than 60,000 according to recent estimates.

West Ashley is a patchwork of old and new neighborhoods and businesses that line the major traffic arteries (US 17 S. and SR 61). Many of the older neighborhoods have graceful old live oaks and spacious, well-tended lawns. And please note, the local residents don't live in West Ashley or at West Ashley, they simply "live West Ashley."

West Ashley is home to Charles Towne Landing State Historic Site, a nature/historic theme park on the site of the original English settlement. It also claims the beautiful Ashley River Road, which leads to Drayton Hall, Magnolia Gardens, and Middleton Place (see Historic Plantations in the Attractions chapter). You'll find Charleston's largest shopping center—Citadel Mall, with well over 100 tenants—in West Ashley. The area also has the "Automile," a strip of new and used car dealerships along Savannah Highway (US 17 S.) and one of the major engines of the local economy.

By far, the largest employer West Ashley (you'll get used to saying it that way) is Bon Secours–St. Francis Hospital. This huge, 32-acre medical complex added 875 new jobs to the area economy, and many other spin-off businesses have followed suit.

James Island & Johns Island

Geographically, James Island, which lies due west of the Charleston Peninsula, is less rural than Johns Island. It is essentially a bedroom community for Charleston, with many shopping strips scattered along the main roads of Maybank Highway and Folly Road.

What remains of James Island's rural character may be threatened by the easy access now made possible by the James Island Expressway (SR 30). This increasingly busy roadway connecting the island to the Peninsula is fueling rapid development—especially along Folly Road toward Folly Beach. The remaining tracts of farmland are likely victims of rising land values and are prime targets for real estate developers.

While Johns Island may be still agricultural in appearance, change is in the air. A recent study showed that Johns Island was home to more than half of the nearly 2,000 people employed on the resort islands of Kiawah and Seabrook (plus most of the 400 more who work there during the busy season). After the opening of The Sanctuary, Kiawah's hotel and spa, the number of James and Johns Island employees jumped considerably.

Folly Beach

This eccentric and diverse beach town likes to call itself "the edge of America." Only 10 minutes from historic Charleston, this is a tourist's world—one where there's plenty to see and do.

First of all, there's the beach—Folly's claim to fame. It runs almost 6 miles along the Atlantic side of the island. Folly has had serious erosion problems in the past. Periodically the beach is "renourished" by mechanically pumping millions of cubic yards of sand back onto the shore. But there's always plenty of sand, sun, fun, and (yes) folly to go around.

The island has a year-round estimated population of 2,617. But the population swells enormously on any summer day, when the hordes of beach lovers, young and old, come out to play. Employment opportunities are almost exclusively limited to the tourist trade.

Crabbing, sunning, surfing, swimming, surf fishing, biking, waterskiing, and sailing are going on nearly year-round. You name it, Folly Beach has it. Folly touts its 1,000-foot fishing pier, complete with snack bar, tackle shop, and full-service seafood restaurant. The pier is reminiscent of the old days when beach pavilions were all the rage for dance bands and swing music. Although there are walk-throughs along the beach that lead from Arctic and Ashley Avenues to the surf for day visitors, it's best to go to the west end of the island and visit Folly Beach County Park. Admission is $7 a vehicle ($10 on summer weekends), but once you're inside, you've got restrooms, showers, drinking water, limited parking, and probably the best open vistas on the island.

You'll find many reasonable short-term accommodations at Folly Beach. There are also seasonal rentals and a lot of interesting full-time residents on the island. It is Charleston's truly original beach playground. (See the Accommodations chapter.)

Kiawah Island

Only 21 miles from Charleston is Kiawah Island, renowned for its natural beauty and environmentally responsible development. The endless acres of marsh, the 10 miles of pristine Atlantic beach, the thick forests, and abundant wildlife are only the beginning. Among all this are championship golf, first-rate tennis, exclusive shopping, and fine dining. Like the beach itself, the opportunities for enjoyment here go on and on.

Golfers have a selection of courses to play. They can choose from Turtle Point by Jack Nicklaus, Cougar Point by Gary Player, Tom Fazio's Osprey Point, and the famed Ocean Course by Pete Dye (site of the memorable 1991 Ryder Cup). (See the Golf chapter for more details.) In November 1997, the Ocean Course hosted the 43rd World Cup of Golf with teams from 32 nations competing. Televised in more than 80 countries, this was the world's most-watched golf tournament to date. In fall 2003, the World Cup returned with 24 nations participating in this much-heralded international golf championship. More excitement returned with the Senior PGA Championship in 2007. The latest major event was the PGA Championship in 2012. Also on Kiawah, tennis buffs have two complete tennis centers with fully staffed pro shops and extensive instructional facilities.

The island's accommodations are all outstanding. Some guests prefer being pampered at The Sanctuary, the island's hotel and convention facility with luxury spa, which opened in 2004. Others prefer the privacy of furnished villas or cottages conveniently scattered around the island. Bear in mind that Kiawah Island is a private community with access limited to property owners, guests of the resort, or designated rental agencies. Full-time residents number 1,626, according to the 2010 census. But seasonal visitors swell this number to more than 7,000. Public access to the beach is available at Beachwalker County Park at the west end of the island. (See the Relocation, Accommodations, and Golf chapters.) For more about Kiawah, start at the Kiawah Island Visitor Center at 22 Beachwalker Dr., open from 9 a.m. to 3 p.m. Mon through Fri.

Seabrook Island

Seabrook Island is on the Atlantic shore just 22 miles south of Charleston. It is unique in that it is totally private and completely owned by its residents. Entry to the island is controlled by a security gate for the privacy of residents and guests. The beauty of the island is striking. Visitors can enjoy 3.5 miles of unspoiled beach along the Atlantic and the banks of the Edisto River, which flows into the ocean at Seabrook.

The Club at Seabrook offers championship golf courses: Crooked Oaks, designed by Robert Trent Jones Sr., and Ocean Winds, designed by Willard Byrd. (See the Golf chapter.) A beach club, a tennis center, and a beautiful Island House Club with restaurants, bar lounges, and a golf pro shop are here. Also unique to Seabrook is its equestrian center.

The island has more than 450 villas available for rent as well as more than 1,700 permanent residents, whose homes are situated along the beach, marshes, lakes, and golf courses.

Bohicket Marina, just outside the Seabrook Island gate, is a superb marina with dockominiums plus an attractive shopping area. About 60 rental slips are available for all sizes of motor cruisers and sailboats. Boat rentals and charters for deep-sea fishing, crabbing, shrimping, or exploring the miles of ocean creeks are also available. (See the Boating & Water Sports chapter.)

GETTING HERE, GETTING AROUND

Visitors to the Trident area who arrive via different modes of transportation are faced with challenges unique to each form. For instance, if you drive, fly, ride the bus, or take the train, how are you going to negotiate the trip into town or—worse yet—out to the fringes? Say you come in on a yacht, or you are a passenger on a cruise ship. What next?

We've answered these questions individually, and the headings identify each transportation mode.

Getting Here by Auto

Thankfully, travel accompanied by GPS has simplified directions into and around Charleston by car. Or local area maps show the major routes for entering the Charleston area such as I-26, I-526, US 52, US 78, US 17 N., US 17 S., and SR 61 (see our maps). With heavy seasonal traffic (in spring, as many as half a million visitors come to Charleston by car), seemingly constant road and bridge work, and a peculiar system of one-way city streets, getting around Charleston is not always simple on first try. A new DASH route serving this area makes a continuous loop from the visitor center around King, Broad, East Bay, Market, and Meeting Streets and, best of all, is free.

> **i** Beware! Many Charleston streets and alleys are one way. With so many interesting distractions vying for your attention, it's easy to miss the signs. So keep a lookout and be careful.

Also, parking is always a problem. The city has made strides toward managing the situation to the benefit of both residents and tourists, with restricted parking hours in residential neighborhoods and parking garages for public use. Metered parking spaces are limited but convenient when you can find them. To avoid costly tickets, a parking garage is your safest bet (see City & County Parking Facilities later in this chapter).

Downtown Charleston

Take a Number

Bombarded by highway designations that seem to be blurring into one another? Confused by well-meaning Lowcountry direction givers who throw out numbers faster than a lottery-ball machine? Take heart! Below is a brief listing of highways and connectors that are often referred to by locals without the state or US prefixes.

For cross-referencing ease and your information, please note these numbers, with a few of their local incarnations:

US 17 N. (the Crosstown, the Bypass, Johnnie Dodds Boulevard, Georgetown Highway)

US 17 S. (Savannah Highway)

US 52 (Rivers Avenue)

US 78 (Summerville Highway)

SR 7 (Sam Rittenberg Boulevard, Cosgrove Avenue)

SR 30 (James Island Expressway)

SR 517 (Isle of Palms Connector)

SR 700 (Maybank Highway)

SR 703 (Coleman, Ben Sawyer, Jasper, and Palm Boulevards)

SR 61 (St. Andrews Boulevard, Ashley River Road)

SR 171 (Folly Road)

I-526 (Mark Clark Expressway)

Remember, don't be afraid to ask for specifics. When true Insiders are pressed for directions, they can almost always find a way to shepherd you from point A to point B.

Getting Here by Air

Charleston is more accessible than ever by air. The Trident area boasts a full-service international airport with major carriers taking off and touching down throughout the day. Major national rental car agencies service the airport, limousine and shuttle services are available, and the terminal has a 1,200-space covered parking garage, plus additional surface parking on-site.

There are also four Lowcountry locations serving the needs of private pilots; one is an auxiliary service of the Charleston International Airport. All are reasonably convenient to the downtown area, and specific amenities are noted below.

Major Airport Service

CHARLESTON INTERNATIONAL AIRPORT, 5500 International Blvd., North Charleston; (843) 767-1100, (843) 767-7009; chs-airport.com. This 280,000-square-foot facility has 10 gates, all served by covered loading bridges. The walking distance from the terminal entrance to the remotest aircraft gate is only about 800 feet. The international area and customs service inspection area have 25,000 square feet of space and process international passengers quickly. Currently, the airport is undergoing phased renovations to add an additional baggage carousel and five new gates along with other improvements. If you're interested in business opportunities at Charleston International Airport, contact the Aviation Authority Development Office at (843) 767-7000 or visit chs-airport.com.

Flight Information

Major airlines serving the Trident's international flight facility include American, (800) 433-7300 (reservations), (800) 535-5225 (baggage); Delta, (800) 221-1212 (reservations), (800) 325-8224 (baggage); JetBlue, (800) 538-2583 (reservations), (866) 538-5438 (baggage); Southwest Airlines, (800) 435-9792 (reservations and baggage); United, (800) 241-6522 (reservations), (800) 335-2247 (baggage); and USAirways, (800) 428-4322 (reservations), (800) 371-4771 (baggage).

The number to call if you want to check an arrival time for an incoming flight is (843) 767-7009. Checking before leaving for the airport can save time and frustration. The airport's information desk always has the most updated flight schedule data available.

Rental Cars/Parking

Chances are your preferred rental car service has an airport outlet in Charleston. The five national companies that serve the airport are Avis, (800) 331-1212 or (843) 767-7031; Budget, (800) 527-0700 or (843) 767-7051; Enterprise, (800) 261-7331 or (843) 767-4557; Hertz, (800) 654-3131 or (843) 767-4550; and National, (800) 227-7368 or (843) 767-3078.

The terminal parking facility offers 1,200 covered spaces for a fee of $15 per day. A surface lot slightly farther away from the terminal offers additional parking at $8 per day. Thirty minutes of parking in both areas is free. A free cell phone waiting area is available for persons picking up travelers who call once they have exited the terminal. A valet parking service is available from 5 a.m. to 1 a.m. (or until the last flight arrives) 7 days a week for $15 per day and can be reached at (843) 767-0990.

Getting to the Airport

As a simple rule of thumb, plan on allowing at least a half hour to get to the airport if you're driving from downtown Charleston. Allow even more time during rush hours or on busy holiday travel dates. You may want to call ahead and get time allowances for security procedures.

Take I-26 west (toward Columbia). Exit off I-26 at exit 212-B marked Airport and I-526 Savannah. Continue approximately a mile on I-526 (toward Savannah), and exit at the Montague Avenue exit. A sign will also read Trident Research Authority, Coliseum, and Airport. Turn right at the light (at the exit to International Boulevard), and continue approximately 1.5 miles to the terminal.

If you are driving south toward the city on I-26, take the Mark Clark Expressway (I-526) exit. The airport exit off this highway is clearly marked, and you'll again head into the terminal area via International Boulevard.

For local residents and those who need ground transportation to the airport from downtown or other locations, there's a central phone number through the Charleston Aviation Authority that will redirect your call to the next available option. Call (800) 750-1311 or (843) 607-5456 for this airport limousine/taxi pick-up information.

Another option for transportation both to and from the airport to the visitor center at Meeting and Mary Streets downtown is to catch route 11 "Dorchester/Airport" on the CARTA bus system (see "Public Transportation" later in the chapter). For schedules check out ridecarta.com.

Taxi, Limo & Shuttle Service from the Airport

Several Charleston area hotels, motels, and bed-and-breakfast inns offer shuttle service to and from the airport. Check with your reservation agent, your inn's concierge, or your hotel for specific details. Near the baggage carousel, you'll find a lighted courtesy board showing several of the area's better hotels, motels, and bed-and-breakfast inns. The attached phone offers speed-dial service to those places offering airport pick-up service.

If you're left to your own resources for transportation into the city, you have a couple of options. Outside the baggage claim area, across the pick-up zone, is a small booth offering taxi and limo (van) rides to Lowcountry destinations. Various cab companies, as a service of the Aviation Authority, take turns picking up fares from this booth. Here's the gist: If you are in a great hurry, a taxi will take you immediately at a metered rate of $2.52 a mile for the first two passengers. Additional passengers will pay $14 each. The average ride from the airport to a downtown hotel will be around $29 to $34. If you're willing to i One way to avoid the somewhat pricey long-term parking fees at Charleston International Airport is to use one of the off-site parking facilities nearby that can deliver you to the front door of the airport in time for your flight and safely store your car while you're gone. Upon return, just call their shuttle for a quick ride to the lot, where your car will be ready and waiting for you. One of the best options is Park & Go, at 3621 West Montague Ave. Call (843) 302-2288, (866) 727-5275, or visit park-go.com for rates and information.

wait about 15 minutes, you can catch a shuttle (really a van) with several other passengers at a much-discounted rate of $14 per person.

Passengers heading to the nearby Charleston Air Force Base can catch an immediate taxi for around $14. A trip for one or two to Kiawah or Seabrook by taxi is about $73 or $75, respectively, for the 30-mile journey. Those heading for Wild Dunes can expect to pay about $59. Other approximate fares are available on charleston-arrives.com. If you want private limousine service and make reservations in advance, you can choose from a number of limousine companies available in the Lowcountry. (See the "Limousines" listing later in this chapter.)

Private Plane Service
Greater Charleston offers four options for private pilots, all convenient and uncongested.

ATLANTIC AVIATION (NORTH CHARLESTON), 6060 South Aviation Ave., North Charleston; (843) 746-7600; atlanticaviation.com. Just across the runway from the Charleston Air Force Base, off Aviation Avenue at Charleston International Airport, Atlantic Aviation's terminal and service facility offer two runways (7,000 feet and 9,001 feet), nine instrument approaches, and 24-hour all-weather service. This is your best choice if you want to land a private plane in close proximity to downtown. Both jet fuel and AV gas are available. Customers not buying fuel are charged nightly tie-down fees and should call for rates and facilities. Atlantic Aviation also offers a wide range of services—from rental cars to limousines to dinner reservations and catering arrangements.

ATLANTIC AVIATION (JOHNS ISLAND) AT CHARLESTON EXECUTIVE AIRPORT, 2742 Fort Trenholm Rd., Johns Island; (843) 559-2401; atlanticaviation.com. Private pilots wanting access closest to Kiawah and Seabrook will most likely want to choose Atlantic Aviation's airport on Johns Island, 12 miles south of the city. Charleston County and the Federal Aviation Administration spent $2.3 million on this facility in 2005, upgrading its landing strips, enlarging its jet park area, and planning for future expansion. It presently offers two runways, 5,350 by 100-feet and 4,313 by 150-feet. The facility offers jet fuel and 100 LL gas. For customers not buying gas, handling fees are charged so contact them for details. There is also a pilot's lounge with a snooze room and showers. Rental cars are available on the premises, and limited limousine service to Kiawah and Seabrook is offered. Travelers heading for The Sanctuary on Kiawah may call the hotel for transportation to the island. Operating hours are 6 a.m. to 10 p.m.

MOUNT PLEASANT REGIONAL AIRPORT, 700 Airport Rd., Mount Pleasant; (843) 884-8837; chs-airport.com. Private pilots have access to the East Cooper area (including Wild Dunes) via the Mount Pleasant Regional Airport in Mount Pleasant. Managed by Atlantic Aviation, this facility offers a 3,700-foot runway, tie-downs, jet fuel, and AV gas service. Rental cars are available on the premises through Enterprise. The office and terminal are open from 6 a.m. to 8 p.m. Helicopters are accommodated on site.

PELICAN AVIATION, 890 Greyback Rd., Summerville; (843) 851-0970. This facility for private pilots flying into the Summerville area and Berkeley County has a 3,700-foot runway. It offers airplane detailing, general maintenance, and flight training, plus jet fuel and AV gas. Tie-downs are $5 per night (with first night waived with purchase of fuel). The office and terminal are open from 8 a.m. to 5 p.m. through the winter and 8 a.m. to 6 p.m. after Apr 1.

Getting Here by Other Methods

By Bus or Train

If you are arriving or departing by bus, the Greyhound Terminal, 3610 Dorchester Rd., is in North Charleston and a routine stop for cabs. Call (800) 231-2222 or (843) 744-4247 or visit greyhound.com for rates and schedules.

The Amtrak Train Station, 4565 Gaynor Ave., (843) 744-8263 or (800) 872-7245, amtrak.com, is also in the north area. Amtrak runs on the CSX

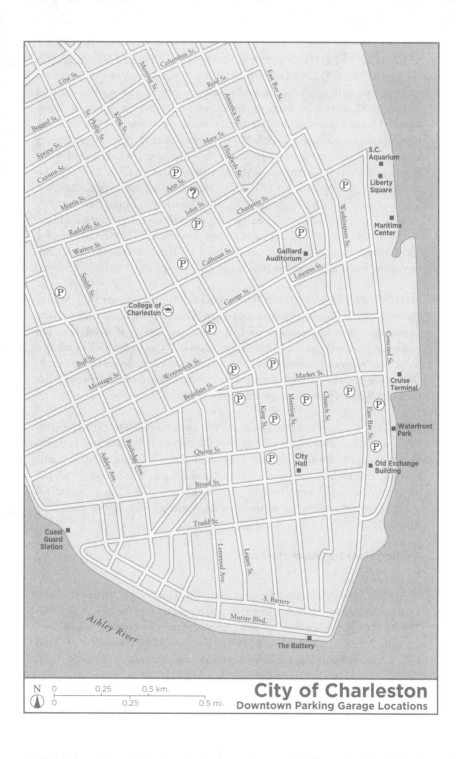

City of Charleston
Downtown Parking Garage Locations

City & County Parking Facilities

Here's the general rule for most city-owned and county-owned parking facilities: It's $1 per half hour. The all-day rate is $16 in city garages. The overnight rate (where offered) is $16 with a hotel registration, and the monthly rate (where available) is $125. City garages near hotel facilities may be slightly higher. In any case, unless your accommodation provides off-street parking or you want to feed a hungry meter, these parking options may turn out to be your only choices:

- **Aquarium Garage,** 24 Calhoun St., (843) 579-7681, 1,093 spaces

- **Camden Exchange Garage,** 47 John St., between John and Hutson Streets off Meeting Street, (843) 720-3866, 308 spaces

- **Charleston Place Garage,** 85 Hasell St., between Meeting and King Streets, (843) 724-7419, 404 spaces

- **Concord-Cumberland Garage,** 1 Cumberland St., corner of Concord and Cumberland Streets, (843) 724-7387, 624 spaces

- **Cumberland-Meeting Garage,** 90 Cumberland St., between Meeting and Church Steets, (843) 724-6786, 958 spaces

- **East Bay–Prioleau Garage,** 25 Prioleau St., between Mid-Atlantic and South Atlantic Streets, (843) 724-7403, 339 spaces

- **Gaillard Municipal Auditorium Garage,** 32 Alexander St., off Calhoun Street and Alexander, (843) 973-7207, 596 spaces

- **George-Society Lot,** 31 George St., off King Street, between George and Society Streets, (843) 724-7384, 146 spaces

- **King-Queen Garage,** off Queen Street, corner of King and Queen Streets, (843) 724-6786, 427 spaces

- **Majestic Square Garage,** Market and Archdale Streets, behind Saks Fifth Avenue, (843) 853-1682, 366 spaces

Continued on next page

- **Marion Square Garage,** 399 King St., just north of the Francis Marion Hotel, (843) 965-4104, 308 spaces

- **Market and Horlbeck Lot,** 131 Market St., in the block between Market and Horlbeck Streets, (843) 724-7385, 118 spaces

- **Queen Street Garage,** 93 Queen St., (843) 965-4981, 323 spaces

- **34 St. Phillip Street Garage,** 34 St. Phillip St., (843) 577-8393, 598 spaces

- **Visitor Center Garage,** 63 Mary St., (843) 973-7290, 723 spaces

- **Visitor Center Lot,** 375 Meeting St., adjacent to the Charleston Visitor Reception and Transportation Center, (843) 724-7174, 62 spaces

- **Wentworth-St. Philip Garage,** 81 Wentworth St., (843) 853-7559, 235 spaces

Railroad lines, and there are two northbound and two southbound stops each day. Call for ticket prices and train schedules.

By Boat

There is a growing leisure craft and passenger ship industry in Charleston.

Cruise ships dock at the passenger terminal off Concord Street in the historic district. In the daytime, walking there is fine, if you have the time and the stamina, but we endorse travel by cabs or limousines at night for safety and convenience. (See the listings for taxis and limousines following.)

Private yachts moor (pending availability) at any of several marinas in the Trident area. (See the Boating & Water Sports chapter for more information.) Cabs or rental cars are the best solution for ground transportation unless you are docked at the City Marina, which is centrally located on the Peninsula near popular destinations and on the DASH route. (See more on the DASH system under "Public Transportation," following.) The nearby Ashley Marina has easy access via walkway to the City Marina and connecting DASH routes.

Charleston Water Taxi

It's hard to go far in Charleston without crossing over water, but here's another option—the Charleston Water Taxi. This water taxi service runs every hour from 9 a.m. to 8 p.m. (more limited hours during the winter) between the Charleston Maritime Center near Aquarium Wharf or the Waterfront Park/ Market Street downtown and the Charleston Harbor Resort & Marina or Patriots Point in Mount Pleasant. Tickets are $10 for an all-day pass; children under 3 are free. What a fun way to catch a harbor boat ride and have a spectacular view of the Ravenel Bridge! Call (843) 330-2989, or visit charleston watertaxi.com for more details.

GETTING AROUND THE LOWCOUNTRY

Taxis, Limos & Rental Cars

Taxis can be scarce here in the Lowcountry, especially at odd hours. Because of that, savvy travelers needing cabs should keep a list of taxi phone numbers in their purse or wallet. The more popular solution is to rent a car from one of the nationally recognized car rental companies, all of which are represented in the area.

Limousines, it seems, are more loosely defined. A limousine can be anything from a stretch Caddy to an airport van. What follows is a list of taxi, limousine services, and rental car options.

Taxis

To get around by taxi, here are some possibilities:

Cabby of Charleston: (843) 763-1603
Charleston City Cab: (843) 879-8180
Charleston Green Taxi: (843) 819-0846
JCW Taxi Services: (843) 452-1100
North Area Taxi: (843) 352-6515

Limousines

Some limousine services available include:

AAA A-1 Airport Shuttle & Limo Service: (843) 834-1998
Above and Beyond Limousine Service: (843) 402-0600, (800) 755-8667

Carey Limousine: (843) 744-8900, (800) 336-4646

Charleston Downtown Limo: (843) 723-1111

Rental Cars

Rental car agencies abound. Companies servicing the area include:

Avis Rent-A-Car: (843) 577-9705, (800) 831-2847

Budget: (843) 577-5195, (800) 221-8822

Dollar Rental Car: (843) 767-1130, (800) 800-4000

Enterprise Rent-A-Car: (843) 723-6215, (888) 305-8051

Hertz Rent-A-Car: (843) 573-2147, (800) 654-3131

National Car Rental: (843) 552-3415, (877) 222-9058

Thrifty Car Rental: (843) 552-1400, (800) 847-4389

Public Transportation

Public bus transportation in the area is a great way to circumvent the city's automobile congestion and parking woes altogether. This service is provided in the Lowcountry by the **Charleston Area Rural Transportation Authority** (CARTA). Under CARTA's auspices is the **Downtown Area Shuttle** (DASH), a separate system generally dedicated to the transportation needs of tourists in the downtown area and historic district. Together, CARTA and DASH operate more than 20 routes linking downtown, West Ashley, Mount Pleasant, and North Charleston.

While the green DASH trolleys are not considered tour vehicles per se, their turn-of-the-20th-century "antique" trolley look is clearly an eye-catcher—and it's one way to quickly identify a DASH vehicle from the more modern-looking (yellow and green) CARTA buses that operate in the metro area. DASH trolleys and metro CARTA buses stop at designated shelters, benches, and trolley signs located throughout the city. For safety reasons, drivers are not allowed to pick up passengers at locations other than the designated color-coded stops.

One-way and all-day CARTA and DASH passes are available on board the vehicles. You are expected to have exact change. One-way fare is $1.75, although those with a senior-citizen or Medicare card can ride for 85 cents each way Mon through Fri from 9 a.m. to 3:30 p.m. or after 6 p.m. and all day Sat and Sun. Disabled riders pay 50 cents. An all-day pass is $6. Transfers are 30 cents. Inside the Visitor Reception and Transportation Center you can buy a 10-ride pass for $14 or 40 rides for $49. A 31-day pass is sold for $50. A student pass is $70. Children under 6 can ride for free when accompanied

> ## Take a Load Off
>
> If you just need to scoot around downtown and you're tired of hoofing it, you can summon one of the handy **rickshaws** that orbit the Market area in the evenings. The three-wheeled (bicycle-like) wonders pedal about the streets starting at 9 a.m. until 2 a.m. 7 days a week. All are "driven" by strong-winded college kids who know the city and the bicycle rules of safety. You can hail one anywhere you see it, or you can call the dispatch number at (843) 723-5685, and one will pedal to your location (approximate response time: 5 minutes). Rates are $5.50 one way (for about a 10-minute ride). More information is at charlestonrickshaw.net.

by a paying adult. Police, guide, signal, and service dogs are the only animals allowed on board.

Call (843) 724-7420, or visit ridecarta.com for more information.

Bicycling

If you plan on spending time on the Peninsula or out on the beaches, why not park the car and consider renting a bicycle by the hour or day? Now you can even put your bike on a CARTA bus (with their new front-loading bike racks) and enjoy the convenience of public transportation. For in-town and Mount Pleasant service, we recommend **The Bicycle and Outdoor Shoppe,** thebicycleshoppecharleston.com, which offers two locations: 280 Meeting St., (843) 722-8168, and 1539 Johnnie Dodds Blvd., Mount Pleasant, (843) 884-7433. These folks rent single-speed adult cruisers and hybrids. Also serving Kiawah and Seabrook Islands is **Island Bike and Surf Shop,** islandbikeandsurf.com, 3665 Bohicket Rd., Johns Island, (843) 768-1158. Another option is **Mike's Bikes,** mikesbikescharleston.com, 709 Coleman Blvd., Mount Pleasant, (843) 884-5884, or on James Island at 808 Folly Rd., (843) 795-3322. For delivery and 3-day or weekly rental to most of the islands, try **Carolina Bike and Beach,** carolinabikeandbeach.com, (843) 747-BIKE.

History

With cultural roots as deep and colorful as the surrounding blue-green waters, Charleston is a rich mixture of early English, Scottish, Irish, French, Spanish, German, Swiss, Santo Domingan, African, Native American, and Caribbean influences.

While each of these cultures left its mark on the city in a unique way, no influence was stronger than that of the British. Archaeologists tell us countless generations of Native Americans lived on and around the land now called Charleston before the first permanent English settlers arrived, but little remains of their occupation outside of the archaeological record in the ground itself. The first English settlers, arriving in the spring of 1670, were adventurers coming to lands granted by King Charles II to eight lords proprietors, who claimed ownership of the "Carolinas"—presumably extending from the Atlantic to the shores of the Pacific.

EARLY HISTORY

As the settlers navigated into what is now Charleston Harbor, they passed enormous mounds of bleached, white oyster shells at the tip of a peninsula where two rivers met and named the area Oyster Point. Seeking higher ground, the colonists sailed farther up one river to a high bank they called Albemarle Point and established the first crude encampment there. They dutifully named the new settlement Charles Towne for King Charles II. The two rivers, called the Kiawah and Etiwan by local tribes, were renamed the Ashley and Cooper, respectively, in honor of one of the lords proprietors, Anthony Ashley Cooper, Lord Shaftesbury. The original settlement area is now a South Carolina state park called Charles Towne Landing State Historic Site. (See the Attractions and Kids chapters.) A decade later, because of their need for protection, the Charles Towne colonists were drawn back to the Oyster Point peninsula between the two rivers—clearly a more defensible location. Here, the foundations of what is now Charleston were first laid.

By 1719, the colonists were tired of being exploited by the proprietary government, and friction ensued. This resulted in the colonists coming under even more discipline from the English crown, which meant forced allegiance to a series of appointed royal governors. This troublesome governmental entity stayed in place for the colonists until the American Revolution.

In 1725 the British sent over a plan for the new settlement called the "Grand Modell," intending to guide the development of 600 prime acres on the peninsula into a proper town. Amazingly, traces of that early English plan are still evident in the plat of today's Charleston Peninsula.

Owing to the great success of this busy English port and its merchant-planter aristocracy, the town soon became a small city. To many, the 18th century will always be Charleston's golden age. Early travelers to this thriving colonial port took back to Europe impressive stories about Charles Towne's elegant architecture, wealthy citizenry, and sophisticated lifestyle. Indeed, during these heady, pre-Revolutionary years, rice and indigo from the plantations were sent out to eager markets all over the world. In exchange, hundreds of boatloads of enslaved Africans were brought to Charleston to ensure a cheap labor force to work the land. In stark contrast to this grim exchange, the arts flourished, and Charles Towne was considered the brightest jewel in England's colonial crown.

Map showing the rivers and harbor during the Siege of Charleston, printed from the Atlas of the battles of the American Revolution *(1845)*

Many of the seeds of the American Revolution found fertile ground here in the Carolina Lowcountry. Political passions ran high, and once war broke out, there were many high-profile Charlestonians deeply involved on both sides of the issue. Actually, the first decisive American victory during the Revolution occurred at the Battle of Fort Sullivan just outside the city. However, at first the war didn't go well. For a while, Charleston fell to the British, and during this time, the city suffered the first of its two unseemly "enemy occupations."

Newly liberated after the war, the city became incorporated in 1783 and adopted a new, shortened name: Charleston. As the 19th century dawned, the young city of Charleston experienced an incredible building boom. Today you can still see an extraordinary number of Adam-style buildings from this remarkable period. Among them are the Joseph Manigault House at 350 Meeting St., built in 1803, and the Nathaniel Russell House at 51 Meeting St., built in 1808. (See the House Museums section of the Attractions chapter.)

As cotton and tobacco were added to the plantation products earning handsome profits in the international marketplace, and even more money flowed into its thriving port, Charleston continued to grow. By the early 19th century, Charleston's flourishing middle class of merchant-tradesmen offered services and locally manufactured goods from small, street-front shops. Many of these shops were clustered along what is now King Street.

> **i** It was (once) all about rice. . . . In the 18th and early 19th centuries, this Lowcountry land and its waters spawned a rich, romantic, fragile culture largely based on a single cash crop—rice. Any real understanding of the Lowcountry and its ethic includes an appreciation for rice and the major role it played in the development of the area.

Some traders sold simple things such as household necessities and fresh produce brought in on wagons from outlying gardens. Others were true artisans in their own right and produced work such as early Charleston-made silver pieces and locally crafted furniture that are highly prized on the antiques market today. This flourishing "wagon trade" on upper King Street preceded the retail stores that make up the present shopping district.

Meet You at "The Four Corners of Law"

The intersection of Meeting and Broad Streets is affectionately known in Charleston as **"The Four Corners of Law."** The old line (mostly used these days by carriage drivers and walking tour guides) is meant to imply that you can do literally everything legally required in life right here at this one important Charleston intersection. On the first corner you can get your mail (at the oldest operating post office building in South Carolina). On the second corner you can get married (at St. Michael's Church, built in 1761 and the place where the visiting George Washington once worshiped). On the third corner you can pay your taxes (at the Charleston County Courthouse). And on the fourth corner—if necessary—you can get divorced (at Charleston's City Hall, built in 1801). This phrase thinly disguises the notorious Charlestonian belief that, indeed, this intersection is the center of the universe. The tongue-in-cheek attitude ranks right up there next to the other one-liner that graciously allows, "The Ashley and Cooper Rivers come together at Charleston to form the Atlantic Ocean."

THE CIVIL WAR & SUBSEQUENT STRUGGLES

Disputes over economics and slavery left unresolved by the young country's founding fathers had festered into a battle between the federal government and individual states by the mid-19th century. In April 1861, Confederate soldiers fired on Fort Sumter in Charleston Harbor, thus signaling the start of the devastating War between the States. After the city's second "enemy occupation," this time by Union troops, Charleston was at its lowest ebb. Years of relentless bombardment, sweeping fires, and economic starvation had taken a terrible toll on the once grand city.

Because Charleston was widely known as the "seat of secession," it is probably true that Charlestonians received especially severe punishment during the

Cannon inside the walls of Fort Sumter

Reconstruction years. Recovery was slow to come and sometimes halfhearted. Some say Charleston never did recuperate from the Civil War until the arrival of the Navy Yard in 1904 and the subsequent economic booms of the two World Wars.

Fires, earthquakes, hurricanes, yellow fever epidemics, and even the boll weevil threatened Charlestonians' health and wealth during the late 19th and early 20th centuries.

After the arrival of the Navy Yard, things started looking better. Phosphate, an organic fertilizer, was mined along the Ashley River and processed in several local factories. This proved to be a significant new source of income

> **i** Insiders tend to find an even kinder welcome if they show an interest in Lowcountry history. Feel free to ask questions and learn more. Most Lowcountry residents are historians at heart—they grew up with it!

for many old plantation families who still owned phosphate-rich lands. Other landowners converted to timber farming as the South slowly rebuilt a working economy.

It has been observed that in the most difficult of times Charleston citizens were "too poor to paint," but they were also "too proud to whitewash." This inability to modernize maintained an almost timeless feeling throughout the city and actually worked to preserve Charleston's now-legendary cache of historic homes and public buildings.

CULTURAL RENAISSANCE & AN ECONOMIC BOOM

In the 1920s, a kind of artistic renaissance occurred in Charleston. The city's now-quaint architectural backdrop inspired a new generation of artists, writers, poets, and musicians who captured regional and national acclaim. (See The Arts chapter for more about this fascinating period in Charleston's history.)

At the same time, the aesthetic and economic value of Charleston's architectural legacy started to be realized. This was when the city's early preservation ethic was first formulated, and it was kept alive through the especially difficult Depression years of the 1930s.

World War II brought another boom to Charleston, with the Navy Yard expanding to produce war materials and more job opportunities than Charleston had seen in decades. After the war ended, many workers drawn here by the Navy decided to stay on and settle down. The sea, the mild weather, and a growing business climate kept pulling newcomers to the Lowcountry through the 1950s and 1960s.

i Charleston has been the scene of numerous historical firsts. The first regularly scheduled passenger train service in America was established here in 1830.

In the 1970s, Charleston's chamber of commerce launched a national advertising campaign based on the simple slogan, "Charleston: America's Best Kept Secret." This, of course, was intended to let this cat out of the bag, and it worked splendidly. With high-profile events such as Spoleto Festival USA and the (almost always sold-out) house tours every spring and fall (see the Festivals & Annual Events chapter), the message was getting out—Charleston was a beautiful, historic, and highly desirable place to visit. Many visitors decided to move here and make the Charlestonian lifestyle their own.

Accommodations

If the Lowcountry knows a thing or two about putting up guests, it's because millions of them visit the Trident each year. Through the years, Southerners have established a reputation for hospitality, and they often compete to maintain the highest standards. Research and experience tell us that Charleston area visitors arrive with varying expectations, and a diverse accommodations industry has evolved to meet those needs.

We have included in this chapter what we consider to be good choices for people who may be looking for vastly different accommodations. We start with Trident area hotels and motels—some for the bargain-minded, some that are large and grand—then discuss the more intimate bed and-breakfasts and atmospheric inns and vacation and beach rentals. Like friends in an eclectic gathering, each accommodations category has something different to offer. Prices vary greatly as well.

Downtown Charleston has the greatest number and the widest variety. We start our listings with downtown properties, then extend our coverage using the geographical order detailed in the How to Use This Book chapter. We end with information specifically helpful to the Lowcountry visitors who arrive by air and those among them seeking accommodations convenient to the airport. Unless we tell you otherwise, expect that these lodgings offer smoking and nonsmoking rooms and access for wheelchairs and that they do not allow pets.

A friendly word of advice: Charleston attracts droves of visitors year-round (there are major events scheduled nearly every month; see the Festivals & Annual Events chapter), and we strongly recommend that you make reservations well in advance. For major events like Spoleto Festival USA and holiday weekends, it's advisable to plan up to 6 months in advance.

Price Code

Although rates are subject to change, we use the following pricing code to indicate the average rate for a one-night stay, in season, for two adults. Note that these rates do not include taxes (14.5 percent accommodations tax or 4 percent for a B&B), gratuities, or add-on services such as room service or premium TV channels. Off-season rates are, of course, lower. Mar through July and Oct through Dec are usually considered peak seasons.

| $ | Less than $90 |
| $$ | $90 to $150 |

A walkway on Kiawah Island

$$$	$150 to $200
$$$$	$200 to $300
$$$$$	More than $300

HOTELS & MOTELS

Downtown Charleston

CHARLESTON PLACE, 205 Meeting St.; (843) 722-4900, (888) 635-2350; charlestonplace.com; $$$$$. In terms of size, Charleston Place Hotel is the granddaddy of Charleston accommodations, with 490 luxury suites and superbly appointed rooms in the massive complex in the city's downtown shopping district. The hotel, with its impressive lobby and reception area, opens into the walkway of a mini-mall that includes such famous stores as Gucci, St. John, and Godiva. (See the Shopping chapter.) The full-service European spa with its on-staff masseur and masseuse has an indoor-outdoor swimming pool among the luxury amenities. Under the auspices of Orient-Express Hotels, the rooms at Charleston Place have taken on the aura of Europe in the 1930s. Expect to find marble bathtubs and gold fixtures in the roomy baths, and notice the little touches in the rooms, such as art deco lighting and the subdued use of color. They add just that much more romance to your lodging experience. Several superb dining options are available right under the Charleston Place roof. Foremost among them is the Charleston Grill on the main floor tucked away among the shops and boutiques. (See the Dining chapter for more on the Charleston Grill.)

COMFORT INN RIVERVIEW, 144 Bee St.; (843) 577-2224, (800) 228-5150; choicehotels.com; $$$. As part of the Comfort Inn chain, the Riverview's 129-room version offers a string of discounts and other standard features plus its most desirable asset, views of the Ashley River. It is just outside the historic district (but still on the Peninsula), and tours are available from the hotel. A fitness room appeals to many travelers, and the outdoor pool with its river view is a big hit with all ages. A hot breakfast is included in the price of the room, and there is no charge for parking. This location makes it a popular option for visitors to The Citadel, area hospitals, and the College of Charleston. Comfort Inn & Suites Airport Convention Center in North Charleston is the north area's option that can be reached at (843) 725-4700, and Comfort Suites West of the Ashley on Savannah Highway is at (843) 769-9850.

COURTYARD BY MARRIOTT HISTORIC DISTRICT, 125 Calhoun St.; (843) 805-7900, (877) 805-7900; marriott.com; $$$$. For almost 40 years, the corner of Calhoun and Meeting Streets was known by frequent Charleston visitors as the location of a convenient and affordable 1960s-style high-rise. It went by a number of names over the years and is now a Courtyard by Marriott. There are 176 guest rooms and suites, a full-service restaurant and lounge, concierge service, a fitness center, valet laundry, an outdoor heated pool, and courtyard. Best of all, it's still just steps away from King Street shopping, Marion Square, the visitor center, and Gaillard Auditorium. Business travelers have Wi-Fi and copy and fax services.

COURTYARD BY MARRIOTT WATERFRONT, 35 Lockwood Dr.; (843) 722-7229, (800) 449-0320; marriott.com; $$$$–$$$$$. Overlooking the Ashley River at the base of the Peninsula, Courtyard by Marriott Waterfront offers 178 spacious guest rooms, all with two-line phones, wireless Internet, voice mail messaging, and a work desk. In-room coffeemakers and movies on demand via cable are some of the other amenities. A waterfront swimming pool, an indoor whirlpool spa, and a fitness center are available, as well as a daily breakfast buffet in the Courtyard Cafe. Golf packages are available for area Lowcountry courses. There's ample on-site parking. This Courtyard by Marriott, which is near the Calhoun Street medical complex, cuts a high profile for those entering Charleston via SR 61, US 17, and SR 30. For a list of additional locations, visit the website.

DOUBLETREE BY HILTON HOTEL & SUITES, Charleston-Historic District; 181 Church St.; (843) 577-2644, (877) 408-8733; charlestondouble tree.com; $$$$. A relative newcomer to the Market area, and formerly known as the Hawthorn Suites, this comfortable courtyard hotel consists of oversize suites. Units have "the Charleston look" and include complete kitchens, separate bedrooms, and living rooms. Life is made easy with a breakfast buffet, and you can unwind in the afternoon with refreshments at the lobby lounge. For those who enjoy burning the calories they consume, there's a fitness center too. When energy levels diminish, the hotel's movie library is available to complement your cable television service. There are 5 suites that are completely wheelchair accessible. The hotel provides valet covered parking for an additional fee.

★ **EMBASSY SUITES HISTORIC CHARLESTON,** 337 Meeting St.; (843) 723-6900, (800) 362-2779; historiccharleston.embassysuites.com; $$$$$. This all-suite luxury hotel is located in the historic district in what was originally The Citadel's first home (ca. 1820). Unmistakably a military building, the echoes of young cadets marching off to the Civil War still seem to bounce off these old walls. Enjoy 153 handsomely furnished 2-room suites with private bedrooms and living rooms. The decor recalls the grandeur of the colonial West Indies. All guest suites open onto a stone-floored atrium with giant palms and a 3-tiered fountain. Amenities include in-room wet bars, telephones with voice mail and dataports, complimentary Wi-Fi, free, cooked-to-order breakfast, and complimentary beverages each evening. This is an ideal location, a stroll from the visitor center, the Charleston Museum, and special events in Marion Square.

★ **FRANCIS MARION HOTEL,** 387 King St.; (843) 722-0600, (877) 756-2121; francismarioncharleston.com; $$$$$. Built in 1924 and beautifully renovated, the Francis Marion is now one of the city's most popular hotels. Named for Revolutionary War general Francis Marion, also known as "the Swamp Fox," the hotel offers all the traditional services of a grand hotel—valet parking, concierge, doorman, bell service, and room service. In all, there are 235 guest accommodations ranging from rooms with 2 double beds to 2-room king suites. All have been handsomely reappointed with custom detailing. At 12 stories tall, the hotel affords visitors a bird's-eye view. It's near upper King Street's fast-developing shopping district, the Charleston Museum, the College of Charleston, and the visitor center. The hotel's signature restaurant, the Swamp Fox Restaurant & Bar, offers a very pleasant atmosphere on the first-floor King Street side. A complete day spa and Starbucks are on-site too. Ample parking is just next door in a city-owned garage.

The old Citadel

HAMPTON INN HISTORIC DISTRICT, 345 Meeting St.; (843) 723-4000, (800) 426-7866; hamptoninn.com; $$$$–$$$$$. There are 171 rooms in the downtown Hampton Inn Historic District, conveniently located across from the visitor center, trolley transportation, and the Charleston Museum. One of downtown Charleston's newer inns, the Hampton offers the attractive features of an older, restored building mellowed with time but beautifully decked out in crisp, new furnishings. The courtyard is probably the largest on the Peninsula, and the large pool is a welcome oasis for travelers. Double rooms have 2 queen beds, and an impressive continental breakfast is part of the deal—muffins, bagels, other breads, cereal, and coffee cake. The Hampton Inn Airport/Coliseum location at 4701 Saul White Blvd. is handy for airport travelers and convention visitors. Visit the website for additional locations.

KING CHARLES INN, 237 Meeting St.; (843) 723-7451, (866) 546-4700; kingcharlesinn.com; $$$$–$$$$$. King Charles Inn is the ideal location for those wanting to explore King Street shopping and the Market area on foot. (See the Shopping chapter.) Those of us who drive past on sweltering Charleston afternoons envy the guests we see frolicking in the second-level outdoor swimming pool. The nearby fountain makes a sparkling show for guests in the dining room. The decor is traditional Charleston, with mahogany reproductions and Lowcountry art. Rooms feature 19th-century-style furniture, and some have adjoining guest rooms or balconies. The parking garage is underground and free for guests.

MARKET PAVILION HOTEL, 225 East Bay St.; (843) 723-0500, (877) 440-2250; marketpavilion.com; $$$$$. This boutique hotel at the corner of South Market and East Bay Streets features guest rooms and suites for tourists and business travelers. For the latter, there are meeting rooms and banquet facilities, and an executive boardroom on tap. Guests have access to a rooftop pavilion with a pool and an open-air bar providing spectacular views from this popular reception area. An upscale restaurant, Grill 225, completes the picture (see the Dining chapter). Valet parking is available, and the location couldn't be more convenient to the Market's shopping adventures and its after-hours nightlife.

MARRIOTT CHARLESTON HOTEL, 170 Lockwood Dr.; (843) 723-3000, (800) 228-9290; marriott.com; $$$$. If you are crossing the Ashley River Bridge into Charleston, look to your left to see the towering 14-story Marriott Charleston Hotel behind riverside Brittlebank Park. There are 340 rooms and suites in this option, many with views of the river, and this venue is a popular one for conventions and meetings. A swimming pool and fitness center are part of the facility, and the rooms have premium channels and movie rentals. Abundant parking is available at no charge. An on-site restaurant called Saffire with American fusion cuisine and a rooftop lounge are part of the sophisticated offerings here.

★ **MILLS HOUSE HOTEL**, 115 Meeting St.; (843) 577-2400, (800) 874-9600; millshouse.com; $$$$–$$$$$. Of the city's grand hotels in the historic district, the Mills probably enjoys the oldest, grandest reputation. It is located on the corner of Meeting and Queen Streets, next door to the imposing white-columned Hibernian Hall (site of many a debutante ball and home of the Hibernian Society). Modern in its comforts and antebellum in its decor, the Mills House has always been a favorite with affluent travelers. The original Mills Hotel (ca. 1853) standing on that site was deemed unworthy of restoration in the early 1960s, so it was razed and replaced with a new, fire-safe structure taller by a couple of floors but with lobby areas and public rooms copied from the original hotel. So exacting are the reproduced details and antebellum appointments that frequently the Mills is used as a backdrop for movies and TV shows needing a period hotel setting. The beautiful courtyard, outdoor pool, and deck add a casual side to the Mills experience. The in-house restaurant and bar, called the Barbados Room, draws local patrons as well as the international set. You'll find live entertainment somewhere on the premises each night, and turndown service is part of the pampering. It's hard to beat the Mills for location, as it is only a stone's throw from the Four Corners of Law, the King Street antiques district, several museums and galleries, plus the bustling Market area.

RENAISSANCE CHARLESTON HISTORIC DISTRICT HOTEL, 68 Wentworth St.; (843) 534-0300, (800) 468-3571; renaissancecharlestonhotel.com; $$$$$. Opened in early 2001 in the heart of the city's downtown business district, the Renaissance is steps away from King Street shopping and area restaurants. The location is ideal for visitors to the College of Charleston campus just a short stroll away. The 166 elegantly appointed rooms are decorated in a Charleston decor with bonnet beds and other charming details. Some rooms open onto the pool deck; others have balconies with city views. The on-site restaurant, The Wentworth Grill, serves a continental cuisine with a Charleston flair. There's a fitness center, a heated outdoor pool, and ample meeting space for business travelers and conventioneers. Hotel valet and self-parking is just across Wentworth Street.

East Cooper

⭐ **CHARLESTON HARBOR RESORT & MARINA**, 20 Patriots Point Rd.; (843) 856-0028, (888) 856-0028; charlestonharborresort.com; $$$$–$$$$$. The 130-room Charleston Harbor Resort was a long time coming to this breathtaking waterfront spot at the very tip of Mount Pleasant overlooking the Holy City. After 13 years, 2 different developers, and a major hurricane, this prime real estate resisted successful completion of a planned resort until Hilton arrived to save the day. Now under new management, the hotel and marina complex is one of Charleston's best destinations for fun, sun, sea, and golf. The resort's decor is maritime—teak-trimmed and nautical. The state-record blue marlin catch is triumphantly displayed in the main foyer. Indoor facilities include meeting rooms, the Indigo Grille restaurant, a cocktail lounge called the Reel Bar, and a ballroom. Suites and rooms are available with king-size or 2 queen beds. Room phones have voice mail. Outdoors there's a swimming pool as well as a man-made, private sandy beach. The USS *Yorktown*, Patriots Point Maritime Museum, and the new Fish House restaurant are just next door. Golfers have discounted greens fees at the Patriots Point course just outside the gate (see the Golf chapter). Guests can take advantage of the 459-slip marina with water taxi service to downtown. (See the Boating & Water Sports chapter.)

HAMPTON INN AT PATRIOTS POINT, 255 Sessions Way; (843) 881-3300, (800) 426-7866; charlestonpatriotspoint.hamptoninn.com; $$$–$$$$. This is a 121-room Mount Pleasant hotel with inside hallways rather than the outside breezeways that characterize many motels. There is no charge for local calls and high-speed wireless Internet. There is a business center for work and a fitness center for working out. The rooms here are a little grander than in most off-highway accommodations. The service says hotel, but the price says motel. A deluxe continental breakfast is on the house. The Hampton Inn on the Isle of

Palms connector features deluxe suites, which are popular with traveling families. It is located at 1104 Isle of Palms Connector (843-856-3900 or 800-426-7866).

> **i** The average daily rate for a room in Charleston County peaks in April. In 2014 that average was $128.83 per night. The occupancy rate for Charleston's hotel and motel accommodations in prime season is a healthy 72 percent.

MAINSTAY SUITES, 400 McGrath Darby Blvd.; (843) 881-1722, (877) 424-6423; mainstaysuites.com; $$$. This 71-unit, 3-floor, all-suite hotel offers unique accommodations to business travelers and vacationers who enjoy traveling as families. Half of the units at MainStay have 2 bedrooms and 2 baths, with doors that separate the kitchen, living area, and bathrooms from the sleeping rooms. The other half are roomy efficiencies, with full kitchens equipped with all the necessities for preparing meals. You'll also find a heated pool, an exercise room, and guest laundry services. There's even a barbecue area for outdoor cooking. The check-in desk is manned only from 6 a.m. to 9 p.m. Mon through Fri. On weekends, it's open until 6 p.m. If you arrive outside of that envelope, follow the check-in instructions in the lobby.

SHEM CREEK INN, 1401 Shrimp Boat Ln.; (843) 881-1000, (800) 523-4951; shemcreekinn.com; $$$$. With views of the shrimp boats moving in and out of their docks and the sun sparkling off miles of marsh, Shem Creek Inn is fun for both children and adults. A large waterfront pool is perfect for relaxing or watching all the creek action. Each of the 50 rooms has a private balcony, and all have microwaves and refrigerators. There is convenient parking under the building, and complimentary continental breakfast is served each morning. All the Shem Creek nightlife goes on close to the inn, and boat dockage is available.

Sullivan's Island & Isle of Palms

These two islands are popular vacation destinations and abound with rental property. With no hotel, motel, condominium, or resort development, Sullivan's Island has less to offer in terms of overnight rental but has an assortment of old and new island homes for rent in weekly or monthly increments.

On the Isle of Palms, in addition to weekly house rentals, Wild Dunes, a major resort, offers flexibility in length of stay (see subsequent listing). Please note: Summer reservations on both islands are often booked by late winter, so start making plans with a rental agency or other entity at least 6 months ahead. Most do not allow pets, but it is always worth asking.

THE BOARDWALK INN AT WILD DUNES, 5757 Palm Blvd., Isle of Palms; (843) 886-6000, (888) 778-1876; wilddunes.com; $$$$–$$$$$. Opened early in 1998, the Boardwalk Inn at Wild Dunes is a $12 million luxury hotel with 93 rooms or suites near Wild Dunes' 2 famous golf courses and 20-court tennis center. All this is situated along 2.5 miles of unspoiled white sand beach. The Boardwalk Inn has an on-site gourmet Lowcountry-style seafood restaurant and lounge plus a tropical pool complex. Even locals enjoy the attractive bed-and-breakfast packages for special occasions.

⭐ **WILD DUNES RESORT,** 5757 Palm Blvd., Isle of Palms; (843) 886-6000, (888) 778-1860; wilddunes.com; $$$$–$$$$$. Rental possibilities at Wild Dunes are widely varied. This 1,600-acre oceanfront golf resort is 20 minutes north of Charleston. Accommodations include 1- to 4-bedroom villas next to the ocean, golf courses, tennis courts, or lagoon. You can rent 3- to 6-bedroom homes with ocean, fairway, and Intracoastal Waterway views. Guests choose their location based on proximity to the beach, pool, tennis courts, marina, or fairways and, of course, on price. The accommodations provide linens, dinnerware, televisions, and washers and dryers, plus a cleaning staff takes care of the messy parts of vacationing. You just focus on the fun. Golf is a big attraction, with 2 excellent courses: The Links, designed by Tom Fazio and ranked as a top course by *Golf* magazine, and the Harbor Course, with holes along the Intracoastal Waterway. There are Har-Tru tennis courts for day and night play, and tennis clinics and lessons are available. Of course, the sandy beach is beautiful, and there are many activities for families. Wild Dunes does not allow pets but will recommend local kennels. (For more about Wild Dunes see our Golf chapter.)

West Ashley

The following West Ashley options provide good value with proximity to the Peninsula. At most, you'll be about 20 minutes from the hustle and bustle of the historic district. Note that most properties are on or near US 17, which is called Savannah Highway throughout this area.

SPRINGHILL SUITES, 98 Ripley Point Dr.; (843) 571-1711, (888) 287-9400; marriott.com/chssh; $$$–$$$$. Across the Ashley just past the round Holiday Inn you'll find this all-suite Marriott hotel, which is popular with boaters tying up at Ripley Light Marina. Close to downtown and SR 61 (out to the plantations), this hotel also offers many luxury amenities. Each suite has a mini-kitchen, a sitting area, cable TV, 2-line telephones with dataports, wireless Internet, voice mail messaging, and a spacious work area. Guests also enjoy a free continental breakfast, outdoor pool and whirlpool spa, and exercise room. Next door is the slightly more upscale (and pet-friendly) Marriott Residence Inn offering 1 or 2 bedrooms, fully equipped kitchens, some suites with fireplaces, and other luxuries. Call (843) 571-7979 or (800) 331-3131 for reservations or more information.

TOWN & COUNTRY INN & SUITES, 2008 Savannah Hwy.; (843) 571-1000, (800) 334-6660; thetownandcountryinn.com; $$$–$$$$. What will strike you first about this West Ashley establishment is the electronic billboard out front that gives a running message about the services within. The regular rooms feature 2 queen beds or 1 king-size bed, and some include kitchenettes. The phones offer voice mail service, and the 37-inch flat-screen TVs all have 56 cable channels, including HBO. Laundry service is an option and, if you are traveling light, efficiencies are available. The restaurant, Trotters, is popular as well (especially with the after-church crowd on Sunday) and runs unusual specials—just check the sign! (See the Dining chapter.)

Folly Beach

Visitors interested in staying on Folly Beach will find a range of accommodations, including an oceanfront high-rise hotel (see listing below) and old-style beach houses available for rent. Again, to rent a beach home, see the list of agents in the Vacation & Beach Rentals section of this chapter.

TIDES FOLLY BEACH, 1 Center St.; (843) 588-6464; follybeachhotel .com; $$$$. This is the only oceanfront hotel, restaurant, and bar in this part of the Lowcountry. All rooms overlook the ocean at Folly Beach, and private "Juliet" balconies make wave watching all the nicer. Standard rooms have either 1 king-size or 2 double beds. Microwaves and refrigerators, voice mail, dataports and complimentary Wi-Fi are some of the many room conveniences. There is an oceanfront pool for those who do not dip in the salt water, and Blu Restaurant and Bar has terrific coastal cuisine and flowing spirits at its bar.

Kiawah & Seabrook

These world-class resort destinations offer some extraordinary rental options that might be just what you are looking for: everything from a private villa to luxury homes to an upscale hotel. Look for descriptions of Kiawah and Seabrook in the Welcome to Greater Charleston and Golf chapters.

Buit in 1876, the Morris Island Lighthouse stands at a distance from Folly Beach.

KIAWAH ISLAND RESORT, 12 Kiawah Beach Dr., Kiawah Island; (843) 768-2121, (800) 654-2924; kiawahresort.com; $$$$–$$$$$. Called "South Carolina's joy of a resort isle" by *Vogue* magazine, Kiawah Island is a 10,000-acre, semitropical island with rental options galore. Choose from villas, cottages, and private homes. Kiawah's newest premier spot is The Sanctuary, a $126 million hotel, spa, and convention complex with 255 rooms. (See following listing.) There are actually three resort areas, or villages, within walking or biking distance of island shopping and dining. Villas and cottages are fully equipped and have as many as 4 bedrooms, while luxury homes for rent in adjacent residential areas have as many as 7 bedrooms and elaborate extras. Other accommodations are basically clustered in the West Beach Village, the East Beach Village, and the Vanderhorst Plantation. In the West Beach Village, villas have views of the forest, ocean, lagoon, tennis courts, or golf courses. East Beach villas are parkside, linkside, courtside, or oceanside and offer some very appealing options. There are 2 pools for guest usage, one of which is an Olympic-size option in the 21-acre Night Heron Park, where guests will also find a covered pavilion, arcade, soccer field, and lake for fishing. The Vanderhorst Plantation is an exclusive gated community with very large homes and ample privacy. Plan to swim, bike, shell hunt, boat, and fish, and explore the many nature trails that encircle the island. Oh, and expect to break out the clubs too. According to *Golf* magazine, Kiawah is one of the best golf resorts in America. It was home of the 1991 Ryder Cup Matches, the 1997 World Cup of Golf, the 2003 WGC World Cup, the 2007 Senior PGA Tournament, and the 2012 PGA Championship. Kiawah's tennis program, with state-of-the art facilities at two centers, also ranks high nationally. Kiawah's kids' programs are a hit with young families.

⭐ **THE SANCTUARY AT KIAWAH ISLAND**, 1 Sanctuary Beach Dr., Kiawah Island; (843) 768-2121, (800) 654-2924; thesanctuary.com; $$$$$. The Sanctuary at Kiawah Island opened in 2004 with much hoopla and anticipation among locals and regular visitors to the Lowcountry. The opening of this 255-room hotel and spa built right on Kiawah's legendary 10-mile, pristine beach came after a decade of planning and construction—marking a new era in luxury accommodations for coastal South Carolina. Guests of The Sanctuary may think of it as a destination unto itself, although the island's world-class golf and tennis programs are major draws. Nearly all the unusually large rooms and suites offer sweeping ocean views, and the hotel's decor harks back to the Gilded Age of beachfront mansions built by America's 19th-century aristocracy. Two dining rooms vie for hungry guests' attention; the Jasmine Porch (with its Lowcountry cuisine) and the Ocean Room (a fine-dining option serving dinner only with a New American menu—see the Dining chapter). An on-site full-service spa tempts guests with an ample selection of relaxing and healthful pamperings available to both men and women. Along with every imaginable beach amenity (including indoor and outdoor pools plus an outdoor bar and grill), The Sanctuary offers guests an arcade of smart shopping boutiques, and an on-site staff of wildlife experts is available to lead guests on a variety of nature adventures—all Kiawah style.

SEABROOK RESORT, 1002 Landfall Way, Seabrook Island; (843) 768-2500, (800) 358-6556; discoverseabrook.com; $$$$–$$$$$. This resort offers family vacations in a residential, island setting. Here you'll find 1-, 2-, and 3-bedroom villas, cottages, and townhomes—some in the maritime forest, others overlooking the marsh or the sea. These properties come equipped with spacious kitchens, sundecks or screened porches, cable hookups, and everything from linens to dinnerware. All are in proximity to one of Seabrook's two golf courses, Ocean Winds and Crooked Oaks. Along with these championship courses, Seabrook has a tennis complex and the area's only resort equestrian center. Swimmers choose between glistening pools and a beautiful stretch of beach along the Atlantic Ocean. Children can enjoy supervised, old-fashioned fun such as puppet shows, finger painting, and ice-cream making while their parents relish precious private time. Seabrook recently completed a 5-year, $31 million renovation, so all facilities are top-notch.

BED-AND-BREAKFASTS

ASHLEY INN BED & BREAKFAST, 201 Ashley Ave.; (843) 723-1848, (800) 581-6658; charleston-sc-inns.com; $$$–$$$$. A real taste of Charleston, this home was built around 1832 and is a mansion even by today's standards—6 bedrooms and a suite, with fireplaces throughout the house and a lovely garden. All rooms have private baths and are tastefully furnished with antique, four-poster pencil-post or canopy rice carved beds. Breakfast is served on the piazza and features such gourmet delights as savory sausage turnovers with cream cheese and chive scrambled eggs or baked cheese blintzes with triple berry sauce. Afternoon wine with homemade treats is part of the hospitality. The inn has bicycles for guests to use and provides off-street parking. This may be the best option for guests wishing access to MUSC facilities. They are literally across the street.

BARKSDALE HOUSE INN, 27 George St.; (843) 577-4800, (888) 577-4980; barksdalehouse.com; $$$–$$$$. This bed-and-breakfast inn is in proximity to King Street shopping and the College of Charleston. In fact, the facility was once a fraternity house. No one would guess that fact today, as the Barksdale House Inn includes 14 beautifully appointed rooms, each one different from the others. All have cable TV, free wireless Internet, and private telephones. Five rooms are equipped with fireplaces and whirlpool baths (oh, what the frat brothers would have given . . .). Continental breakfast is served in your room or in the rear garden, and a nightly turndown service and afternoon tea or sherry are included. Free parking is available.

BATTERY CARRIAGE HOUSE INN, 20 South Battery; (843) 727-3100, (800) 775-5575; batterycarriagehouse.com; $$$$–$$$$$. The Battery Carriage House (ca. 1843) is located right on the Battery, Charleston's very best address for a couple of hundred years. You couldn't be closer to the picturesque, historic park and beautiful views of Charleston Harbor. The 11 guest rooms to the rear and under the piazza are small, but completely charming—most with queen-size canopy beds and interesting furnishings. Three rooms are available with king-size beds. All rooms have cable TV with HBO and wireless Internet access, and you'll find individual controls for heating and air-conditioning. Some rooms have large steam showers; others have whirlpool tubs. Fluffy terry cloth robes and down pillows add to the pampering. Silver-service continental breakfast is served in the room or in the garden under the loggia, your choice.

Happy hour wine is served in the lobby. The service here is very cordial, the ambience very European—a bit like an Italian pensione. There's usually plenty of parking just across the street.

CANNONBORO INN BED & BREAKFAST, 184 Ashley Ave.; (843) 723-8572, (800) 235-8039; charleston-sc-inns.com; $$$–$$$$. This historic 1853 home has 8 beautifully decorated rooms for guests—all of which offer antique four-poster or canopy beds. The all no-smoking rooms are done in a handsome palette of pastels that complement the original hardwood floors. The house is furnished with an assortment of period antiques, and all rooms have air-conditioning and private baths. Guests have cable TV, wireless Internet, and private telephones, too. Complimentary wine is served each afternoon along with an assortment of home-baked goods. Awake to the aroma of sizzling sausage and freshly baked biscuits. A full gourmet breakfast is served each morning on the columned piazza overlooking a Lowcountry garden and fountain. Off-street parking is provided, and complimentary touring bicycles—an especially nice option in this part of town—are available for guests.

Historic Bed-and-Breakfasts

Historic Charleston Bed & Breakfast, (843) 722-6606 or (800) 743-3583 (historiccharlestonbedandbreakfast.com), is a local business that has been matching guests with in-home accommodations since 1981. The reservation service books more than 50 different private homes and carriage houses within the historic district. With very few exceptions, these accommodations date from 1860 or earlier. Agents for Historic Charleston Bed & Breakfast know each property intimately. They know which ones are appropriate for children, which ones are accessible to persons with disabilities and the elderly, and they can arrange for late arrivals and special transportation. Historic Charleston Bed & Breakfast also sends out excellent pre-arrival materials, including maps and shopping and dining recommendations.

Accommodations booked through Historic Charleston Bed & Breakfast can range from $95 to $295 for 2 adults in a 1-bedroom setting, an average of $275 for a 2-bedroom accommodation, and as high as $500 to $600 for luxury 3-bedroom offerings during high season. Rates can be slightly higher for special events and peak weekends like Cooper River Bridge Run, Spoleto Festival USA, and New Year's. Off-season rates are, of course, lower. Mar through July and Oct through Dec are usually considered peak season.

CHARLOTTE STREET COTTAGE, 32 Charlotte St.; (843) 577-3944; charlestoncottage.com; $$$$$. Ever wish for your own private, separate house when visiting downtown Charleston? Here is a great choice. The Charlotte Street Cottage is an elegant, historic guest home available by the day, week, or month. This beautifully restored brick cottage is an original kitchen house built in 1820. It is centrally located in the historic district just off East Bay Street and near the Gaillard Auditorium and other Spoleto venues, the Charleston Museum, the Aquarium, and attractions at Liberty Square. Bicycles are provided for easy access to other historic district destinations. A kitchen (with the original fireplace), breakfast nook, living room, and half bath are downstairs, and two bedrooms, full bath, and washer/dryer are upstairs. Just step out of the kitchen door onto your private patio and garden. Cable TV, telephone, and high-speed and wireless Internet access are all a part of the complete package. There is complimentary gated parking.

1837 BED & BREAKFAST AND TEA ROOM, 126 Wentworth St.; (843) 723-7166, (877) 723-1837; 1837bb.com; $$$–$$$$. Two artists have restored this historic (ca. 1837) house near the College of Charleston and King Street shopping. All 9 rooms and the brick carriage house have air-conditioning and are beautifully decorated. Guests are treated to a sumptuous gourmet breakfast and have access to off-street parking. Afternoon tea for registered guests is complimentary. Rooms have private entrances and baths, refrigerators, and televisions. To quote the *New York Times,* it is "a perfect place to unwind."

FANTASIA BED & BREAKFAST, 11 George St.; (843) 853-0201, (800) 852-4466; fantasiabb.com; $$$–$$$$. Here in this 1813 classic Charleston Single House, you'll find a charming bed-and-breakfast in Charleston's tradition of hospitality. The main house's two bedroom suites are upstairs over a pair of first-floor drawing rooms that give visitors the feel and flavor of Charleston life before the Civil War. The piazza with its lazy hammock overlooks a handsomely landscaped garden accented with fountains and a cobblestone drive. A carriage and kitchen house with another bedroom actually sleeps four with a pull-out couch. A full Southern breakfast is served in the main house, and a continental breakfast is available for carriage house guests. Off-street parking is available, and short-term lease agreements are offered for the carriage and kitchen house facilities.

★ **15 CHURCH STREET: THE PHILLIPS-YATES-SNOWDEN HOUSE BED AND BREAKFAST,** 15 Church St.; (843) 722-7602; bedandbreakfast .com; $$$$–$$$$$. Homeowners Jack and Annelise Simmons welcome guests to a truly Charleston experience in their lovely 1840 home. A full breakfast is served either in the dining room or on the piazza (side porch) or in the garden. The fluffy Virginia pancakes or crustless sausage quiche are signature items, but special dietary restrictions can be accommodated as well. After a day of sightseeing the piazza is once again a welcome spot to relax with wine and cheese and share your adventures with your hosts who, by the way, speak both English and French. When it's time to retire, there is a choice of king or queen bedrooms on the third floor of the main house with beautiful views of the harbor or antebellum rooftops. A king bedroom (convertible to two twins) on the ground floor has a private entrance. Each room has a private bath, telephone, fireplace, and Wi-Fi. The carriage house (parts of which date to 1759) is perfect for families with two bedrooms, one-and-a-half baths, living room, dining room, full kitchen, and washer/dryer. Off-street parking is another plus here. As you enter the property note the two cannonballs mounted on the gateposts which were two of the four that struck the house during the Civil War.

4 UNITY ALLEY—A B&B, 4 Unity Alley; (843) 577-6660; unitybb.com; $$$$. Unity Alley is steeped in history; according to legend, George Washington quartered his horse here on his visit to Charleston back in 1791. Today, this quiet alley in the bustling French Quarter boasts a renovated warehouse beautifully transformed into a grand home with charming guest accommodations. Furnished with antique and reproduction furniture, the building surrounds a restful atrium garden perfect for entertaining and dining. Opened in 1998, 4 Unity Alley offers three suites, each with a private bath. A full breakfast is served each morning, and rarest of all, there's indoor parking available for guests.

KING GEORGE IV INN, 32 George St.; (843) 723-9339, (888) 723-1667; kinggeorgeiv.com; $$–$$$$. At this 4-story, federal-style house with decorative fireplaces, wide-planked hardwood floors, and 3 porches, you're just off King Street with its many antiques shops and fashion boutiques. And Charleston's colorful City Market is only a 5-minute walk away. This was originally the 1790s home of Charleston writer and early newspaper publisher Peter Freneau. Freneau was of Huguenot descent, and his brother Philip was called the "poet of the Revolution." All 10 rooms are furnished with antiques, cable TVs, and telephones, and have air-conditioning and Wi-Fi. Eight of the rooms have private baths. Each morning, a full Southern breakfast is served until 10:30 a.m. in the Breakfast Room, or you may choose to eat on the porch. There is free off-street parking for guests.

LOWNDES GROVE PLANTATION BED-AND-BREAKFAST, 266 Margaret St.; (843) 853-1810, (877) 307-9243; lowndesgrove.com; $$$–$$$$. Now listed on the National Register of Historic Places, Lowndes Grove (ca.

1786) is the only plantation on the Ashley River actually within today's city limits. The house and grounds, with spectacular views of the water, make a lush setting for wedding receptions and other festivities. There are three air-conditioned guest rooms with private baths and a two-bedroom, air-conditioned guest cottage for families (babysitting is available). As elegant as the house is, the spacious grounds, pool, Jacuzzi, and river dock also make it a comfortable, almost rural setting. The house is especially convenient to The Citadel and Hampton Park, once the site of the 1901 West Indies Exhibition, a World's Fair–like extravaganza that attracted dignitaries from all over the world. At the time, Lowndes Grove hosted former president Theodore Roosevelt.

MERHAVEN BED, NO BREAKFAST, 16 Halsey St.; (843) 577-3053; $$. Although this listing doesn't fit the bed-and-breakfast category in the strictest sense, it's a close relation. In fact, this is what the *New York Times* called "the no-frills option" in Charleston. You'll find two large, light-filled, air-conditioned rooms with a private entrance but, sorry, no eggs and grits. Actually, coffee, tea, and a refrigerator are available in each room, which means you can easily prepare your own breakfast. Both rooms are nonsmoking, and there's a shared bath. Guests have their own TV and an in-room extension of the family phone line. There's a delightful courtyard, too, with a comfy chaise lounge that's ideal for an afternoon siesta. Guests appreciate the off-street parking and the fact that the College of Charleston and MUSC and the hospitals are within easy walking distance. No credit cards.

OLD VILLAGE POST HOUSE, 101 Pitt St., Mount Pleasant; (843) 388-8935; oldvillageposthouse.com; $$–$$$. There are 6 bedrooms in the newly renovated Post House, formerly the Guilds Inn (ca. 1888), each beautiful and typically "Old Village." Every room has a private bath, and the on-site restaurant offers gourmet meals for dinner. A continental breakfast, cable TV, wireless Internet access, and daily newspapers are complimentary. There's even a full-service tavern, too. Rooms vary in size; there's an executive suite, and honeymooners can request the special bridal suite with oversize whirlpool tub. Guests enjoy the charm of this quaint neighborhood, where evening walks are a popular pastime. (For more on the Old Village Post House restaurant, see the Dining chapter.)

THE PALMER HOME BED & BREAKFAST, 5 East Battery; (843) 853-1574; thepalmerhomebandb.com; $$$$–$$$$$. This bed-and-breakfast is in one of the most high-profile mansions on the Battery. The huge pink Italianate single house (sometimes called the "Pink Palace") offers spectacular views.

From the piazza, guests can see across all of Charleston Harbor, with Fort Sumter silhouetted on the horizon. There are four guest rooms on the third floor, one on the second (stair climbing is required), and a swimming pool in the garden for cool refreshment. There's also a more expansive carriage house with two bedrooms that can accommodate up to eight adults. A full Southern breakfast buffet is served in the dining room or on the piazza at your choosing. Afternoon wine and cheese in the drawing room allows the opportunity to meet the other guests. There's plenty of off-street parking, too. Their sister property, Palmer's Pinckney Inn at 19 Pinckney St., offers 5 additional suites near the Market Street area.

★ THIRTY-SIX MEETING STREET BED & BREAKFAST, 36 Meeting St.; (843) 722-1034; 36meetingstreet.com; $$$–$$$$. This handsome (ca. 1740) home is only a little more than a block off the Battery and offers 3 guest suites, each with its own private entrance. One is on the ground floor of the carriage house and another is on the second floor, each with 2 bedrooms and a sitting area and private baths. In the main house there is an exterior spiral staircase that leads to 1 bedroom and bath on the second floor. All rooms have four-poster mahogany queen beds and kitchenettes, and there's an inviting walled-in garden with tables and chairs for relaxing after a busy day. A continental breakfast is provided in the kitchenette—ready whenever guests rise and wish to partake, and the morning newspaper is left at your doorstep. Off-street parking and bicycles are available.

THE THOMAS LAMBOLL HOUSE, 19 King St.; (843) 723-3212, (888) 874-0793; lambollhouse.com; $$$. Named in honor of colonial-era judge Thomas Lamboll, this Charleston single house (ca. 1739) is now a private home with 2 lovely third-floor guest rooms offered to bed-and-breakfast guests. Each is elegantly furnished with reproduction and antique furniture, has central air-conditioning, a fireplace, cable TV, and a telephone. French doors lead onto the third-floor piazza with distant views of Charleston Harbor over the treetops. Continental-plus breakfast is offered in the formal dining room every morning. Children are welcome, and off-street parking is available.

21 EAST BATTERY BED & BREAKFAST, 21 East Battery; (843) 556-0500, (888) 721-7488; 21eastbattery.com; $$$$$. Within the urban compound of Charleston's historic 1825 Edmundston-Alston House (see House Museums in the Attractions chapter), is this charming bed-and-breakfast created in the property's former stables, carriage house, and slave quarters. The old hayloft is now the master bedroom overlooking a lovely garden. Where carriages were once stored are now a spacious living room and a dining room with hidden kitchen facilities—stocked for a gourmet breakfast. Additional rooms in the museum house's rear dependency can accommodate up to a total of 10 people. This high-end option located right on Charleston's famous High Battery is ideal for multiple couples celebrating a special event or traveling families.

TWO MEETING STREET INN, 2 Meeting St.; (843) 723-7322, (888) 723-7322; twomeetingstreet.com; $$$$–$$$$$. This elegant 1890 Victorian mansion is at the intersection of Meeting Street and South Battery facing White Point Garden. Guests stay in one of 9 air-conditioned rooms, each with a private bath. The rooms are all different, but each carries out the Victorian theme in every detail. A hot Southern breakfast is served in the garden or the formal dining room, depending on the weather. Or you may decide to lounge in your luxury cotton bathrobe (provided with the room) and have breakfast delivered

ACCOMMODATIONS

to your guest room. Afternoon tea and evening sherry are included in the rate. Much of Two Meeting Street's charm comes from the lacy Queen Anne–style veranda stretching across the front of the inn. Its lazy ceiling fans and rocking chairs make the scene an inviting option for afternoon tea. No credit cards.

VENDUE SUITES, 30 Vendue Range; (843) 723-2228; bedandbreakfast .com; $$$–$$$$$. Located close to Charleston's picturesque harbor and near many of the city's best restaurants, Vendue Suites is tucked away just off East Bay Street. This B&B-style inn has 3 guest suites for short or extended stays. There is a 1-bedroom, 1-bath with satellite TV, Wi-Fi, air-conditioning, ceiling fans, and a fully stocked refrigerator complete with continental breakfast each morning. The other suites are 2-bedroom with one and a half baths with whirlpool tubs in addition to the other amenities. Repeat guests have praised the comfort, cleanliness, and superb location in their reviews. The suites give the feel of having your own apartment mere steps away from Charleston's charms. Native Charlestonians Tradd and Weesie Newton are the proprietors here and have a reputation for quality hospitality offerings with close attention to detail. (Read about their Fleet Landing Restaurant in our Dining chapter.)

★ **ZERO WATER STREET, 31 East Battery; (843) 723-2841; zerowaterstreet .com; $$$$–$$$$$.** Zero Water Street is actually a quiet, private entrance to 31 East Battery, one of Charleston's classic mansion houses built on the Battery in 1836. Water Street is in the very heart of the old city's historic district, and 31 East Battery directly overlooks Charleston Harbor and Fort Sumter. Your room (with its private bath) and the adjoining piazza will offer spectacular views. The guest suite has 12-foot ceilings, air-conditioning, private telephone, cable TV, wireless Internet, and off-street parking. A continental plus breakfast is provided either in your room or in the lovely Victorian garden with its antique play house. Children over age 12 are welcome. A 2-night minimum is required. No credit cards.

INNS

Many inns in Charleston offer some of the same personalized touches that make the bed-and-breakfasts special, but on a larger scale. Most, but not all, operate in modernized facilities either renovated or built specifically for lodging. You can usually expect a great deal of charm along with complimentary continental breakfast, afternoon wine or sherry, and evening turndown service. What distinguishes one from another is location, authenticity of decor, trendy amenities, and management style. Prices per night vary with the seasons, and our price guides reflect the same coding ranges and caveats used for the bed-and-breakfasts. Unless otherwise indicated, all addresses are in Charleston.

ANDREW PINCKNEY INN, 40 Pinckney St.; (843) 937-8800, (800) 505-8983; andrewpinckneyinn.com; $$$$–$$$$$. The Andrew Pinckney Inn is at the corner of Church and Pinckney Streets on the very edge of Charleston's historic Market. All of the Market's famous diversions—quaint shops, craft stalls, nightclubs, and fine restaurants—are nearby. Even the horse-drawn carriage tours are just a few steps away. The recently remodeled and expanded inn features a rooftop garden terrace for catching Lowcountry sunsets, and the attentive concierge service can arrange special golf and fitness packages on request. A continental breakfast is part of the package, and all rooms feature handsome West Indies–style furnishings. There's even a fully equipped business center available for business or group travelers.

⭐ **ANSONBOROUGH INN,** 21 Hasell St.; (843) 723-1655, (800) 522-2073; ansonboroughinn.com; $$$$–$$$$$. The award-winning Ansonborough Inn is at the end of Hasell Street off East Bay. There are 37 suites that have been cleverly fashioned out of a turn-of-the-20th-century warehouse. Heart-of-pine exposed beams (measuring 12 inches by 12 feet) and locally made red brick have been incorporated into the decor to give the inn a remarkably warm feeling, even with its magnificent 16- and 18-foot ceilings. The facility's 3 floors are wheelchair-accessible and surround an open central atrium. The suites are equipped with full kitchens, and some have lofts. There's an on-site English-style pub and rooftop bar. Guests receive complimentary afternoon wine and a 24-hour monitored parking lot is available. One favorite amenity is the continental breakfast with fresh-baked breads. Choose from banana, strawberry, and blueberry muffins delivered each morning from Saffron, a popular bakery just down the street (see the Dining chapter). The business traveler is treated to multiple dataports, wireless Internet, and on-site conference facilities.

> **i** When negotiating your way through Charleston streets, you may encounter several street names that Charlestonians choose to pronounce in their own inimitable fashion. Here's a quick translation: If somebody mentions "Le-GREE" Street, it's Legare Street. And when directed to Hasell Street, note it is called "Hazel."

ELLIOTT HOUSE INN, 78 Queen St.; (877) 727-0369; elliotthouseinn
.com; $$$$. Elliott House is next to the popular 82 Queen restaurant (see the
Dining chapter) and across the street from the Mills House Hotel. This is life
as it should be in the refined fast lane—breakfast served on silver service, afternoon wine and cheese reception in the courtyard, and a large hot tub at night.
Guests stay in one of 25 air-conditioned rooms, complete with Oriental rugs
and reproduction period furniture. Since 82 Queen draws a big (but respect-
able) crowd to its bar, the action is just a few strides away for Elliott House
guests. Complimentary bicycles are available for exploring the neighborhood,
and parking is across the street in a city garage.

FRENCH QUARTER INN, 166 Church St.; (843) 722-1900, (866) 812-
1900; fqicharleston.com; $$$$$. Located in Charleston's original French Quar-
ter district in the historic Market and Church Streets area, this independent
offering opened in Jan 2002. There are 50 rooms and suites elegantly appointed
with an eclectic array of French pieces, Provençal beds, European-style bed dress-
ings, and a pillow menu of seven different comfort choices. Some of the rooms
feature working fireplaces, whirlpool tubs, and balconies overlooking the festive
Market area. Amenities include silver service breakfast in the room, afternoon
wine and cheese, turndown service, and complimentary 24-hour coffee, tea, and
snacks. Valet laundry and parking are part of the upscale service.

FULTON LANE INN, 202 King St.; (843) 720-2600, (800) 720-2688;
fultonlaneinn.com; $$$$–$$$$$. This cozy inn is a nonsmoking facility nes-
tled just off King Street in the heart of Charleston's fascinating antiques district. Built post–Civil War by Confederate blockade runner John Rugheimer,
the inn is a fascinating taste of a time gone by. The 45 rooms are decorated in
Southern plantation style and some feature fireplaces, king-size canopy beds,
luxury baths, and whirlpool tubs. Nightly turndown service and a continental
breakfast delivered on silver service are part of the hospitality here. Public parking is available just outside the door. This inn is part of the Charming Inns of
Charleston group.

THE GOVERNOR'S HOUSE INN, 117 Broad St.; (843) 720-2070,
(800) 720-9812; governorshouse.com; $$$$–$$$$$. Built in 1760 by John
Laurens, this is the oldest house in Charleston currently being used as a bed-
and-breakfast. Edward Rutledge, the youngest signer of the Declaration of
Independence and once governor of South Carolina (1798–1800), lived here.
Today, the house boasts 11 elegantly appointed guest rooms. The Grand rooms
feature 12-foot ceilings with fireplaces and private verandas. The Roofscape

room provides lovely views over the area's historic architecture. The Kitchen House suite has a separate living room, private porch, wet bar, and an original 1760 fireplace. A Southern gourmet breakfast is served, as are afternoon tea and evening sherry. The location is ideal from several standpoints. You're at the edge of the original Grand Modell city and today's prestigious Below Broad residential area, and you're within easy walking distance of King Street's shopping and antiques district.

Last-Minute Reservation

If you arrive in Charleston without reservations, help is available at the Charleston Visitor Reception and Transportation Center at 375 Meeting St. Open daily from 8:30 a.m. to 5:30 p.m., the visitor center offers help finding rooms at inns, hotels, and motels in the Greater Charleston area. This is, in effect, a clearinghouse of last-minute accommodations and a real lifesaver for those impromptu visitors to the city. Later in the business day, these rooms are often offered at discounted rates. The desk personnel cannot secure reservations for you via phone; you must be there in person. They can, however, make a room reservation using your credit card once you're there.

ACCOMMODATIONS

HARBOURVIEW INN, 2 Vendue Range; (843) 853-8439, (888) 853-8439; harbourviewcharleston.com; $$$$. This is one of Charleston's best luxury inns right in the heart of the downtown historic district. Its location, directly across from Waterfront Park, is one attraction. The 52 high-end, luxury rooms and suites close to the area's many fine restaurants, shops, galleries, and nightclubs are another. The inn, with its handsome nautical appointments throughout, offers nightly turndown service, elegant in-room continental breakfast, all-day snacks, and afternoon refreshments in the atrium. Top-floor rooms have spectacular views over Charleston Harbor—hard to find on the Peninsula. Ask about the "Celebrate Romance" package for a special weekend with your significant other.

INDIGO INN, 1 Maiden Ln.; (843) 577-5900, (800) 845-7639; indigoinn .com; $$$$. The Indigo Inn fronts on Meeting Street and is across from a bustling shopping and restaurant district not far from Charleston Place. The 3-story inn has 40 rooms around a private courtyard and fountain, and it prides itself on impeccable service. The traditionally decorated rooms feature massive four-poster beds and evoke a plantation atmosphere. A hunt (continental-plus) breakfast and the morning paper are complimentary, as is the on-site parking, a blessing in the heart of the city. Well-behaved pets are welcomed at an additional charge.

THE JASMINE HOUSE, 64 Hasell St.; (843) 577-0041, (888) 913-0488; jasminehouseinn.com; $$$$. This classic Greek Revival (1843) mansion sits in the historic Ansonborough neighborhood, between the Market and Gaillard Auditorium. Six guest rooms are in the main house and feature 15-foot ceilings, Italian marble baths, and original architectural details. Four others in the carriage house open onto the private courtyard and Jacuzzi area and have charming brick floors and second-level piazzas. Guests enjoy a hot continental-plus breakfast and complimentary parking. Rooms in the main house are handsomely decorated in themes appropriate to the period of the house and Charleston's pre–Civil War heyday. Check-in is handled at the sister property, Indigo Inn, at the corner of Maiden Lane and Meeting Street.

Waterfront Park in downtown Charleston

★ **JOHN RUTLEDGE HOUSE INN,** 116 Broad St.; (843) 723-7999, (800) 476-9741; johnrutledgehouseinn.com; $$$$–$$$$$. Built in 1763 by John Rutledge, a signer of the US Constitution, the house at 116 Broad St. has been completely renovated and transformed (as part of a three-building complex) into a swank inn with 19 rooms in all. The house is a designated National Historic Landmark, and the National Trust for Historic Preservation named it among the top 32 Historic Hotels of America for good reason. George Washington himself had breakfast here and was one of many patriots, statesmen, and presidents who came to call on Mr. Rutledge. The main residence contains elaborate parquet floors, Italian marble mantels, and molded plaster ceilings. Rooms have been modernized to include private baths, refrigerators, televisions, and individual climate controls. Afternoon tea is served in the ballroom, and evening turndown service includes chocolates at bedside. Continental or hot breakfast and a newspaper are delivered to guests each morning. The Rutledge House is dog-friendly for an additional fee. This inn is part of the Charming Inns of Charleston group.

KINGS COURTYARD INN, 198 King St.; (843) 723-7000, (800) 845-6119; kingscourtyardinn.com; $$$$–$$$$$. The Kings Courtyard Inn has an interesting history in that the building has come full circle in its lifetime. The Greek Revival building, dating from 1853, began as an inn catering to 19th-century plantation owners and businessmen. Then it was a private residence; after that, the downstairs housed some of Charleston's most fashionable shops; and now it once again serves guests with luxury accommodations. The inn, with its garden oasis, is nestled among many fine antiques shops on King Street. Rooms and suites are modernized with air-conditioning and private baths, and no two are exactly alike. Some offer canopy beds; others feature fireplaces, and many offer views of a lovely courtyard below. You may expect a continental breakfast and a newspaper delivered to you each morning, or you can have breakfast in the courtyards or the breakfast room. Cocktails are available in the courtyard bar, and sherry is provided each evening on the first floor. This inn is part of the Charming Inns of Charleston group.

MEETING STREET INN, 173 Meeting St.; (843) 723-1882, (800) 842-8022; meetingstreetinn.com; $$$$–$$$$$. In the heart of the city on bustling Meeting Street, this is a convenient option for a Charleston inn experience. The front portion of the inn is over 140 years old, while the back section is a recent addition. Four-poster rice beds in every room add to the 19th-century ambience of this elegant accommodation, convenient to many fine restaurants, antiques shops, and the colorful City Market area. Continental breakfast may be taken in your room or out in the courtyard. The courtyard's heated Jacuzzi is popular with guests at any time of the day. Afternoons at the Meeting Street Inn include complimentary seasonal refreshments and bar service in the lobby. Evening turndown service means a freshened-up room and bath plus a delicious chocolate on your bedtime pillow.

★ **MIDDLETON INN, 4290 Ashley River Rd.; (843) 556-0500, (800) 543-4774; theinnatmiddletonplace.com; $$$–$$$$.** In our estimation, Middleton Inn is the kind of place you really want to write home about. Situated on the grounds of one of the most beautiful and historic plantations in the South, Middleton Inn overlooks the Ashley River and the nation's oldest landscaped gardens and is just 14 miles from downtown Charleston. Guests have access to the nature trails, gardens, house museum, and stableyards. You'll also find an outdoor pool, horseback riding, bicycling, kayaking, and an on-site cafe for continental breakfast. Middleton Place's famous restaurant is just a stroll away through the woods. The facility itself is of national award-winning design, contemporary and starkly modern in its simplicity. It has 55 rooms with charming fireplaces and European baths. (See the Attractions chapter for more about Middleton Place.)

PLANTERS INN, 112 North Market St.; (843) 722-2345; plantersinn.com; $$$$–$$$$$. As charming and roomy as an antebellum Charleston home, this inn has a European flavor and an understated elegance that radiates quality. It came as no surprise to us some years back when Planters Inn captured *Lodging Hospitality* magazine's first-place award in the guest room category. From four-poster beds to mahogany armoires, authentic Charleston reproductions are showcased in spacious rooms with traditional high ceilings. The inn is in the colorful City Market area and is home to the popular Peninsula Grill (see the Dining and Entertainment chapters). Silver-service breakfast is delivered to your room, or a gourmet breakfast is served in the dining room. A nightly turndown service sends you sweet dreams with a chocolate and a weather card to plan tomorrow's activities. Parking is available—a rarity for this busy location.

THE VENDUE, 19 and 26 Vendue Range; (843) 577-7970, (800) 845-7900; thevendue.com; $$$$–$$$$$. Situated between East Bay Street and the famous "walk through" fountain of Waterfront Park is this upscale, boutique-style hotel with one of the best reputations for fine service and attention to detail. Completing a $5 million renovation in the spring of 2014, The Vendue offers 85 rooms in its two properties, The Vendue and 26 Vendue, across the street from each other. Art lovers especially will enjoy the exhibits located in its gallery spaces throughout the property. The rotating exhibitions are curated by Robert Lange Studios, a local art gallery. A rooftop terrace and bar offer one of the best views in the city (see the Entertainment chapter), and The Vendue's on-site restaurant, the Drawing Room, is one of Charleston's intimate dining adventures. Wine and cheese are available every afternoon, and milk and cookies show up at 9 p.m. until they are gone. A new coffee shop on the East Bay Street corner is called The Press, a reference to the *South Carolina Gazette* newspaper published here in the late 18th century.

★ **WENTWORTH MANSION**, 149 Wentworth St.; (843) 853-1886, (888) INN-1886; wentworthmansion.com; $$$$$. This elegantly refurbished inn was built from 1885 to 1887 as one of Charleston's few great Victorian townhomes. Articulated in what is called the Second Empire style of architecture (after a French fashion popularized during the reign of Napoleon), it was originally the private estate of Francis Silas Rodgers. Rodgers was a Charleston cotton merchant who made a fortune in phosphate after the Civil War. His mansion survives today as the city's most opulent ode to the long-lost Gilded Age. Remarkably unchanged, the property features 21 rooms and suites individually decorated and furnished with 19th-century antiques. All rooms have king-size beds and baths with oversize whirlpool tubs. Most have working gas fireplaces. Guests enjoy the mansion's common rooms such as the Rodgers Library, the Harleston Parlor, and the atrium-like Sun Porch—where guests savor leisurely elegant breakfasts, afternoon sherry, and evening wine and hors d'oeuvres. Local guides lead guests on tours of the city, and an on-site fine dining restaurant, Circa 1886, offers seasonal specialties. (See the Dining chapter.) With its private spa, Wentworth Mansion brings a whole new level of service to Charleston's already renowned tradition of unparalleled hospitality.

VACATION & BEACH RENTALS

Beach rentals, especially those on the barrier islands of Kiawah, Seabrook, Sullivan's Island, Isle of Palms (home of Wild Dunes Resort), and Folly Beach, are considered a real estate specialty here in the Lowcountry.

AVOCET PROPERTIES, 38 Center St., Folly Beach; (843) 588-6699, (800) 951-2470; avocetproperties.net. This company has a new name but has handled real estate for over 16 years in the West Ashley area. Avocet focuses on vacation rentals, property management, and real estate sales on Folly Beach with friendly, reliable service. Its office is in the first 2-story building you'll see on Center Street as you come off the bridge to the island. It offers a wide variety of accommodations ranging from the casual basics to oceanfront luxury condominiums and homes. The company hopes to be your "key to a lifetime of memories." Write or call for a brochure of Folly Beach properties.

BEACHWALKER RENTALS, 140 Gardener's Circle, PMB 162, Johns Island; (843) 768-1777, (800) 334-6308; beachwalker.com. This independent resort-rental company specializes in Kiawah and Seabrook Island vacations. With more than two decades of experience, the company has built a solid reputation for value and friendly service. Many loyal families return to Beachwalker year after year, with these folks handling all the arrangements from bike rentals to golf. Call for the annual catalog of beachfront and nearby properties, and ask about the off-season discounts. Online booking is available on the website.

CARROLL REALTY, 103 Palm Blvd., Isle of Palms; (843) 886-9600, (800) 845-7718; carrollrealtyinc.com. This family-owned firm, which started in 1981, specializes in the sale and rental of resort homes on Isle of Palms, including Wild Dunes, and Sullivan's Island. Offerings range from 1-bedroom condos to 10-bedroom mansions. Its offices are between the islands on Palm Boulevard.

DUNES PROPERTIES OF CHARLESTON, 31 Center St., Folly Beach; (843) 588-3800, (888) 843-2322; dunesproperties.com. Specializing in coastal real estate and vacation rentals, Dunes Properties of Charleston has been doing business in the Lowcountry since 1989. They handle rentals on Folly Beach and the Isle of Palms/Wild Dunes. About half this company's business comes from repeat customers who use its services year after year. Vacation planners can view and book Dunes Properties' rental listings online.

FRED HOLLAND REALTY, 50 Center St., Folly Beach; (843) 588-2325; fredhollandrealty.com. Experience is the key word for Fred Holland Realty when it comes to Folly Beach real estate and rentals. The company has been finding vacation homes for Folly visitors for more than 30 years. It handles a range of beach rentals from 2- and 3-bedroom condos to oceanside beach houses and even small apartments. The agents also arrange many long-term (yearly) leases annually. Most of their business is repeat customers coming back for more. The website features the year's offerings for summer rentals. Call or visit for more information.

ISLAND REALTY, 1304 Palm Blvd., Isle of Palms; (843) 886-8144, (866) 380-3983; islandrealty.com. Since 1977, this firm has been a major player in property sales and resort rentals on Isle of Palms (at Wild Dunes), Goat Island, Sullivan's Island, and Mount Pleasant. Island Realty's staff prides itself on meeting your vacation needs. We especially like their user-friendly website with links for rentals that are pet-friendly or come with a private pool, a dock, or an elevator.

PAM HARRINGTON EXCLUSIVES, 4343 Betsy Kerrison Pkwy., Johns Island; (843) 768-0273, (800) 845-6966 Kiawah Rentals; (843) 768-0808, (888) 718-7949 Seabrook Rentals; pamharringtonexclusives.com. This company, with headquarters just before the traffic circle leading to Kiawah and Seabrook, does a lion's share of business on Kiawah and Seabrook Islands. It's been helping visitors secure luxury accommodations and premium real estate on Kiawah, Seabrook, and Johns Island since 1978. For sales information, call (843) 768-3635.

Dining

Believe it or not, you won't have to go very far to find a Charlestonian who will tell you that as recently as 25 years ago there were only a few white tablecloth restaurants in the entire city. That seems incredible today, when there are easily two dozen truly fine dining options to choose from on any given evening out on the town.

With the revitalization of our downtown area and the draw of people to all places South, there has been an accompanying influx of outstanding new culinary talent and the interest to match. In fact, Charleston has been home to some of the country's most respected culinary institutions. This deepens the talent pool for dining establishments all over the Lowcountry. Now establishments and styles fit almost every whim while making a true effort to share and preserve the traditional cuisine of the Lowcountry. We have included information, typical fare, and opinions in this chapter that may help you with your selections. Menu items are frequently seasonal and subject to change.

Red beans and rice

OVERVIEW

The list here is not exhaustive but gives, we feel, a fair representation of what is available on the downtown Peninsula, in Mount Pleasant, on the islands east of the Cooper, and in the areas and islands west of the Ashley River. Not included in our descriptions are the familiar national restaurant chains. Eateries are categorized by type of food offered. Bear in mind that many of the downtown restaurants are housed in old and historic buildings that may not be wheelchair accessible. If that's an issue for you or your party, it's always good to call ahead.

Whatever your budget, we feel confident you'll find in the following listings the perfect setting for enjoying Lowcountry meals that will augment your stay in the Trident area.

Price Code

The reference guide should be used to translate the average price ranges of dinner for two persons, minus cocktails, wine, or gratuity. We caution that prices, hours, menus, and means of payment are frequently subject to change, so if you have any doubts about an important issue, call ahead. Since most restaurants will accept cash, traveler's checks, and all major credit cards (but almost never personal checks), we inform you only of those establishments that do not take plastic.

Here are our breakdowns for average entree prices for two and the correlating symbols.

$	Less than $20
$$	$20 to $35
$$$	$35 to $60
$$$$	More than $60

AMERICAN

CALIFORNIA DREAMING RESTAURANT AND BAR, 1 Ashley Pointe Dr.; (843) 766-1644; californiadreaming.com; $–$$. You can go to California Dreaming by car or by boat (yes, you can tie up at a dock), and it's always an adventure. The kids pretend it's an old fort (although it isn't), and the views of the Ashley River are mesmerizing. The restaurant and the bar do an incredible, nonstop business year-round. The interior is colorfully decorated with flags and divided into two dining levels, with seating for 260 (and the place is often full). The little ones are welcome and can order from a special menu. Patrons really go crazy for the soft, buttery croissants and the house salad (topped with eggs, almonds, ham, and bacon—almost a meal in itself). All fish is fresh and local, and the burgers, ribs, and house special prime rib are popular. A decadent dessert list includes the fabulous house special—apple walnut cinnamon pie. Lunch and dinner are served every day, and hours are extended on weekend nights. Reservations are suggested. (See the West Ashley section of the Entertainment chapter.)

EASTERBY'S FAMILY GRILLE, 2388 Ashley River Rd.; (843) 556-5707; easterbysfamilygrille.com; $$. Easterby's on Ashley River Road (SR 61) is a comfortable, affordable place for casual dining and local seafood. It's a popular lunch stop for tourists heading out to the plantations along the highway (see our Attractions chapter). Dinner patrons enjoy the seafood (fried or not), steaks, and pastas, barbecue, crab legs, and Cajun mixed grill. Spirits are available, and reservations are not necessary unless you're in a large group. Lunch and dinner are served Mon through Thurs until 9 p.m., Fri and Sat until 10 p.m.

FISCHER'S SPORTS PUB & GRILL, 1883 Andell Bluff Blvd., Johns Island; (843) 243-0210; $. If Ernest Hemingway were alive today, you'd find him at Fischer's. This authentic, family-owned pub at the Bohicket Marina is a perfect place to rub shoulders with the locals. Come in flip-flops straight from the beach and enjoy the best fried shrimp/oyster baskets anywhere around; even the french fries are exceptional. Whether you're watching the game on the big-screen TVs, shooting a round of pool, or just throwing back a cold beverage, Fischer's is a hangout you'll enjoy frequenting any day of the week from 11:30 a.m. to 2 a.m.

THE ISLANDER, 160-B Fairchild St., Daniel Island; (843) 388-6366; theislanderdi.com; $$–$$$. Those who remember the pirate decor of the former Queen Anne's Revenge will be surprised to see the new light, bright, and airy interior of The Islander. Now, the island vibe of the restaurant injects a little vacation feeling for the residents and visitors to Daniel Island. The bar is on the expanded patio creating outdoor and indoor service where live music is played on weekends—with maybe even a steel drum or two. The main dining room features a driftwood finish on the beautiful woodwork of the former mahogany bar adding to the tropical elegance of the setting. The fresh seafood is presented in ceviche, sushi, salads, and traditional Caribbean and Gullah fare sourced with South Carolina produced ingredients whenever possible. The house-ground burgers are also a favorite here. A family-friendly atmosphere is preserved with a kid's menu of sandwiches, soups, and mini fish tacos. The Islander is open for lunch, dinner, and Sunday brunch.

★ **MUSTARD SEED,** 1036 Chuck Dawley Blvd., Mount Pleasant; (843) 849-0050; dinewithsal.com; $$. This simple, yet sophisticated, eatery is a big hit with the vegetarian crowd—although the Mustard Seed offers pork, chicken, and seafood, too. Clearly, not everyone who frequents "the Seed" has abandoned beef; they simply enjoy the varied and creative menu offered here. In addition to a regular menu, there's a blackboard with daily specials that shows why there's sometimes a waiting line out the door. The sweet potato, Gorgonzola, walnut, and parsley ravioli are one example. The huge and authentic Greek salad is another. Desserts are very special, too. Coconut cream cake and chocolate cream pie are superb. A conservative but adequate wine list keeps customers amused if, in fact, a short wait is necessary. Be patient; it's worth it, and the food is a good value, too. Lunch is Mon through Sat 11 a.m. to 2:30 p.m. Dinner is served from 5 to 9:30 p.m. on weekdays and to 10 p.m. on weekends. An additional location is at 1970 Maybank Hwy. (843-762-0072).

THE ORIGINAL MS. ROSE'S, 1090 Sam Rittenberg Blvd.; (843) 766-0223; msroses.com; $$–$$$. The casual, fine dining options in West Ashley are somewhat limited. That's why it's good to know there's Ms. Rose's on Sam Rittenberg Boulevard across from the Park Center office complex. This trendy, eclectic-style restaurant with an outdoor deck is popular with business folk at lunch and locals after work and when the dinner hour comes. The snack menu is enticing with dirty rice fritters and Jamaican meat pies. But more ambitious appetites are well served by entrees like their braised pork shoulder or Rose's fried chicken. Steaks, ribs, and a daily market fish round out the menu offered every day from 11 a.m. The weekend crowd enjoys their Saturday and Sunday brunch.

SULLIVAN'S RESTAURANT, 2019 Middle St., Sullivan's Island; (843) 883-3222; sullivansrestaurant.org; $$. A favorite with the islanders and others in the know, Sullivan's is a family restaurant with affordable, good food. Not fancy, Sullivan's is just what the regulars want—a place to order delicious, traditional specials that include steaks, burgers, shrimp and grits, or oysters and scallops with two sides for less than $20. Dinner is served every day starting at 5 p.m. There is a children's menu, and Sunday brunch is served from 10:30 a.m. to 2 p.m.

T-BONZ GILL & GRILL, 1668 Old Towne Rd.; (843) 556-2478; tbonz gillandgrill.com; $–$$. Another vibrant, happening spot with a couple of locations throughout the city, T-Bonz serves a wonderful filet mignon (when you say rare, they take you at your word) as well as fresh gourmet burgers, and even seafood. There's plenty of beer on tap, including T-Bonz's own custom-brewed ales like Cooper River Red and Lowcountry Light Lager. Photographs of regular customers and Western paraphernalia adorn the walls, and you can't miss the enormous painting of the renegade cowboys on horseback. Regular customers order side veggies (sautéed and delicious) and feel comfortable having the kids along. Takeout is another option. They're ropin' 'em in for lunch and dinner 7 days a week. A second location is at 80 North Market St. (843-577-2511).

TOAST, 155 Meeting St.; (843) 534-0043; toastofcharleston.com; $$. Toast has accomplished an alchemy that few Charleston restaurants have been able to achieve. Here's a simple, convenient, friendly place to get an amazingly hearty breakfast, lunch, or dinner that's unpretentious, yet creatively prepared and, best of all, affordable. Toast is that rare find that's become almost extinct in downtown Charleston. The chalkboard outside the door lists an array of daily specials that are American and Lowcountry favorites. Come hungry; portions are generous. Toast is open daily starting at 6 a.m. for those who want to get an early jump on the day.

TRIANGLE CHAR & BAR, 828 Savannah Hwy.; (843) 377-1300; triangle charandbar.com; $–$$. With its 2-story-tall windows, the Triangle Char & Bar is a fun, open place to meet friends for an evening meal or just to enjoy the great desserts, cordials, and specialty coffees at the bar. Situated on a triangular piece of land between Savannah Highway and Magnolia Road, it offers plenty of outside seating for pleasant summer evenings. From the live charcoal grill, you can order the daily specials that may include fresh fish, chicken, pork, or steaks. Don't miss the chicken liver appetizer with a fried egg and tasso gravy over grits or the SC grass-fed beef burgers. Sandwich favorites include the fish tacos and the classic Cuban. Sunday brunch is from 11 a.m. to 3 p.m. Dinner is served Mon through Sat starting at 4:30 p.m., and lunch runs from 11 a.m. to 2 p.m. A second location is in Mount Pleasant at 1440 Ben Sawyer Blvd. (843-606-2900). (See the Entertainment chapter.)

TROTTERS RESTAURANT, 2008 Savannah Hwy.; (843) 571-1000; the townandcountryinn.com; $$. Trotters Restaurant, in the Town & Country Inn & Suites, is a good find for an all-out buffet—breakfast and lunch as well as Friday nights. Sunday brunch is popular with the after-church crowd. The buffet table always groans with a wide selection of meats, seafood, vegetables, and desserts. There's no Saturday lunch or Sunday dinner, but Trotters is open for all other meals every day. (See the West Ashley section of the Accommodations chapter.)

VICKERY'S BAR & GRILL, 1313 Shrimp Boat Ln. (Shem Creek), Mount Pleasant; (843) 884-4440; vickerys.com; $$–$$$. Vickery's Bar & Grill is on Shem Creek and is as talked about for its unusual bar as for its good food. There's always an eclectic bunch of interesting folks to meet—young professionals and rebels with a cause. The fare here is vaguely Cuban, with a Southern twist. The original Vickery's is in Atlanta and has always earned good reviews there. Grab a booth or a table, inside or out, and order a burger (with piping hot, hand-cut fries) or a delicious seafood entree. Vickery's is open for lunch and dinner 7 days a week. (See the Entertainment chapter.)

ASIAN

MAMA KIM'S KOREAN AND JAPANESE RESTAURANT, 349 King St.; (843) 577-7177; $–$$. Mama Kim's Korean and Japanese Restaurant offers authentic Korean food for lunch and dinner 7 days a week. The food is well prepared and a delight for the palate. Choose either the beef or pork bulgogi with the spicy Korean sauce, a house favorite. Sushi fans will find creative options here too. Takeout is available, and reservations are not required.

MIYABI JAPANESE STEAK HOUSE AND SUSHI BAR, 688 Citadel Haven Dr.; (843) 571-6025; miyabicharleston.com; $$–$$$. This Japanese steak and seafood restaurant rates high on the family entertainment scale because of the hibachi style of tableside preparation and the knife-juggling Japanese chefs. Meals include a light soup, salad, and entree, and the food is consistently good. If you have never experienced this form of dining, be advised you may be sharing grill and dining space with strangers. Try the steak and shrimp for a sample of what the hibachi does for surf and turf. Try the sushi bar if you like yours untouched by the flame. A children's menu is available too. Dinner and drinks are served 7 nights a week, and early-bird specials are common. Call for reservations.

OSAKA JAPANESE AND CHINESE, 100 Folly Rd.; (843) 852-9979; charlestonosaka.com; $–$$. Osaka is nestled in the South Windermere Shopping Center in West Ashley. In addition to many choices of a la carte sushi, there is a varied appetizer menu including spring rolls, shrimp tempura, and steamed or fried dumplings. Complete dinners range from mango chicken or beef curry to Chinese specialities such as Szechuan chicken and shrimp with cashew nuts. If you like your seafood unscathed by the flame, this is the place for Japanese sushi delicacies all beautifully presented. There's even a private room for group gatherings. Osaka is open for lunch and dinner Mon through Sat and dinner only on Sun.

DINING

BARBECUE

BESSINGER'S BARBECUE, 1602 Savannah Hwy.; (843) 556-1354; bessingersbbq.com; $. Bessinger's serves tasty Southern meals featuring ribs, chicken, fried catfish, pot roast, and of course their famous barbecue with various sauces. The Southern buffet is a favorite on weekends (Fri through Sun), as is the next-door sandwich shop, which is open daily, late morning to late evening. There's drive-through service when you're on the run. The catering operation, aptly named "When Pigs Fly," can be reached by calling the number above.

FIERY RON'S HOME TEAM BBQ, 1205 Ashley River Rd.; (843) 225-7427; hometeambbq.com; $–$$. Bring up the subject of whose Southern barbecue is best and you can always count on an argument. In fact, we don't even agree on how to spell the subject—but we sure like to eat it. One place getting a lot of business from barbecue lovers is this little gem tucked away West Ashley on SR 61. Fiery Ron's Home Team BBQ, as the name suggests, offers 6 different Fiery Ron's housemade BBQ sauces to fire up your generous plate full of food. Their specialty is Memphis-style dry-rubbed barbecue ribs, chicken, and pork shoulders and all the fixins that go with them. We're talking Brunswick stew, rib platters (you can order in half or full racks), smoked turkey, collards, mac 'n cheese, poppyseed coleslaw, and corn bread. There are salads, tacos, sandwiches and wraps, and a kids' menu too. This place is nothing fancy, just a BBQ shack/juke joint atmosphere with indoor and outdoor seating and lots of TVs to catch your favorite team in action. Beer, wine, and drink specials help cool down the fire and add to the mix of good food, good music (live bluegrass on Thurs, Fri, or Sat), and good times. Home Team BBQ is also a caterer, so many folks choose them for parties and family get-togethers where barbecue is a staple. It's open for lunch and dinner Mon through Sat and Sunday brunch. A second location is at 2209 Middle St., Sullivan's Island (843-883-3131).

MELVIN'S SOUTHERN BBQ & RIBS, 925 Houston Northcutt Blvd., Mount Pleasant; (843) 881-0549, (888) 635-8467; melvinsbbq.com; $. The delicious barbecue, coleslaw, onion rings, hamburgers, and vegetables at Melvin's make it a good bet for a quick meal. This has been a Lowcountry outlet for barbecue since 1939. The prices are quite reasonable, too. Melvin's is open Mon through Sat for lunch and dinner. A second location is at 538 Folly Rd. (843-762-0511).

STICKY FINGERS, 341 Johnnie Dodds Blvd., Mount Pleasant; (843) 856-7427, (800) STICKYS (784-2597); stickyfingers.com; $–$$. Any day (or night, for that matter) is great for ordering Sticky Fingers' famous ribs. They come in about every style possible: Tennessee Whiskey, Carolina Sweet, Memphis, and Habañero Style, to name a few. You may even want to take home a bottle of one of their five signature barbecue sauces after chowing down here. The eatery also serves chicken, salads, and sandwiches. A $4.99 kids' menu includes an entree, side, drink, and sweet treat. It offers a full bar and is open 7 days a week for lunch and dinner. Two more locations are at 235 Meeting St. (843-853-7427) and 1200 North Main St. in Summerville (843-871-7427).

CAFES & DELIS

BEAR-E-PATCH CAFE, 1980-A Ashley River Rd.; (843) 766-6490; beare patchcafe.com; $–$$. Every once in a while a simple, affordable, neighborhood restaurant strikes gold with the right combination of good food, generous portions, nice atmosphere, and friendly service. And that's what the Bear-E-Patch has going for it. This relatively small and unpretentious eatery is popular with locals. The breakfast menu is so hearty and creative with several specials offered daily that it's available until 3 p.m. and makes a dandy lunch. A deli-like lunch menu is offered also, along with grilled burgers and such. But at least one down-home special is right out of Grandma's Lowcountry cookbook. An on-site bakery turns out fresh bread (sourdough is a specialty) and pies, which adds to the allure. Dinner is served Mon through Fri until 9 p.m. and Sat until 8 p.m. The cafe is closed on Sun.

★ **BLOSSOM CAFE,** 171 East Bay St.; (843) 722-9200; magnolias-blossom -cypress.com; $$–$$$. Blossom Cafe is another see-and-be-seen place downtown but offers the bonus of being as affordable or extravagant as your budget allows. The cafe, open every day, has indoor and outdoor dining, an in-house bakery, a cappuccino bar, and an extensive New American menu with Italian and Mediterranean influences. Each menu for lunch, dinner, and late-night dining, features pastas, seafood entrees, and gourmet pizzas from the oak-burning oven. Sunday brunch is another option here. An added bonus is free parking just next door (after 5 p.m. on weekdays and all day Sat and Sun).

CARPENTIER'S WINE AND DINE DELI, 976 Houston Northcutt Blvd., Mount Pleasant; (843) 884-9386; carpentierscatering.com; $. Insiders know the deli at Carpentier's is a gourmet's delight. Choose from prepared meats, European breads and cheeses, homemade pâté, and daily specials. The distinctive aroma of roasted coffee and fresh-baked cookies and pastries fills the air. A selection of imported beers and fine wines is available, and there are a few small tables for dining in the store. Carpentier's is open for breakfast and lunch Mon through Sat. Gift baskets can be ordered by calling (843) 830-3042.

CHARLESTON'S CAFE, 1039 Johnnie Dodds Blvd., Mount Pleasant; (843) 856-7796; charlestonscafe.com; $–$$. Charleston's Cafe serves wonderful fare at breakfast and lunch and sells freshly baked goods. Located in the Queensborough Shopping Center, this cafe offers some serious omelets, eggs Benedict, and french toast, along with its signature potato casseroles. Lunch might be a crab melt, fish tacos, jerk chicken salad, and fried green tomatoes. Their weekend specials like the breakfast burrito and the farm hash are especially tantalizing. Take home some fried cinnamon rolls to enjoy later. The cafe opens at 8 a.m. daily. Closing time is 2:30 p.m. weekdays and 2 p.m. on Sat and Sun.

CRU CAFE, 18 Pinckney St.; (843) 534-2434; crucafe.com; $$–$$$. There's nothing quite like Cru Cafe in Charleston. Sure, we have other restaurants in single houses, and you can dine on the porch at those as well. But Cru Cafe is unique. The menu features "upscale comfort food" that's nourishing and desirable to the palate and the eye—but not so exotic as to be intimidating. For instance, there's their buttermilk fried oyster salad, Thai seafood risotto, pan-seared duck breast, and BBQ Berkshire pork osso buco. Lunch and dinner are served Tues through Sat. Seating is limited, so we recommend that you avoid the peak hours of noon to 1 p.m. Reservations are suggested.

JACK'S CAFE, 41 George St.; (843) 723-5237; $. The turnaround at Jack's is fast, and the food is as typically American as the no-frills apple or peach cobbler. College of Charleston students, professors, and alumni as well as King Street merchants frequent Jack's for old-fashioned burgers (served in plastic baskets) and milk shakes. The value is definitely part of the draw, but so is the vegetable soup (and, in fact, all of the food). People eat at booths, the counter, or around a few tables. It's all very low-key and functional. Take-out service is available. Jack's is open weekdays only for breakfast and lunch. No credit cards.

KAMINSKY'S BAKING CO., 78 North Market St.; (843) 853-8270; kaminskys.com; $. Kaminsky's is an A-plus addition to the list of indulge-thyself Peninsula eateries. The surprise is its just wonderful desserts and the right coffees and spirits to accompany them here. The handsome brick walls of the Market Street location make a backdrop for a nice showcase of art, and the cafe's intimate size contributes to its appeal. Try an exotic coffee or nonalcoholic drink with a delicious dessert. The milk shakes, for instance, are legendary. Be prepared to face a dilemma: There are 150 other choices. Relax with a martini or hot toddy. Kaminsky's is open from 2 p.m. until late night Mon through Wed, and Thurs through Sat beginning at noon. (See the Entertainment chapter.)

LAURA ALBERTS, 891 Island Park Dr., Daniel Island; (843) 881-4711; lauraalberts.com; $$–$$$. A welcoming atmosphere beckons from Laura Alberts on Daniel Island's Island Park Drive. The neighborhood place to stop for a little Lowcountry cuisine with a bit of flair, Laura Alberts fills the bill. This mother/daughter–founded cafe is also a place for fine wine, craft beers, and gifts. They serve lunch Mon through Sat plus a Sat brunch menu from 10 a.m. to 3 p.m. An ample selection of warm and cold sandwiches, pastas, salads with seafood or other toppings, and tasty appetizers are all prepared with fresh local and South Carolina–grown products. Dinner is offered on Wed nights only to help you get "over the hump." Wednesday is also host to their "Growler Hour" from 5 to 7 p.m. where you can taste what's on tap from their selection of over 100 craft beers. Their boutique-quality wines are extensive with over 27 varietals and 600 distinct labels. This is a great stop too for picking up boxed lunches for a picnic or boating adventure.

LONG ISLAND CAFE, 1515 Palm Blvd., Isle of Palms; (843) 886-8809; longislandcafesc.com; $$–$$$. Long Island Cafe became a local favorite soon after its doors opened way back in 1986, and it still has a loyal following. The changing menu is always interesting. The stuffed shrimp baked with crab, Parmesan-crusted salmon, and filet mignon with demi-glace are all popular with patrons. A nice selection of soups, salads, and sandwiches is also available. Long Island is open every day for dinner from 5 p.m. "'till" and lunch Mon through Sat. Its Sunday brunch, where the oysters Dupuis eggs Benedict is a favorite, is from 11 a.m. to 2 p.m.

★ **THE MED BISTRO,** 90 Folly Rd.; (843) 766-0323; themedbistro.com; $$–$$$. Talk about your neighborhood magnets. The Med Bistro is a real draw for West Ashley and downtown diners. Not only is the food good and predictable (the menu doesn't change, and favorite specials are repeated), but it's also just 5 minutes from the city, and parking is no trouble. Connoisseurs of spirits will enjoy the great selections of wine and imported beers here. Regulars are partial to the pita pocket sandwich with fried green tomatoes or black bean soup at lunch. For dinner, try the pasta specials; there are plenty of variations on the theme. There is live music on weekend evenings. The Med Bistro is open from late morning to 10 p.m. every day but Sun when they serve brunch from 9:30 a.m. to 3 p.m.

METTO COFFEE & TEA, 354 West Coleman Blvd., Mount Pleasant; (843) 216-8832; $. For a delightful treat, try Metto's salads, paninis, pastries, and bagels, and the like while taking advantage of the large selection of fresh-brewed coffees and teas. One exciting plus is that Metto's has a drive-up window to make it handy for pick-up lunches or java-to-go. There's outdoor seating too. It's open Mon through Sun from early morning until late afternoon. (See Coffeehouses in the Entertainment chapter.)

★ **THE PALMETTO CAFE**, 130 Market St., Charleston Place; (843) 722-4900; charlestonplace.com; $$$. This restaurant is inside the large Charleston Place complex and serves breakfast and lunch in a relaxed but upscale cafe atmosphere. The breakfast buffet on Sat and Sun is a very elaborate event with several choices of entree and salad, fresh vegetables and fruits, plus desserts. The garden atmosphere is particularly attractive and convenient to those staying in the hotel or shopping downtown. It falls in the pricier category, but everything is beautifully presented, and it is well worth the price on a special occasion (like your first visit to Charleston). For lunch, there's nothing like the seared scallops with heirloom tomatoes and feta cheese. Follow that with filet mignon with romesco sauce, roasted broccoli, and Spanish goat cheese. This stylish restaurant features optional courtyard dining and is open daily.

SAFFRON CAFE & BAKERY, 333 East Bay St.; (843) 722-5588; eatatsaffron .com; $–$$. This is a light and airy restaurant, contemporary in design and good for solo ventures or joining friends. The pitched-roof, modern building is divided into a gourmet product section with imported pastas and olive oils; a full bakery (you'll be seduced by the scent and leave with a loaf of bread); and a dining room with booths and tables scattered about and an outdoor patio. Popular menu items include the Middle Eastern salads and appetizers, pasta and kebab dishes, and the classic carrot cake. It's open for breakfast, lunch, and dinner 7 days a week. A pizza and salad buffet is offered weekdays. Saffron does a Sunday brunch from 9:15 a.m. to 2 p.m.

SEA BISCUIT CAFE, 21 J. C. Long Blvd., Isle of Palms; (843) 886-4079; seabiscuitcafeiop.com; $. This is one petite charmer—complete with a tiny front porch, substantial side porch (for dining), and really good island fare. The Sea Biscuit, tucked away on one of Isle of Palms' less chaotic streets, serves breakfast or brunch with the house specialty: fabulous biscuits. Try shrimp and gravy with grits and eggs, seafood omelets, french toast, and even eggs Benedict. The cafe serves a delicious house tea, and there's even a "treehugger" special of homemade granola, yogurt, and fresh fruit. Get there early, or expect a wait. Lunch is served after breakfast Mon through Fri; breakfast only is served Sat and Sun. No credit cards.

WILD WING CAFE, 36 North Market St.; (843) 722-9464; wildwingcafe .com; $. Wild Wing Cafe is popular with the younger-than-30 bar crowd, but also has appeal to those of us who have topped out the age group but not our attraction to a good time. Wild Wing serves a wonderful platter of chicken wings (of course), dressed in all kinds of herbs and spices—from the Ginger Wing to the Flying Fajita. There are great dips, sandwiches, burgers, and salads as well as weekday happy hour specials for a table packed with thirsty friends. The little ones are not forgotten with their Wild Child Menu. Wild Wing is open for lunch and dinner every day. Visit the website for additional locations.

YE OLE FASHIONED ICE CREAM AND SANDWICH CAFE, 474 Savannah Hwy.; (843) 766-4854; yeolefashioned.com; $. This is a quick stop but a change from the usual fast food. There are several locations within our coverage area and a few more beyond. This cafe serves triple-decker sandwiches, homemade soups, and, of course, lots of ice cream. There are scores of flavors. Their 10-slices-of-bacon BLT and the all-beef hot dog are big hits, too. If you use the drive-through window, you may want to call ahead for soup and sand-wich take-out orders. All the food is delicious, and local kids love this place. Hours are midmorning through late night daily. Check their website for more area locations.

FRENCH

FAT HEN, 3140 Maybank Hwy., Johns Island; (843) 559-9090; thefathen .com; $$–$$$. Chef-owner Fred Neuville, formerly of Rue de Jean and Coast has created a neighborhood restaurant on Johns Island that is packing them in. Just the right balance of a relaxed atmosphere and his signature French-inspired Lowcountry cuisine draws locals and tourists here from downtown and the Kiawah and Seabrook resorts. Try the scallops wrapped in bacon with pome-granate BBQ sauce and herb salad for an appetizer. Dinner favorites like the coq au vin braised in red wine with bacon and swiss chard or the seared grouper served over butter beans, corn, and tomatoes more than satisfy. And, of course, to pair with this is an impressive wine list with well- and lesser-known labels. Don't miss the Pluff Mudd Pie with chocolate mousse, Oreo cookie crust, and Chantilly crème. They are open daily for dinner starting at 5:30 p.m., and a bar menu starts at 4 p.m. They even have a kids' menu. Sunday brunch is served from 10 a.m. to 3:30 p.m. Limited reservations are accepted for dinner and brunch.

GAULART & MALICLET (FAST AND FRENCH), 98 Broad St.; (843) 577-9797; fastandfrenchcharleston.com; $–$$. Tucked neatly into what was once a long, narrow doctor's office, with lovely old molding, G&M (called Fast and French by locals) is a tiny Parisian-style cafe serving delicious, contemporary French fare. The counter-style service offers cheese plates, salads, and house specials. The owners (French, of course) know what they are doing and are pleasant while doing it. Some favorites are the sesame chicken and the Swiss fondue with French bread. They serve breakfast, lunch, and dinner almost every day except Sun. No dinner is served on Mon.

⭐ **39 RUE DE JEAN**, 39 John St.; (843) 722-8881; 39ruedejean.com; $$–$$$. Here's a little bit of Paris on South Carolina soil. That is, this restaurant is all about French food served in the best tradition of the genre. Located across John Street from the visitor center, this is a great place to begin a dining tour of Charleston. It's known for braised short ribs with espagnole sauce and steamed mussels available in six different presentations. If you want, a large assortment of French wines is available, but domestic labels are offered too. The full-service bar is a popular stop for locals as well as first-time visitors to our city. A favorite dessert is the crème brûlée. Rue de Jean is open for lunch or dinner every day from 11:30 a.m. until 11 p.m. or late night on Fri and Sat. Their Sunday Brasserie Brunch is served 10 a.m. to 3 p.m.

GREEK & MEDITERRANEAN

ATHENS GREEK RESTAURANT, 1939 Maybank Hwy., James Island; (843) 795-0957; athensofcharleston.com; $$. The line moves quickly at Athens, in the Athenian Village, where there is usually a crowd eager to dine. Specialties at this popular Greek place include Greek chicken, spanakopita, lemon chicken soup, Greek salad with feta cheese, and baklava. A full range of spirits is available. Athens is open every day for lunch and dinner. Dashing diners will appreciate their Express Cafe for a quick bite or takeout, located next door in the same building. The delivery phone number is (843) 302-8888.

OLD TOWNE GRILL AND SEAFOOD, 229 King St. (across from Charleston Place); (843) 723-8170; oldtownerestaurant.com; $$. Owners Spiros Fokas and Steve Ferderigos have been serving authentic Greek lunches and dinners here daily for more than 30 years. The menu includes seafood, salads, Greek chicken, and the ever-popular Super Special—a sampler, good for the whole gang. Pictures of classical Greece line the walls, and a grill in the front window offers a tempting display of chicken being roasted on a turning spit. Another location is called Zeus Grill and Seafood at 725 Johnnie Dodds Blvd. in Mount Pleasant (843-388-9992).

SERMET'S DOWNTOWN, 276 King St.; (843) 853-7775; sermetsdowntown .com; $$$. After the success of his first eatery west of the Ashley, Sermet's creative artist and chef opened a new location on King Street several years ago to rave reviews and standing-room-only crowds. The cuisine is Mediterranean-influenced, with spicy pastas and fresh green salads, and it's a refreshing option on the King Street luncheon and dinner scene. Look for their lavender honey–glazed duck breast with thyme-roasted fingerling potatoes. The desserts are straight from heaven. There's a chocolate ganache cake that is definitely to die for. Sermet's is open daily from 11 a.m. to 3 p.m. for lunch; and it reopens for dinner starting at 4 p.m. Upstairs the Mezz Charleston Jazz Bar offers additional restaurant and bar seating where jazz talent performs while you dine or enjoy a glass of wine. (See the Entertainment chapter.) A second location called Sermet's Courtyard is at 115 River Landing Dr., Daniel Island; (843) 471-1777.

IRISH

THE BLUEROSE CAFE, 652 St. Andrews Blvd.; (843) 225-2583; blue rosecafecharleston.com; $$. This little bit of Ireland may seem out of context, located as it is just across the Ashley from downtown Charleston. But the Bluerose Cafe is a welcome find for all who seek it out. Chef-owner Denis O'Doherty has all the blarney you'd expect of a true son of the Emerald Isle, but he makes true believers of a growing list of happy locals who know his skills in the kitchen are the real thing. The key word here is value. Luncheon specials are always well under $10 and range from Irish curry chicken salad with golden raisins to grilled prime rib sandwiches. Dinner entrees include a shepherd's pie that's hearty and nourishing, as is the seafood chowder with scallops, shrimp, and salmon. There's also a choice of chops or chicken in a number of presentations, and there's always plenty of soda bread, scones, and authentic Irish jams to satisfy the palate. A choice of imported wines and beer is offered if you like. It's open for breakfast and lunch Mon through Sat. Dinner is served on Thurs, Fri, and Sat from 5 to 9 p.m. Sunday brunch is from 9 a.m. to 2 p.m.

TOMMY CONDON'S IRISH PUB AND SEAFOOD RESTAURANT, 160 Church St.; (843) 577-3818; tommycondons.com; $–$$. The most authentic Irish pub in Charleston, Tommy Condon's has live Irish music Wed through Sun and serves a variety of imported beers and ales, such as Bass and Guiness Stout. The menu is a mixture of Irish and Lowcountry items, including shrimp and grits, seafood jambalaya, and fresh fish of the day. There is a covered deck for outside dining, and patrons are welcome for lunch or dinner any day of the week. The kitchen closes at 10 p.m., but the bar stays open until 1 a.m. (2 a.m. on weekends). (See the Entertainment chapter.)

ITALIAN

BOCCI'S, 158 Church St.; (843) 720-2121; boccis.com; $$–$$$. This cozy Northern Italian family restaurant near the Market keeps them coming back for more calzones, salads, pizza, and pasta. Mozzarella lovers go for the hand-pulled cheese. Another favorite is flounder involtini with blue crab stuffing over Parmesan risotto. Try the veal marsala, too. There is a front-room view looking onto historic Church Street. Bocci's is open every day for lunch and dinner.

FULTON FIVE, 5 Fulton St.; (843) 853-5555; fultonfive.com; $$$. Fulton Five is an authentic taste of old Italy tucked away on Fulton Street, just off King Street in the heart of the antiques district. The building looks Old World enough to be European, and the alfresco dining experience is definitely continental in feel. An upstairs dining area adds another perspective on the charms of quaint and narrow Fulton Street. The menu is constantly changing with new and more exciting entrees, but if the following dishes are available, we heartily recommend them. Start with antipasto Spoleto (grilled fresh mozzarella and prosciutto rolled into a romaine leaf with balsamic and tomato vinaigrette). Next, move to the ravioli di maiale stuffed with ricotta and shredded pork. Then enjoy the grilled veal chop with cannellini bean puree and sautéed spinach. For a light, sweet touch, order a grapefruit, orange, or tangerine ice made in-house or tiramisu—the perfect finale. A fine selection of Italian and other wines is always on hand. Fulton Five is open only for dinner Mon through Sat starting at 5:30 p.m. Reservations are suggested.

VINCENT CHICCO'S, 39-G John St.; (843) 203-3002; vincentchiccos.com; $$–$$$. If you're looking for old-fashioned Italian American fare, look no further. Vincent Chiccos is a new offering from the restaurant group that has successfully delivered for years at Coast and 39 Rue de Jean nearby (see listings). Celebrating classic flavors through the handmade pastas and rich homemade sauces on their menu, popular items include appetizers like the roasted tomato bisque and the bruschetta with house focaccia bread and local tomatoes. The *ragù alla Bolognese* and lamb *sugo* pastas and the veal and chicken piccatas are some of the traditional dishes that even an Italian mother would endorse. It might be hard but save room for dessert—the blueberry mascarpone cheesecake and chocolate torte are superb. Vincent Chiccos serves dinner nightly starting at 5 p.m.

WILD OLIVE, 2867 Maybank Hwy., Johns Island; (843) 737-4177; wild oliverestaurant.com; $$–$$$. Smack-dab in the middle of the Johns Island farming community, the Wild Olive makes the most of the nearby Lowcountry bounty in their Cucina Italiana. The chefs here work to transform the seasonal produce and local products into regional Italian classics with their own house-made pastas and house-cured salami. Start with crispy calamari with marinara, garlic aioli, lemon, and parsley or ravioli with local beets, goat cheese, pistachio dust, and aged balsamic. Move on to veal scalloppine with marsala, Mepkin Abbey mushrooms, peas, and mashed potatoes or local shrimp with *nduja*, over roasted tomatoes, spinach, and Geechie Boy polenta cake. Finish off with Venetian apple cake or the daily gelato accompanied by a nice dessert wine. Wild Olive is the first restaurant in South Carolina to become a Certified Green Restaurant, showing their commitment to not only purchasing locally, but to recycling and composting 85 percent of their waste. For those of us watching our carbon footprint, this is a destination that feels good all around. They are open daily serving a bar menu starting at 4 p.m. and dinner starting at 5:30 p.m. Reservations are recommended in this small, intimate spot.

LOWCOUNTRY CUISINE

Lowcountry cuisine is the cooking style found along the coastal areas of South Carolina and Georgia. Charleston, in particular, has embraced this culinary

Fresh pasta sale at a Charleston farmers' market

identity incorporating its plentiful seafood, game, produce, and rice culture with a blending of French, English, Caribbean, and African influences. Some of the traditional favorites include shrimp and grits, hoppin' John, frogmore stew (Lowcountry shrimp boil), and she-crab soup.

82 QUEEN, 82 Queen St.; (843) 723-7591, (800) 849-0082; 82queen.com; $$$–$$$$. This multi-award-winning restaurant has several personalities— one of which is sure to please. Exploring the 11 dining rooms at 82 Queen is an adventure in itself. The grounds include three 18th-century town houses, 2 inside bars (one full-service and one just for shots), an outside raw bar that is a very popular hangout for the after-work crowd, a partly glassed-in romantic gazebo, and outdoor tables for dining. Lowcountry seafood, beef, lamb, and fowl are specialties of their updated traditional Southern cuisine. Farm-fresh herbs and vegetables are locally grown for their kitchen. The wine list includes more than 140 selections. Lunch and dinner are served daily. Weekend brunch is especially nice in this pleasant atmosphere. Reservations are encouraged. (See the Entertainment chapter.)

FIG, 232 Meeting St.; (843) 805-5900; eatatfig.com; $$$. Locals fondly remember an affordable Italian restaurant at the corner of Meeting and Hasell Streets that is no more. But in its place came FIG (Food Is Good), a new and delightful offering spearheaded by Michael Lata, formerly of Anson. He brings an equally pleasing menu to FIG, inspired by his frequent travels in France, where fine dining is a way of life. Local farmers supply the freshest ingredients at peak flavor, and the results are reflected in every meal served. Vegetarians love the fresh plate of today's best produce specially prepared by the chef for maximum enjoyment. The ever-changing menu frequently includes a tomato and onion tart with creamy goat cheese or steamed Capers Inlet clams as starters. Look for Keegan-Filion Farms chicken liver pâté—or if you like, have corn flour–dusted snowy grouper with Yukon Gold puree.

Seasonal desserts like Edisto Meyer lemon pudding make a rewarding finale. Wines—domestic and imported—are plentiful and served by the glass or bottle. They're open Mon through Sat for dinner only starting at 5:30 p.m.

HIGH COTTON, 199 East Bay St.; (843) 724-3815; high-cotton.net; $$$– $$$$. In the mix of Charleston's array of fine eateries along the East Bay corridor just north of the Exchange Building is High Cotton. This is another one of the Maverick Southern Kitchens' restaurants (which also brings us Slightly North of Broad across the street and Old Village Post House over in Mount Pleasant). They call this one "an unabashedly masculine and American saloon," but don't look for anything Wild West about it. Instead, there's dark mahogany woodwork, exposed brick walls, lots of alligator skin upholstery, and a hearty menu of meats, game, and fresh fish. Local dishes may include South Carolina rabbit loin, duck breast, and shellfish. The spirits served and the service rendered are up to Maverick group's high standards. Happy hour begins at 4 p.m.

daily. Dinner hours are 5:30 p.m. until late night seven days. Brunch is served Sat and Sun from 10 a.m. to 2 p.m. Local jazz each evening and during Sunday brunch is popular, too. Call for reservations.

> **i** Check the menu or specials board at Lowcountry eateries for Beaufort stew (sometimes called frogmore stew), a hearty one-dish supper that's a staple meal on the Sea Islands. It's smoked sausage, fresh ears of corn, and shrimp all boiled together with special spices. This fare is often served at Lowcountry oyster roasts as an alternative menu item.

★ **HOMINY GRILL,** 207 Rutledge Ave.; (843) 937-0930; hominygrill .com; $$. On Rutledge Avenue, within a stroll from the huge MUSC hospital and medical office complex, there's a small but worthwhile cafe that's anything but institutional. This is a favorite with the medfolk, as you would imagine, so the best time to find a table is off the peak meal rush hours—although breakfast, lunch, and dinner are all offered. The cuisine is contemporary Southern, with several attractively served specials listed daily on the chalkboard menu. Look for some Lowcountry favorites like classic shrimp and grits. Or, there's a catfish creole in tomato and ham sauce over jasmine rice. Desserts are terrific, and the buttermilk pie and chocolate pudding are special treats. Hominy Grill serves breakfast from 7:30 until 11:30 a.m., when the all-day menu picks up through 9 p.m. Their popular weekend brunch goes from 9 a.m. to 3 p.m.

HUSK RESTAURANT, 76 Queen St.; (843) 577-2500; huskrestaurant .com; $$$–$$$$. Garnering accolades right from the get-go, Husk was named *Bon Appétit's* best new restaurant in America in 2011. *Southern Living* readers felt the same way. And what makes it so good? Well, maybe it's due to the James Beard Award–winning Chef Sean Brock and Lowcountry native Chef Travis Grimes, who explore what they call "ingredient-driven cuisine" using heirloom food products from the bounty of the South. This means that the menu changes daily but might include fare such as Blue Ridge bison short rib with sweet onion relish, Ambrose spinach, and cider glacé or cornmeal-dusted NC catfish with fried cabbage, green tomato chow chow, and Appalachian tomato gravy. Who could resist a Southern side dish like smoky butterbean and tomato with heirloom kale and Carolina Gold rice or a skillet of corn bread with TN bacon? To satisfy that down-south sweet tooth, finish off with bourbon pound cake or NC apple crisp. No wonder Husk continues to delight. They are open for dinner every day, lunch Mon through Sat, and brunch on Sun.

JASMINE PORCH, 1 Sanctuary Beach Dr., Kiawah Island; (843) 768-6253, (800) 654-2924; thesanctuary.com; $$$–$$$$. The Sanctuary at Kiawah has one dining option that revisits a much-loved tradition for those who know Kiawah from years ago. That's a dining room known as Jasmine Porch—a reincarnation of the first dining room from Kiawah's former Inn. Here the cuisine is Lowcountry fare—kicked up a notch or two. The emphasis here is on the purest and finest ingredients, so when you order shrimp and grits, the shrimp is the freshest caught available, and the grits are organic and cooked to perfection. Same is true for the she-crab bisque and the oysters on the half-shell. Same goes for the flourless chocolate torte and the apple cake. Breakfast, lunch, and dinner are served daily, and spirits are on call. Sunday brunch is a special treat with chilled Champagne mimosas and live music setting the stage for the sumptuous fare. It doesn't hurt that Jasmine Porch with its outdoor terrace overlooks The Sanctuary's spectacular pool area and the Atlantic Ocean. Nearby is the Loggerhead Grill, offering additional outdoor dining when the weather permits.

★ **MAGNOLIAS UPTOWN/DOWN SOUTH**, 185 East Bay St.; (843) 577-7771; magnolias-blossom-cypress.com; $$–$$$. Magnolias tops the list of hot restaurants on the Peninsula. In fact, *Travel + Leisure* called it *"the* place in downtown Charleston." This is new American-Lowcountry cuisine, and the chef's specialties include shellfish over creamy white grits with fried spinach, and the down-south egg roll stuffed with chicken, tasso ham, and collard greens. The expansive menu will remind you of the restaurant's California, Tex-Mex, and Cajun inspirations, but the atmosphere is strictly refined New South. Enjoy eating in the beautiful dining rooms at Magnolias, but also try your hand with Magnolias' recipes at home: *Magnolias Southern Cuisine* is a hot-selling cookbook. Lunch and dinner are served daily. Reservations are definitely encouraged.

OLD VILLAGE POST HOUSE, 101 Pitt St., Mount Pleasant; (843) 388-8935; oldvillageposthouse.com; $$–$$$. This is one of the dining options presented by Maverick Southern Kitchens, Inc. This one is combined with a 6-room inn nestled in the heart of Mount Pleasant's quaint Old Village. (See the Accommodations chapter.) The beautifully restored 1888 structure now houses 2 dining rooms and a charming tavern available to inn guests or a la carte visitors looking for fine food at affordable prices. For starters, you can expect to find Lowcountry favorites on the menu like shrimp and grits, but check out the beef carpaccio with soft-boiled egg and black truffle vinaigrette. The main dishes making a hit with patrons include pan-roasted grouper with Carolina Gold risotto and roasted fennel. Along with the grilled salmon with butternut squash puree, you can find steaks and duck breast on the creative and varied bill of fare. It's open for dinner nightly from 5:30 p.m., and serves a popular brunch on Sun from 10 a.m. to 2 p.m.

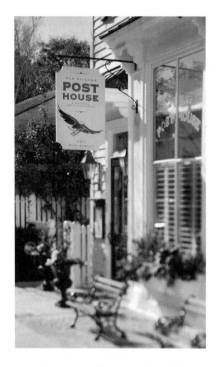

POOGAN'S PORCH, 72 Queen St.; (843) 577-2337; poogansporch .com; $$–$$$. Poogan's Porch is in a charming old Charleston house where lunch and dinner can be enjoyed fireside or outside beneath the stars on the porch or patio. Expect casual, intimate dining with such Lowcountry favorites as Chef Issac's she-crab soup, fried green tomatoes, crispy-skinned snapper, buttermilk fried chicken, seafood specials, and even—on the wilder side—an occasional alligator dish. A wine cellar stocked with 1,500 bottles makes it a connoisseur's dream. Lunch is served weekdays, and dinner 7 days a week; reservations are recommended for dinner. Saturday and Sunday brunch is from 9 a.m. to 2:30 p.m.

★ **ROSEBANK FARMS CAFE,** 1886 Andell Bluff Blvd., Seabrook Island; (843) 768-1807; rosebankfarmscafe.com; $$–$$$. Here's a delightful place to get typical Lowcountry cuisine (in other words, "Suh-thun cookin'") done with a modern twist. Rosebank Farms Cafe is in the marina atmosphere of Bohicket Creek. This spot is especially popular during fishing tournaments at Seabrook. Along with choice steaks, local seafood, pastas, and fresh vegetables, try the honey and buttermilk fried chicken. The blue plate lunch specials for $10.75 are a great deal. And if you saved any room, their triple chocolate oatmeal brownie is to die for. A children's menu is available too. Rosebank is open for lunch daily and reopens for dinner at 5 p.m. every night.

★ **SLIGHTLY NORTH OF BROAD**, 192 East Bay St.; (843) 723-3424; slightlynorthofbroad .net; $$–$$$. In one of the many 19th-century cotton warehouses that line East Bay Street, there's this trendy option for S.N.O.B. types. Cute name notwithstanding, the folks here are very serious about good food. It's what they call a "maverick Southern kitchen" with multicultural overtones. The grilled rib eye filet and pan-seared flounder are divine. The $10.95 express lunch of the day is a hit too. This restaurant is a favorite of those who want to lunch with friends (Mon through Fri) or have a special evening on the town (any day of the week). Reservations are encouraged.

NOUVELLE AMERICAN

Nouvelle American is a modern style of cooking based on nouvelle cuisine that originated in France in the 1970s. It emphasizes a lighter, healthier cuisine over the richer, heavier French haute cuisine that preceded it. Nouvelle American stresses light sauces and purees, and quickly cooked fresh vegetables using regional, seasonal produce, seafood, and meats in smaller portions with an artful, elegant presentation.

★ **ANSON**, 12 Anson St.; (843) 577-0551; ansonrestaurant.com; $$$. This elegant restaurant on Anson Street is between the Market and the trendy Ansonborough neighborhood. Anson is as well appointed as it is deserving of its reputation for fine food and good service. The nouvelle American menu includes a decadent whole crispy flounder with apricot shallot sauce that should not be missed. If you're among those who enjoy beef carpaccio, Anson's consistently gets rave reviews. Other temptations include outstanding first-course shrimp and grits with bacon, roasted tomatoes, and Anson's grits. When it's time for dessert, look for their dense, moist

DINING

house-made chocolate cake. Dinner is served 7 nights a week; reservations are recommended.

⭐ **CHARLESTON GRILL,** 224 King St. (in Charleston Place); (843) 577-4522, (800) 237-1236; charlestongrill.com; $$$–$$$$. This is the grande dame restaurant in Orient Express's Charleston Place. In this recently renovated and traditionally decorated eatery, quality is the byword. Service is exuberant, for those who demand close attention, and the wine list can compete with any in the South. It isn't exactly stuffy, but the atmosphere is definitely upscale. The food is simply superb. Its nightly specials are always as billed, but the regular menu is abundant in attractive choices. Try the Black River caviar or venison tartare for starters. And the grilled domestic lamb rack with mint chimichurri makes for a delectable entree. Desserts are announced nightly for those with a taste for excess. Live jazz begins at 6:30 p.m. (7:30 p.m. on weekends) and adds a cool balm to the well-orchestrated scene. Dinner is served nightly, and the bar opens at 5 p.m. Reservations are welcomed.

CIRCA 1886, 149 Wentworth St.; (843) 853-7828; circa1886.com; $$$–$$$$. When the giant landmark Victorian town house on Wentworth Street opened as a high-end B&B, the whole concept for the genre in Charleston expanded upwardly—in more ways than one. Not only would the envelope for luxury accommodations be expanded, an on-site restaurant of similar caliber would be opened for the convenience of the mansion's guests and other discerning diners. Thus, Circa 1886 was born (about a year later), and it seems well worth the wait. Named for the date of the Wentworth Mansion's construction, this small and intimate dining venue in what was once the carriage house offers seasonal cuisine that conceivably might have been served to the home's owner at that time. Executive Chef Marc Collins rotates the menu seasonally—presenting his unique and modern take on old Charleston recipes. Look for the antelope loin with butterbean succotash and Meyer lemon anglaise. Another find is their lemon pepper–brined swordfish with rosemary potatoes and mushroom glacé. Desserts sure to please include pistachio crème brûlée or bittersweet chocolate soufflé.

An intimate bar and attentive but unobtrusive service add to the ambience here—and Circa 1886 provides a quiet evening of fine dining clearly intended to be a cut above the rest of the downtown restaurant crowd. An impressive wine list with more than 250 labels is available. Dinner is served Mon through Sat from 5:30 to 10 p.m. Reservations are suggested.

CYPRESS LOWCOUNTRY GRILLE, 167 East Bay St.; (843) 727-0111; magnolias-blossom-cypress.com; $$$$. Many Charleston visitors have tried Magnolia's on East Bay Street and raved about it. Here's another restaurant from the same owners and chefs with a slightly different twist. Cypress is contemporary American cuisine with Asian overtones, and the result is delightful. Wine lovers will appreciate the 21-foot-tall "wine wall" with choices for the most discriminating palate. The 4,500 bottles kept on hand make a stunning background for a memorable evening. The 1834 building that houses Cypress retains a Charleston feel, while the decor is smart and trendy by any standard. The menu is large; for instance, you choose from more than a dozen different appetizers. The grilled portobello flatbread and almond fried brie are popular options. Among the dozen or so main dishes, smoked salmon Wellington with cauliflower, basil gremolata, and mustard butter is divine. The desserts are equally attractive. Try the Tahitian vanilla bean crème brûlée with a milk chocolate bonbon. The pecan financier with sweet potato ice cream is memorable, as well. Cypress is open for dinner daily starting at 5:30 p.m. Reservations are preferred.

⭐ **LANGDON'S,** 788 Shellmore Blvd., Ste. 105, Mount Pleasant; (843) 388-9200; langdonsrestaurant.com; $$$. A popular choice with Mount Pleasant residents is this small restaurant and wine bar in what locals call the Bi-Lo Shopping Center. The decor is upscale, or "urban chic," if you please. The crowd is young and hip, thus so is the menu. For starters, try the seared foie gras over tempura-fried shiitake mushrooms. Or, you might ask for the arugula salad topped with goat cheese, pear slices, and smoky bacon vinaigrette. When it comes to entrees, look for the local market fish over leek and sweet corn risotto. The boneless pork chop with tomato-brie grits and horseradish-apple slaw is another favorite. The dessert menu changes seasonally, but you can usually find the berry crisp with fresh blueberries and orange liqueur a la mode. The global wine list is ample with more than 100 varieties offered. How 'bout that for a shopping center location? This surprisingly refreshing dining adventure is open weekdays for lunch and Mon through Sat for dinner. Dinner reservations are strongly recommended—especially Wed through Sat.

MCCRADY'S, 2 Unity Alley; (843) 577-0025; mccradysrestaurant.com; $$$–$$$$. McCrady's experienced a new incarnation several years ago that retains much of the old tavern's charm but adds new space and sophistication. The dark wood and exposed brick interiors hark back to the days when George Washington supposedly supped here, and the huge fireplaces add their own charm. But the service and—most of all—the cuisine are the reasons to go there. Here, fine dining is a major event. The menu changes daily, but McCrady's serves appetizers like aged squab with sunchoke and huckleberries. Sometimes there are South Carolina clams too. For entrees, try the black bass with swiss chard, beet, fennel, and tangelo. But delicious variations of duck, chicken, beef, pork, and lamb are always on the menu. If you're still able, try a dessert like the carrot crémeux. The sommelier's wine list is extensive and impressive. It's open daily for dinner. (See the Entertainment chapter.)

THE OCEAN ROOM, 1 Sanctuary Beach Dr., Kiawah Island; (843) 768-6253, (800) 654-2924; thesanctuary.com; $$$$. The signature dining venue at The Sanctuary, Kiawah's luxury hotel and spa complex, is the Ocean Room. Up a dramatic staircase from the lobby is a handsome bar that introduces the Ocean Room's dining adventure, where expansive views overlooking the Atlantic give the place its name. Elegant decor and excellent service are expected here—the cuisine is New American with an emphasis on beef entrees, and presentation is one of the points of focus. Chef de Cuisine Jason Rheinwald brings his special touch to the ever-changing menu, which includes some favorites like the lobster bisque with cognac foam, or the steak tartare with spiced chips, capers, anchovies, and fried herbs. Favorite entrees include the seared Atlantic salmon and the Ocean Room fillet with spinach, potato puree, and bordelaise. Of course, the sommelier directs guests through an extensive wine list to recommend the perfect accompanying vintage. The pastry chef presents a tantalizing array of fantastic desserts for the Ocean Room's finale. Reservations are definitely recommended. (For more on The Sanctuary, see the Accommodations chapter.)

> i The footsore traveler who's already enjoyed a full dose of Charleston's charm may be in the mood for a brief respite for some tea and sympathy. The Charleston Tea Company, at 24-B Ann St., across from the visitor center, has just the right medicine—a glass of refreshing mint tea (locally grown right here on Wadmalaw Island) or a cup of coffee and soups or sandwiches or other light fare. There's also a breakfast menu of pastries and hot breakfast sandwiches if the early riser needs a jump start. In any case, you'll be sustained for further adventures in the Holy City.

⭐ **PENINSULA GRILL, PLANTERS INN,** 112 North Market St.; (843) 723-0700; peninsulagrill.com; $$$–$$$$. The restaurant in the Planters Inn is the Peninsula Grill, an elegantly simple and altogether comfortable dining experience that has "extraordinary" written all over it. For instance, half the menu is devoted to the Champagne Bar, which offers an old-world selection of Champagnes by the glass and a list of mixed cocktails that reads like a page from Noel Coward's *Private Lives*. The Champagne Bar menu includes a full selection of oysters, lobster (fresh from Maine), and other seafood specialties. Try the roasted rack of domestic lamb or the pan-seared Carolina trout. The steaks, chops, and accompanying side dishes are equally fine, and you're tended to by a courteous and capable staff. As for wine, there's an extensive list—mostly from France and California. Several labels are available by the glass. Their "Ultimate Coconut Cake" is so popular that they will ship one overnight anywhere in the US. Peninsula Grill is open Mon through Sun for dinner only starting at 5:30 p.m. Reservations are suggested. (See the Entertainment chapter.)

SEA ISLAND GRILL, THE BOARDWALK INN, Wild Dunes Resort, 5757 Palm Blvd., Isle of Palms; (843) 886-2200; wilddunes.com; $$$–$$$$. Located within the Boardwalk Inn, the premier restaurant at the upscale Wild Dunes Resort is called the Sea Island Grill, formerly the Grill. As the name implies, the cuisine features the freshest Lowcountry seafood creatively presented by Chef Jeff Miller and his culinary team. In addition to the wide

DINING

selection of seafood dishes, entrees include seasonal presentations of steaks, chops, and poultry. Try the Lamb "Charleston Chop" with blue cheese–beet ravioli or Atlantic black grouper served with crawfish, and tasso and potato hash. If you are up to it, finish off with the Chocolate Symphony Cake, a thick slice of a rich, multilayered chocolate cake made with dark chocolate mousse and raspberry jam. The Sea Island Grill is open for breakfast, lunch, and dinner daily. Call ahead for dinner reservations and the required gate pass for entrance into Wild Dunes.

TRISTAN, 10 Linguard St.; (843) 534-2155; tristandining.com; $$$– $$$$. Located in the Market Street area within the French Quarter Inn (see the Accommodations chapter), Tristan offers an alternative to the Lowcountry dining experience abounding here. Right when you enter, you'll see the difference in a decor that is decidedly contemporary, yet comfortable, and an atmosphere that is reminiscent of fine dining in a sophisticated New York or Paris restaurant. Following in that same tradition the service is superb and the fare exceptional here. You may choose from a seasonal a la carte menu or the chef's tasting menu perfectly paired with a complementary wine. There is a nod to the local delicacies with locally sourced oysters, Lowcountry carbonara with Carolina quail, and pine-smoked day-boat scallops all beautifully presented with an innovative twist. Or venture out with their Scottish salmon with carrots cooked in embers and roasted shallot or house-made pumpkin tortellini with buffalo-milk Parmesan and Alba hazelnuts. Desserts complete the scene with choices like milk chocolate crémeux or a sorbet tasting of vanilla, mango, plum, and coconut lychee. The lounge opens at 5 p.m. daily, and dinner is served Mon through Sat starting at 5:30 p.m. Reservations are recommended. Complimentary valet parking is available at the 10 Linguard St. entrance.

PIZZA

ANDOLINI'S PIZZA, 414 West Coleman Blvd., Mount Pleasant; (843) 849-7437; andolinis.com; $–$$. Fine dining is one thing, but sometimes nothing beats a good pizza. Especially when the kids are involved or when appetites of the young-at-heart come to the fore—a good pizza is a joy forever. Here in Mount Pleasant is one of the best pizza parlors around. Andolini's Pizza uses marinated hand-tossed dough, homemade sauces, and the best cheeses in its array of pizzas, calzones, and salads. It's open for lunch and dinner Mon through Sun. Check out their website for more area locations.

MELLOW MUSHROOM, 309 King St.; (843) 723-7374; mellowmushroom .com; $–$$. Some visitors to Charleston may be familiar with the earlier version of this specialty pizza den that was a big draw in Atlanta when it first opened in the 1970s. Our version is new to the King Street crowd and the College of Charleston kids who weren't around for the "groovy" version in Hot 'lanta. In addition to the specialty pizzas, like their Mega-Veggie with a garden's worth of fresh nonmeat ingredients, their dough is made with spring water. Calzones, hoagies, and salads are on the bill as well. The location is ideal for students, but MM attracts out-of-towners, too. It's especially popular with late-nighters and lunchtimers from King Street's business district. They're open daily for lunch and dinner, and the bar stays open until late night. Additional locations are at 3110 SR 17 N. in Mount Pleasant (843-881-4743) and at 19 Magnolia Rd. in West Ashley (843-747-4992).

SEAFOOD

A. W. SHUCK'S SEAFOOD & OYSTER BAR, 70 State St.; (843) 723-1151; a-w-shucks.com; $$–$$$. More than a decade has passed since Shuck's first opened its doors, and a lot has changed in the Market area since then—at Shuck's in particular. What was originally a cozy, popular bar packed with locals has become a bigger, fancier eating establishment where the bar is no longer the major draw. Shuck's features both indoor and outdoor dining. Oyster connoisseurs will be interested to know the mollusks are sold raw or steamed at market price. Beef, fowl, shrimp, mahimahi, scallops, flounder, and children's plates are all on the menu. A. W. Shuck's is open daily for lunch and dinner. Locals and visitors alike enjoy the abundance of early artwork by local painter John Doyle throughout the restaurant.

THE BOATHOUSE AT BREACH INLET, 101 Palm Blvd., Isle of Palms; (843) 886-8000; boathouserestaurants.com; $$$. Right on the stretch of water known as Breach Inlet, with spectacular sunset views, is this unique restaurant. The decor is nautical but nice, and the menu includes pastas, grilled fresh fish, and house specialties such as coastal crab cakes with green Tabasco sauce and fried red onions, and the fresh catch of the day. The sides are as interesting as the entrees. Look for stone-ground grits, blue cheese coleslaw, and collard greens. Parking is free and dinner is served 7 days a week. Sunday brunch is from 11 a.m. until 2 p.m.

CHARLESTON CRAB HOUSE, 145 Wappoo Creek Dr., James Island; (843) 795-1963; charlestoncrabhouse.com; $$–$$$. On the Intracoastal

Waterway, the Charleston Crab House is open for lunch and dinner every day. The restaurant specializes in their crab pot, steamed garlic crabs (cooked until they are red, then placed before you for what locals call a "crab crack"). There is a raw bar, and outside tables for dining are close to the water. You can arrive by boat and moor at the restaurant dock, and they even will prepare your own catch. No reservations are necessary. There's a "fiddler crab" (kids') menu, and Mom and Dad may enjoy frozen tropical drinks. (See listing in the James and Johns Islands section of the Entertainment chapter.) Another location is at 41 South Market St., Charleston (843-853-2900).

COAST, 39-D John St.; (843) 722-8838; coastbarandgrill.com; $$–$$$. Tucked away on Hutson Alley behind Rue de Jean (on John Street) is this seafood restaurant making big waves with locals as well as out-of-towners. When the question arises, "Where will you find good seafood?" this is always a great answer. The menu lists dozens of options—all prepared in different as well as traditional ways. Some of the favorite coastal dishes from our own Lowcountry waters are the seared rare tuna, Carolina crab cakes, and braised grouper. A full raw bar is part of the scene, but you can order your seafood wood-grilled, steamed, smoked, or fried with a choice of ten sauces. Dessert is not to be missed here. Open daily for dinner starting at 5:30 p.m.

FISH, 442 King St.; (843) 722-3474; fishrestaurantcharleston.com; $$–$$$. As the name implies, this is a small restaurant on upper King Street that's mostly about (but not exclusively dedicated to) seafood. You can count on the fact that none of the seafood brought to table will be more than 36 hours from its native waters. The fun decor is part of the charm. You enter through a courtyard past a fountain and discover an environment that's creative and unusual without being too cute. The menu changes seasonally, but look for the sweet chile calamari in sesame tempura batter or the mussels du jour. If you're game for it, choose four items like crab spring roll, duck confit, goat cheese panini, and rice cake from their dim sum menu. You might like to try the bouillabaisse, a traditional steam pot in lemongrass broth, suitable for two seafood lovers. The dessert they're all talking about is the "monkey bar" with chocolate shortbread, caramelized banana, and marshmallow ice cream. Fish is open for lunch Mon through Fri. Dinner is served daily 5:30 to 10 p.m., and the bar opens at 4:30 p.m.

FLEET LANDING RESTAURANT, 186 Concord St.; (843) 722-8100; fleetlanding.net; $$–$$$. Curiously, there are not a lot of waterfront dining establishments on Peninsula Charleston. Fleet Landing addresses that problem. They are not only on the waterfront, their building juts out over the marsh and water on a reinforced pier offering up a wonderful view of Charleston Harbor and all its shipping and boating activity. This 6,000-square-foot concrete structure built in 1942 served as a debarkation point for US Navy sailors, thus the name "Fleet Landing." Today the chic maritime decor and classic yet contemporary Southern seafood menu make a perfect combination for a fun dining experience. Dine inside or hit the deck. Some of the regular menu items include Carolina lump crab cakes, pimiento cheese rib eye, and pan-seared tilapia. Seasonal items may include tempura-fried softshell crab, bacon-wrapped shad roe over creamy grits, and Johns Island tomatoes. They have a nice selection of regular and specialty beers, creative cocktails, and interesting martinis. Fleet Landing is open daily for lunch and dinner and brunch on weekends. Some parking is available in their lot in front or nearby metered parking or a parking garage across the street.

> **i** A sweating glass of sparkling iced tea is a Southern tradition, and most restaurants will gladly refill your glass gratis. Be sure to let them know, however, if you are specifically looking for our good old-fashioned sweet tea.

GILLIGAN'S SEAFOOD RESTAURANT, 1475 Long Grove Rd., Mount Pleasant; (843) 849-2244; gilligans.net; $$–$$$. Gilligan's restaurant has a great family atmosphere and delicious fresh steamed or fried seafood. There are burgers, steaks, and chicken as well. The blue plate lunch specials are a bargain at $7.99, and the kids' menu for ages 10 and under starts at $4.99. Crayons are available so the kids can draw while they wait. Their seasonally all-you-can-eat oyster clusters by the trayful are a hit with locals. Gilligan's is open for lunch and dinner every day. Check out their website for more area locations.

HANK'S SEAFOOD RESTAURANT, 10 Hayne St.; (843) 723-3474; hanksseafoodrestaurant.com; $$$–$$$$. Old-time Charleston insiders remember a place called Henry's, which was part and parcel of this city's colorful "renaissance era" in the 1920s and '30s. It was a seafood joint down in the Market (which was a whole lot rougher in those days), and among other distinctions, old Henry's served liquor throughout Prohibition with (apparently) no interference from the city fathers. Hearty "receipts" for seafood soups and dishes laden with cream and flavor were always offered at Henry's, and generations of Charlestonians were raised on it. Hank's is today's reincarnation of that tradition, with a lot of sophistication added to the mix. An old warehouse has been carefully outfitted with a quasi-period-looking fish-house decor without being too cute about it. And several of the old Henry's dishes have been reproduced or improved upon for patrons with modern palates who now flock there from all over the world. This is where she-crab soup is done right (lovingly flavored with crab roe and sherry), and oysters are still served on the half-shell atop beds of crushed ice. Tackle Hank's Seafood Tower of shellfish from the oceans of the world, if you like, or try the specialties (like sea scallops or seared tuna). There are several fried seafood platters that feature a variety of old Lowcountry receipts, as well. Spirits are still high and served at Hank's willingly. Dinner is served daily starting at 5 p.m., and reservations are suggested.

HYMAN'S SEAFOOD COMPANY, 215 Meeting St.; (843) 723-6000; hymanseafood.com; $$. A casual, always-crowded seafood dining experience for lunch or dinner, Hyman's offers a large selection of fresh-caught fish and a wide variety of shellfish. A raw bar and lounge are upstairs. Hyman's regularly fries in vegetable oil for those who want traditionally fried seafood. But you can order your fish broiled or blackened. Try the Lowcountry gumbo, for a hearty starter. The she-crab soup is award-winning. Open every day, the restaurant serves meals all day long from 11 a.m. to 11 p.m. We suggest parking in the Charleston Place garage.

LOCKLEAR'S LOWCOUNTRY GRILL, 320 Coleman Blvd., Mount Pleasant; (843) 884-3346; locklearsrestaurant.com; $$–$$$. Locklear's has been one of the most popular seafood restaurants in Mount Pleasant for years. But it's known for the chicken salad plate and she-crab soup as well. It's also considered a bargain. Now there is a Folly Beach location on the Folly pier, too (101 East Arctic Ave.; 843-588-6412). Call ahead for take-out lunch. Locklear's is open 7 days a week for lunch and dinner, and breakfast Mon through Sat. This is a popular spot for Sunday brunch starting at 10 a.m. Reservations are accepted.

MARINA VARIETY STORE & RESTAURANT, City Marina, 17 Lockwood Dr.; (843) 723-6325; varietystorerestaurant.com; $$. Enjoy good food as well as a magnificent view of the Ashley River at what regulars call the Variety Store. Offering breakfast, lunch, and dinner in a very casual setting, the restaurant serves basic, good food. For instance, you can order eggs, bacon, and toast for breakfast after church and come back for a tuna salad sandwich and cup of okra soup after the noon regatta. If you want to return that night, a dinner of fresh fish with red rice and a salad is a distinct possibility. Spirits are available, and children are welcome. Takeout is a popular option for City Marina guests and locals. Open daily, except there's no dinner service on Sun.

NOISY OYSTER, 24 North Market St.; (843) 723-0044; noisyoysterseafood .com; $$–$$$. Locally owned and operated for more than a decade, this restaurant offers fresh seafood and a casual atmosphere. Noisy Oyster always has a number of daily specials with fresh shrimp, scallops, and fish. Look for the oysters Rockefeller or the Lowcountry fish stew. Dining is possible inside and out, and spirits are available. Lunch and dinner are served daily. (See the Entertainment chapter.) Another location is at 7842 Rivers Ave., North Charleston (843-824-1000).

RED'S ICE HOUSE, 98 Church St., Mount Pleasant; (843) 388-0003; reds icehouse.com; $$. Another casual spot where diners get a view of Shem Creek, Red's Ice House is landmark along the popular restaurant row on both sides of the creek. You'll enjoy oysters, scallops, fish, and shrimp, as well as landlubber fare such as hamburgers and chicken. But make no mistake—right-off-the-boat shrimp and fish are the main draw here. Red's is right on the water, where shrimp boats dock and boaters cruise, to see and be seen. Red's colorful atmosphere makes this a happenin' place for young singles, especially on weekend nights. Red's is open daily from 11:30 a.m. to 10 p.m., or 11 p.m. on Fri and Sat, and the bar is open late night. Their Bohicket Marina location (1882 Andell Bluff Rd.; 843-518-5515) has a spectacular dockside setting too.

SALT AT STATION 22, 2205 Middle St., Sullivan's Island; (843) 883-3355; saltstation22restaurant.com; $$–$$$. Salt is the new incarnation of the former longtime Station 22 Restaurant in the middle of Sullivan's Island. Retaining the casual atmosphere, but not quite flip-flops and a T-shirt, SALT offers variety on its menu with creative salads, chowders, burgers, pizza, pastas, and of course, seafood. They even kept the island history on its walls, which showcase dozens of photographs of turn-of-the-20th-century Sullivan's Island. The menu changes daily but look for appetizers like the selection of seasonal oysters from the raw bar or the daily ceviche of brown shrimp, sheepshead with *leche de tigre*, and crispy yam chips. For an entree, try the pan-roasted local wreckfish with Carolina Gold rice, house-made sausage, and shrimp, or the braised beef short rib bourguignon with Parmesan polenta. Save room for their signature Station 22 coconut cake. Open every day from 5 p.m. for dinner and Sunday brunch from 11 a.m. to 2 p.m. A happy hour menu is offered weekdays from 5 to 7 p.m. and Sun 3 to 5 p.m., which can be enjoyed on their patio or porch. Valet parking is in their private lot directly across the street.

SALTY WATERS RAW BAR & GRILL, 520 Folly Rd.; (843) 762-9252; saltywatersrawbarandgrille.com; $$. This attractive little bistro is located in the Merchant Village Shopping Center on Folly Road. The restaurant's digs sport a strictly casual feeling. Salty Waters offers a full gamut of sandwiches, salads, and pasta dishes. Appetizers include shrimp bruschetta and a crab cake tower. Entrees range from blackened mahi to Cajun chicken pasta. Of course, there's always an extensive raw bar selection. The place is open for lunch and dinner Mon through Sat. It's a pleasant option for Sunday brunch, too. There's a full bar with ample varieties of beer including their very own Deep Sea Ale on tap.

SHEM CREEK BAR & GRILL, 508 Mill St., Mount Pleasant; (843) 884-8102; shemcreekbarandgrill.com; $$–$$$. To experience dining out the way the locals enjoy it, go to Shem Creek Bar & Grill (just Shem Creek to the regulars) and you'll find yourself surrounded by loyal Lowcountry patrons. (See the Entertainment chapter under East Cooper.) The menu has something for everyone, from burgers and steaks to lobster and grilled seafood specials, and Sloppy John's Oyster Bar is always a temptation. During the warmer months, Shem Creek is the hangout for the boating set, many of whom arrive by power craft. There is casual dining inside and out, with views of the creek from most seats. It's open daily for lunch and dinner and has brunch on Sun. The owners also operate the Banana Cabana on the Isle of Palms. (See the Entertainment chapter.)

WATER'S EDGE, 1407 Shrimp Boat Ln., Mount Pleasant; (843) 884-4074; waters-edge-restaurant.com; $$$. Water's Edge is an upscale seafood and beef restaurant on Shem Creek. Specialties include local seafood, prime rib, burgers, pastas, and paella. You'll also find one of the most comprehensive wine and Champagne lists in Mount Pleasant. Patrons park themselves, if possible, at a table next to the window for a view of the shrimp boats. Or come by your own boat and dock at the cabana bar. Water's Edge is open for lunch and dinner every day and serves a nice Sunday brunch as well.

THE WRECK OF RICHARD AND CHARLENE, 106 Haddrell St., Mount Pleasant; (843) 884-0052; wreckrc.com; $$–$$$. Tucked between Magwood and Wando seafood companies in the Old Village of Mount Pleasant, the red nun 106 (buoy marker) at the entrance to the parking lot and two flags out front (there's no official sign or designation) will help find The Wreck. The restaurant is very unpretentious, and you can arrive by your own boat if you don't mind crawling around on the docks to disembark. You may dine either on the deck or the screened-in porch dining area (the porch is sealed up and heated in the winter months). Try the seafood platter or the lightly fried oysters. The shrimp and scallops may be grilled, boiled, or fried, according to taste. Portions come in either Richard's size (large) or Charlene's size (not as large, but plenty), so order to match your appetite. Beer and wine are available except on Sun. The Wreck is open every day for dinner beginning at 5:30 p.m.

STEAK HOUSES

GRILL 225, 225 East Bay St.; (843) 266-4222; grill225.com; $$$$. When the Market Pavilion Hotel opened near the Market on East Bay Street, they promised a restaurant of distinction, and clearly, it was a promise they kept. Fashioned in the style of the great steak houses of yore, Grill 225 prides itself on garnering the freshest and highest-quality beef, veal, lamb, and seafood available. The fare is deliberately simple in its creation, proportion, flavor, and presentation—so the exceptional quality of each ingredient can (and does) carry the day. For starters, try their tuna tower, and then tackle their generous cut of prime beef or double-cut lamb chops. From the sea come jumbo lump crab cakes and, of course, lobster of almost any size you specify. If you're willing, the dessert menu tempts with banana bread pudding or flaming baked Carolina. Reservations are recommended, and they can be made online. Dinner is served daily from 5:30 p.m. Lunch is from 11:30 a.m. to 3 p.m. Mon through Sat. Sun lunch is from 11 a.m. to 2 p.m.

MICHAEL'S ON THE ALLEY, 39-E John St.; (843) 203-3000; michaels onthealley.com; $$$–$$$$. Serious meat lovers will embrace the high-quality cuts of USDA prime, Angus, and choice steaks, wet- or dry-aged, presented at Michael's on the Alley. The bacon Gorgonzola butter or horseradish beetroot crust to accompany your selection can take it to the next level. Updated menu favorites from the turn-of-the-20th-century steak house heydays include oysters Rockefeller, shrimp cocktail, Maine lobster tail, bone marrow, caviar, and beef tartare. The fresh seafood, prime rib, and tableside salad prep are other reasons to choose to dine here for a special evening out. The wooden-clad and brick dining room walls, white tablecloths, and tufted leather banquette seating add to the classic steak house feel. At the very least share one of their enticing desserts to linger a little longer. Dinner service starts at 5 p.m. every night.

OAK STEAKHOUSE, 17 Broad St.; (843) 722-4220; oaksteakhouserestaurant .com; $$$–$$$$. What locals remember as the little luncheon eatery called BJ's took on a whole new identity when the 1840s-era building (originally a bank) went through a $3 million renovation and expansion, which took 7 months to complete. When done, the stage was set for high drama, and a New York–style steak house par excellence opened its doors. This is an upscale source for steaks, chops, seafood, and even vegetarian specialties—all served with flair. They use only prime Angus beef, and you may order from a number of specially prepared sauces to complement your selection. Among the favorite starters is the steak tartare with quail egg, herb aioli, cornichons, and crostini. A popular steak for the hearty appetite is the marinated 16-ounce bone-in rib eye. For those not in a beef state of mind, there's free-range roasted chicken breast and whole fried lobster. The wine selection is served up from a vault that in an earlier life held Confederate bonds (before the "Recent Unpleasantness"). There's also a tasty bar menu to accompany one of their specialty cocktails or martinis. Valet parking is offered along busy Broad Street, which is a welcome gesture of true hospitality. Reservations are definitely called for, as space is limited. They're open daily from 5 to 10 p.m. (11 p.m. on Fri and Sat).

Entertainment

When the sun goes down, not all the people in Greater Charleston pack it in. In fact, locals and visitors who seek nighttime entertainment are met with an abundance of choices.

If you are interested in listening to live contemporary music, dancing, or just hitting the bar scene, start with the sampling of spots we've described below—you won't be bored. If you like beer and want to sample it straight from the folks who create it, try one of the brewpubs. Many of the nightspots are actually lounges at restaurants where dining is the primary focus, and many of these places are described in greater detail in the Dining chapter. We also have a category called Dinner Cruises for those who want to spend an evening on the waters of Charleston Harbor cruising and dining with live music and dancing as after-dinner options.

While Charleston is affectionately called the "Holy City" in reference to its many lovely churches, it also has a reputation for entertaining where socializing has a long and rich tradition. If you plan on enjoying a few beers or cocktails as part of the fun, be aware of the legal restrictions in the Charleston area, and know that area police departments actively enforce these laws. The minimum drinking age is 21 in South Carolina, and open containers are not allowed on the streets or in moving vehicles. A charge of driving under the influence may be levied against anyone whose blood alcohol content is measured at .08 percent or higher. In the city of Charleston, last call for liquor is usually 1:30 a.m., and closing is mandatory at 2 a.m.

For information about other entertainment options and cultural happenings, we suggest consulting the Arts and Festivals & Annual Events chapters.

DOWNTOWN CHARLESTON

BLIND TIGER PUB, 36 and 38 Broad St.; (843) 577-0088; blindtiger charleston.com. If you are looking for British pub atmosphere, escape into this friendly environment with its dark English mahogany walls and cast-iron stools. Order Bass Ale or Guinness Stout, or try a Black and Tan (Bass on bottom, Guinness on top). Fear not: The beer is chilled appropriately for Charleston, not served lukewarm as in England. A nice selection of appetizers is available until 10:30 p.m. There is live music some nights and a crowd that just keeps coming back. The back courtyard is a nice option when weather permits.

82 QUEEN, 82 Queen St.; (843) 723-7591, (800) 849-0082; 82queen .com. A long-standing, favorite hangout for the local Broad Street business set and others, the bar at 82 Queen is narrow (but comfortable enough) and a good place to see friends. You'll find a fine mix of people there knowing and not knowing each other's names. Patrons especially like the back bar if the weather is nice. They enjoy hanging out in the courtyard while waiters zip by with tempting appetizers, and outdoor diners enjoy their fare beneath the stars.

i Late-night revelers who need a rule of thumb to remember Charleston's bar-closing hours, try this: All bars in the Market area close at 2 a.m. If you feel the need to party even later than that, you'll have to go elsewhere.

THE GRIFFON, 18 Vendue Range; (843) 723-1700; griffoncharleston.com. A popular hangout for young professionals is The Griffon, a cozy English pub with an easy, friendly atmosphere. Especially busy at lunchtime, workers from the financial and legal offices on East Bay and Broad Streets stop here for simple but hearty sandwiches and maybe a cool brew. Others check in for happy hour, and some stay for dinner. It's open each evening and attracts a nice mix of locals and tourists out and about on East Bay.

HENRY'S BAR & RESTAURANT, 54 North Market St.; (843) 723-4363. Henry's used to be known for its Old Charleston meals and clubby side bar. Today, under different ownership, it has updated trappings and a new reputation for light food and live music nightly. The ambience is contemporary New Orleans, and the rooftop deck and dance floor are great for letting loose. This is a happening place for the Market Street crowd.

KAMINSKY'S BAKING CO., 78 North Market St.; (843) 853-8270; kaminskys.com. Kaminsky's Cafe tempts the minute you enter the door with their case full of "most excellent" desserts. In addition to specialty coffees, wine, beer, and liquors are on the menu. Kaminsky's serves from noon until late night.

★ **MCCRADY'S,** 2 Unity Alley; (843) 577-0025; mccradysrestaurant .com. Neatly tucked down Unity Alley, off the hustle and bustle of East Bay Street, is this small but attractive haven for a quiet drink. It lays claim to the fact that George Washington tipped a few here back in 1791. Today, this beautifully turned-out restaurant and upscale bar are a favorite with downtown business types and professionals because of the cozy atmosphere. The extensive wine list and premium bar serve happy-hour specials to please the after-work crowd. And its popular dining room close by makes a natural progression from an after-work respite to an evening on the town.

THE MEZZ CHARLESTON JAZZ BAR, Sermet's Downtown, 2nd Fl.; 276 King St.; (843) 853-4515; mezzdowntown.com. Just above Sermet's Downtown restaurant on the corner of King and Wentworth, the Mezz Charleston Jazz Bar serves up local and national jazz talent to include the Charleston Latin Jazz Collective and the ever-popular Quentin Baxter Quintet. Music enthusiasts may enjoy dinner from the restaurant, drinks, or wine or Champagne by the glass or bottle while watching the show. A $15 to $20 cover charge applies and dress is business casual. Visit the website to check out the lineup of musicians and make reservations.

★ **MILLS HOUSE HOTEL,** 115 Meeting St.; (843) 577-2400; millshouse .com. Easily the best location in Charleston if you're looking to be at the center of things, the Mills House Hotel is home to two nightspots that deserve your consideration. The handsome First Shot Lounge (in honor of the first shot fired at Fort Sumter in the Civil War) just off the Barbados Room Restaurant is a classic Southern setting that oozes charm. There's a grand piano, and often someone is on hand to play your favorite Gershwin tune. The Best Friend Lounge (named for the nation's first steam locomotive originating in Charleston) is a separate, more intimate bar with quiet entertainment Tues through Sat.

MUSIC FARM, 32 Ann St.; (843) 577-6989; musicfarm.com. Now in its second decade on the Peninsula, one of the most popular nightspots for contemporary music enthusiasts is the Music Farm—affectionately referred to by regulars as the Farm. The beat goes on at nearly nightly gigs when live bands—yes, favorite city sons Hootie and the Blowfish were once among them—perform here. The Farm's website has more information about upcoming entertainment and ticket prices. The college crowd is thick, but also expect to see 30-somethings, 40-somethings, and older-somethings elbowing their way toward the bar. The Farm is across the street from the visitor center, and parking is available on the street as well as in the nearby garage.

NOISY OYSTER, 24 North Market St.; (843) 723-0044; noisyoysterseafood.com. Located on bustling Market Street, this friendly little bar offers libations that seem to taste better in the salty sea air of the nearby Cooper River. The restaurant always has a number of seafood specials sure to please. Lunch and dinner are served daily.

⭐ **PENINSULA GRILL,** 112 North Market St.; (843) 723-0700; peninsula grill.com. The Peninsula Grill at the Planters Inn offers a very beautiful, romantic, upscale bar tucked inside the restaurant. In warm weather, we recommend a drink here before and after dining outdoors in the gaslit courtyard. This bar always attracts a well-dressed, attractive crowd and is a classy oasis amid the carnival atmosphere of the Market at night. The delightful Champagne Bar carries an extensive list of labels, and several are sold by the glass. The bar opens daily starting at 4 p.m.

ROOF TOP RESTAURANT & BAR, 23 Vendue Range; (843) 414-2341; thevendue.com. On the roof of The Vendue in downtown Charleston is this rare find on the Peninsula—a place (for cocktails) with a rooftop view and refreshing sea breezes. (See The Vendue in the Accommodations chapter.) Recently renovated, the Roof Top Bar remains a hit with locals. This place is a lovely location for starting a summer evening catching the sunset over the rooftops of Charleston. The service is friendly, and you can enjoy live entertainment most nights.

SOUTH END BREWERY AND SMOKEHOUSE, 161 East Bay St.; (843) 853-4677; southendbrewery.com. Here's a restaurant with its own microbrewery. Ice-cold handcrafted brews, made on the premises, are served with baby-back ribs, oven-baked pizzas, and specials off the wood-burning grill. The glass elevator takes you up to their third-floor Harborview Bar with a billiard and game room with spectacular views over the city. South End has live entertainment on weekends and serves both lunch and dinner 7 days a week.

STARS ROOFTOP & GRILL ROOM, 495 King St.; (843) 577-0100; starsrestaurant.com. Stars Rooftop is one of the most popular spots in the thriving Upper King Street district, and it's easy to see why. One look at the 360-degree view of downtown Charleston makes for an enchanted evening as the sun sets and the stars pop out. The wicker furniture and reclaimed tiger-wood bar set the scene for a Lowcountry feel while sipping one of their specialty cocktails, craft beers, or international tap wines. Space heaters take care of any cool evenings during Charleston's mild winters. You may want to follow cocktail hour with a Carolina cuisine dinner downstairs in the Grill Room featuring their live firewood cooking and exhibition kitchen. The Saturday and Sunday brunch with Bloody Marys and mimosas are a hit, too.

TOMMY CONDON'S IRISH PUB AND SEAFOOD RESTAURANT, 160 Church St.; (843) 577-3818; tommycondons.com. Every day is St. Paddy's Day at Charleston's only authentic Irish pub owned by an Irish family. In fact, families are indeed welcome here. Tommy Condon's has traditional Irish sing-alongs Wed through Sun and serves Irish spirits as well. The layout of the facility, with its big horseshoe bar, makes for a good party flow, and people mix and mingle all around.

WET WILLIE'S, 209 East Bay St.; (843) 853-5650; wetwillies.com. Across the street from the Custom House is this watering hole that's popular with the young professionals working up and down East Bay Street. Tourists are lured in as well, because it's right on the street and very inviting by day or night with its big, wide open doors. Live music cranks up every night with dancing on Fri and Sat nights. Wet Willie's will ask you to support global cooling by drinking one of their famous frozen daiquiris.

EAST COOPER

Mount Pleasant

Although Mount Pleasant is still a family-oriented community, there are plenty of exciting destinations for grown-ups when the sun goes down. The tremendous growth of the Mount Pleasant area and the subsequent boom in population have created a whole new market for after-hours entertainment. That's especially true now that all bars in Charleston are mandated to close at 2 a.m. The days when this quiet East Cooper neighborhood was strictly a bedroom community for downtown Charleston are over. Some of Mount Pleasant's nightspots howl until late night. Mind you, this is no passport to drive irresponsibly or misbehave, and the Mount Pleasant fuzz are out and about at all hours to prove it.

CHARLESTON HARBOR RESORT & MARINA, 20 Patriots Point Rd.; (843) 856-0028, (888) 856-0028; charlestonharborresort.com. This Mount Pleasant hotel on the Point, which extends into Charleston Harbor, is a delightful venue for sunset watching and a taste of coastal nightlife. (See the Accommodations chapter.) Every Fri during the spring months, hotel employees construct added outdoor bars and light bonfires in the sand for "Party on the Point," and hundreds of people come to enjoy the music, spirits, and invigorating night air. Charleston Harbor Resort & Marina brings in entertainment from near and far. Jazz, rock, beach music—it's all here at one time or another. They start pouring signature drinks at 6 p.m. and continue until long after sunset. Light dining options may include beachside barbecue and a seasonal seafood raw bar. Located just over the Cooper River Bridge, this is a popular destination for Peninsula folk and East Cooper residents alike.

SHEM CREEK BAR & GRILL, 508 Mill St.; (843) 884-8102; shemcreek barandgrill.com. High on the list of casual nighttime destinations, Shem Creek is one of the most popular watering holes in the area. It certainly has some great things going for it—the dockside bar overlooking the marsh, the raw bar inside, and the salty characters who make it their home away from home. The mood is usually upbeat, and the munchies are delicious.

VICKERY'S BAR & GRILL, 1313 Shrimp Boat Ln.; (843) 884-4440; vickerys.com. Vickery's is a popular spot for a drink with friends. The restaurant does a booming daytime business with its Cuban-American cuisine, and there's a festive Latin flavor in the bar at night. There's a large outdoor seating area for imbibing or dining. Vickery's is in the lively mix of restaurants and nightspots located on scenic Shem Creek.

Sullivan's Island & Isle of Palms

Although the islands east of the Cooper River are considered family beaches, there are several notable watering holes nestled behind the dunes. A word of warning: Don't let the casual setting lull you into ignoring the open container laws. In other words, don't stroll outside with an unsealed alcoholic beverage. Police officers take it seriously.

BANANA CABANA, 1130 Ocean Blvd., Isle of Palms; (843) 886-4360; thebananacabanasc.com. The Banana Cabana is open 7 nights a week and offers lots of cool, refreshing libations, and munchies or full lunches and dinners if you're looking for more. Wine and beer along with tropical concoctions and pitchers of drinks are on hand. Locals and visitors seem to delight in visiting this place after a day at the beach. Sometimes this is where you'll find macho men and their female friends fresh from the beach boasting their perfect tans.

DUNLEAVY'S PUB, 2213-A Middle St., Sullivan's Island; (843) 883-9646; dunleavysonsullivans.com. A welcome watering hole for the island, Dunleavy's is an Irish pub with indoor and outdoor dining. The outdoor picnic tables are replete with dog bowls for patrons on a leash. The bar regularly attracts the

All That Jazz . . .

If anything about Charleston is known and recognized the world over, it has to be the 1920s dance craze that swept the country and set the tone for America in the Jazz Age. Relatively few people, on the other hand, know the origins of the dance or the story of how it captured the imagination of an American generation bursting with pent-up energy after the so-called war to end all wars (World War I). The popular dance known as **"the Charleston"** is said to have begun on the street beside Charleston's Fort Sumter Hotel (near the Battery) with the energetic dance steps of the **Jenkins Orphanage Band.** In 1892, the Rev. Daniel Jenkins founded an orphanage in the city for homeless black children. To fund his charity, he organized the kids into a band that played on street corners for pennies donated from passersby. These young musicians were a delight to locals and visiting tourists alike. Eventually several bands and choirs evolved that were invited to perform in Florida, the northern states, and eventually Canada and Europe. The Jenkins Orphanage Band and its jaunty jazz tune called the "Charleston" spawned the careers of several great jazz musicians who eventually played in the world-class bands of jazz greats like Count Basie, Louis Armstrong, and Duke Ellington.

beach crowd, and it's very family-oriented at the dinner hour. On weekends it features live music (and some Tuesdays feature bluegrass). Bill Dunleavy is usually on hand and makes one and all feel welcome.

POE'S TAVERN, 2210 Middle St., Sullivan's Island; (843) 883-0083; poes tavern.com. No brooding here, even though this friendly tavern is named for writer Edgar Allan Poe, who actually spent time on the island back in 1827. He was stationed at nearby Fort Moultrie for 13 months and wrote a story about buried treasure called "The Gold Bug" that was inspired by his stay. Paying homage to his literary career, scrumptious Angus beef burgers are named for some of his other stories and poems called the Raven, Pit & Pendulum, Tell-Tale Heart, and Annabel Lee. This charming little beach cottage-turned-tavern serves up a nice selection of bottled and draught beers and wine indoors and out along with appetizers like quesadillas and Edgar's Nachos. The kitchen closes at 10 p.m., but the bar is open until midnight. Take note that no one under 18 years old is allowed in the bar area after 8 p.m.

WEST ASHLEY

Nighttime activity west of the Ashley River is often on or near the water, in settings that are attractive but casual. Most nightspots are part of restaurants, and some with docks cater to the boating crowd.

CALIFORNIA DREAMING RESTAURANT AND BAR, 1 Ashley Pointe Dr.; (843) 766-1644; californiadreaming.com. This is the fortlike restaurant whose lights beckon from across the Ashley at night. After sundown, the scene is busy, lively, and fun. The bar is a great place to have a drink with a friend or a group of friends. You can see the lights of the Ashley and City Marinas, and it's adjacent to Ripley Light Marina, so the view is breathtaking. Because diners come here by droves, the bar is also a natural place to wait for a table. There's even a small floating dock for boat tie-ups.

GENE'S HAUFBRAU, 817 Savannah Hwy.; (843) 225-4363; geneshaufbrau .com. This West Ashley spot claims to be Charleston's oldest bar established in 1952. Nothing luxurious, the new place is a comfortable neighborhood bar, friendly and spacious, with pool, shuffleboard, darts, good pub food, and more than 150 beers and a chalkboard full of drafts from which to choose. This bar is popular with the after-work crowd who toil across the Ashley River Bridge. And it's still close enough to The Citadel to draw the thirsty (and legal) cadets who can smell a beer at 40 paces.

TRIANGLE CHAR & BAR, 828 Savannah Hwy.; (843) 377-1300; triangle charandbar.com. Stop by the Triangle Bar after work or a long day seeing the sights and enjoy the lively crowd and drink specials. Happy hour is Mon through Fri, 4 to 7 p.m. Starters and sandwiches are available in the bar too, or entrees are served on the restaurant side if your appetite calls for more. Their Mount Pleasant location is rockin' too, at 1440 Ben Sawyer Blvd. (843-606-2900).

JAMES & JOHNS ISLANDS

CHARLESTON CRAB HOUSE, 145 Wappoo Creek Dr., James Island; (843) 795-1963; charlestoncrabhouse.com. This popular spot on the Intracoastal Waterway near the Wappoo Cut Bridge has dockside tables and space for mooring boats. Happy hour drink and food specials are snapped up in their Tag & Release Lounge, Mon through Fri from 4 to 7 p.m. There is live entertainment on weekends after Memorial Day, and it always seems to be packed during the summer months. The deck is a lot of fun for drinks, appetizers, and watching those giant yachts go by. Another location is at 41 South Market St., Charleston (843-853-2900).

COFFEEHOUSES

EAST BAY MEETING HOUSE BAR & CAFE, 160 East Bay St.; (843) 723-3446; eastbaymeetinghouse.com. Located in the heart of the French Quarter District on East Bay Street, the East Bay Meeting House brings a touch a European elegance to Charleston's charm. Their intimate bar serves gourmet coffees along with a full selection of wines, cocktails, and signature martinis. You may want to linger a while to try one of their soups, appetizers, hot paninis, or desserts from the After Dark menu. In keeping with nostalgia for a salon society, Mon night features an open mic for poets and singer/songwriters. The Meeting House is open 7 days a week from 7 a.m. to 2 a.m.

METTO COFFEE & TEA, 354 Coleman Blvd., Mount Pleasant; (843) 216-8832. Here's a trendy coffeehouse that's actually a cross between a place to grab some tasty hot java or tea and a drive-through dry cleaner. Instead of freshly laundered shirts, they dispense coffee, panini sandwiches, salads, pastries, and desserts—to go. It's a favorite with morning commuters, who can buy a newspaper while waiting in line for their coffee and/or lunch. It's open 6 a.m. to 6 p.m. every day. The fare here is far more creative than fast food and almost as convenient.

MUDDY WATERS COFFEE BAR, 1739 Maybank Hwy., James Island; (843) 795-0848; muddywaterscoffee.com. Owned by a couple of Seattle natives, this independent coffeehouse brews Counter Culture Coffee, which purchases coffees from growers dedicated to sustainable coffee farming from around the world. This means they have taken "freshly brewed" to a new level. A variety of pastries are on hand to accompany your coffee all set in a cozy atmosphere of leather sofas, small tables, and chairs, with local artists' works showcased on the walls. Located in the James Island Shopping Center, parking is available in the shopping center lot.

THE HAVE NOTS! THEATRE 99, 280 Meeting St., 2nd Fl.; (843) 853-6687; theatre99.com. A very popular improv comedy troupe known as The Have Nots! has found a permanent home at Theatre 99 on the second floor of 280 Meeting, above The Bicycle Shoppe. This three-member troupe has built a strong following in Charleston by finding the funny bone of local audiences and those out-of-towners who came for Piccolo Spoleto alike. Somehow, they always manage to take the ordinary and turn it into the absurd from point-blank audience suggestions. Having their own space gives them an option of using creative lighting as a prop, which seems to be a trick all their own. Audiences range from teens to tourists of the senior persuasion. Everybody seems to have a great time. They sometimes tour, so call ahead to be sure they're playing at their home venue. Other comedy programming is offered every Wed, Fri, and Sat. Admission ranges from $5 to $12.50.

DINNER CRUISES

SPIRITLINE DINNER CRUISE, 40 Patriots Point Rd., Mount Pleasant; (843) 722-2628, (800) 789-3678; spiritlinecruises.com. Dining and dancing aboard this 96-foot luxury tour boat while cruising historic Charleston Harbor

View of a bridge and boats and marina of Charleston, South Carolina

make for one of those quintessential Charleston experiences. The *Spirit of Carolina* serves a 3-course meal of she-crab soup, house salad, and a choice of five entrees such as beef short ribs, porterhouse-cut pork, chicken, or seafood (also vegetarian and vegan) per prior request. All menu items are served with a nod toward the Lowcountry tradition of cooking. The boat makes its rounds up and down the waterways at sundown and is always a lot of fun. Live music and dancing are part of the weekday bill of fare. Entertainment is provided by a live band who can perform jazz, blues, shag, and country music as per your request. *Spirit of Carolina* is part of the Fort Sumter Tours group and conveniently departs from the docks at Patriots Point Naval and Maritime Museum, where there's parking at the clearly marked boarding dock for a cash fee. The boarding begins at 6:30 p.m., and the cruise departs at 7 p.m. and returns at 10 p.m. Rates and schedules change seasonally, but tickets are around $53 for adults (Sun through Thurs) and around $59 on Fri and Sat and must be purchased in advance. (See the Cruise & Boat Tours section of the Tours chapter.)

MOVIE THEATERS

CINEBARRE; 963 Houston Northcutt Blvd., Mount Pleasant; (843) 884-7885; cinebarre.com. If you are looking for dinner and a movie, here's the place—and all under one roof. As soon as you enter the lobby, you'll see the difference as you step into a lounge and bar offering a dozen or so domestic and imported draft and bottled beers. Wines by the bottle or the glass as well as daiquiri and margarita pitchers are options here too. Casual food like sandwiches, burgers, and pizzas are delivered to your movie seat (with a small table) as efficiently and quietly as can be done. Showing a mix of first-run films along with mainstream and art-house movies on 11 screens, this is a movie-lovers haven. No children under 3 are allowed and all children under 18 must be accompanied by an adult, cutting down on the disruptive atmosphere of some other cinemas.

TERRACE THEATER, 1956 Maybank Hwy., James Island; (843) 762-9494; terracetheater.com. In the Terrace Oaks shopping center, this first-run, wide-screen movie house features current hits, classics, and independent and foreign films in an upscale and comfortable atmosphere. Its cafe and lounge features gourmet snacks, coffee, and microbrews on tap. Desserts, wine, and Champagne are also available to accommodate every taste. Call the information line (see above) to hear what's on the current bill or visit the website for matinee and nightly showtimes.

CONCERT INFORMATION & VENUES

Greater Charleston's appetite for entertainment and artistic diversions is satisfied by a wide range of performance venues today. From the rafter-filling rock concerts attracting thousands to the most intimate recitals at the College of Charleston, we have a concert hall or a major facility that can handle the crowd.

Ticketmaster is one of the high-tech ways to get tickets to almost any concert or special event in the Lowcountry. This company, with nationwide ticket distribution, adds a surcharge for the convenience of buying tickets through them. But the added cost is worth it for some. Most of the events have their own sites as well for purchasing tickets online. Others prefer to shop for their tickets to Spoleto and other hot concerts the old-fashioned way, by standing in line at the ticket window. You can access Ticketmaster by visiting ticketmaster .com or calling (800) 745-3000.

- **Gaillard Municipal Auditorium,** 77 Calhoun St.; (843) 577-7400; charleston-sc.gov

- **North Charleston Coliseum,** 5001 Coliseum Dr., North Charleston; (843) 529-5000; coliseumpac.com

- **North Charleston Performing Arts Center,** 5001 Coliseum Dr., North Charleston; (843) 202-2787; coliseumpac.com

- **The Sottile Theatre,** 44 George St.; (843) 953-5623; sottile.cofc.edu

ENTERTAINMENT

Shopping

For a city that's famous for all that's old and historic, Charleston offers shoppers today easier-than-ever access to things that are new and exciting. The variety ranges in size from specialty shop enclaves in downtown nooks and crannies to major shopping centers and the seemingly endless random strip malls. To provide a useful index for your shopping needs, we've categorized these shopping adventures by location and merchandise.

We'll start with the major shopping areas of downtown Charleston—**King Street, Meeting Street & the City Market,** and **Broad Street.** Some of these famous old streets have been shopping meccas for 200 years. Other streets have only recently become decidedly commercial. Much of downtown's historic district houses a mix of shops and homes and every other aspect of daily life—with a certain deference made to keeping the historic fabric of the city intact.

Within each of the three major shopping areas we've categorized stores by the type of merchandise that's dominant there. Included are the most exclusive boutiques and the just-as-welcome discount stores catering to the dollar-conscious consumer. In each case, we've tried to identify businesses with items of particular interest for our visitors and those frequented by a local clientele.

In general, we've omitted descriptions of most major chain retailers with which you are already familiar. Some of the best of these are the high-end shops featured in The Shops at Charleston Place. We do encourage you, however, to venture off the beaten path from time to time—new and hidden surprises are everywhere!

KING STREET

Let's start with King Street, one of the leading Charleston shopping districts. This is the essence of downtown shopping, and it has been for a couple hundred years. While the street actually begins high on the Peninsula and ends as a narrow throughway past an extraordinary collection of pre-Revolutionary private homes, the real business and shopping district begins at about Mary Street and continues with greater intensity until it crosses Broad Street.

Listed below, by category of merchandise, are some of the more unusual shops you'll find on or near King Street.

Close-up

Finding Antiques in Charleston

For the insider who wants to buy, sell, study, or just window shop for antiques, Charleston is a mother lode. Because it was first an English city, the Charlestonian sense of taste in antiques is decidedly British. Fittingly, Charleston's many antiques shops and galleries, many of which are clustered along King Street, tend to reflect that English bias.

The affluent, British-educated, 18th-century Charlestonians proudly decorated their homes with the latest in English good taste as an obvious symbol of their cultural status and social position. If they couldn't import their heart's desire for finery and furniture, they imported tradesmen who could re-create it for them on this side of the Atlantic. Eventually, Charleston produced a new generation of silversmiths and cabinetmakers who earned their own reputations for fine craftsmanship. Indeed, early furniture from Charleston is among the best of the pre-1830 furniture crafted in this country. But it's safe to say that long after Britain ceased being a political factor in the colonies, Americans still looked to Mother England for direction in taste. In fact, this artistic and cultural codependency has lingered in Charleston for more than 200 years.

Today, Charleston no longer relies on furnishings from local homes and the misfortunes of its old families to fill today's antiques shops and galleries. Local dealers and buyers attend auctions and estate sales up and down the

Antiques

ALEXANDRA, 156 King St.; (843) 722-4897; alexandrafrenchantiques .com. Walk through the King Street doorway to discover this exclusive shop of 18th- and 19th-century European furniture, decorative wares, fine linens, pillows, china, and oil paintings—many reflecting the French Provençal ambience now gaining popularity in Charleston.

A'RIGA IV, 204 King St.; (843) 577-3075. Open since 1976, this shop carries a wide assortment of interesting early ceramics, decorative arts, and period accessories. There are no reproductions here at all. Look for an eclectic assortment of

Eastern Seaboard, and some make regular buying trips to Europe. Ships carrying 40-foot containers filled with early- to mid-19th-century English antiques arrive regularly in Charleston Harbor. Much of the merchandise is sold in local shops, while some of it goes to discerning dealers all over America. Still, Charleston enjoys the lion's share of the top-quality merchandise, largely because of the demand. Many of Charleston's old homes were built to showcase such furnishings, and each new owner cherishes the opportunity to refurbish his or her home appropriately.

From St. Michael's Alley and King Street to the shops in Mount Pleasant and along Savannah Highway, there are dozens of opportunities to shop for some of the best antiques sold in America.

One particular section along King Street, between Beaufain and Queen Streets, is sometimes referred to as the Antiques District, where you'll find a high concentration of quality shops and fascinating merchandise. But shoppers who really want to "do" the antiques market in Charleston will have to expand their search well beyond King Street these days. Quality shops are found tucked away in nearly all the commercial areas, plus small areas of West Ashley, Mount Pleasant, and James Island. Seeing them all is getting to be something of a crusade. Lookers are almost always welcome, but if you're a serious collector or a dealer, be sure to talk to the proprietor and make your wishes known. Often, there are back rooms or upstairs galleries available only to those interested enough to ask.

At the corner of King and Queen Streets is a good place to start. Walking north from there, you'll find some of the best antiques stores the city has to offer. Most shops are open Mon through Sat, but hours of operation can be as eclectic as the selections at many of these shops, so if in doubt, call ahead.

17th- through 19th-century furniture. A'riga IV is best known, however, for its fascinating assortment of antique medical and scientific instruments. This is a special treat for the many docs and nurses who come to Charleston for medical conventions.

DAVID SKINNER ANTIQUES & PERIOD LIGHTING, 177 King St.; (843) 853-3104; davidskinnerantiques.com. This wonderful resource of fine antiques and period lighting moved to King Street in 2009 from its former location on President Street. Owner David Skinner has a large selection of American, English, and French furniture as well as Jamaican, West Indian, and

Cuban pieces. The lighting may include chandeliers, sconces, torchieres, and table and floor lamps. Decorative accessories, paintings, mirrors, and garden accoutrements round out the many finds to browse here. The showroom is open Mon through Sat from 10 a.m. to 5 p.m. or by appointment.

★ **GEORGE C. BIRLANT & COMPANY,** 191 King St.; (843) 722-3842, (888) 247-5268; birlant.com. This is one of Charleston's oldest and largest antiques stores, having been around since 1929. The owners are direct importers of 18th- and 19th-century English furniture and faithful English-made reproductions. They also specialize in antique silver, china, crystal, and brass. Birlant is the exclusive source for replicas of a Charleston Battery Bench like those found in White Point Garden. They actually own the original cast-iron molds.

GOLDEN & ASSOCIATES ANTIQUES, 206 King St.; (843) 723-8886; goldenassociatesantiques.com. Clearly, this is one of King Street's largest displays of imported and locally acquired pieces. The vast array of American and European merchandise includes, but is not limited to, furniture, mirrors, chandeliers, sconces, fireplace accessories, and garden items from the 18th and 19th centuries. There are 19th-century Caribbean pieces here too.

KHOURY ORIENTAL RUGS, 71 Wentworth St., Ste. 102; (843) 720-7370; khouryorientalrugs.com. This retailer, just off King Street, handles the finest in hand-knotted Oriental rugs. The selection is considerable, with something for every discerning shopper. Here you'll find old and antique Persian rugs, Indian tea-stained rugs, kilims, and Oushak, as well as needlepoints from China and assorted tapestries. Free shipping is available for out-of-state buyers.

MOORE HOUSE ANTIQUES, 143 King St.; (843) 722-8065; moorehouseantiques.com. Here is a delight for fanciers of Chinese export porcelain. There's always a fine assortment of Canton, Rose Medallion, Fitzhugh, and others from the early 19th century. Look for the shop's 18th- and 19th-century American furniture, including rare Charleston-made pieces. This merchandise is beautifully documented, and safe shipping to anywhere is never a problem. Owner Bryan Riddle has been serving Charleston Antique District shoppers for many years.

THE SILVER VAULT OF CHARLESTON, 195 King St.; (843) 722-0631, (843) 571-4342; silvervaultcharleston.com. The Silver Vault specializes in the purchase and sale of American, Continental, British, and French silver as well as jewelry and decorative arts pieces. This shop is also a hard-to-find resource for silver-plating, repairs, and full restorations of all metals, including brass and pewter. This is the companion shop of the Brass & Silver Workshop at 758 Saint Andrews Blvd.

Bookstores

Please note that bookstore browsers will find the familiar chain stores such as **Barnes & Noble** at locations in 7620 Rivers Ave., Charleston, (843) 572-2322; 1716 Towne Centre Way, Mount Pleasant; (843) 216-9756; 160 Calhoun St., Charleston (843) 953-5518. **Books-A-Million** is located at 2150 Northwoods Blvd., Charleston; (843) 764-2377.

BLUE BICYCLE BOOKS, 420 King St.; (843) 722-2666; bluebicyclebooks .com. This upper King Street bookshop buys, sells, and trades books. While popular reading material is the main thrust of the store, rare books, collectibles, Lowcountry memorabilia, and souvenirs are also for sale. Local author book signings are popular events here. Mind you, this store is a fooler. Its tiny storefront belies the seemingly endless series of rooms housing a vast selection of reading matter for every taste. It's even open until 7:30 p.m. Mon through Sat and till 6 p.m. on Sun.

COLLEGE OF CHARLESTON BOOKSTORE, 160 Calhoun St.; (843) 953-5518; bookstore.cofc.edu. The College of Charleston's bookstore in the Lightsey Center, actually on Calhoun Street just off King, is operated by Barnes & Noble as the campus bookstore. It carries a nice section representing local authors and local interest books as well as faculty publications. It's also fun to poke around in the college textbook sections just to see what's happening these days. Time flies.

⭐ **PRESERVATION SOCIETY OF CHARLESTON BOOK & GIFT SHOP,** 147 King St.; (843) 722-4630; preservationsociety.org. The Preservation Society of Charleston Bookstore has what may be the most comprehensive area collection of books about Charleston, the Lowcountry, and all things Southern. Many Charleston and Lowcountry authors are represented here. You also can shop for art books, academic works, entertaining literature, and even some recorded material. (See the Attractions chapter for more on The Preservation Society of Charleston.)

UNIVERSITY BOOKS OF CHARLESTON, 360 King St.; (843) 853-8700; ubc-cofc.com. This bookstore is not officially affiliated with the College of Charleston, but is a popular source for college students and a place to browse for interesting academic titles. They also sell textbooks for the Charleston School of Law. Along with textbooks and reference materials, University Books sells school logo items—everything from T-shirts to bumper stickers for your favorite college team.

Children's Clothing

KIDS ON KING, 195 1/2 King St.; (843) 720-8647; kidsonking.com. Travel the world by shopping at Kids on King where the children's clothing comes from the most prestigious international fashion destinations. The owners have carefully selected unique styles from New York and around the world to bring to their Charleston store. Some of the brands include Alessia, Biscotti, Peruvian Trading, Hartstrings, Anavini, deux par deux, Glorimont, Haute Baby, and Elephantito shoes. They cater to infants, girls, boys, and preteen girls. Unusual gifts and collectibles can be found here too for all those childhood special occasions.

WORTHWHILE, 268 King St.; (843) 723-4418; shopworthwhile.com. This boutique sells 100 percent cotton clothing and accessories for infants, children, and adults. (See the Women's Clothing section under King Street in this chapter.) Shop here for earth-friendly, contemporary clothes that feel comfortable in the Charleston heat. In addition to their clothing lines, they have decorative accessories with a touch of whimsy for the home, bed and bath linens for cozy nesting, and personal care products for a sensual delight.

Flowers

TIGER LILY FLORIST, 131 Spring St.; (843) 723-2808, (800) 844-8199; tigerlilyflorist.com. Oftentimes, visitors to the Lowcountry are especially impressed with the floral displays that grace private parties, special events, and hotel lobbies throughout the city. When asked who did the arrangement, the answer is frequently, "Tiger Lily." This creative and popular florist is located at the corner of Spring Street and Ashley Avenue (a short drive from upper King Street). It's in what was once an art deco–styled auto dealership from the 1930s. The creativity the company brought to rehabbing this distinctive building can be found in its floral arrangements, which range from the most elaborate affair to the single rose on the pillow of a honeymoon bed. One nice touch to Tiger Lily's marketing is the website, which shows shoppers an array of creative displays recently produced by the shop's designers. Clients can choose or modify their orders from a visual starting point, which is very helpful. Tiger Lily also carries accessories and furnishings for outdoor gardens and patios where flowers and design are the main focus. A second location is at the The Sanctuary on Kiawah Island.

Gifts

PRESERVATION SOCIETY OF CHARLESTON BOOK & GIFT SHOP, 147 King St.; (843) 722-4630; preservationsociety.org. Along with all that's printed on Charleston and the Lowcountry, this terrific store offers local crafts, art prints, even recordings of Lowcountry lore told in the local Gullah dialect. Here, too, are the architectural drawings of Jim Polzois, whose studies of the city's architectural vernacular are beautifully done. They're simply the best available. (See previous listing under Bookstores.)

THE SMOKING LAMP, 401-B King St.; (843) 577-7339, (800) 745-7465; smokinglamp.com. Forget the NO SMOKING signs. Right across from Marion Square, this always-fragrant tobacco shop features a complete selection of fine pipes, cigars, tobacco, cigarettes, and smoking accessories. Coffee, beer, and wine are offered here too. Another location is at 1890 Sam Rittenberg Blvd. in West Ashley.

VIEUXTEMPS, 180 King St.; (843) 723-7309; vieuxtemps.net. When it's time to shop for a wedding or anniversary gift, this should be your first stop. Vieuxtemps deserves a gold star for its complete selection of crystal and fine china. It carries Waterford, Herend, Mottahedeh, William Yeoward, and Towle, as well as a wonderful collection of accent pieces and decorating accessories. This is where many Charleston brides register their china and sterling patterns.

Home Accents & Decor

LE CREUSET, 241 King St.; (843) 723-4191; lecreuset.com. Most folks don't know that the famous French enameled cast-iron cookware known as Le Creuset has a manufacturing plant right here in the Lowcountry. It's in Yemassee, South Carolina, about an hour's drive from Charleston, and the good news is the factory outlet is on King Street. The ordinarily pricey cookware is considerably discounted here—a boon to gourmets who happen across this downtown store. You're likely to pick up some wine and Champagne accessories, too, along with some nifty cooking gadgets.

MORRIS SOKOL FURNITURE, 510 King St.; (843) 722-3874; morris sokol.com. Since 1921 Morris Sokol Furniture has furnished homes in Charleston and across the Southeast. Located in the Upper King Street Design District, which has emerged around their long-standing 37,000-square-foot showroom, this store offers a large selection of traditional, contemporary, or tropically inspired furniture and accessories. Some of the lines carried here are American Drew, Bernhardt, Century, Charleston Forge, Gloster, Lane, Lexington, and Tropitone. They also have Sterns & Foster bedding. Whether you are looking for a houseful or just one accent piece, the sales staff is quite helpful, and they have designers on hand to help create and implement your vision. Free parking is around the corner on Reid Street across from the store.

YVES DELORME, The Shops at Charleston Place, 197 King St.; (843) 853-4331; yvesdelorme.com. This is the store for fine French linens—everything for the bed, bath, and table. All the merchandise is natural fiber—either linen or Egyptian cotton. Yves Delorme also carries goose-down duvets and pillows that veritably evoke pastel mornings on the Left Bank. To complete the scene, the shop carries a variety of handpainted porcelain and other table graces. If you love Paris, there's a little bit of it here.

Jewelry

⭐ **CROGHAN'S JEWEL BOX,** 308 King St.; (843) 723-3594; croghans jewelbox.com. This is a shop that some will remember as a tiny space unobtrusively tucked away behind a small awning on King Street but filled with quality merchandise. It's tiny no more. After more than 100 years as a Charleston shopping institution, this family-owned jewelry store finally has the space to show its worth. Now expanded into the space next door, Croghan's carries exquisite jewelry and wonderful gifts for all the important occasions. The rings are to die for, and there seems to be no end to the trays of earrings, shelves of silver and crystal, and other delights. Don't miss the estate and antique pieces here too. A Croghan's package delivered to your door or under the tree—sometimes the smaller, the better—is cause for real excitement.

DAZZLES, 202 King St.; (843) 722-5997; dazzlesjewelry.com. This family of jewelry stores is best known for its 14-karat-gold slide bracelets that have the look, style, and feel of an heirloom. Dazzles has a large selection to choose from, or you may design one of your very own. Gold slide bracelets can be set with diamonds and precious stones in various shapes and motifs. Dazzles also has a large selection of jewelry from internationally known designers such as Hidalgo, Alwand Vahan, Monte Carlo, Konstantino, and Lalique. Another location is at 86 Queen St. (843-722-5950).

> ℹ Along King Street at about Wentworth Street, you'll note a section of roadway paved in bricks bearing the names of individuals and businesses. In the early 1980s, the construction of Charleston Place required a complete rebuilding of the immediate area's infrastructure. City leaders initiated a fund-raising campaign to cosmetically revitalize the area, and the bricks of the street commemorate those who donated to the cause.

JOINT VENTURE ESTATE JEWELERS, 185 King St.; (843) 722-6730, (800) 722-6730; jventure.com. This is the area's largest estate and pre-owned fine jewelry consignment shop. The inventory ranges from the most elaborate Victorian ornaments to a very modern, contemporary look. Variety is the strong suit here—with more than 1,200 consignors offering jewelry, flatware, and hollowware for every taste and pocketbook. Specialties found here are platinum, diamonds, sapphires, emeralds, rubies, pearls, and a large assortment of vintage watches. Repairs, restorations, and appraisals are done on-site.

Men's Clothing

BEN SILVER COLLECTION, 149 King St.; (843) 577-4556, (800) 221-4671; bensilver.com. Here is a must-see, whether you're shopping for men's or women's clothing. Ben Silver maintains shops only in Charleston and London, so here's your one chance on this side of the Atlantic. Along with ultra-fine British and American clothes and furnishings, you'll discover exclusive blazer buttons for virtually every college or university in the US and abroad. In fact, Ben Silver carries button sets for more than 600 fraternal organizations and military schools. It's a classy place for a nifty gift idea.

★ **BERLIN'S CLOTHIERS, 114 King St.; (843) 722-1665, (877) 722-1665; berlinsclothing.com.** Since 1883, Berlin's has been a Charleston institution. Four generations of young Charleston gentlemen have purchased their first good suit from Berlin's. You can find all the classics here, from wing-tip shoes to navy blazers, knit shirts to madras shorts. Look for European designer names, too, among the classics, such as Armani, Coppley, Canali, Hickey-Freeman, Peter Millar, and more. Berlin's offers custom sizing, a complete formal-wear department, and a big-and-tall section. Patrons love the convenient free parking across the street for their own shopping or shopping for something nice for the lady in their life from Berlin's for Women next door. (See listing under Women's Clothing.)

GRADY ERVIN & CO., 313 King St.; (843) 722-1776; gradyervin.com. The sign reads Classic Clothiers to Gentlemen, and that pretty much sums it up for this shop. This smart store is among King Street's collection of fine men's shops, and it's a real contender. You'll find a complete selection of traditional blazers, yachting wear, sports clothes, and accessories. Expect quality, style, and gracious old-world service.

M. DUMAS & SONS, 294 King St.; (843) 723-8603; mdumasandsons .com. Charleston men and boys have been buying their outdoor sports clothes at M. Dumas since 1919. This store is all about practicality mixed with style and boasts one of the most complete inventories—hunting jackets, camouflage hats, flannel shirts, corduroy pants, shoes, and even snakeskin boots—in town. Dumas was doing the "hunting look" before doing the hunting look was cool.

319 MEN, 316 King St.; (843) 577-8807. This shop is a favorite among discriminating shoppers whose tastes edge toward Italian designs. The owners of 319 Men claim to carry the most recognizable designer labels in town, and they probably do. You can always count on personalized service and a pleasant shopping experience.

Natural Beauty

SPA ADAGIO, 387 King St.; (843) 577-2444; spaadagio.com. This is one of those places you can go for those special pamperings that bring back harmony to your life. The Spa Adagio therapists know just the song your sore muscles need to hear (through massage). Their soft aromas sing to your senses, and their relaxing sounds soothe your soul. You'll find Spa Adagio in the lower level of the Francis Marion Hotel. (See the Accommodations chapter.)

STELLA NOVA, 292 King St. (esthetique, makeup studio, and salon); (843) 722-9797; stella-nova.com. Stella Nova sells Aveda pure plant products and services for the hair, skin, and body. In their 3,000-square-foot location at 292

King St. (call 843-853-6161 for the salon only), they offer a large inventory of specially selected fragrances, makeup, and bath, hair, and men's products from around the world. Check out the natural solutions to stress, ranging from aromatherapy to basic, old-fashioned pampering. Call (843) 723-0909 for day spa appointments at their 78 Society St. location. Visit the website for additional locations.

Shoes

BOB ELLIS, 332 King St.; (843) 722-2515; bobellisshoes.com. Experience the shoe store phenomenon that is Bob Ellis. People from all over the country make the pilgrimage to Charleston to do just that. Suffice it to say that the store's three telephone lines into the women's section say something about their popularity. High fashion, a huge selection, and friendly, highly qualified sales folk create the magic. The store carries women's sizes 4 to 12 AAAA, AAA, AA, and B. In men's, you'll find sizes 7 to 14. If you love shoes (and fine matching bags), don't miss Bob Ellis.

RANGONI OF FLORENCE SHOES, 270 King St.; (843) 577-9554; rangoni shoes.com. Many think the level of personal service here is simply the best in town. Rangoni's fine collection of Italian-designed shoes for men and women is superb in both quality and style. For women, the store carries (even in hard-to-find sizes) the elegant Rangoni Amalfi shoes. For just the right accessory to complement those stylish new shoes, choose from one of the largest selections of handbags in town. Men's lines of footwear include Mezlan, Robert Zur, Moreschi, Auri, Anatomic, and Bacco Bucci, among others. They also carry men's shoes in exotic skins such as crocodile and lizard.

Sports

THE EXTRA MILE, 336 King St.; (843) 853-9987; theextramileinc.com. This is a service-oriented, specialty sports shop with products preferred by competitive runners and swimmers. The store is owned and operated by athletes who are competitive runners and triathletes, so they know a thing or two about running needs. The Extra Mile sells Nike, New Balance, Asics, Saucony, Mizuno, Body Glide, and other name brands.

HALF MOON OUTFITTERS, 280 King St.; (843) 853-0990; halfmoon outfitters.com. When friends were gearing up to travel through South America one Christmas season, where did they head first? That's right—Half Moon. They were after brands such as Patagonia, North Face, Chaco, Mountain

Hardwear, Keen, and Smartwool. Half Moon carries other lines in its wide assortment of supplies for outdoor sports and adventure-seeking activity. Two more locations are at 425 Coleman Blvd., Mount Pleasant (843-881-9472) and 94 Folly Rd. (843-556-6279).

Women's Clothing

ANNE'S, 312 King St.; (843) 577-3262; annesdowntown.com. Anne's has developed a loyal following among petites in the community because of the wonderful selection, all the way down to size 3. There are happy customers in all the other sizes as well, because Anne's carries name-brand merchandise and gives personalized service. Shop here for contemporary clothing appropriate for business and casual occasions as well as evening attire. There is free customer parking in the city lot behind the store.

★ BERLIN'S FOR WOMEN, 116 King St.; (843) 723-5591; berlinsfor women.com. At the corner of King and Broad is family-owned Berlin's, one of Charleston's oldest and nicest clothing stores. Established in 1883, Berlin's built a reputation as a fashion landmark specializing in sportswear, lifestyle, and special-occasion dressing. It carries one of the largest selections of evening and special-occasion dresses in the Southeast and attracts customers from all over. Some of its designer lines include Nicole Miller, Zelda, Bagley Mischka, and Rene Ruiz. A beautifully renovated store, excellent service, and free parking across the street make it a pleasure to shop here.

★ BITS OF LACE, 302 King St.; (843) 577-0999, (800) 842-3990; bits oflace.com. For sexy, pretty lingerie, visit Bits of Lace. Please note: These are undergarments that should be treated with care. In fact, many are silk and should be washed only by hand. Most items are simple, top-of-the-line articles of clothing that definitely give the impression that someone cares.

CHRISTIAN MICHI, 220 King St.; (843) 723-0575. At the corner of King and Market Streets, Christian Michi offers collections for women by fashion designers such as Qi Cashmere, Piazza Sempione, Chan Luu, Hoss, and Sachi & Babi. The shop also sells assorted home furnishings like imported crystal and Diptyque candles. Check out the handmade 22-karat-gold jewelry.

ELLINGTON, 473 King St.; (843) 722-7999. Classic style with a new arrangement is Ellington's claim to fame. Located on upper King Street, the retailers say they are to clothing and furniture what jazz is to music. Some of the chic lines of women's clothing available are Babette, Planet, Georgina Estefania,

Crea, and Emelle. Look for great accessories to accentuate your outfit with their jewelry, belts, and purses. Things for the home include lamps (new and old), bedding, and some American and European antiques (from couches to accent tables). Ellington ships anywhere.

THE FINICKY FILLY, 303 King St.; (843) 534-0203; thefinickyfilly.com. The shop of exquisite women's fashions is a delight for the discerning shopper on King Street. In addition to private-label jackets and accessories, look here for Italian fashions and leathers, Parisian couture, and cashmere items. The hand-embellished silks are the inspiration for many a formal ensemble worn here and in other fashionable places. Some of the names you'll find are Etro, Lela Rose, Tory Burch, Nanette Lepore, and Ciao Milano. An in-store fashion consultant is available for private appointments. Check out their sister store, Haute Hanger, at 307 King St. for the younger set.

LUNA, 334 King St.; (843) 853-5862; shopluna.com. Like its sister store in Charlotte, North Carolina, this King Street shop features clothing, jewelry, accessories, shoes, candles, Mexican pottery, and home furnishings. Eclectic style, lots of color, and sheer exuberance are the keynotes here.

NANCY'S, 342 King St.; (843) 722-1272; nancysofcharleston.com. Nancy's is another interesting, upscale boutique on King Street that's a must-see for ladies with a strong sense of style. Look here for a unique collection of contemporary apparel. Of special note are the one-of-a-kind metal bracelets imported from Europe exclusively for Nancy's. Belts of leather, chain, and even rhinestones are among the accents found here. The look is chic but timeless—appropriate for the young and the merely young at heart.

THE OOPS CO., 326 King St.; (843) 722-7768; theoopsco.com. This shop is every catalog shopper's dream come true. It exclusively features the clothing overruns and irregulars from your favorite name-brand mail-order catalogs. The prices here are about half the regular fare when you order from the book, and the merchandise is plentiful for folks of all ages and sizes. It also carries a nice collection of South Carolina logo items, such as polos, T-shirts, caps, belts, key fobs, and pet accessories. This may be the "find" of your whole shopping day. There is a second location at 696 Coleman Blvd., Mount Pleasant (843-881-6935).

RTW, 186 King St.; (843) 577-9748; rtwcharleston.com. For interesting clothes that are always on the cutting edge of fashion, visit RTW. Look for designers such as Marc Jacobs, Peter Cohen, and Lanvin, and others who present trunk shows here with some frequency. RTW is diagonally across King Street from George C. Birlant & Company. (See the previous listing under Antiques.)

WORTHWHILE, 268 King St.; (843) 723-4418; shopworthwhile.com. Selling unique casual and contemporary clothing made from only natural fibers, Worthwhile is, well, a worthwhile boutique on Charleston's trendy King Street. Look for brand names such as FLAX, Morgan, and Krista Larson, and shoes by Marsell and Guidi. (See the previous Children's Clothing listing in this chapter.)

i If you happen to be in town on the second Sunday of the month, enjoy strolling King Street between Queen and Calhoun without concern about vehicular traffic. From 1 to 5 p.m. cars are prohibited, and the pedestrian traffic delights in taking in the dining spots and shops along the route. Free 2-hour parking vouchers are available at 2ndsundayonkingstreet.com.

MEETING STREET & THE CITY MARKET

The cross street that, along with Broad Street, defines the "Four Corners of Law" is Meeting Street, another wide avenue of history, prosperity, and faith. Here, after all, is the location of the original church that gave the street its name (see the Historic Churches section of the Attractions chapter). Meeting Street runs virtually the length of the Peninsula and ends at White Point Garden.

Meeting Street takes you smack-dab into the historic Market, one of the most colorful and popular tourist destinations in the city. The Market's shopping area is flanked by busy, one-way streets (called North and South Market Streets) and East Bay Street.

The Market may be one of the oldest "shopping malls" in the US. It was built on land that Charles Cotesworth Pinckney, who was a signer of the US Constitution, ceded to the city in the 18th century for use as a public market. Made up of low brick buildings that have survived hurricanes, earthquakes, tornadoes, fires, and even Civil War bombardment, these sheds also were used by vendors selling fish, meat, and vegetables in bygone days.

The Great Hall, stretching from Meeting to Church Streets, recently underwent a $5.5 million renovation and houses a string of new specialty shops, boutiques, and eateries. Here, vendors of all types rent spaces and booths to hawk their wares.

The Market is a must-see for every Charleston visitor, and its magic seems to lie in its eternal spontaneity. It's an ever-changing kaleidoscope of things and smells and sounds and people who all seem to be in a carnival mood. It's different every day, and it's always the same. The Market is a Charleston enigma. Don't miss it.

Bookstores

⭐ **THE SHOPS OF HISTORIC CHARLESTON FOUNDATION**, 108 Meeting St.; (843) 724-8484; historiccharleston.org. This store, as you might expect, stocks books regarding preservation and restoration. From beautiful coffee table books to fascinating reference material, choose from works about everything from gardening to selecting Victorian house colors. The store's selection of gift items also is keyed to the Charleston taste with brasses and china accents and linen tableware. The Historic Charleston reproduction furniture by Baker is shown here as well. (For more, see the Attractions chapter and the Home Accents & Decor listings in this section of this chapter.)

Candy

GODIVA CHOCOLATIER, INC., The Shops at Charleston Place, 142 Market St.; (843) 722-6045; godiva.com. Tucked seductively inside Charleston Place's trendy shopping arcade, this is where you'll find those famous Godiva chocolates loved the world over by serious chocoholics. Go all out, and take home a whole box, or taste just the individual confections that catch your eye. Be prepared for the not-too-subtle aromatherapy when you walk in the door. It's very beguiling.

MARKET STREET SWEETS, 100 North Market St.; (843) 722-1397; river streetsweets.com. As if the distractions of the Market aren't enough, here's a candy store that hands out free samples. Woe to the poor dieter who happens to pass by here. Market Street Sweets opened in this location in 1984 selling gourmet Southern candies. The devil has had his way with sweet-tooth sufferers here ever since. The shop is most famous for its pralines but also turns out beautiful bear claws, chocolates, and other homemade specialties. This is a first stop for many Charleston visitors who have passed this way before. Market

Street Sweets ships anywhere, so no one is really immune. A second location is at 270 King St.

Gifts

ALPHA DOG OMEGA CAT, 40 Archdale St.; (843) 723-1579; alphadog omegacat.com. In Majestic Square on the corner of Market and Archdale Streets, this shop is strictly for the dogs (and cats). Gifts range from gourmet pet biscuits, designer collars, and leashes to jewelry, toys, and clothes. We're talking indulgence here, and this shop is serious about it all. Only a pet lover would really understand.

CHARLESTON CHRISTMAS COLLECTIBLES, 188 Meeting St., Ste. 111; (843) 722-8002. For those travelers who like to find a year-round Christmas shop and buy that special ornament for the tree that's sure to recall their Charleston vacation, here's a shop that nicely fills the bill. This store, tucked away in the Market between Meeting and Church Streets, is a division of Light Be and features exclusive lines of handpainted, locally made ornaments with a Charleston theme. Collectible lines include Byers' Choice, Annalee, Jim Shore, and Fontanini, among many others. Even on the hottest days of summer, there's a little bit of the North Pole here.

CHARLESTON LEATHERGOODS, 61 South Market St.; (843) 577-4773; charlestonleather.com. Down in the Market where all the action can be quite distracting, there's a very nice resource for leather goods of all kinds. The shop carries a number of brand names, including Fossil, Rolfs, Dopp, and Scully for leather items. This collection of duffles, totes, and travel gear can take you to your next destination in style.

THE CHARLESTON MUSEUM GIFT SHOP, 360 Meeting St.; (843) 722-2996; charlestonmuseum.org. Here in America's oldest municipal museum, there's a gift area that's both comprehensive and tasteful. The emphasis is on items (such as books, jewelry, models, textiles, and educational toys) that have some connection to Charleston and the Lowcountry. It's an ideal place to pick up a souvenir from your vacation while visiting the must-see museum. (See the Museums & Other Sites section of the Attractions chapter as well as the Kids chapter.)

⭐ **GIBBES MUSEUM OF ART SHOP,** 135 Meeting St.; (843) 722-2706; gibbesmuseum.org. The shop at the Gibbes is just inside the front doors of the museum and is open to the public with no admission charge. This is one of the Lowcountry's best stops for art books, jewelry, stationery, small reproductions, and art prints of all kinds. Many locals go in early November for the best selection of fine Christmas cards in the city. (For more on the Gibbes Museum of Art, see the Attractions and Kids chapters.)

KITES FLY'N HI, 40 North Market St., Rainbow Market; (843) 577-3529; kitesflynhi.com. Something about flying a kite brings out the best in people. That's the philosophy behind this colorful little shop in Rainbow Market that is all about kites—of every kind and size. Look here for diamonds, deltas, boxes, and dragons plus wind socks and flags of fantastic design. The shop even has stunt kites for advanced fliers. Put the products to use here on the Lowcountry beaches or take them home to your own sky.

MARKET LEATHER OF CHARLESTON, 40 North Market St., #11, Rainbow Market; (843) 722-1156; marketleather.com. Here's a shop in the Rainbow Market that's all about leather accessories for men and women. You'll find several lines of imported ladies' handbags and work-totes for the home or office. For men, there's a wide selection of billfolds, duffles, and utility kits. Look for leather backpacks, passport covers, attachés, briefcases, garment bags, wallets, and computer briefs, plus handsome cases for cell phones. This is a gold mine of gift ideas when holidays and birthdays come around.

O'HARA & FLYNN, LTD., 225 Meeting St.; (843) 534-1916; oharaand flynn.com. Here's a direct importer of fine wines and gourmet cheeses plus fresh pâtés, smoked salmon, and saucissons for the discerning connoisseur. With a downtown location near Charleston Place, it's handy for tourists and locals who know their tastes and want the best. There are even in-shop tastings at the wine bar and live music on most weekends.

Home Accents & Decor

THE SHOPS OF HISTORIC CHARLESTON FOUNDATION, 108 Meeting St.; (843) 724-8484; historiccharleston.org. The Shops of Historic Charleston Foundation is the showroom for home furnishings, accessories, and giftware authorized by the foundation. All items for sale have an accompanying product card explaining the item's historical significance to Charleston's history and the Charlestonian lifestyle. The shop features Baker Furniture's Historic Charleston collection of 18th- and 19th-century reproductions of furniture from famous Charleston homes. It also carries dinnerware patterns and brass

Close-up

Lowcountry Tradition: Sweetgrass Baskets

There is an art form practiced here in the Lowcountry that has been recognized and celebrated virtually all over the world. Examples of this rare craft are found in the art museums of New York and Rome and among the Smithsonian collections in Washington, D.C., yet the work is evident all along the sidewalks of Charleston's Four Corners of Law at Meeting and Broad Streets. You'll easily find it downtown in the Market and in makeshift stalls along Lowcountry highways—especially US 17 N.

We're talking about the weaving of **sweetgrass baskets,** a traditional African-American art practiced here in the Lowcountry since the early 18th century. These baskets are handmade of long bunches of sweetgrass, pine needles, and bulrush that are bound together with fiber strips from native palmetto trees. The bunches are coiled and formed to create a variety of baskets—all shapes and sizes, each one unique. The baskets are both functional and beautiful. Creating these baskets requires skilled craftsmanship and long hours of hard work. A simple, average basket may require 12 hours or more to make, while larger, more complicated versions may take up to 2 or 3 months. The craft of weaving sweetgrass baskets has been a part of the Lowcountry since the earliest days of slavery. The skills are largely passed on from generation to generation. Traditionally, the men harvest the fiber and other plant material from the local marshes and swamps, and the women weave the baskets.

accessories, fabrics, and wallpaper, as well as rugs, books, and jewelry. Because of its nonprofit status, no sales tax is charged. (See the previous listing under Bookstores.)

Jewelry

NICE ICE FINE JEWELRY, 145 Market St.; (843) 577-7029. Cross Market Street from Charleston Place to find Nice Ice. Check out the many cases of

While the bulrush, pine needles, and palmetto strips are indigenous to and traditionally obtainable throughout the Lowcountry, coastal land development has begun to threaten the artisans' supply. Today, some weavers have to travel as far as Florida and along the Savannah River in Georgia to find natural stands of sweetgrass growing in roadside marshes. Because of this threat to one of the Lowcountry's most endearing traditions, Historic Charleston Foundation sponsored a test project on James Island to cultivate the growing of sweetgrass as a crop. It is hoped the sweetgrass basket tradition will continue to be an integral part of the Charleston experience. Each sweetgrass basket is utilitarian and beautiful, rich in the natural tones of the varied grasses and elegant in its ethnic simplicity. The baskets are true objects of art, and so they're not cheap. We feel the investment (usually $50 or $60 for a standard basket) is very worthwhile. Be sure to discover the wonderful sweetgrass baskets of the Lowcountry for yourself.

costume designs along with displays of the real stuff. Expect to be a bit surprised by the good prices. Some of the most unusual pieces seen around town have been created by Nice Ice. Look here for Slane & Slane, Druzy, Judith Ripka, Charriol, and many more.

Women's Clothing

EVERYTHING BUT WATER, 195 Meeting St., The Shops at Charleston Place; (843) 722-5884; everythingbutwater.com. If you are looking for a bathing suit, try Everything But Water in Charleston Place. The store carries contemporary swimwear, cover-ups, and accessories by such designers as Trina Turk, Becca, Juicy Couture, Michael Kors, and Nanette Lepore in sizes 0 through 24.

EAST BAY STREET

This was once a street of bustling cotton warehouses in the mid-19th century, where silks and satins from exotic lands were bought and sold by the rice and indigo merchants who prospered here. The old warehouses that survived the rigors of war and economic stagnation were "rediscovered" in the late 1970s, when a new epoch for the street began. Below Broad Street, East Bay can claim the famous Rainbow Row of town houses and the High Battery along Charleston Harbor. Above Broad you'll find a concentration of galleries, nightclubs, restaurants, and shops along East Bay between Market and Broad Streets. Beyond this area, other clusters of stores have emerged worth noticing. Here are some of the shopping venues you won't want to miss.

Antiques

★ ACQUISITIONS, 273 East Bay St.; (843) 577-8004; acquisitionsinteriors
.com. This shop offers full interior design services and specializes in English pine originals and beautifully made reproductions of English mahogany and antique painted furniture. It is a great resource for accent pieces as well. These designers are very popular with the Kiawah and Seabrook Island crowd, and one look at their handsome displays tells you why.

Gifts

INDIGO, 4 Vendue Range; (843) 723-2983; indigohome.com. If you gravitate toward the eclectic, you'll love Indigo. The inventory ranges from metal art to bike bells to wooden animals. In this shop, you'll find village baskets nestled near wine bottle candles next to handmade glassware and sea glass jewelry. You'll never fail to find something wonderful here.

Home Accents & Decor

★ CHARLESTON COOKS!, 194 East Bay St.; (843) 722-1212; charleston
cooks.com. For gourmet cooks and those who just love cooking, Charleston Cooks! is a little bit of heaven right here on East Bay Street. The concept is part kitchen store, part cooking school—where Lowcountry visitors can take one-time-only classes in how to prepare those Southern dishes that are so tasty.

The Maverick Southern Kitchens group heads up a program of daily classes that feature guest chefs from restaurants all over the city and beyond. The model kitchen where classes take place holds 40 students, with a video overview allowing close-up observation of the magic at hand.

Next door is the retail side of the operation, with a complete array of fine cooking utensils, cutlery, pots and pans, small appliances, and many cookbooks (some locally inspired). You'll even find some delicious prepared Southern accent foods like relishes, jams, and sauces. Shoppers don't necessarily have to be enrolled in the cooking classes to take away some culinary souvenirs. But to enroll in the classes, call the number above, or visit the website.

Jewelry

★ GEISS AND SONS JEWELERS, 116 East Bay St.; (843) 577-4497; geissjewelers.com. Geiss is on the first floor of a charming little 18th-century brick building on East Bay just south of Broad. Their selections include Roberto Coin, Kwiat, A. Link, and Nanis designer jewelry. They were awarded Couture Jeweler status, one of only 170 jewelry stores nationwide to receive this recognition. The shop sells custom-designed diamond and colored stone rings. Watch and jewelry repair, and jewelry redesign are special services here. Complimentary parking is on East Elliot Street.

Natural Beauty

EARTHLING DAY SPA, 245 East Bay St.; (843) 722-4737; earthlingdayspa .com. Earthling Day Spa is a great source for skin and body products and books and tapes on health and well-being. Earthling also offers the unique Pilates method of conditioning. With Pilates, clients work out with trained professionals who guide them through a therapeutic body-conditioning regimen of stretching, strengthening, alignment, and toning exercises. There are other gifts for the mind and spirit, such as aromatherapy candles, spa treatments, therapeutic massage, and a nice selection of natural cosmetics.

BROAD STREET

This is the major Charleston thoroughfare that crosses King, Meeting, and Church Streets, ending at East Bay with the impressive facade of the Exchange Building (see the Attractions and Kids chapters). It is the one made famous by the adage "Below Broad Street," which indicates the mother lode of pricey Charleston real estate south of this line. Historic Broad Street has always been a center of business and political activity since colonial days, but recently the street is primarily commercial between East Bay and King—home to many banks, law offices, and real estate firms. Nowadays, you'll also find a few high-end art galleries and restaurants in the mix, plus a few creative retail venues.

Gifts

THE BOUTIQUE, 47 Broad St.; (843) 722-1441. Without a doubt, the Lowcountry's most gorgeous nightgowns, bathrobes, slips, and the like come from The Boutique. It is also a source for the authentic Charleston bonnet donned by many a Charleston baby. This store, located at the corner of Church and Broad, is where the "hat man" is painted on a wall. The shop also sells fine costume jewelry, linens, and other quality gift items.

CABBAGE ROW SHOPPE, 13 Broad St.; (843) 722-1528, (888) 722-1528; cabbagerowneedlepoint.com. Needle artists in the know say this is a great place to find cross-stitch and needlepoint supplies. Look for antique samplers and charts, kits, and handpainted canvases of Old Charleston and the South. Brand names include DC Designs, Needledeeva, and Strictly Christmas—to name a few. Look here for fine linen, needlework stands, and reference books.

★ **THE RSVP SHOPPE, 141 Broad St.; (843) 577-9740.** For over 30 years this shop has been considered the premier place for fine stationery and invitations. Their move from King Street to Broad a few years back allowed the new owners to expand their merchandise in an attractive location a little off the beaten path. They carry the exclusive Black Label line, candles, gourmet food, cocktail linens, and frames. They have what you need to entertain with panache.

THE SILVER PUFFIN, 43 Broad St.; (843) 723-7900, (888) 723-7900; silverpuffin.com. This Broad Street gift shop has a large selection of cards, mirrors, pottery, jewelry, prints, and glassware. International gourmet foods and Charleston goodies are other draws here. Some of the charming merchandise is domestic, some imported. The owners ship anywhere, so tourists can buy without having to carry things around during their Charleston adventures. Their sister store, Bartons Toys, carries educational and quality toys and games and is located at 708 South Shelmore Blvd. in Mount Pleasant.

THE WINE SHOP, 3 Lockwood Dr.; (843) 577-3881; thewineshopof charleston.com. Sometimes, there's nothing like having a nice bottle of wine to enjoy in your hotel, yacht, or B&B room at night after a day of shopping or sightseeing in Charleston. This shop, next to the City Marina, is the place to find just the right vintage. It carries a wide selection of wines and Champagnes for all budgets as well as cheese, glassware, and wine accessories. It's a good resource for finding a nice gift bottle for a friend or house sitter keeping the pets back home.

Women's Clothing

FABULOUS FROCKS, 100 Church St.; (843) 754-1855; fabulousfrocksof charleston.com. It should come as no surprise that Charleston has become one of the most popular destination wedding sites in the country. And who wouldn't want to tie the knot in this charming and romantic city? Local and brides from away have some dreamy choices at Fabulous Frocks for their perfect wedding gown. And even better this is a consignment shop carrying only the highest quality gowns from leading bridal designers at reduced prices. In-house alterations and personal attention from the staff make for a relaxing, yet exciting shopping experience for that special day. Fabulous Frocks is open Tues through Sat and suggests you make an appointment. It is located just below Broad Street on Church.

Attractions

However varied the attractions of the Lowcountry and Greater Charleston may be, this is a place where people are drawn to, captured by, and never completely released from the clutches of history. In fact, it's fair to say we focus more on history—a deeper, richer, more romantic history (and more of it)—than any other colonial city in America. At least, that's the traditional and prevailing Charlestonian attitude.

Whether you're a newcomer to the Lowcountry (and soon to be an Insider yourself) or just a visitor to this gentle land, it's easy to be overwhelmed by the amount of history offered here and the seriousness with which Charlestonians deal with it in their daily lives.

Tourism and Charleston have a long working (if sometimes strained) relationship. Charleston and tourist management, on the other hand, are relatively recent and wary acquaintances. In other words, the sheer volume of visitors (especially during the past decade) has begun to seriously impact the fragile charm Charlestonians have stubbornly held on to for the past 200 years.

The quaint, genteel, quiet residential flavor of the 18th-century peninsular city (even with its 19th- and 20th-century scars) is by definition threatened by the economic, cultural, and environmental consequences of 4+ million tourists visiting annually. This collision of mores and economics has resulted in a very carefully planned and closely monitored tourism experience for today's Charleston visitor. We, as the city's guests (whether for a week or a lifetime), are very much the fortunate winners in this tug-of-war between then and now.

Because we truly care, and because it helps to preserve our city's unique cultural identity, Charleston's historic attractions are, for the greatest part, well organized, highly accessible, and intelligently interpreted. In short, there are delightful experiences in Charleston for visitors of all ages and all areas of interest.

In this chapter, we will begin by steering you to visitor centers and information outposts. Then we'll take you on a written tour of the Lowcountry's brightest and best attractions, beginning with the house museums, followed by plantations and gardens, forts, historic churches, and other museums. There is a lot to see and do here, and we hope this guide will help you plan well and miss nothing of interest to you. Unless otherwise noted, all addresses are in Charleston.

Price Code

The following price code table is provided to give you an idea of the price of admission to those establishments that charge an admission fee. Please note that prices, means of payment, and hours change often and may vary seasonally, so call ahead for details. If no price code is designated, there is no charge to enter, but there may be other fees.

$	Less than $6
$$	$6 to $10
$$$	$10 to $20
$$$$	More than $20

VISITOR INFORMATION

CHARLESTON VISITOR RECEPTION AND TRANSPORTATION CENTER, 375 Meeting St.; (843) 853-8000, (800) 774-0006; charlestoncvb .com. Because parking in the old historic district is nearly always a problem, visitors are encouraged to make their first destination the Charleston Visitor Reception and Transportation Center. Its location on upper (meaning the northern end of) Meeting Street offers visitors a welcome opportunity to leave their cars behind and see Charleston's large historic district (mostly on the southern end of the Peninsula) by any of several alternative transportation options. This is the major, general information resource site in Charleston proper, and when we make a general reference to "the visitor center" in our guide, the Visitor Reception and Transportation Center is the place to which we refer. Once you've taken in the city's overview of itself, it's time to go out and see the real thing. It's always best to start with a professional tour of some kind. If you're new to Charleston, this will be your only first impression, so why not make it an informed one with a guided tour? Guided walking tours usually begin in the morning and last from 1 to 2 hours. They start from various central locations in the historic district—at most of the large hotels and bed-and-breakfast inns. The cost is about $20 per person. You may also choose to ride in a comfortable, air-conditioned minibus. These guided, motorized tours take about an hour, and prices range from $20 to $25. Or you might want to take one of Charleston's famous carriage tours and see the city at a clip-clop pace. (See the chapter on Tours for complete information on tour options and prices.) Inexpensive and convenient motorized shuttle buses called DASH (Downtown Area Shuttle System) cost $1.75 per ride, leave the old depot behind the center at 15- or 20-minute intervals, and carry passengers to the old City Market in the heart of downtown. Some routes are even free. So, it's very possible to "do" the city and leave your car at the visitor center lot or garage. The visitor center is open daily from 8:30 a.m. to 5 p.m. except Thanksgiving, Christmas, and New Year's Day.

PRESERVATION SOCIETY OF CHARLESTON, 147 King St.; (843) 722-4630; preservationsociety.org. Another friendly informational oasis for the sore-footed traveler (especially handy for those touring the many antiques venues scattered along King Street) is the Preservation Society of Charleston. Its Book & Gift Shop offers a fine collection of books, reference materials, and gift items pertaining to Charleston and the Lowcountry. The accommodating staff of volunteers offers free tourist information as well. Every fall the Preservation Society's tours of private homes and gardens are very popular. This is a lovely time of year to see the city. Tickets are priced at $50 a tour and often sell out early, but you might check here at the bookshop at the last minute and still be able to join one of these self-guided, neighborhood walking tours. (See the Festivals & Annual Events chapter for more on the tours.) The 147 King St. location serves as headquarters and resource center for the organization (founded in 1920) originally known as the Society for the Preservation of Old Dwelling Houses, one of America's premier preservation organizations. The Preservation Society Book & Gift Shop is open from 10 a.m. to 5 p.m. Mon through Sat., 10 a.m. to 4 p.m. Sun. (See the Shopping chapter.)

THE SHOPS OF HISTORIC CHARLESTON FOUNDATION, 108 Meeting St.; (843) 724-8484; historiccharleston.org. Those who find themselves downtown in the vicinity of 108 Meeting St. (across from the Mills House) have another option for starting their historic Charleston odyssey. The Shops of Historic Charleston Foundation is its official name, but it's the Historic Charleston Foundation's version of visitor orientation. You'll find a well-planned cultural and architectural overview and free and friendly tourist advice. The shop carries a fine array of merchandise, including many items from the foundation's Reproduction Collections. You'll find a comprehensive selection of books and reference materials relating to preservation, restoration, and Charleston's 18th- and 19th-century cultural life. You can also buy tickets for the foundation's signature house museums, the Nathaniel Russell House and the Aiken-Rhett House, and Middleton Place Foundation's Edmondston-Alston House. (See the House Museums section of this chapter.) They also handle tickets sales for the Spring Festival of Houses and Gardens and the Charleston Antiques Show (see the Festivals & Annual Events chapter). The Shops of Historic Charleston Foundation is open Mon through Sat from 9 a.m. to 6 p.m., Sun hours are from noon to 5 p.m. Admission is free.

HOUSE MUSEUMS

Peninsular Charleston contains thousands—yes, *thousands*—of historic buildings considered "architecturally significant." Overwhelming as that may seem, it's even more amazing to realize the vast majority of those buildings are private homes. Of these homes, literally hundreds could legitimately qualify as house museums—not only for their exterior architectural sophistication, but also for their sumptuous interiors. In fact, preserving these homes and their remarkable collections of art, china, fine furniture, and fabrics has become an integral part of today's Charleston lifestyle.

While most of these historic homes remain in private hands and are rarely opened to public tours, six Charleston house museums offer visitors unique adventures behind normally closed doors.

Most of the following house museums are open year-round and operated by various nonprofit preservation organizations in the city. Others are privately owned and run as businesses. In either case, Charleston's house museums afford a fascinating glimpse into the style of the city's interiors during a number of heydays in the development of American decorative arts.

From 18th-century Georgian to late-19th-century Victorian, Charleston's house museums have it all. As a quick reference for those who don't happen to keep the eight basic architectural styles of historic Charleston constantly top-of-mind, the following definitions (courtesy of the Historic Charleston Foundation and the National Trust for Historic Preservation) are offered:

- **Colonial** refers to the period from 1690 to 1740. Look for a very low foundation, beaded clapboard siding, a high-pitched gable roof (sometimes with flared eaves), hipped dormers, and raised panel shutters. A good Charlestonian example is the John Lining House, 106 Broad St. at King Street.

- **Georgian** refers to the architectural style popular in England during the reign of Anne and the four Georges. Here in America, the style is generally assigned to the years 1700 to 1790. Look for a hipped roof, box chimneys, triangular pediments (often with oval lights), columns, a raised basement, and a belt course between floors. An excellent Charleston example is the Miles Brewton House, 27 King St.

- **Federal** is the American architectural style seen chiefly between the years 1790 and 1820. In England, the style is called Adam, in reference to the English-Irish architect Robert Adam. Look for geometric rooms, ironwork balconies, a low-pitched roof, decorative bands around interior rooms, exterior trim, spiral stairs, and elliptical fan lights. The Nathaniel Russell House, 51 Meeting St., is a fine Charleston example.

- **Classical Revival** is the architectural return to the lines and look of ancient Greece (and later, Rome). It was popular in America from about 1820 to 1875. Look for large, heavy columns and capitals, temple pediments, triglyph and guttae, and all the other details in classic Greek architectural order. In Charleston, a great example is Beth Elohim Synagogue, 90 Hasell St.

- **Gothic Revival** refers to the period between 1850 and 1885, when many American building designs borrowed from the upreaching lines of western European architecture between the 12th and 16th centuries. Look for pointed arches, buttresses, stone tracery, and finials. At 136 Church St., the French Huguenot Church exemplifies this style.

- **Italianate** is shown in the popular building style seen here between 1830 and 1900. Look for paired brackets and round head arches, balustrades, a low-pitched roof, and the loggia (or veranda). A classic Charleston example is the Col. John Algernon Sydney Ashe House, 26 South Battery.

- **Victorian** refers, of course, to England's Queen Victoria, who reigned from 1836 to 1901. In American architecture, however, it was a popular style between the years 1860 and 1915. Look for a multi-gabled roof, elaborate wood bracket work (sometimes called gingerbread), turrets, and roof decorations. A rare Charleston example is the Sottile House, on the College of Charleston campus at Green Street.

- **Art Deco** is exemplified in the highly stylized look that many American buildings took during the years between the world wars, roughly 1920 to 1940. Look for decorative panels, narrow windows, flat roofs, and multicolored bands. Charleston's most outstanding example is the beautifully restored Riviera Theater, 225–227 King St.

AIKEN-RHETT HOUSE (1818, 1833, 1857), 48 Elizabeth St.; (843) 723-1159; historiccharleston.org; $$. Unlike any other house museum in

Charleston, the Aiken-Rhett house is a time capsule of Charleston's history and taste. It was the home of Gov. William Aiken from 1833 through 1887, and it owes most of its eerie charm to him. The structure was built in 1818 by John Robinson as a typical Charleston single house, much like many others built in the city at the time. However, under the later ownership of South Carolina railroad magnate Aiken (who was governor at the time of the Civil War), the house was drastically altered and enlarged. In 1833 it was remodeled to conform to the bold Greek Revival style popular then. Again in 1857, alterations were made, this time in the heavily ornamented Rococo Revival style that was gaining popularity in antebellum Charleston. Rococo Revival, which was popular in 18th-century France, is noted for curvilinear lines, as in shells, foliage, and scrolls. Here again, an uncanny amount of furnishings and other objects belonging to Governor and Mrs. Aiken can still be found, including portraits, statuary, library volumes, and elaborate chandeliers the couple brought back from Paris in the 1830s. The difference here is that much of the house is unrestored. It is instead preserved, largely as it was presented to the Charleston Museum in 1975 by descendants of the Aiken family. As a result, the visitor can almost feel the presence of Jefferson Davis, president of the Confederacy, who was a guest in the house in 1863. You can easily picture Confederate general P. G. T. Beauregard using the house as his headquarters during the almost relentless Union bombardment of Charleston in 1864. The haunting, life-size portrait of Mrs. Aiken dressed in her finery belies the emotional and economic hardship she suffered after the war when the governor was arrested and briefly imprisoned for treason. Another miracle of the Aiken-Rhett house is the remarkably well-preserved slave quarters and outbuildings (including stables and a privy) to the rear of the house. A high masonry wall surrounding the stableyard and slave quarters somehow managed to keep out the forces of time and change. They're shown as they are, unromanticized, making an eloquent statement about slavery and the sociology of the 19th-century South. If woodworking detail is any measure of worth and respect, the horses at the Aiken-Rhett house were more important than the slaves who worked as house servants. The horse stalls have Gothic arches and turned pillars; no such adornment graces the utilitarian slave quarters. The fragile textures of time and the changing fortunes of war very much show in this remarkable house museum. Surely this is its most romantic and tragic charm. Now owned and operated by the Historic Charleston Foundation, the Aiken-Rhett House is a must-see. The 45-minute audio house tours are given from 10 a.m. to 5 p.m. Mon through Sat. Last tour starts at 4:15 p.m. On Sun, tours begin at 2 p.m. A combined ticket that includes admission to the Nathaniel Russell House is available.

CALHOUN MANSION (1876), 16 Meeting St.; (843) 722-8205; calhoun mansion.net; $$$. This house museum is one of Charleston's few great Victorian-era palaces. Architecturally, it represents a brilliant expression of the Italianate style, which became extremely popular in America during the last

The Calhoun Mansion was built in 1876.

half of the 19th century. This style is a rarity in Charleston's rich display of domestic architecture, possibly because when it was built, in 1876, the city's economy was still devastated by the loss of the Civil War. During the postwar period known as Reconstruction, very little mansion building was going on in Charleston. But the builder, George Walton Williams, a wholesale grocer and banker, was financially undaunted by the war. Unlike most wealthy Southerners, he had invested heavily in England and in the North before the war. When Mr. Williams's huge, new Charleston home was completed, newspapers in New York, Atlanta, and Charleston immodestly described it as "the handsomest and most-complete home in the South, if not the country." Indeed, it is still the largest privately owned home in Charleston with its 35 rooms, 24,000 square feet of living space, 23 fireplaces, 3-tiered piazza, Italian water gardens with fountains, and a cupola soaring 90 feet in the air overlooking Charleston Harbor. The Calhoun name comes from the fact that the builder's son-in-law, Patrick Calhoun—grandson of John C. Calhoun, "The Great Nullifier"—lived here until 1929, when he lost the house and his fortune in the stock market crash of that year. Subsequent owners failed to find a viable use for this venerable old mansion. It slowly slid into decline until it was finally condemned by the City of Charleston in the 1970s. A young local attorney bought it and spent a considerable fortune and much of the next 25 years restoring its structural and artistic integrity. Today, it houses a new owner's extensive personal collection of English and American furniture of the 18th and 19th centuries—with an emphasis on Southern decorative arts. In addition, his fine collection of impressionist art, Chinese ceramics, and other objets d'art look amazingly at home in this huge Victorian-era forum originally designed to create an impressive display. The Calhoun Mansion has been featured in many national magazines and used as a set for the very memorable television miniseries *North and South*. Guided tours of the main 2 floors take place on the hour and half hour starting at 11 a.m. until 5 p.m., seasonally Tues through Fri and by appointment. A new Grand Tour tours the entire mansion including the cupola and costs $75 per person with advance reservations. Toddlers must be carried by a supervising adult; no strollers allowed. In-house photography is prohibited.

EDMONDSTON-ALSTON HOUSE (1825, 1838), 21 East Battery; (843) 722-7171; middletonplace.org; $$$. In 1825, Charles Edmondston, another wealthy merchant and wharf owner, built this handsome dwelling where he could enjoy an uninterrupted view over the expanse of Charleston Harbor. In 1828 the house was bought by Col. William Alston, a rice planter. His son, Charles, redecorated the house in the 1830s, favoring the fashionable

Greek Revival style. Incredibly, today's visitor can still find many family documents, portraits, silver pieces, and fine furnishings—including Charles Alston's almost-intact library—in place. Much of it dates back to the 1830s. The house is notable for its unusual Regency woodwork, as well as its uncompromising views of the harbor. The intimacy and authentic details of the house may leave guests feeling as if the Alstons only recently left the property, perhaps on a visit to the country. The Edmondston-Alston House is owned by Middleton Place Foundation. Tours are offered from 10 a.m. to 4:30 p.m. Tues through Sat and 1 to 4:30 p.m. Sun and Mon. Admission is charged, but it's free for children age 5 and younger.

HEYWARD-WASHINGTON HOUSE (1772), 87 Church St.; (843) 722-2996; charlestonmuseum.org; $$.
This handsome, early Charleston "dwelling house" is now known by two names because of two prominent Americans associated with it—one an owner, the other a distinguished guest. It was built in 1772 by Daniel Heyward, a wealthy rice planter and the father of Thomas Heyward Jr., a South Carolina signer of the Declaration of Independence. It is documented that the younger Heyward lived in the house until 1794. In 1791 President George Washington made a grand tour of the new nation and included Charleston on his itinerary. In anticipation of this distinguished visitor, the city rented Heyward's house for Washington's accommodations, and Heyward was thus displaced to his country house for the duration. In Washington's diary, he recorded his visit to the property, saying, "The lodgings provided for me in this place were very good, being the furnished house of a gentleman at present residing in the country; but occupied by a person placed there on purpose to accommodate me." Today the house is furnished with a magnificent collection of period antiques, especially some fine Charleston-made furniture of the 18th century. Look for the famous Holmes bookcase that still bears the scars of an incoming British mortar from the days of the American Revolution. This is the only 18th-century house museum in the city with original outbuildings (kitchen, carriage house, and necessary) still a part of the courtyard. You'll also find a small formal garden, in keeping with the period of the house. Heyward-Washington House was saved from destruction in the early 1920s by the Preservation Society of Charleston. It is now a National Historic Landmark owned and operated by the Charleston Museum. It's open daily, Mon through Sat from 10 a.m. to 5 p.m. and Sun from 1 to 5 p.m. No entry is allowed after 4:30 p.m. Note that the Charleston Museum offers discounted combination ticket prices for this house and the Joseph Manigault House.

★ **JOSEPH MANIGAULT HOUSE (1803)**, 350 Meeting St.; (843) 723-2996; charlestonmuseum.org; $$. At the beginning of the 19th century, Charleston architecture was still very much dominated by what was fashionable in Mother England. This house, designed and built in 1803 by Charleston gentleman-architect Gabriel Manigault for his brother Joseph, was certainly no exception. Today it remains one of America's most beautiful examples of the graceful Adam style. Both Manigault brothers were wealthy rice planters with sophisticated tastes. Gabriel had studied in Geneva and London, where the Adam influence was at its height, and he maintained an extensive architectural library of his own. The house is distinguished by one of the most graceful staircases in the city and displays an outstanding collection of Charleston, American, English, and French furniture of the period. Don't miss the charming gate temple in the rear garden. During the 1920s, when the Manigault House was very nearly torn down in the name of progress, Gabriel Manigault's classical gate temple was used as the restroom for an oil company's service station, then on the garden site. Later, during World War II, the house served as a USO canteen for servicemen passing through Charleston's busy Navy Yard en route to battle stations overseas. Today it is a National Historic Landmark owned and operated by the Charleston Museum. Hours are 10 a.m. to 5 p.m. Mon through Sat and 1 to 5 p.m. on Sun. The last tour begins at 4:30 p.m.

★ **NATHANIEL RUSSELL HOUSE (1808)**, 51 Meeting St.; (843) 724-8481; historiccharleston.org; $$. Prominent shipping merchant Nathaniel Russell decided to build his great "mansionhouse" on Meeting Street, practically within sight of the busy wharves that produced his wealth. When his house was completed in 1808, Russell was 71, and he had reportedly spent $80,000 on the project—an enormous sum at that time. Like the Manigault House, Russell's new home was inspired by the work of English architect Robert Adam, whose delicate style was influenced by the airy classical designs only recently uncovered (literally) in the Italian excavations of Pompeii and Herculaneum. Today's visitor is immediately dazzled by the dramatic, free-flying, elliptical stairway floating up through 3 floors without any visible means of support. Finely proportioned, geometric rooms are furnished with another outstanding collection of Charleston, English, and French pieces, including rare china, silver, and paintings. Unlike most other Charleston house museums, the Russell House has never been through a sad period of decline and disrepair. First as a fine town house, then as the home of a South Carolina governor, and later as a school for girls and even a convent, 51 Meeting St. has always been a respected and cared-for landmark. Today it is owned and operated by Historic

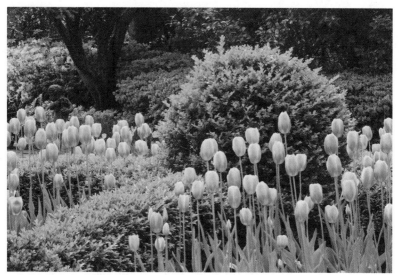

Nathaniel Russell House gardens in full bloom

Charleston Foundation, an organization that has done much to preserve and illuminate the city's architectural heritage. The house is open for tours Mon through Sat from 10 a.m. to 5 p.m. and Sun from 2 to 5 p.m. The last tour begins at 4:30 p.m. The house is closed on Thanksgiving, Christmas Eve, and Christmas Day. A combination ticket for this and the Aiken-Rhett House at 48 Elizabeth St. is available. Call (843) 724-8481 for tickets and group tour information.

PLANTATIONS & GARDENS

Here's a suggested route you may want to take: Starting on the Peninsula, take US 17 S. Once across the Ashley River Bridge, you'll drive through some of Charleston's post–World War II urban sprawl. You may choose to start your plantation tour at the very beginning—at Charles Towne Landing State Historic Site, South Carolina's unique state park at the site of the colony's original settlement. There, you'll explore a reconstruction of an early settler's cabin and see the "experimental garden" where test crops of various kinds held the settler's best hope for survival in this brave new world.

Next, you may want to take the same architectural quantum leap Charlestonians did—from that early, crude settler's cabin to the classical grandeur of

Drayton Hall (begun in 1738), which was built along the Ashley River's west bank only a generation later.

At Middleton Place (developed ca. 1740) and Magnolia Plantation (started in the 1680s, then expanded about 1840), you can explore the vast gardens so important to these early planter families. Magnolia's informal design (typical of 19th-century gardens) makes an interesting contrast to Middleton's strict geometric patterns (so popular in 18th-century France).

In the spring, you'll want to include Cypress Gardens, originally part of Dean Hall plantation on the Cooper River. Follow SR 61 from Middleton Place to SR 165, join US 17-A through Summerville to Moncks Corner, and follow the signs. There, in a 163-acre blackwater cypress swamp, is an incredible azalea garden started in the 1920s and now owned and operated by the City of Charleston Department of Parks. You'll find charming little bateaux (flat-bottomed boats) to use, and there are 3 miles of walking paths through the vibrant spring colors reflected in the mirrorlike waters.

After your initial excursions into the Lowcountry's plantation past along the Ashley River, you will not want to miss the opportunity to visit some of the vast plantations that once flourished along the Cooper River in Mount Pleasant. First is Snee Farm, country home of one of America's founding fathers, Charles Pinckney (1757–1824); then comes one of America's most photographed plantations, Boone Hall.

To find Snee Farm, cross the 4-lane highway (US 17 N.) opposite Christ Church to Long Point Road, and look for the sign. Less than a mile up Long Point Road on your left is the entrance to Snee Farm.

Back along US 17 N. is Boone Hall, the picturesque, 738-acre plantation used extensively in the ABC-TV miniseries *North and South,* filmed in and around Charleston. Boone Hall's best features include the famous avenue of live oaks and the original "slave street" of 9 brick slave cabins (ca. 1743).

You won't be able to visit all these plantations in a single day. If you must select only a sampling of Greater Charleston's plantation culture, the following in-depth review of these sites should help you choose.

You won't regret the investment of time and travel it takes to digest these plantations and gardens. They're so much a part of the city, so vital to its development, that to see just one side of Charleston life and not the other might seriously handicap your understanding of the area as a whole.

BOONE HALL PLANTATION, 1235 Long Point Rd., Mount Pleasant; (843) 884-4371; boonehallplantation.com; $$$. Boone Hall Plantation dates back to the 1680s, when the Lords Proprietor made this sizable land grant to an early English settler, Maj. John Boone. During the 18th and 19th centuries, Boone Hall was

Boone Hall Plantation, old brick slave quarters site

a thriving cotton plantation covering more than 17,000 acres. The original Boone Hall mansion was lost in a tragic fire. The present structure dates from the mid-1930s. Admission includes the plantation house tour, the plantation coach tour (weather permitting), the slave street and history tour, "Black History in America" exhibit, a self-guided garden tour as well as seasonal educational performances and the Butterfly Pavilion in the spring and winter months. The property is open every day except Thanksgiving and Christmas but closes Jan 2 through mid Feb for the winter. Hours are Mon through Sat from 9 a.m. to 5 p.m. and Sun from noon to 5 p.m. From mid Mar through Labor Day, hours extend to 8:30 a.m. to 6:30 p.m. on weekdays. Many special events take place here, so check their website and plan your visit accordingly. (For more on Boone Hall, see the Tours chapter.)

CHARLES TOWNE LANDING STATE HISTORIC SITE, 1500 Old Towne Rd. (between I-26 and SR 171); (843) 852-4200; southcarolinaparks .com; $$. Surely this is one of the most unusual state parks in South Carolina, if not America. Charles Towne Landing State Historic Site was created as part of South Carolina's 300th anniversary celebration in 1970. The vast acreage is devoted to re-creating and interpreting the first English settlement in the Carolinas, which existed on this site back in 1670. Start at the visitor center that includes extensive interactive exhibits describing how settlers, slaves, traders, and Native Americans came together at this location to begin the first

European colony in the Carolinas. Along the river, you may explore a full-scale replica of a typical 17th-century trading vessel called the *Adventure,* docked at the landing in Old Towne Creek. The Animal Forest boasts a 20-acre natural habitat zoo with wolves, pumas, bears, bison, snakes, and alligators—all part of the Lowcountry landscape when settlers first arrived in the 1670s. The Settlers' Life Area, with its replica colonial buildings, is a handsome example of what early colonists saw every day. You'll see candle making, open-fire cooking, woodworking, and, depending on the season and the weather, even the colony's first printing press in action. Charles Towne Landing is open all year except Christmas Eve and Christmas day. The hours are 9 a.m. to 5 p.m. daily. Picnic tables, a snack bar, and a gift shop are all on-site. The park is largely accessible to visitors with disabilities. Visitors age 6 and older are charged an admission fee. Wheelchairs and strollers are available free of charge.

CYPRESS GARDENS, 3030 Cypress Gardens Rd., Moncks Corner (off US 52, 8 miles south of Moncks Corner); (843) 553-0515; cypressgardens.info; $$. For those with time and the inclination to go even farther afield, there's yet another treat in store. Discover the beauty and wonder of Cypress Gardens—a true Southern cypress swamp and a 162-acre water forest of uncommon natural beauty. You'll find meandering footpaths for hikers, but the traditional way to see Cypress Gardens is by bateau—a flat-bottomed boat poled or paddled by expert young boaters who are always on hand to do the work for a small price. You have the option of rowing yourself if you like, but the serenity of the black waters mirroring springtime azaleas, dogwoods, daffodils, and wisteria deserves your undivided attention. Scenes from the movies *The Patriot* and *The Notebook* were filmed here. In a separate building, Cypress Gardens' 24,000-gallon "swamparium" features fish and reptiles native to the Lowcountry. There's also a butterfly house and a large greenhouse to explore. Cypress Gardens is open daily except Thanksgiving, Christmas Eve, Christmas, and New Year's. Call ahead for seasonal hours and special admission prices. Hours are usually 9 a.m. to 5 p.m. No admittance is allowed after 4 p.m. Admission is free for children younger than 6.

DRAYTON HALL, 3380 Ashley River Rd.; (843) 769-2600; draytonhall .org; $$$. Not a tour of a reconstructed working plantation or the collected decorative arts from a bygone era, Drayton Hall offers an adventure in architecture. Yes, architecture and a great deal more. If for no other reason, Drayton Hall should be seen and experienced as the sole survivor of the ugly 1865 rampage by Union troops, who looted and burned nearly every other plantation house along the Ashley River. But there is more to Drayton Hall, as it also stands as a survivor of many other changes, influences, forces, and times. It was built between 1738 and 1742 as the country seat (primary home) of John Drayton (1716–1779). The house is considered one of the oldest and finest examples of Georgian-Palladian architecture in America. The structure remains almost untouched as an eloquent statement about 18th-century thinking, craftsmanship, technology, and design. It's one of the few sites left in colonial America so pure, unaltered, and uncompromising. Visitors will find the Drayton Hall story—how it all came to pass—interpreted by a small group of professional guides who lead you through 250 years of time, family genealogy, architectural history, and a smattering of the economic and social realities of the plantation system. The staff has recorded oral histories of the Drayton family as well as the African Americans so closely associated with the house and its survival. A map is provided to visitors for a self-guided nature walk through the Drayton property including marsh, riverfront, and forest areas. Major portions of the nature trails are wheelchair-accessible. This historic site is now owned by the National Trust for Historic Preservation. Admission prices include a professionally guided tour of the historic house and a self-guided tour of the grounds, including the African-American cemetery and their interactive Connections program. Tours are offered on the half hour from 9:30 a.m. to 3:30 p.m. Mon through Sat and 11:30 a.m. to 3:30 p.m. Sun. A written tour in English, French, or German can be purchased. Admission is always free to members of the National Trust and Friends of Drayton Hall who show their membership cards. (See the Festivals & Annual Events chapter for information on the Annual Spirituals Concert at Drayton Hall.)

ℹ Looking to add a splash of color to your spring visit to Charleston? Wade into the vast sea of fuchsia, pale pink, and white azalea blossoms during the annual spring bloom at Magnolia Plantation and Gardens. It's truly an overload for the senses.

MAGNOLIA PLANTATION AND GARDENS, 3550 Ashley River Rd.; (843) 571-1266, (800) 367-3517; magnoliaplantation.com; $$$–$$$$. This is where Thomas Drayton Jr., father of Drayton Hall's John Drayton, settled when he came to Charles Towne in 1679. Early on, the home that Drayton, a successful English planter from the island of Barbados, built for himself and his family was destroyed by fire. The house built to replace it was subsequently burned by Union troops in 1865. The present structure is said to have been

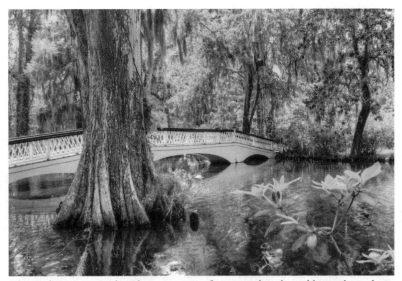

The gardens at Magnolia Plantation were first opened to the public in the early 1870s and are the oldest unrestored gardens in America.

a Drayton family hunting lodge that was moved down the Ashley River in 1873 and placed atop the foundations of the old plantation house. Magnolia Plantation is the original (and continuing) home of the Drayton family, now owned and managed by a 12th-generation descendant. It is famous for its expansive, informal, English-style gardens, which are the legacy of the Reverend John Grimke-Drayton, the plantation's owner during the Civil War. In 1843, Grimke-Drayton imported numerous specimens of *Camellia japonica,* and in 1848, *Azalea indica.* Look for the garden called Flowerdale. Here is Magnolia's earliest garden area (planted in the late 1680s), and it was possibly the inspiration for Grimke-Drayton's larger, more ambitious plan a century and a half later. Today, the gardens boast 250 varieties of azaleas and 900 varieties of camellias. These, plus many other flowers added through the years, keep Magnolia Gardens in colorful bloom all year long. Its most spectacular season, however, is spring, when the dazzling, vibrant azalea colors seem to vibrate on the landscape as far as the eye can see. Visitors can get an overview of the property in a 12-minute video on the plantation's history shown at regular intervals in the orientation theater. Magnolia Plantation offers additional activities for nature lovers. Canoes can be rented to glide through the eerie beauty of its 125-acre waterfowl refuge. There are walking and bicycle trails, plus a wildlife observation tower that's very popular with bird-watchers. There's an herb garden,

Close-up

Ashley River Road: Back Road to the Plantation Life

Before Hurricane Hugo struck the Lowcountry in September 1989—destroying an estimated 7 million board feet of prime, standing lumber—the **Ashley River Road** (SR 61 from Church Creek to Bacons Bridge Road) was oak-lined, moss-laden, sun-dappled, and almost unbearably beautiful. Certainly, that's how many Lowcountry old-timers remember it.

Most of the huge oak trees were hundreds of years old and stood so close to the road they became a hazard to speeding cars. So, for several years, every serious accident (and there were many) became a new excuse to remove more trees and more of the road's ambience. Then came the slow but relentless encroachment of commercial businesses and the addition of more and bigger real estate developments, each taking an even higher toll on the once scenic highway.

In the late 1990s, however, preservationists woke up to the fact that old SR 61 was a unique natural resource—of Lowcountry history and beauty—and it was quickly vanishing in the name of progress and development. Turning back these forces, once under way, turned out to be nearly impossible. But through years of planning and negotiation, a new plan has emerged that hopes to preserve as much of the old road's ambience as possible. Ashley River Road was designated a South Carolina State Scenic Byway in 1998 and a National Scenic Byway in 2000.

The stretch between Drayton Hall and Middleton Place still has the densest tree canopy. The live oaks reach up and over the road, creating a sun-filtered canopy through which you'll feel you're driving into the past.

Remember, the Ashley River itself is always on your right—sometimes just through the trees. Bear in mind, too, that the old road (originally a trail

a horticultural maze, newly opened antebellum slave cabins, a typical Ashley River rice barge, and even a petting zoo for children (as well as adults). You'll find picnic areas, a snack shop, and a gift shop there, too. (See the Kids chapter.) The Audubon Swamp Garden encompasses a 60-acre, blackwater cypress and tupelo swamp. The visitor has the opportunity to see an otherwise inaccessible for Native Americans) was only a back road to the Ashley's colonial plantations. It was slow, rutted, and practically impossible to navigate in wet weather. Most social and business traffic to and from the far-flung plantations went by water. Thus, the great houses were actually built facing the river, the avenue to all agricultural wealth. Still, European settlers are recorded using the back road as early as 1707.

If you look carefully, you'll notice some unexplained low ridges along the roadside. Chances are, these are old rice dikes indicating where the land was flooded and the fields cultivated for rice.

In other places through the forest you'll see larger, unnatural-looking mounds—especially noticeable in the wintertime. These are the outcroppings from old, abandoned phosphate mines. After the Civil War, during the late 1870s, phosphate (an early fertilizer product) was discovered in the ground along the west bank of the Ashley. For a brief but reckless period, this entire landscape was crudely strip-mined. As ecologically careless and harmful as these practices were, the phosphate era provided desperately needed income for a few of the old planter families that had somehow managed to hold on to their properties through the war and Reconstruction.

If the phosphate mining years were not the Ashley River's finest hour, at least they helped rescue what little was left of the plantations after the cataclysmic year of 1865. In February of that year, as the war was winding down, Union troops advanced toward Charleston on the Ashley River Road, looting and burning as they came. Of all the great houses once standing along the high, west bank of the river, only Drayton Hall survived.

Once, there were scores of plantations along the Ashley. They had wonderful, lyrical names: MacBeth and Runnymede, Millbrook and Schieveling. Today, three of the old properties are open to the public. These are Drayton Hall, Magnolia, and Middleton Place. (See entries in text.) Each is unique and remarkable in a different way, and each offers special insight into the Ashley River's fascinating plantation story.

natural area via boardwalks, dikes, and bridges that provide an intimate view of the horticultural beauty and wildlife, including a few alligators. The swamp garden gets its name from the great 19th-century American naturalist and wildlife artist John James Audubon, who visited Magnolia in search of waterbird specimens during his many lengthy stays in Charleston. This attraction is a

1-hour self-guided walking tour. The property is open daily from 8 a.m. to 5:30 p.m. (9 a.m. to 4:30 p.m. Nov through Feb). A basic admission is charged, with additional fees added for the Plantation House, Nature Train/Boat, Slavery to Freedom tour, and Audubon Swamp.

★ **MIDDLETON PLACE, 4300 Ashley River Rd.; (843) 556-6020, (800) 782-3608; middletonplace.org; $$$$.** Middleton is one of the Lowcountry's most famous plantations and another National Historic Landmark along the rich and fascinating Ashley River. This was the home of Henry Middleton, president of the First Continental Congress, and his son Arthur, a signer of the Declaration of Independence. The sheer size and scope of Middleton's gardens tell a great deal about the man and his grand vision. The 12-acre greensward, with its grazing sheep and strutting peacocks, creates an unforgettable image for the first-time visitor. Not to be missed is the view of the Ashley River from the high terraces of the gardens. The green grass ripples down the hillside to the graceful butterfly lakes below. This bucolic, pastoral scene belies the frenzy of activity and the vast labor force needed to maintain this busy world. On the Middleton Place grounds is Eliza's House, an actual freedman's dwelling. At the lively plantation stableyards, with active displays of day-to-day life, you'll find a blacksmith, a potter, weavers, and carpenters all busy at work and eager to explain and demonstrate their skills. The main house, built sometime before 1741, was—like Magnolia's—burned in 1865 by Union troops. The south flanker building (added about 1755) was least damaged by the fire, and it was essentially rebuilt in the early years of the 20th century in its present form. The Restaurant at Middleton Place serves authentic Lowcountry cuisine, and a daily lunch is available to visitors from noon to 3 p.m. At night, from 6 to 9 p.m. Fri and Sat and until 8 p.m. Tues through Thurs and Sun, the restaurant serves a delightful candlelight dinner, and there's no admission charge for entry to the property after 5:30 p.m. with dinner reservations. (See the Middleton Place website or call 843-266-7477 for details on dining there.) Just past the rice mill, a path leads into the forest and up a hill to the Middleton Inn, a 55-room riverside oasis for discerning overnight travelers. With vine-covered stucco and unblinking modern glass walls, each suite looks out over a green, woodland setting or the quiet waters of the Ashley River. (See the Accommodations chapter for more.) Middleton Place is open daily. Hours are 9 a.m. to 5 p.m. for the gardens and stableyards. House tours begin at 10 a.m., except on Mon, when they begin at noon. House tour admission adds $15 per person to Middleton Place rates. An optional carriage ride through the property adds to the admission charge for adults and children. (See the Festivals & Annual Events chapter for special events at Middleton.)

⭐ **SNEE FARM (CHARLES PINCKNEY NATIONAL HISTORIC SITE)**, 1254 Long Point Rd., Mount Pleasant; (843) 881-5516, (843) 883-3123; nps.gov/chpi. Let's begin with Charles Pinckney, the man. He began his public career at age 22, when he was admitted to the South Carolina Bar and the South Carolina General Assembly. Pinckney served as one of four South Carolina delegates at the Constitutional Convention in Philadelphia. He served as governor of South Carolina, was ambassador to Spain from 1801 to 1805, and held seats in both the state and national legislature. He retired from public life in 1821 and died 3 years later. Originally, Snee Farm was part of a 500-acre royal grant awarded in 1698 to Richard Butler. By 1754, the farm comprised 715 acres and was purchased that year by Pinckney's father. The property was the family's "country seat" and an integral part of Charles Pinckney's life. Like many other Charleston aristocrats, Pinckney relied on slave labor (mostly imported from West Africa) to raise the "Carolina gold" (rice) that grew on Snee Farm. (For more on African-American history at Snee Farm, see the Tours chapter.) The present house on the remaining 28-acre site, built in the 1820s, is an excellent and charming example of the type of coastal cottage once common here in the Lowcountry. Guests will find interesting interpretive exhibits in and around the house. There's an informative 20-minute video telling of Charles Pinckney, Snee Farm, George Washington's colonial era visit to the property and the US as a young, emerging nation. Park hours are from 9 a.m. to 5 p.m. daily. Closed Thanksgiving, Christmas, and New Year's Day. Admission is absolutely free, a real bargain.

FORTS

Among the most visited attractions in the Lowcountry are the area's famous forts—standing today in mute testimony to the great strategic role Charleston Harbor played during the conflicts of the past 300 years.

Of course, the most famous of these fortresses is legendary Fort Sumter, where the Civil War began. But Greater Charleston has a number of other forts and former military fortifications that offer fascinating stories, both for the serious historian and for us regular Insiders too. There's Fort Moultrie on Sullivan's Island, Fort Johnson on James Island (now site of the South Carolina Wildlife and Marine Resources Center), and Battery Wagner on Morris Island.

We'll sketch brief histories of these sites—just enough to send you off to see the real thing with a taste of the very real drama and sacrifice associated with these places.

View looking down on Fort Sumter

FORT JOHNSON WILDLIFE AND MARINE RESOURCES CENTER,
217 Fort Johnson Rd.; (843) 953-9300; dnr.sc.gov/marine. Fort Johnson
is another Charleston area fortress steeped in history and adaptively reused
for modern needs. Since the early 1970s, the waterfront James Island site has
been the home of the South Carolina Wildlife and Marine Resources Division,
which researches and promotes the state's marine industries. But savvy military buffs know Fort Johnson in another role. Like Fort Moultrie, this site has
military significance that dates back several hundred years. No trace now exists
of the original Fort Johnson that was constructed on the site in about 1708. It
was named for Sir Nathaniel Johnson, proprietary governor of the Carolinas
at the time. A second fort was constructed in 1759, and small portions of
that structure remain as tabby ruins there today. (Tabby is an early building
material made from crushed oyster shell and lime.) Records show the fort was
occupied in 1775 by three companies of South Carolina militia under the leadership of Lt. Col. Motte. During the American Revolution, the fort remained
in colonial hands until 1780, when the British forces advancing on Charleston
reported finding it abandoned. A third fort was built in 1793, but a hurricane
destroyed it in 1800. Some work on Fort Johnson was done during the War
of 1812, but the following year another storm destroyed that progress. Shortly
afterward, Fort Johnson was dropped from official reports of US fortifications.

During early 1861, South Carolina state troops erected mortar batteries and an earthwork of three guns on the old fortress site. Unbeknownst to most Americans, the actual signal shot that opened the bombardment of Fort Sumter and marked the beginning of the Civil War was fired from the east mortar battery of Fort Johnson on April 12, 1861. Fort Sumter was fired upon, not vice versa. During the Civil War, building activity increased until Fort Johnson became an entrenched camp, mounting 26 guns and mortars. However, apart from routine artillery firing from the site, the only major action at the fort occurred on July 3, 1864, when its Confederate defenders repulsed two Union regiments totaling about 1,000 men. The Union forces sustained 26 casualties and lost 140 men as captives. The Confederate loss was one killed and three wounded. On the night of February 17, 1865, Fort Johnson was evacuated during the general Confederate withdrawal from Charleston Harbor. After the Civil War, Fort Johnson became a quarantine station operated by the state and the City of Charleston. It continued to be used in that capacity until the 1950s. Today's inhabitants at the site (the Marine Resources folks) do not prohibit exploration, so you might find this history-drenched spot worth a visit. There is no charge to visit.

FORT MOULTRIE, 1214 West Middle St., Sullivan's Island; (843) 883-3123; nps.gov/fosu. From the earliest days of European settlement along the Eastern Seaboard, coastal fortifications were set up to guard the newly found, potentially vulnerable harbors.

In this unique restoration, operated today by the National Park Service, visitors to Fort Moultrie can see two centuries of coastal defenses as they evolved. In its 171-year history (1776 to 1947), Fort Moultrie defended Charleston Harbor twice. The first time was during the Revolutionary War, when 30 cannons from the original fort drove off a British fleet mounting 200 guns in a ferocious, 9-hour battle. This time, Charleston was saved from British occupation, and the fort was justifiably named in

Fort Moultrie, the grave of Major General William Moultrie

honor of its commander, William Moultrie. The second time the fort defended the city was during the Civil War. For nearly 2 years, the Charleston forts (and the city itself) were bombarded from both land and sea. The walls of Forts Sumter and Moultrie crumbled under the relentless shelling, but somehow the forts were able to hold back the Union attacks. Today, the fort has been restored to portray the major periods of its history. Five different sections of the fort and two outlying areas each feature typical weapons representing a different historical period. Visitors move steadily back in time from the World War II Harbor Entrance Control Post to the original, palmetto log fort of 1776. Fort Moultrie is open from 9 a.m. to 5 p.m. year-round. It is closed on Thanksgiving, Christmas, and New Year's Day. Groups should make reservations for guided tours. Pets are not allowed. Admission is free.

★ **FORT SUMTER NATIONAL MONUMENT,** Charleston Harbor; (843) 883-3123, (800) 789-3678; nps.gov/fosu, fortsumtertours.com; $$$. Almost every Charlestonian knows the story by heart: The year was 1861. South Carolina had seceded from the Union. And yet, just a few miles east, there at the mouth of Charleston Harbor, Union forces were still stationed at Fort Sumter. The Confederacy officially demanded that Fort Sumter be vacated, but the North adamantly refused. At 4:30 a.m. on the morning of April 12, a mortar shell burst over the fort, fired from nearby Fort Johnson. The Civil War had begun. At first—largely as a matter of honor—the Union forces defended Fort Sumter. But after 34 hours, they surrendered. It was practically a bloodless battle—no one was killed, and only a few men were wounded. Amazingly, the Confederates held the fort for the next 27 months, against what was the heaviest bombardment the world had ever seen. Over the course of almost 2 years, no fewer than 46,000 shells (about 3,500 tons of metal) were fired at the island fort. In the end, the Confederate troops abandoned Fort Sumter, but they never surrendered. It was February 17, 1865. By April, the war and the cause would be lost. Today, Fort Sumter is a national monument administered by the National Park Service of the US Department of the Interior. It is still accessible only by boat, and the only public tour of this tiny man-made island and world-famous fort is offered through Fort Sumter Tours, Inc. You can board the Fort Sumter tour boat at the National Park Service's new facility at Liberty Square at the foot of Calhoun Street on the Cooper River. The impressive $15 million interpretive center took 3 years to build and adds a dramatic new dimension to the Fort Sumter experience. Here, visitors are immersed in the Fort Sumter story with interactive displays and graphics, while Park Service rangers are on hand to answer questions. Among the sights found here, you'll find the actual 33-star Garrison Flag that flew over the fort that historic first night of the Civil War. The trip out to Fort Sumter takes about 2 hours and 15 minutes (including 1 hour at the fort). The boat ride affords delightful views of Charleston's waterfront and includes a narrated history of Charleston Harbor given en route. Another departure location is at Patriots Point in Mount Pleasant. The specially built sightseeing boats are clean, safe, and have on-board restrooms. Once you're at Fort Sumter itself, you can walk freely about the ruins. There's another interpretive museum area on-site with National Park Service rangers there to answer any questions you may have. You'll need to check in for your tour at least 30 minutes early for ticketing and boarding. Departure times vary according to the season and the weather, so call the toll-free number listed for departure information. During the busy summer season, there are usually 3 tours a day. No tours on Thanksgiving, Christmas, and New Year's Day. Children younger than 4 are admitted free, but a boarding pass is required for them. Wheelchair access is available. Group rates are available, but advance reservations for groups are encouraged. (Visit spiritlinecruises.com or see the Tours and Kids chapters for additional information.)

Battery Wagner, Morris Island

Of all the forts and battlegrounds that dot the Lowcountry landscape and pay quiet tribute to the area's military history, perhaps the most muted one is Battery Wagner on Morris Island. The story is a brief one in the long struggle of the Civil War, but it is a significant one that is especially poignant today. In 1989, the story of Battery Wagner was portrayed in the acclaimed film *Glory,* which starred Matthew Broderick, Denzel Washington, and Morgan Freeman.

Time and tides have long since removed all traces of Battery Wagner. Today, Morris Island is vacant and uninhabited. It is hoped that one day Morris Island will become a National Historic Landmark and interpreted for visitors as the battleground and graveyard it is. Although a monument at Battery Wagner is planned, the site remains remarkably overlooked by the public for now. But whatever its future may hold, the story of Morris Island will always include the story of Battery Wagner and the 54th Massachusetts Regiment.

Because Charleston was the "cradle of Secession," it was a primary target for the Union's high command. On June 16, 1862, the Union forces' first attempt to capture the city failed at the Battle of Secessionville on James Island. Union commanders decided to mount a two-pronged attack using both land and naval forces. There were two possible lines of approach to the city: through Sullivan's Island, which was heavily defended, or through Morris Island, which was more lightly guarded. On Morris Island, the main defense was Battery

Wagner, a quickly built fortification with thick sand walls and more than a dozen cannons.

Choosing the Morris Island approach, Union forces landed on July 10, 1863, and opened fire the following day with little success. A week later, they tried again. Even after a 10-hour artillery bombardment, Battery Wagner stood firm.

At dusk on July 18, the Union infantry advanced up the beach toward heavily defended Battery Wagner. Spearheading the attack was the 54th Massachusetts Regiment under the leadership of Col. Robert G. Shaw, the 25-year-old son of a wealthy Boston abolitionist. The regiment under Shaw's command was made up entirely of free blacks from the North. It was one of the 167 black units that fought against the Confederacy in the Civil War.

The bloody, hand-to-hand struggle at Battery Wagner saw 272 men from the 54th (more than 40 percent of the unit) fall dead, and 1,500 Union forces were lost, including Col. Shaw. The valor and courage displayed in the battle proved once and for all to Northern and Southern leaders that black soldiers could and would fight. The story of the 54th was widely publicized at the time, and as a result, the Union army began to enlist blacks in growing numbers. By 1865, a total of 178,895 black soldiers had enlisted, which constituted 12 percent of the North's fighting forces.

The fight for Battery Wagner continued for 10 more weeks until the Confederates finally abandoned the work on September 6. The 54th continued to serve along the southeast coast for the remainder of the war. It was mustered out of service in Mount Pleasant on August 20, 1865.

HISTORIC CHURCHES

In a city that was a major contributor to the American ethic of religious freedom, there's a deep reverence for church architecture. The "Holy City," as it likes to be called, has dozens of beautiful 18th- and 19th-century churches that bear witness to this history and the 21st-century pride that goes with it.

Several churches are notable because of their early dates of construction, while others impress with their architectural grandeur. Some are survivors of cataclysmic events; a few speak volumes about their ethnic and sociological origins. Here are some churches whose history enriches Charleston and its citizenry, but remember, they are only a few of many. Unless otherwise noted, all are in the downtown vicinity and are still active houses of worship. They are listed in alphabetical order.

CATHEDRAL OF ST. JOHN THE BAPTIST (1890–1907), 120 Broad St.; charlestoncathedral.com. The first Cathedral of St. John the Baptist was completed in 1854. It was an outstanding example of Gothic architecture, built of Connecticut sandstone with a 200-foot spire. The building was completely lost in the great fire of 1861. By 1890, work had begun on what is almost an exact duplicate of the 1854 building. It was designed by P. C. Kelly of Brooklyn, New York, and followed closely the plans for the original structure. The exception is the square tower that, for monetary reasons, replaced the tall spire. A new spire and three bells were added atop the tower 103 years later, completing the reconstruction of the old building. The newer building is made of Connecticut brownstone. The nave is tiled, measures 150 by 80 feet, and seats 700 people.

CATHEDRAL OF ST. LUKE AND ST. PAUL (1815), 126 Coming St.; your-cathedral.org. The church that is now the Cathedral Church for the Anglican Diocese of South Carolina was originally known as St. Paul's, Radcliffeborough. It was organized as a mission in 1806. This building, designed by the architects James and John Gordon, was completed in 1815. At the time of its building, the load of the tower proved too heavy for the supporting walls, and the tower was dismantled. A lighter, Gothic Revival–style parapet was added, which is in contrast to the Classical Revival building below. Inside, the original color schemes have been reproduced as part of the intensive restoration of the building following severe damage in Hurricane Hugo in 1989.

CHRIST CHURCH (1726, 1788), 2304 US 17 N., Mount Pleasant; christch.org. Here's your first chance to encounter one of the Lowcountry's most charming undiscovered treasures, one of the little-known but much-loved chapels of ease. Millions of tourists visit the area and never even know these little testimonies to the Lowcountry's bygone plantation era still exist. Amazingly, they do exist, in various forms and in varied states of repair and use. First, however, a little background information is required. The colony of Carolina was founded with the Anglican Church as its established religious force. Early on, Anglican congregations received financial assistance from the British government to construct houses of worship. These first Anglican churches also tended to benefit from the generosity of wealthy planters in their congregations. As a result, these churches were built with greater architectural sophistication than the early buildings of other religious organizations, and it's mostly these better-built, early Anglican structures that survive today as mute witnesses to the strength of religion in the early colonies and the isolation of plantation life. Christ Church Parish was one of 10 parishes established by the Church

Act of 1706. The following year, a wooden building was in place on this site, serving a slowly growing number of communicants. After fire destroyed the wooden building in 1725, a brick structure was completed in 1726. In 1782, British soldiers burned the church to the walls during the Revolution, and it was rebuilt six years later. In 1865, during the Civil War, fire all but destroyed the church again, and although it was once more rebuilt, regular services were discontinued by 1874. Finally, in 1925, both the structure and the congregation were restored by caring descendants of early Christ Church Parish families. Despite its long, hard struggle for survival, Christ Church is a viable, active congregation today.

CIRCULAR CONGREGATIONAL CHURCH (1891–1892), 150 Meeting St.; circularchurch.org. This church was originally called the Independent Church of Charles Towne and was established in 1681 by some of the first settlers of Charleston. It was one of the first two congregations created in the settlement (the other being St. Philip's Church; see subsequent listing). The first building was of white brick and was known by locals as the White Meeting House. It is from this early euphemism that Meeting Street takes its name. That building was outgrown and replaced in 1804 by the first "Circular Church," an impressive structure designed in the Pantheon style by Charleston's famous architect Robert Mills. It is said to have seated 2,000 people, both black and white. The great fire of 1861 swept across the city and took this building with it. The ruins stood mutely until the earthquake of 1886 turned them to rubble. A third (and the present) building on this site was completed in 1892 and is circular in form but Romanesque in style. The church's graveyard is the city's oldest, with monuments dating from 1695. This is the burial ground of Nathaniel Russell. (See the Nathaniel Russell House listing under House Museums in this chapter.)

EMANUEL A.M.E. CHURCH (1891), 110 Calhoun St.; emanuelame church.org. The African Methodist Episcopal Church had its beginnings in 1787 in Philadelphia with the founding of the Free African Society, based on the doctrines of Methodism and the teachings of John Wesley. A similar organization was founded in Charleston in 1791 by the Rev. Morris Brown, a free black preacher affiliated with another Methodist church in the city. This show of independence from the blacks led to a secession from the Methodists and the founding of three black churches in Charleston, known as the Bethel Circuit. The Emanuel A.M.E. congregation is one of those churches. The original building was in the Hampstead neighborhood in the east side of the city. By 1818, it had 1,000 members. In 1822, Denmark Vesey, a carpenter who bought himself out of slavery, laid plans in the church for a slave insurrection. Word of the rebellion leaked out, and Vesey and some of his followers were executed. The Hampstead church was burned to the ground. By 1834, all black churches in South Carolina were closed by the state legislature. During the years following the Denmark Vesey incident, some of the congregation returned to white churches, but others continued the traditions of their African church and met underground. The congregation resurfaced in 1865—3,000 strong. Today's building was completed in 1891. The original gas lamps that line the sanctuary have been preserved. With seating for 2,500, the church has the largest seating capacity of Charleston's African-American congregations.

FIRST BAPTIST CHURCH (1822), 61 Church St.; fbcharleston.org. Here is the oldest Baptist church in the South. The congregation originally emigrated from Maine to the Carolinas in 1696. The building was designed by the first American-born architect, Robert Mills, in the popular Greek Revival style. Mills didn't mince words, saying of his creation, "[it is] the best specimen of correct taste in architecture in the city. It is purely Greek in style, simply grand in its proportions, and beautiful in its detail." Wood for the solid mahogany pulpit was brought from the West Indies for the staggering sum (in 1822) of $1,000. First Baptist's fabulous organ dates from 1845 and was made by Erben.

FIRST (SCOTS) PRESBYTERIAN CHURCH (1814), 53 Meeting St.; first-scots.org. The Scots Kirk (or Scots Meeting House) was organized in 1731 by 12 Scottish families who believed in a strict subscription to the Westminster Standards (church laws) and the Presbyterian form of church government. Their first simple structure on this site was built in 1734. It was replaced in 1814 by the present structure, which is the fifth-oldest church building in Charleston. By unanimous vote of the congregation, the church bell was donated to the Confederacy in 1862 and was only recently replaced by an English bell made in 1814. Although the church was badly damaged by a fire in 1945, it was lovingly repaired. In the window over the main door appears the seal of the Church of Scotland, the burning bush, with a Latin motto that reads, *Nec Tamen Consumbatur (Nevertheless it was not consumed)*.

⭐ **FRENCH HUGUENOT CHURCH (1845)**, 136 Church St.; huguenot-church.org. French Huguenots were followers of the 16th-century French reformer John Calvin. After Louis XIV revoked the Edict of Nantes (1685), there was an enormous flight away from France by Protestants, many of whom came to the Carolinas. The Huguenot Church in Charleston was organized in 1681, and groups of believers arrived in this area between 1680 and 1763. In 1706 the

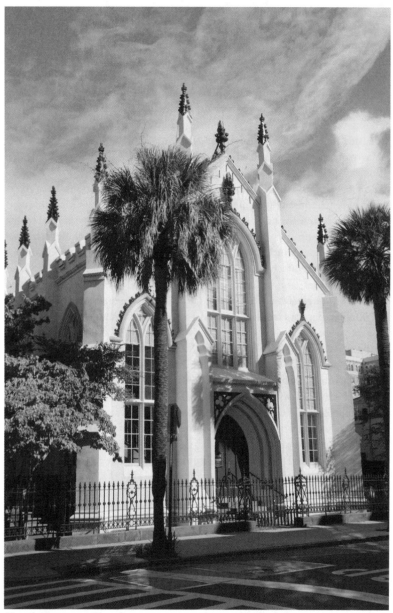

French Huguenot Church

Church Act established the Anglican Church as the official religion in South Carolina, and slowly, most Huguenot churches were absorbed into what became Episcopal congregations. The Huguenot Church in Charleston is the outstanding exception; it is the only remaining independent Huguenot congregation in America. This church was the city's first to be built (1845) in the Gothic Revival style. It was designed by Edward Brickell White, a noted Charleston architect who is credited with popularizing the Gothic style in America. The church was damaged by shelling during the Civil War and nearly demolished by the 1886 earthquake. Each time, it was painstakingly restored. The building underwent a major refurbishing in 1997. The church's famous Tracker organ, restored in 1967 by the Preservation Society of Charleston and the Charleston chapter of the American Organists Guild, is one of the city's true musical treasures. It is one of the last of its kind anywhere in the country.

> **i** Some downtown churches are open to visitors who respectfully wish to see these historic interiors during weekday daytime hours. The schedules may be erratic because these are active, working religious organizations with busy calendars of church events scheduled for the congregations. However, if the doors are open, the sanctuary is deserted (usually there's a sign posted for visitors), and you know you're disturbing no one, feel welcome to quietly enter and briefly look around.

GRACE EPISCOPAL CHURCH (1848), 98 Wentworth St.; gracechurch charleston.org. Another magnificent example of Gothic-style church architecture in Charleston is Grace Episcopal Church, designed by Edward Brickell White. This building was completed in 1848. The memorial windows in Grace Church are teaching windows, each containing scenes from the life of Christ as well as laypersons and clergy associated with the church. The largest window, over the rear doorway, took more than a year to complete and contains more than 10,000 pieces of glass. A small window on the Epistle side of the narthex contains an angel with the face of a small girl who drowned on Sullivan's Island. Grace Church was closed for a year in 1864 because of the terrible bombardment from Morris Island, but it reopened soon after the evacuation of Charleston, during Federal occupation.

KAHAL KADOSH BETH ELOHIM (1840), 90 Hasell St.; kkbe.org. This is the oldest synagogue in continuous use in the US. The present congregation was organized in 1749. It is also the longest surviving Reform synagogue in the world. Beth Elohim is acknowledged as the birthplace of Reform Judaism in the US, tracing its origins back to 1824. This is a branch of Judaism that places more emphasis on traditional religious and moral values, instead of rigid ceremonial and ritualistic detail. The present 1840 Greek Revival structure was designed by Cyrus L. Warner. The graceful but massive wrought-iron fence that faces onto Hasell Street dates back to the original 1794 synagogue.

ST. JOHN'S LUTHERAN CHURCH (1817), 10 Archdale St.; stjohns charleston.org. This is Charleston's mother church of Lutheranism, with a history spanning more than 250 years. The congregation was organized in 1742 and worshiped in various places until the present structure was completed in 1817. Frederick Wesner was the architect. The steeple is said to have been designed earlier by famous Charleston miniaturist Charles Fraser and was constructed in 1859. The original bell was given to the Confederate cause (bells were often melted down for use in ammo, cannons, ships, firearms, and the like) and was not replaced until 1992.

ST. MARY'S CATHOLIC CHURCH (1838–1839), 89 Hasell St.; catholic -doc.org/saintmarys. Called "the Mother Church of the Carolinas and Georgia," St. Mary's was the first Catholic church established in the English colony. Its first pastor came from Ireland in 1788. Originally known as the Roman Catholic Church of Charleston, St. Mary's officially took its present name in 1837. The Greek Revival building on the site today was consecrated in 1839, replacing an earlier edifice lost in the city's great fire of 1838. Early communicants were mostly Irish immigrants and French refugees from the West Indies. In fact, church records were kept in French until 1822.

Gaslights and steeples that define the character of Charleston

Today, the crowded churchyard contains gravestones written in Latin, French, and English representing a congregation that spanned 17 nationalities, three continents, and two centuries. Inside, over the main altar, hangs a painting of the Crucifixion executed in 1814 by John S. Gogdell, a noted Charleston artist. The current organ is a Jardine (built in 1874 and restored in 1980) that is often featured in Piccolo Spoleto concerts held in May.

ST. MATTHEW'S LUTHERAN CHURCH (1872), 405 King St.; smlccharleston.org. The huge influx of German immigrants to Charleston during the first half of the 19th century caused the city's second-oldest congregation of Lutherans to greatly expand their house of worship. The magnificently Gothic church, with its tall, German-made stained-glass windows, was finished in 1872 with a 297-foot spire that stands taller than any other in the state. It was designed by John H. Devereaux. In a spectacular 1965 church fire, the spire collapsed into the street below—the very point, in fact, piercing the sidewalk just to the left of the church's front door. That steeple point is still there (encased in concrete) and commemorated by a plaque honoring the congregation's courage and determination to restore the architectural treasure.

★ **ST. MICHAEL'S CHURCH (1752–1761),** 80 Meeting St.; stmichaels church.net. While St. Philip's can claim to be the oldest congregation in Charleston, St. Michael's lays claim to having the oldest church structure. There is some mystery as to whom the actual architect of St. Michael's might have been, but there's no question that this magnificent edifice is one of the great treasures of the city. The church has remained essentially unchanged over the centuries, with the exception of a sacristy added in 1883. However, the structure has undergone major repairs several times because of natural and manmade disasters. In the earthquake of 1886, the steeple tower sank 8 inches, and the church cracked in several places. St. Michael's was damaged by a tornado in 1935 and again in 1989 by Hurricane Hugo. During both the American Revolution and the Civil War, the spire was painted black to make it less visible as a target for enemy gunners. During his visit to Charleston in 1791, President George Washington worshiped at St. Michael's, where he sat in the Governor's Pew—so marked by a small plaque. In later years, the Marquis de Lafayette and Gen. Robert E. Lee sat in that same pew. Buried in St. Michael's churchyard are several distinguished members of the congregation, including Gen. Charles Cotesworth Pinckney, Revolutionary hero, signer of the Constitution, and Federalist presidential candidate; and John Rutledge, signer of the Constitution and member of the US Supreme Court.

⭐ **ST. PHILIP'S CHURCH (1835–1838)**, 146 Church St.; stphilipschurch sc.org. St. Philip's is the mother church of the Diocese of South Carolina, and for more than 300 years, this church has been a vital force in the life of Charleston. Today, there are more than 1,500 communicants. It is believed the name is derived from the Anglican parish in Barbados, the island from which many early Charleston planters came after immigration from England. The first St. Philip's was built in 1680–1681 on the site of what is now St. Michael's Church at Meeting and Broad Streets. A new edifice was authorized for what was considered to be the "new" gates of the city (the present site on Church Street) in 1710. This building was destroyed by fire in 1835. The present building was designed by Joseph Nyde, who was influenced by the neoclassical arches inside London's St. Martin's-in-the-Fields Church (1721) designed by James Gibbs. The history of Charleston is traceable just by reading the names of the memorial plaques around the walls of the sanctuary and in the churchyard outside. Buried here are Col. William Rhett, officer of the Crown; Edward Rutledge, signer of the Declaration of Independence; Charles Pinckney, signer of the US Constitution; and the Hon. John C. Calhoun, statesman and vice president of the US. Here, too, is the grave of DuBose Heyward, author of *Porgy* and collaborator with George Gershwin on the libretto for the folk opera *Porgy and Bess*.

St Philip's Church

UNITARIAN CHURCH IN CHARLESTON (1780, 1854), 8 Archdale St.; charlestonuu.org. The first building on this site was under construction when the American Revolution began. During the British occupation of the city, the church was used as quarters for the British militia, and its newly installed pews were destroyed. The church, of Georgian design, was finally repaired and in use by 1787. For the next 30 years, it formed one corporate body with the Meeting Street Independent Church (now Circular Church; see previous listing), but in 1839, this congregation was rechartered as the Unitarian Church. Charleston was experiencing a period of great prosperity in the 1850s, and the Unitarians hired the young architect (and church member) Francis D. Lee to remodel the building in the popular Gothic Revival style. He was commissioned to incorporate the old walls and tower into his new design. Lee was inspired by the Henry VII chapel at Westminster Abbey—especially the delicate and lacy fan tracery ceiling there. He duplicated that amazing ceiling in this church, and it is considered to be some of the finest Gothic Revival work extant in America.

MUSEUMS & OTHER SITES

AMERICAN MILITARY MUSEUM, 2070 Sam Rittenberg Blvd., Ste. 216B; (843) 577-7000; americanmilitarymuseum.org. Located inside Citadel Mall near Dillards is the American Military Museum, which will be of interest to dedicated reenactment buffs. Here you'll find hundreds of uniforms, patches, and insignia plus legions of military miniatures and toy soldiers. The museum's collection includes items from Iraq, Afghanistan, and Desert Storm, the Vietnam and Korean wars, World Wars I and II, the Spanish-American War, Indian wars, the Civil War, and the American Revolution. There is no admission charge, but donations are welcomed. Hours are noon to 6 p.m., Mon through Fri. Sat/Sun hours are from 1 to 5 p.m. or by appointment.

⭐ **THE BATTERY,** East Bay Street and Murray Boulevard. One can argue that Charleston's White Point Garden, which most people know as the Battery, shouldn't officially be called an "attraction," like a museum or a fort. On the other hand, it's a darn good bet that no first-time visitor to the city ever left here without making it a point to walk there or at least drive by. In a city where almost every other building or street holds some significance, few sites have afforded a better view of Charleston's 300-year history than the Battery. That seaside corner of land at the end of East Bay Street, where it turns and becomes Murray Boulevard, is now a pleasant park with statues and monuments, long-silent cannons, and spreading live oak trees. There's even a Victorian bandstand that looks like it could sport a uniformed Sousa band any Sunday afternoon. But the atmosphere on the Battery hasn't always been so serene. The Battery has been a prominent feature in Charleston since the earliest days of the English settlement. Then, it was known as Oyster Point because

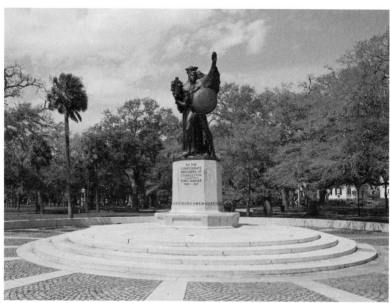

The Battery: Confederate Soldier Memorial White Point Gardens

it was little more than a marshy beach covered in oyster shells—bleached white in the Carolina sun. At first, it was mostly a navigational aid for the sailing vessels going into and out of the harbor. The peninsula was still unsettled, and the first colonial effort was farther upstream on the banks of the Ashley River at what is now called Charles Towne Landing (see earlier listing under Plantations & Gardens). Later, when the settlement was moved to the much more defensible peninsula site, the point was a popular fishing area—too low and too easily flooded to be much of anything else. Charts used during the years 1708 to 1711 show only a watch tower on the site and just a few residences built nearby. Remember, Charles Towne was still a walled city at that time, the southernmost wall being several blocks north, near what is now the Carolina Yacht Club on East Bay Street. The point was definitely a "suburban" location. The area took a decidedly higher public profile about a decade later, when the pirate Stede Bonnet (pronounced bo-NAY) and some 40 or 50 scalawags like him were hanged there from makeshift gallows. These executions were apparently quite effective in bringing an end to the pirate activity that had plagued the Carolina coast. The first of several real forts built on the site came along as early as 1737. This and subsequent fortifications were crudely built, however, and none lasted long against the tyranny of the sea. By the time of the American Revolution, White Point was virtually at the city's door and no longer considered a strategic site for defense. Hurricanes in 1800 and again in 1804 reduced whatever fortification remained there to rubble. Another fort, this version constructed for the War of 1812, apparently gave White Point a popular new name—the Battery. At least, the new name appears on maps beginning about 1833. The seawall constructed along East Battery (the "high" one) was built after a storm in 1885. Storms and repairs have traded blows at the seawall for many years—in 1893, 1911, 1959, and, of course, with Hugo in 1989. The area's use as a park dates back to 1837, when the city rearranged certain streets to establish White Point Garden. It was from this vantage point that Charlestonians watched the battle between Confederate fortifications across the river and the small band of Union troops holed up in Fort Sumter on April 12, 1861. This, of course, was the beginning of the Civil War. Once the war had started, this peaceful little garden was torn up and convulsed into two massive earthwork batteries—part of Charleston's inner line of defense. And while one of these battery sites housed a huge Blakely rifle (one of the two largest weapons in the Confederacy), neither battery ever fired a shot in anger. (Some incoming artillery rounds probably landed here during the extended bombardment of the city from late 1863 until Charleston fell in February 1865.) The end of the Civil War was the end of the Battery's role in Charleston's military defense, although several subsequent wars have left poignant souvenirs behind for remembrance. Today no fewer than 26 cannons and monuments dot the Battery's landscape, each of which is described on a nearby plaque or informational marker. Over the years, the Battery has become something of a balm for the Charlestonian soul. In 1977, Warren Ripley wrote a detailed booklet called "The Battery," which is still available through *The Post and Courier* offices. In it, Ripley sums up the reasons the Battery is so special: "It has watched the elaborate drill of colonial militia and the 'goose step' of Hitler's sailors on parade before WWII. It has suffered through 'reenactments' of historic events it witnessed in the first place, seen parades, air shows, and fireworks displays without number. It has observed three centuries of ocean traffic, watched the evolution from sailing ship to steam and nuclear propulsion as warships and cargo slipped in and out of port. It has echoed Sunday afternoon band concerts and heard the weekday cries of street vendors hawking wares to the neighborhood homes. It has harked to the whispers of countless lovers and warmed to the daylight shouts of happy, playing children." For Charlestonians, clearly the Battery is more than a pleasant little park. Far more, indeed.

Close-up

Charleston's Museum Mile: A Stroll through History

With the plethora of attractions that historic Charleston has to offer, many tourists wonder where to start. After a stop at the visitor center to collect the brochures of greatest interest, perhaps you are still without a plan. **Charleston's Museum Mile** is a way to begin your journey into history in a simplified and focused manner. The designated 1-mile section of Meeting Street (and nearby side streets) leads to 6 museums, 5 nationally important historic houses, 4 scenic parks, a Revolutionary War powder magazine, numerous historic houses of worship, and 6 historic public buildings—that's right, in only 1 short mile!

A natural beginning is the **Charleston Museum** across from the visitor center and its museum house nearby, the **Joseph Manigault House.** Other significant houses not to miss are the **Aiken-Rhett, Heyward-Washington, Nathaniel Russell,** and **Edmonston-Alston** houses. These are a special treat for those who appreciate fine architecture and the decorative arts. More architecturally significant edifices to take in are the **South Carolina Historical**

THE BELLS OF ST. MICHAEL'S, Meeting and Broad Streets. If your timing is lucky, a visit to the very heart of Charleston and its "Four Corners of Law" at the intersection of Broad and Meeting Streets (see the Close-up in the History chapter) will be delightfully punctuated by the resonant chime of mighty church bells ringing overhead. Indeed, the bells of St. Michael's Episcopal Church make more than just a pleasant sound. Their ringing is very much a part of Charleston—one of its oldest and most endearing attractions. In fact, their ringing is another of Charleston's object lessons in faithful perseverance, stubborn Southern survival, and the fleeting passage of time. St. Michael's Episcopal Church, built in 1761, is the oldest church edifice on the Peninsula and the second-oldest congregation in the city. (See previous listing in the Historic Churches section of this chapter.) This is the church where George Washington worshiped on his famous 1791 presidential tour that included a stay in Charleston (see Heyward-Washington House listing in

ATTRACTIONS

Society, City Hall, and the **Charleston County Courthouse.** (See our close-up on "Meet You at 'The Four Corners of Law'" in the History chapter.)

If military history is your hobby, **The Washington Light Infantry, Confederate Museum, Old Slave Mart Museum, Old Exchange and Provost Dungeon, Postal History Museum,** and the **Powder Magazine** are sure to delight. The artist in you will appreciate the collection at the **Gibbes Museum of Art,** and the little ones will enjoy a stop at the **Children's Museum of the Lowcountry.** And you'll soon understand why Charleston is called the "Holy City" as you pass by nearly a dozen historic churches, many of which are open to visitors.

If you need a brief respite from all this sightseeing **Wragg Square, Marion Square,** and **Washington Park** offer a lovely, shady setting to contemplate your next move. Most of the sites charge admission as noted in our individual descriptions within this chapter, but some do not. Of course, you pay only at the ones you visit, and you may start at any point along the **Museum Mile.** There are Museum Mile packages ranging from $27.50 to $35, children $15 to $19, and Museum Mile Weekend in late Sept offers 13 sites for $25 (participating site tickets purchased separately would cost over $100). DASH trolleys provide public transportation for free along the route. Or, you may stroll by foot at your own pace. Museum Mile flags are placed along the way to aid in your explorations. Visit the website charlestonsmuseummile.org for more details and take a walk through history.

the House Museums section of this chapter). The eight bronze bells hanging in St. Michael's spire were originally cast at the Whitechapel Foundry of London in 1764. Church records say the bells first sounded here in Charleston on September 21 of that same year, having safely made their first journey across the Atlantic Ocean. Amazingly, the bells have made that long journey back to England three times since. Their first journey "home" was in 1782 during the War of Independence. The bells had rung in defiance of the Crown during Charleston's protest of the Stamp Act in 1765, and British soldiers confiscated them as a punishing prize of war. Once back on English soil, however, the bells were purchased by a private speculator and promptly returned to Charleston and again placed in St. Michael's steeple. In 1862, during the Civil War, seven of the bells were removed from the steeple and taken to Columbia for what was hoped to be safekeeping. Charleston was such a likely target that many of the city's treasures were sent to Columbia at that time to escape the Union's wrath. Only the large tenor bell was left behind, to ring the alarm for Charlestonians still in the city. In 1865, the year Charleston fell, the bell rang dutifully until it cracked. Meanwhile, Gen. William T. Sherman's Union army selected upstate Columbia as an artillery target, and South Carolina's entire capital city burned in what was one of the most dramatic episodes of the war. In 1866, St. Michael's vestry arranged to have the seven charred bells from Columbia and the one cracked bell remaining in the church returned to England to be recast once more in their original molds at the Whitechapel Foundry. When they were returned in 1867, church records show that the melodies of "Home Again" and "Auld Lang Syne" rang from St. Michael's steeple. The last journey of the bells back to England and the Whitechapel Foundry—still in business after all these years—was in 1993. Their recasting, once more in the original molds, was part of St. Michael's $3.8 million restoration and repair project undertaken as a result of damages suffered in Hurricane Hugo. The bells of St. Michael's rang anew on July 4, 1993, in a special, daylong hand-ringing ceremony done in the English style. Nostalgic Charlestonians from all denominations made special trips past St. Michael's all day to hear the bells celebrate Independence Day and to acknowledge another homecoming for the bells of St. Michael's at the Four Corners of Law.

THE CHARLESTON MUSEUM, 360 Meeting St.; (843) 722-2996; charlestonmuseum.org; $$. Directly across Meeting Street from the Visitor Reception and Transportation Center is one of Charleston's finest jewels: the Charleston Museum. Because it is the first and oldest museum in America, having been founded in 1773, the museum's collection predates all modern thinking about what should be kept or discarded in preserving the artifacts of a culture. Instead, the Charleston Museum is heir to the collected memorabilia of real American patriots, early Charlestonian families, and early colonial thinkers, explorers, scientists, and planters. It is their opinion of what mattered then, and what they thought should matter to us today. Although the collection is housed in modern buildings and has the benefit of modern conservation methods and enlightened interpretation, the collection is uniquely eloquent. It speaks of a city that already knew it was great and sought early on to record itself for posterity. That difference alone makes the Charleston Museum a must-see. The museum's scope is the social and natural history of Charleston and the South Carolina coastal region. Objects from natural science, cultural history, historical archaeology, ornithology, and ethnology are presented to illustrate the importance each had in the history of this area. The Charleston Silver Exhibit contains internationally recognized work by local silversmiths in a beautifully mounted display. Pieces date from colonial times through the late-19th century. Visitors will see what the museum's many archaeological excavations have revealed about some of the city's best and worst times. Some artifacts date from the early colonial period, while others are from the Civil War years. Some exhibits focus on early Native Americans who lived in this region. Others trace changes in trade and commerce, the expansive rice and cotton plantation systems, and the important contributions made by African Americans. Children will be intrigued by the Kidstory exhibit with amazing things to touch, see, and do. They'll see toys from the past, games children played, the clothes they wore, furniture they used, and more. The photographs, ceramics, pewter, and tools reveal a very personal portrait of Charlestonians from the past. Because the Charlestonian lifestyle is so much a part of the city and its history, the two house museums owned and operated by the Charleston Museum are an important part of its offering. (See previous listings for Heyward-Washington House and Joseph Manigault House in the House Museums section of this chapter.) In these appropriate settings, you'll see some of the museum's remarkable collection of antique furniture and other decorative arts. The Charleston Museum is open Mon through Sat from 9 a.m. to 5 p.m. and 1 to 5 p.m. on Sun. See the Kids chapter for more on children's programs. Combination tickets, which include admission for the two house museums, are available for two sites or for all three.

THE CITADEL MUSEUM, 171 Moultrie St.; (843) 953-6846; library.citadel.edu/archives. This museum showcases The Citadel, the Military College of South Carolina. The museum covers the history of the school from 1842 to the present. Various displays represent the military, academic, social, and athletic aspects of cadet life. Chronological exhibits feature photographs, memorabilia including class rings from 1895 to the present, cadet uniforms, and arms. The museum is on campus, on the third floor of the Daniel Library—the first building on the right inside The Citadel's main gates. Look for the side entrance facing the front entrance guard station. Hours are

The Citadel Military College

Mon through Sun from noon to 5 p.m. and Mon through Thurs only in the summer months. The museum is closed for college, national, and religious holidays. There is no charge for admission.

★ **GIBBES MUSEUM OF ART,** 135 Meeting St.; (843) 722-2706; gibbesmuseum.org; $$. Established in 1905 by the Carolina Art Association, the Gibbes Museum of Art stands one block north of the Four Corners of Law. As locations go, that's fairly close to what Charlestonians traditionally believe to be heaven. And clearly, the Gibbes represents Charleston's most uplifting experiences in art. Museum members, residents of the city, and visitors all have access to a distinguished and growing collection along with year-round exhibitions, educational programs, and special events. The building itself stands as a memorial to James Shoolbred Gibbes, a wealthy Charlestonian who bequeathed funds to the city of Charleston and the Carolina Art Association to create a permanent home for the association's collection. Today that rich and fascinating collection includes American paintings, prints, and drawings from the 18th century to the present. There are landscapes, genre scenes, views of Charleston, and portraits of notable South Carolinians. Faces associated with history (and architectural landmarks all over the Lowcountry) seem to come to life here. You'll find Thomas Middleton painted by Benjamin West and Charles Izard Manigault painted by Thomas Sully. There's John C. Calhoun painted by Rembrandt Peale, plus an outstanding collection of more than 400 exquisite, handpainted miniature portraits of 18th- and 19th-century Charlestonians. The Gibbes also has an outstanding collection of early Japanese woodblock prints in a special Oriental gallery. In addition to the regular schedule of exhibitions on loan from international, national, and regional collections, the Gibbes presents major exhibitions in the visual arts during Spoleto Festival USA every May through June. Members and the public are invited to join museum tours, gallery talks, lectures, seminars, and meet-the-artist events, and to see films and videos made for schools and community groups. One of the most popular aspects of the Gibbes is the museum shop, which offers an excellent selection of art books, posters, note cards, jewelry, and other gift items. Museum members receive a 10 percent discount on all purchases. Admission to the shop, which is open during regular museum hours, is free. The Gibbes provides professional instruction in everything from painting and photography to textile silk screening and jewelry making. Classes and workshops are designed for all ages and levels of experience. Contact the Gibbes at (843) 722-2706, ext. 41 for additional information. Guided tours are available by appointment. Ask for the education department to make arrangements. Members are admitted free. Museum hours are Tues through Sat from 10 a.m. to 5 p.m. and 1 to 5 p.m. Sun. The museum is closed on Mon and national holidays. The Gibbes is fully wheelchair accessible. Please note: The museum is undergoing an extensive renovation beginning in the fall of 2014, so check the website or call the number above to locate their ongoing exhibitions, programs, and classes. (For more on the Gibbes, see the Kids chapter.)

CSS *H. L. HUNLEY,* Warren Lasch Conservation Center, 1250 Supply St., Bldg. 225, North Charleston; (877) 448-6539, (843) 743-4865, ext. 10; hunley.org; $$$. In 1864, the CSS *H. L. Hunley* was the first submarine in history to successfully sink an enemy warship when it launched an attack against the Union ironclad *Housatonic* off the coast of Charleston. The *Hunley* and its eight-man crew never returned to home port, however, and its fate remained unknown until divers located the sub in 1995. It was discovered partially buried in mud not far from the scene of its 1864 triumph. In August 2000, the *Hunley* made national headlines as it was carefully raised from its watery grave and brought back to Charleston for several years of painstaking conservation and analysis. It rests, for now, at the high-tech Warren Lasch Conservation Center on the former Charleston Navy Base, where scientists are slowly unlocking the mysteries of its disappearance, including how and when the crew died. Tours are available every Sat from 10 a.m. to 5 p.m. and Sun from noon to 5 p.m. Advance reservations are required to view the sub in its tank and see the fascinating exhibits of its contents and ingenious technology. Call or visit the website for available tour times, tickets, and directions.

JOHN RIVERS COMMUNICATIONS MUSEUM, College of Charleston, 58 George St.; (843) 953-5810; cofc.edu/~jrmuseum. The College of Charleston's John Rivers Communications Museum offers a unique opportunity to explore the world of broadcasting and communications. John M. Rivers was a Charleston-born banker, businessman, and broadcasting executive who introduced television to the Lowcountry in 1953. Visitors to the museum can hear early sound recordings from the Kenneth Hanson Collection, learn about the lives of famous inventors such as Marconi and Edison, and trace the advancements in science from the magic lantern to television, from the phonograph to radio. The museum is open Mon through Fri from noon to 4 p.m., except during College of Charleston holidays. Summer hours may vary, and group tours are conducted by appointment only, so call the museum for scheduling. Admission is free, but donations are appreciated.

KARPELES MANUSCRIPT LIBRARY MUSEUM, 68 Spring St.; (843) 853-4651; karpeles.com. This is one of 12 museums in the US funded by California businessman David Karpeles. They are all nonprofit endeavors to "preserve the original writings of the great authors, scientists, statesmen, sovereigns, philosophers, and leaders from all periods of world history," according to the museum's mission statement. Scholars, educators, students, and lovers of books and manuscripts are invited to enjoy these collections free of charge. This unusual but fascinating collection is housed in the former St. James United Methodist Church (1856), one of Charleston's best 19th-century replicas of a classical Roman temple. Special exhibits change from time to time, but the permanent collection includes some of the rare, original writings that helped build our country's unique form of government. Among the Karpeles manuscripts is one of the four original drafts of the Bill of Rights and the Emancipation Proclamation amendment to the Constitution. The museum is open Tues through Fri from 11 a.m. to 4 p.m. For more information on exhibits or special programs, contact the museum. Admission and parking are free.

MAGNOLIA CEMETERY, 70 Cunnington Ave.; (843) 722-8638; magnolia cemetery.net. One of the most telling places in all of Charleston has to be the remarkably distinctive 19th-century cemetery at the north end of the Peninsula, not far off East Bay Street (which becomes Morrison Drive). Not on any contemporary beaten path, and clearly not a tourist destination, Magnolia Cemetery is the quiet, final resting place of many important Charlestonians and other players in the city's long-running and colorful drama. It is also an intriguing collection of Southern funerary art in an almost unbearably romantic setting. The site was originally on the grounds of Magnolia Umbria Plantation, which dates back to 1790 and where rice was the principal crop in the first half of the 19th century. By 1850, however, a 181-acre section of that land on the edge of the marsh had been surveyed for a peaceful cemetery, dedicated on November 19, 1850. From that time on (even to the present), many of Charleston's most prominent families chose Magnolia as the place to bury and commemorate their loved ones. Many of the city's leaders, politicians, judges, and other pioneers in many fields of endeavor are interred beneath the ancient, spreading live oaks of Magnolia. Among them are five Confederate brigadier generals. There is a vast Confederate section, with more than 1,700 graves of the known and unknown. The 84 South Carolinians who fell at the Battle of Gettysburg are included and the *Hunley* crew was interred there after the raising of the submarine in 2000 (see previous listing). There are literally hundreds of ornate private family plots, many of which bear famous names. You will find the monument of Robert Barnwell Rhett, "Father of Secession," US senator, attorney general of South Carolina, and author. There's also the grave of George Alfred Trenholm, a wealthy cotton broker who served as treasurer of the Confederacy and organized many a blockade run for the cause. Trenholm is thought by many to be the man on whom *Gone with the Wind* author Margaret Mitchell's Rhett Butler was based. Among the famous artists and writers buried in Magnolia are Charleston's Alice Ravenel Huger Smith and John Bennett. Magnolia's gates are open daily from 8 a.m. to 5 p.m.

OLD EXCHANGE AND PROVOST DUNGEON, 122 East Bay St.; (843) 727-2165, (888) 763-0448; oldexchange.org; $$.

A public building has stood on this site at East Bay and Broad Streets since Charles Towne was moved from its original settlement to its present location in 1680. The early settlers built their court of guard here. They imprisoned pirates and Native Americans in the building's lower level and held their town meetings upstairs in the hall. The British built the present building to create an impressive presence in the bustling colonial port. With its striking Palladian architecture, the Exchange surely did just that. It was completed in 1771 and quickly became the social, political, and economic hub of the growing city. From its steps, the independent colony of South Carolina was publicly declared in March 1776. During the Revolution, the building was converted to a British prison, where signers of the Declaration of Independence were to be held. In 1788 the convention to ratify the US Constitution met in the building, and President George Washington was lavishly entertained here several times during his Southern tour. From 1815 to 1896, the building served both the Federal and Confederate governments as the Charleston post office. In 1913 Congress deeded the building to the Daughters of the American Revolution of South Carolina. During an excavation of the dungeon in 1965, part of the original seawall of Charles Towne was discovered. Today, the Old Exchange and Provost Dungeon is leased to the state of South Carolina and open to the public as a museum. The building has two halls that are available to rent for private events. Hours are 9 a.m. to 5 p.m. daily. Admission is free for kids younger than 7.

PATRIOTS POINT NAVAL AND MARITIME MUSEUM, 40 Patriots Point Rd., Mount Pleasant; (843) 884-2727, (866) 831-1720; patriotspoint .org; $$$.

Patriots Point is the name given to a huge maritime museum complex that consists mainly of three in-situ ships (permanently situated): a submarine, a destroyer, and an aircraft carrier with 25 vintage aircraft. There's also a replica of a Vietnam Support Base and a Cold War Submarine Memorial. As home of the Congressional Medal of Honor Society, it showcases their official Medal of Honor Museum. For this complex, one of Charleston's major attractions, you'll need comfortable shoes and plenty of time. Considering all there is to see, Patriots Point Naval and Maritime Museum is a real bargain. Admission is free for children younger than 6. There's a $3 discount for senior citizens and anyone with a military ID. Parking is $5. Plan on spending the better part of your day at Patriots Point; it's open from 9 a.m. to 6:30 p.m. except Christmas Day. Gift shop hours are from 9 a.m. to 5:30 p.m. Below is a detailed rundown of the ships on display.

USS *CLAMAGORE* (SUBMARINE). The World War II submarine *Clamagore* (SS-43) was commissioned on June 28, 1945, and operated in the Atlantic and Mediterranean throughout its entire career, patrolling tense Cuban waters during 1962. Twice modified, the *Clamagore* survived as one of the US Navy's last diesel-powered subs until it was decommissioned in 1975. The *Clamagore* tour route covers the control room, berth and mess areas, engine rooms, maneuvering room, and displays of submarine warfare. *Note:* Spaces are very cramped onboard. Visitors with health problems or claustrophobia are strongly cautioned.

USS *LAFFEY* (DESTROYER). The heroic destroyer *Laffey* (DD-724) was commissioned on February 8, 1944, and participated in the giant D-Day landings of Allied troops at Normandy four months later. Transferred to the Pacific, she was struck by five Japanese kamikaze suicide planes and hit by three bombs during one hour on April 16, 1945, off Okinawa. The *Laffey's* gallant crew not only kept the ship afloat but also managed to shoot down 11 planes during the attack. After World War II, the *Laffey* served during the Korean War and then in the Atlantic Fleet until she was decommissioned in 1975. A tour route on the *Laffey* lets you see the bridge, battle stations, living quarters, and various displays of destroyer activities.

USS *YORKTOWN* (AIRCRAFT CARRIER). No one comes or goes through Charleston via US 17 across the Cooper River Bridge without noticing the giant aircraft carrier moored off Mount Pleasant. It dominates—no, commands—a vast stretch of the Cooper's Mount Pleasant shore at the very gates into Charleston Harbor. She is none other than the USS *Yorktown* (CV-10), the famous "Fighting Lady" of World War II and the proud flagship of Patriots Point, the world's largest naval and maritime museum. Of the three vessels permanently anchored and open to the public, the *Yorktown* is the most impressive. Commissioned April 15, 1943, in the darkest days of the war, the ship fought valiantly in some of the worst engagements ever witnessed at sea, inflicting heavy losses against the Japanese at the Truk and Mariana Islands, and supporting the American ground troops in the Philippines, at bloody Iwo Jima, and Okinawa. Shortly after the ship was commissioned and sent into battle, 20th Century Fox put a film crew onboard to

The World War II era aircraft carrier USS Yorktown

record—on then-rare Technicolor film—the continuing war story of a typical Navy carrier in action. The spectacular footage shot at unnamed, secret locations during then-unnamed battles became the Academy Award–winning documentary film feature of 1944. The film was called *The Fighting Lady,* and it is shown daily at the *Yorktown*'s onboard theater at regularly scheduled intervals. Don't miss it. Nothing brings the World War II drama of the *Yorktown* to life like this amazing celluloid time capsule. The terrible explosions and blistering fires, the fierce fighting, and all the brave young faces who served on the *Yorktown* are there to be seen and appreciated by generations then unborn. But the *Yorktown* story doesn't end there. Not at all. The ship went on to patrol the western Pacific during the cold war and even fought in Vietnam. In fact, the *Yorktown* received the crew of *Apollo 8,* the first manned space flight around the moon, in 1968. The flight deck, hangar deck, and many of the *Yorktown* crew's living and working quarters are open to visitors today. You'll find actual carrier aircraft and Vietnam-era antisub planes on display—25 aircraft in all. And there are other fascinating exhibits on everything from mines to shipbuilding. Another exhibit is the true-to-scale Vietnam Naval Support Base, showing the living conditions and work areas of a typical support base during the Vietnam War. You'll also find the

Angel Oak:
A Lowcountry Treasure

Don't laugh, but we're about to suggest taking a drive to the countryside of Johns Island for the sole purpose of seeing . . . a tree.

That's right, a tree. It's an oak tree, but it's a very special one, a very old one, and a very famous one.

The tree is called **Angel Oak,** and everything about it is pure Lowcountry. No visitor has really seen the Charleston area without making the trip out to the island to be summarily awed and embraced by the Angel Oak's mighty outstretched arms.

Let's start with some background information.

Live oak trees (*Quercus virginiana*) are native to the Lowcountry and found throughout the area, but they are especially common on the Sea Islands. During the 18th and 19th centuries, lumber from the live oak forests was highly valued for shipbuilding. In fact, most of the area's ancient live oaks were harvested during those two centuries.

This live oak, however, survived. Angel Oak has been reported to be hundreds of years old, although the exact age is difficult to calculate. Very old live oaks are prone to heart rot (they become hollow at the center), which makes core sample ring-counting unreliable. This much is documented: Angel Oak is only 65 feet tall, yet its circumference is 25½ feet. The area of shade under this huge canopy is an incredible 17,000 square feet, and the longest

newly renovated and expanded Medal of Honor Museum, featuring displays representing the different eras of our military history in which the Medal of Honor was awarded. The new interactive displays include a tunnel of murals depicting battles with flashing lights and booming guns. You'll see actual Medals of Honor and some of the artifacts related to their original recipients. Mercifully, you'll find a snack bar onboard the *Yorktown* and another in the riverside gift shop, so excited youngsters and foot-weary veterans can stop for lunch and a rest.

outstretched limb reaches out 89 feet and has a circumference of more than 11 feet. Clearly, the Angel Oak is quite old. It knew the Lowcountry long before the English settlers arrived. It was already an old tree when the Kiawah tribe lived on this land and no doubt enjoyed its shade. It knows more than any of us ever will about hurricanes, wars, fires, earthquakes, and time. To see it is to gain worthwhile perspective on the entire Lowcountry environment.

The property where the Angel Oak stands was originally part of a land grant to Abraham Waight in 1717. Waight became a prosperous planter with several plantations in the Lowcountry, including one known as the Point, where the Angel Oak stands. The property passed through generations of the Waight family, acquiring the Angel name when Martha Waight married a Justis Angel in 1810. The Angel family plantation was sold in 1959 to the Mutual Land and Development Corp., but a small parcel of land and the old tree itself were held back and leased to the South Carolina Agricultural Society for $1 a year. The society cared for the tree until 1964, when it became the property of an S. E. Felkel, who eventually fenced in the tree and charged visitors a small fee to view it. The City of Charleston acquired the Angel Oak property in 1991, and it was opened to the public with no admission fee on September 23, 1991.

Generations of Charlestonians have journeyed to the property for picnics, family reunions, weddings, and private parties. Permits are required for large events and the consumption of alcoholic beverages at the site. You won't regret making the effort to visit the old Angel Oak. It's part and parcel of the Lowcountry experience. To get there, take US 17 to Main Road, looking for the signs to Kiawah and Seabrook. After Main Road crosses Maybank Highway to become Bohicket Road, look for Angel Oak Road on your right. Signs mark your route to this magnificent tree of life. For more information, call (843) 559-3496. Admission is still free.

POSTAL HISTORY MUSEUM, Meeting and Broad Streets. Unknown to most of the tourists who pass through the intersection of Meeting and Broad Streets (See "Meet You at 'The Four Corners of Law'" in the History chapter), there's a fine and fascinating little gem right there, deftly tucked into one of the corners. The Postal History Museum is a special room inside the Charleston post office showing visitors some of the interesting tidbits of postal history associated with this coastal colonial town. For instance, Charleston's first postmaster (on the job before 1694) was actually known as the city's "powder receiver." Not only was he responsible for the mail, he also collected a percentage of gunpowder from every ship that arrived (see subsequent listing for Powder Magazine). He was required to post incoming letters in a public room in his house for 30 days and collected his commission only when the letters were picked up by the recipient. Imagine being in London in 1700, addressing a letter to "John Doe, Charles Towne, Carolina," and it actually getting here. This little museum is a must for philatelists or anyone else who ever wondered how 18th- and 19th-century mail was handled. It is open during regular US post office hours, and admission is free. It's a great excuse to see Charleston's elaborately detailed 1896 post office building, the oldest continuously operating post office in the Carolinas.

POWDER MAGAZINE, 79 Cumberland St.; (843) 722-9350; powder mag.org; $. Only a couple of blocks from the bustling market area is, quite simply, the oldest public building in the Carolinas. And yet, as Charleston attractions go, the Powder Magazine is relatively unknown to tourists and to some locals as well. Perhaps the site is overlooked because it's dramatically upstaged by Charleston's sumptuous house museums and romantic streetscapes. And in truth, the utilitarian Powder Magazine actually predates Charleston's legendary aesthetics. It was built for a time when the still-new English settlement was predominantly interested in self-defense and basic survival. In the early years of the 18th century, Charles Towne was still threatened by Spanish forces, hostile Indians, rowdy packs of buccaneers, and an occasional French attack. It was still a walled city, fortified against surprise attack. In August 1702, a survey of the armament in Charles Towne reported "2,306 lbs. of gunpowder, 496 shot of all kind, 28 great guns, 47 Grenada guns, 360 cartridges, and 500 lbs. of pewter shot." In his formal request for additional cannons, the royal governor requested "a suitable store of shot and powder . . . [to] make Carolina impregnable." And so, in 1703, the Crown approved and funded such a building, which was completed in 1713 on what is now Cumberland Street. The Powder Magazine was the domain of the powder receiver, a newly appointed city official entitled to accept a gunpowder tax levied on all merchant ships entering Charleston Harbor during this period. The building served its originally intended purpose for many decades, but eventually, in an early colonial version of today's base closings, it was deemed unnecessary (or too small) and sold into private hands. This multi-gabled, tile-roofed, architectural oddity was almost forgotten by historians until the early 1900s. In 1901 it was purchased by The National Society of The Colonial Dames of America in The State of South Carolina. It was maintained and operated as a small museum until 1991, when water damage, roof deterioration, and time had finally taken too high a toll. In an agreement whereby the Historic Charleston Foundation did the needed work under a 99-year lease, the Powder Magazine underwent a $400,000 preservation effort, its first ever. This included a temporary roof over the entire structure, allowing the massive walls to dry out before necessary repairs could even begin. Much-needed archaeological and archival research was also done on the site. The Powder Magazine was reopened to the public in the summer of 1997 by the NSCDSC. Inside, a new, interactive exhibit interprets Charleston's first 50 years—a time when it was still a relatively crude colonial outpost of the British Empire. A nominal admission is charged. Hours are 10 a.m. to 4 p.m. Mon through Sat and 1 to 4 p.m. on Sun.

SOUTH CAROLINA AQUARIUM, 100 Aquarium Wharf, Calhoun at Concord Streets; (843) 577-3474, (800) 722-6455; scaquarium.org; $$$$. In May 2000, after years of planning, controversy, and nervous anticipation, Charleston's $69 million South Carolina Aquarium opened to rave reviews as a major new attraction in the Lowcountry. This nonprofit, self-supporting institution is dedicated to educating the public about and helping to conserve South Carolina's unique aquatic habitats. Its mission is to display and interpret the state's diverse range of habitats—from rushing mountain streams to the oceanic depths of the Atlantic. It was the first aquarium in the country to open with a complete Education Master Plan in place. Admission is free for South Carolina schoolchildren enrolled in the aquarium's academic programs. Extensive field studies and outreach programs are also in place. Among the 60 exhibits in the 93,000-square-foot building are more than 6,000 plants and animals, representing more than 500 species. The aquarium is home to otters, birds, turtles, fish, venomous snakes, other reptiles and amphibians, aquatic invertebrates, and insects. The exhibit path leads visitors through five major regions of the Southeast Appalachian Watershed as found in South Carolina—the Mountain Forest, the Piedmont, the Coastal Plain, the Coast, and the Ocean. The aquarium uses a variety of media to enhance the visitor experience. Some are interactive, some are for very young children, some are education "stations" for discovery labs and classrooms. Advance tickets are available by visiting the website or calling the numbers above. Hours vary according to time of year. The aquarium is closed on Thanksgiving and Christmas Day and closes at noon on Christmas Eve. Parking is available across Concord Street from the aquarium's entrance. (For more on the aquarium see the Kids chapter.)

Tours

Upon first impression, visitors to Charleston are usually taken with the city's architectural charm. Part of that fascination comes from the unspoken questions that leap to mind about Charleston's early good times. People want to know more about how a city of such wealth and architectural sophistication did, in fact, evolve.

The next impulse many visitors have is to seek out some kind of tour to find answers to some of those questions. Understandably, people want a visual, geographic, or ethnic overview, a point of reference, some kind of perspective. But most of all, they want to hear the stories about Charleston when everything old was shiny and new, political independence was still a dream, and the name of Charles Towne was world famous as the brightest jewel in the British colonial crown.

That's why the telling of Charleston's story has literally become an industry. In fact, it's so important that to become an officially licensed tour guide here, one must take a city-sponsored course (and pass very tough written and oral exams). Charlestonians, you see, care enormously that their story be told well. That's simply because the real truth is interesting enough to make mere half-truths, downright lies (told by unscrupulous tour guides), and corny amateurism wholly unnecessary. It's deceitful, unnecessary, and not at all Charlestonian.

Tours of the city are available in several forms. Most of the walking or riding (be that in a carriage, car, or van) tours depart from the Charleston Visitor Reception and Transportation Center on Meeting Street (simply referred to as the "visitor center" hereafter) or from the City Market area. You may also choose to meet a private guide at your inn or hotel and depart from there. Ask your hotel clerks or concierges to book your tour reservations—they have plenty of experience doing so.

We've listed categories of tours alphabetically, so we'll start with a little background information to help you explore Charleston's rich African-American heritage.

AFRICAN-AMERICAN HISTORY

As we've mentioned in several places in this book, no visit to Charleston would be complete without gaining a better understanding of and appreciation for the strong African influences on this society, past and present. The folkways, lifeways, culture, and achievements of African Americans have been infused into every fiber of the Charleston experience since the very beginning of the 1670 English settlement.

Among the first settlers in Charles Towne were black and white indentured servants and enslaved Africans. Within a decade, the English settlers had implemented the plantation system (already flourishing in Barbados) to sustain themselves here and create a product for economic exchange. Their labor force came from Africa—particularly the West Coast of Africa—from areas now known as Sierra Leone, Ghana, and Benin.

European and American traders plied the Atlantic waters off these areas, capturing Africans and imprisoning them until they could be boarded onto slave ships. Typically, each African was afforded a mere 4 square feet of living space while chained down in the hold. Under these grim and inhumane conditions, untold numbers of Africans died en route to the New World. From coastal Africa, the ships would sail to the West Indies, where some of the human "cargo" would be sold into slavery. The rest were brought to the South Carolina coast.

Awaiting the slave ships on Sullivan's Island off the coast from Charles Towne were crude structures called "pest houses" (see the Close-up in this chapter). Here, the unwilling passengers would be held for a period of at least 40 days to be checked for diseases and infections, during which they would be also

Baskets being woven from sweetgrass

groomed for sale. If maladies were suspected or discovered, the captives would be quarantined onboard their ships.

In just the five years between 1803 and 1808, an estimated 40,000 Africans were imported to America. The sheer volume of incoming slaves became a cause for concern among the relatively few white slaveholders, who feared an uprising. In 1808 the importing of additional slaves was banned. However, this ban did little to stem the flow, and slave trade continued as late as 1858.

Once sold, most of the Africans would toil in the fields. Their labor made the early plantation life of coastal South Carolina not only possible but highly profitable. Africans also brought with them vital knowledge of rice and indigo production, cattle tending, boatbuilding, and ironworking. Eventually, their foods, languages, religions, and music all mingled with the European traditions to create the Lowcountry culture called "Gullah" we celebrate today.

Not all Africans living in America were enslaved. From 1690 on, a few free people of color were living in Carolina. They were mostly multiracial and usually lived in the urban areas where they could find work in various trades. There were cobblers, carpenters, wheelwrights, brick masons, and smithies. Some became wealthy and owned slaves themselves.

With the Emancipation Proclamation and the end of the Civil War, all African Americans were technically free. However, the opportunistic postwar Reconstruction period and the advent of Jim Crow laws led to constitutional struggles over the 13th, 14th, and 15th Amendments. The much-longed-for freedom of African Americans in Charleston was shallow, indeed.

Many people of color left their rural homes and sought a better life in urban settings (sometimes moving to large Northern cities), where opportunities for work and education were better. Those who remained behind tended to live in small, rural, self-sustaining villages that were clustered around their beloved churches—mostly free of white control. Visitors to the Lowcountry today can see evidence of this social pattern in communities such as Snowden, in Mount Pleasant, and Maryville, west of the Ashley. During the civil rights movement of the 1960s, Charleston blacks gathered at sites like the old cigar factory at 701 East Bay St. and Moving Star Hall on Johns Island to organize and peacefully gain rights granted to all Americans by the US Constitution.

Because more than one-fourth of the African slaves shipped to the 13 original American colonies before the Revolution came through Charleston, this city's role in African-American history can hardly be overstated. In the years between 1700 and 1775, an estimated 200,000 slaves were put ashore on Sullivan's Island. One expert on slave history has even dubbed Sullivan's Island the "Ellis Island of black Americans" (in the symbolic, if not the literal, sense). Clearly, the Africans brought to South Carolina as slaves did not come as free-willed immigrants (like those arriving at Ellis Island). But Charleston was their point of entry, and, like Ellis Island, this location was the beginning of the American experience for countless African Americans. Yet, until very recently, this fact was little known by most contemporary Americans—even South Carolinians.

Realistically, this was not a popular subject for Charleston tour guides in the pre–civil rights era. History buffs felt awkward describing the tragedy of 18th- and 19th-century slave trade along with the city's upbeat tourist attractions. In the past, Charleston was criticized in the national media for taking a shortsighted view of its own black history. Today, that history is being explored and celebrated. The annual MOJA Arts Festival in Sept is Charleston's official celebration of its African and Caribbean culture. (See more about MOJA in the Festivals & Annual Events chapter.)

The African American National Heritage Museum is a multisite, cooperative educational effort undertaken by the Avery Research Center for African-American History and Culture, the City of Charleston, Historic Charleston Foundation, and the South Carolina African American Heritage Council. At four primary historic sites, these entities are working together to provide insight into the Greater Charleston African-American experience. At these sites, visitors can start to explore the origins of the culture and the role African Americans played in shaping Charleston, the South Carolina Lowcountry, and the nation. Historical exhibits, living history demonstrations, site interpretation, and cultural events are offered at the following venues.

i For a more extensive look at the hidden historical treasures of the Charleston area, check out one of the day-long excursions planned annually by the South Carolina Historical Society. Every year, the membership is invited to participate in a caravan tour deep into the Lowcountry hinterlands, touring private plantations and fascinating little-known sites. For membership details, you can write the society at 100 Meeting St., Charleston 29401 or visit schistory.org.

★ **AIKEN-RHETT HOUSE**, 48 Elizabeth St.; (843) 723-1159; historic charleston.org. It is rare, indeed, that a property of such prominence and historic importance as this would survive to this day in so authentic a state.

TOURS

But here is a house museum that affords the uncanny opportunity to view an "urban" household of great privilege as it was on the eve of the Civil War. The central section of the Aiken-Rhett House (see House Museums in the Attractions chapter) was built in 1818 in the federal style popular at that time. However, when William Aiken Jr. and his wife obtained the property in 1831, they did an extensive remodeling of the first floor in the robust Greek Revival style, which was all the rage at that time. When Mr. Aiken was elected governor of South Carolina, wings were added with a dining room and ballroom for formal entertaining, and even an art gallery eventually came along. But in effect, the decor of the house was arrested in 1857, shortly before the Civil War began. Because of the war's drastic impact on Governor Aiken and his family, the house and the outbuildings that supported it (including the on-site slave quarters) remained remarkably unchanged from that point on. In fact, the house came into the hands of the Charleston Museum in 1975 almost as a sealed time capsule of pre–Civil War taste and technology. Most notable are the servants' quarters to the rear of the house, which are in sharp contrast to the rest of the property—far more plain and utilitarian than the horse stables and even the privies. A portable prerecorded tape with appropriate sound effects is available for self-guided tours of the property, and docents are on hand to answer any questions you may have. The museum house is open from 10 a.m. to 5 p.m. Mon through Sat. Sun hours are from 2 to 5 p.m. The last tour starts at 4:15 p.m. Admission is $10; children 6 to 16, $5; free for those under 6.

AVERY RESEARCH CENTER FOR AFRICAN-AMERICAN HISTORY AND CULTURE, 125 Bull St., College of Charleston; (843) 953-7609; cofc .edu/avery. In Charleston, the rich culture of South Carolina's African Americans is recognized for its unique national significance. However, the materials that document this culture have been widely scattered over time and much has already been lost. The College of Charleston's Avery Research Center for African-American History and Culture was established to document, preserve, and make public the unique historical and cultural heritage of this significant group for this and future generations. In October 1990, the center was established at 125 Bull St. in Charleston's historic district. Here, at long last, a growing archival collection and on-site museum could share the purpose of gathering together these valuable materials and encouraging scholarship on the subject. The research center is on the site of the former Avery Normal Institute, the local normal school (for teachers-to-be) and college preparatory school, that served Charleston's black community for nearly 100 years. Avery Normal Institute was organized in October 1865 by black minister F. L. Cardozo of the American Missionary Association for (in his words) "the education of colored children." In 1868 the school moved into the Bull Street building just 5 blocks west of the College of Charleston. There, for nearly a century, the school produced teachers for the community and gifted leaders for South Carolina and the nation. Today, the center is actively soliciting manuscript collections: the personal and professional papers of individuals and organizations, oral and video histories, photographic records, and other related documents. Donors may be assured their gifts will receive the care needed to store and preserve them properly. The archival collections are regularly used for exhibits and educational programs for the public. These activities are planned in conjunction with local and national African-American celebrations and holidays. The Avery Research Center reading room is open to the public Mon through Fri 10 a.m. to 5 p.m. and Sat from noon to 5 p.m. Walk-in visitors can enjoy tours of the building and the museum galleries during these same hours. Group tours are available by appointment. For more information, call the number listed above. Written inquiries should be addressed to Avery Research Center for African-American History and Culture, 66 George St., Charleston, SC 29424.

i If you're going to be in Charleston during the spring or early fall, chances are you can find tickets to Charleston's two most famous house and garden tours of private properties. In the spring, the Historic Charleston Foundation sponsors its annual Festival of Houses and Gardens from mid-March through mid-April when the city's flowers are at their peak. During the month of October, the Preservation Society of Charleston sponsors its Fall Tours of Homes and Gardens after the long-anticipated cooler days have returned to the Lowcountry.

Battery Wagner, Morris Island

The first Union regiment of free black soldiers, the now-famous 54th Massachusetts Volunteer Infantry Regiment, fought on Morris Island during the Civil War. The bloody battle was an undeniable confirmation of the bravery, courage, and valor of the black soldiers and their willingness to fight for the North. Although the site is not yet memorialized formally, the island can be viewed briefly during Fort Sumter harbor tours, which leave from Patriots Point in Mount Pleasant or the tour boat facility at Liberty Square near the South Carolina Aquarium. What

Close-up

Gullah: A Language, an Ethic, a Lowcountry Folklore

Part of our country's growing trend toward ethnic self-awareness has been a renewed interest in Gullah, the colorful language and accompanying lifestyle that once flourished on the South Carolina Sea Islands from Georgetown to Daufuskie.

Researchers reported that as late as 1979, 100,000 South Carolinians spoke Gullah. Current estimates count 7,000 to 10,000 people speaking Gullah at home. Without intervention, the Gullah language will soon live only in scholarly textbooks and on fragile academic recordings.

The origins of Gullah date back to a sad chapter in America's past. When slave traders sailed to West Africa and stuffed their ships full of men, women, and children to be sold as slaves to Southern planters, Gullah was conceived. As that black culture meshed with the white, Gullah was born. A thick, lilting mix of African and English dialects, it started as a makeshift second language used among the Sea Island slaves, and it slowly evolved into the unwritten native tongue of their descendants.

you'll see are just small hills that were originally built as artillery fortifications, a few shanties, and truck farm areas. Call (800) 789-3678 or visit fortsumtertours .com for departure times. Fort Sumter Tours are generally from 9:30 a.m. to 5 p.m. Mon through Sun depending on the season. The fare is $18 for adults and teens, $16 for seniors, and $11 for children ages 6 to 11. No tours go out to the fort on Thanksgiving, Christmas, or New Year's Day. (See more on Battery Wagner in the Forts section of the Attractions chapter.)

⭐ BOONE HALL PLANTATION, 1235 Long Point Rd., Mount Pleasant; (843) 884-4371; boonehallplantation.com. Once one of the largest cotton plantations in the South, Boone Hall dates back to the 1680s. At one time Boone Hall was home to more than 1,000 slaves. Nine of the original slave houses still stand on the plantation's "Slave Street." These structures, now frequently used by filmmakers for their stark authenticity, are open to the public

TOURS

Oddly, slavery and the antebellum South fed energy to the language. Gullah served a very practical transitional purpose, and its use and culture actually developed during those years. After the Civil War, however, the separation between the black and white cultures became highly exaggerated for nearly a century and a half. Cut off from the cultural homogenization that occurred everywhere else in America, life along the Sea Islands changed very little. Sea Islanders still fished the coastline, shrimped the marsh, hunted for game in the woods, and spoke their native tongue unashamedly.

Gullah stubbornly survived in this splendid isolation, until the outside world rediscovered the islands and invested millions of dollars to develop them as resorts. Suddenly, bridges were built that introduced paved roads, indoor plumbing, better education, and access to higher paying mainland jobs. Gullah became thought of as "bad English." Soon it was something to be ashamed of or denied. Then television, the greatest homogenizing influence of all, came along and nearly snuffed the language out altogether.

Finding true Gullah today is like finding gold. It's rare, and it's kept hidden from "outsiders." Still, there are a few islanders determined to keep it alive. There still are those who knit their own fishing nets, who still cook the Gullah receipts (recipes) and serve their families whole meals fresh from the sea. Thankfully, there are still those who take what's left of the sweetgrass from the riverbanks and fashion baskets of great skill and beauty—just as their ancestors did back in Sierra Leone (see photo on page 181).

TOURS

on this still-working farm. Boone Hall is open Mon through Sat from 8:30 a.m. to 6:30 p.m. and Sun from noon to 5 p.m. mid Mar through Labor Day. After Labor Day until Jan 1, and mid Feb to mid Mar, hours are 9 a.m. to 5 p.m. Mon through Sat, Sun noon to 5 p.m. Jan 2 through mid Feb Boone Hall is closed for the winter. Admission is $20 for adults and teens and $10 for children ages 6 to 12. Seniors 65 and over pay $18. (See the Attractions chapter for more on Boone Hall Plantation.)

CABBAGE ROW (CATFISH ROW), 89–91 Church St. This downtown area was claimed as the inspirational setting for DuBose Heyward's 1925 book *Porgy* and for George and Ira Gershwin's beloved folk opera *Porgy and Bess,* which premiered in 1935. Cabbage Row, the scene of the story, took its name from the vegetables regularly sold from carts and windowsills by the area's black residents. Heyward named it "Catfish Row" in the book, so today a hanging sign designates it as such. Now, this section houses quaint little shops, but anyone familiar with the opera and its distinctive stage settings will readily see that this place and the alleys around and behind it could easily have been the story's original scene. Was the story based on truth? Was there ever a crippled vendor named Porgy who won, then lost, the love of a troubled woman named Bess? Many older Charlestonians recall a poor, crippled man who lived here in the early 1920s and used a small goat cart to get around. His name was Samuel Smalls. The other details of the story are hard to pin down, but Charleston certainly had enclaves of black families who struggled against very difficult circumstances, and their sagas of survival and social interdependence were not unlike Porgy's. Charleston obviously experiences the wrath of hurricanes, and in those days, terrible storms struck with little warning. And surely then, as now, the ugly specter of drugs and violence dramatically influenced the lives and loves of these people. We may never actually know if Heyward ever heard of Samuel Smalls, but the connections are intriguing, and the story is timeless. More avid music lovers and Porgy fans may want to visit Smalls's grave, which is well marked in the churchyard of James Island Presbyterian Church, about a 6-mile drive from the Charleston Peninsula on Folly Road. The grave was unmarked for many years, until an anonymous but concerned Charlestonian took the responsibility of funding a suitable marker for this legendary Charleston icon. To get to the church, take the James Island Connector (SR 30) over the Ashley River, and turn left on Folly Road. The church is at 1632 Fort Johnson Rd., the intersection of Folly and Fort Johnson Roads. Look for the marker to Porgy just outside the fenced churchyard.

THE CHARLESTON MUSEUM, 360 Meeting St.; (843) 722-2996; charlestonmuseum.org. America's first museum, founded in 1773, has exhibits and art depicting African-American life in the South Carolina Lowcountry. Additional photographs and valued information on African-American history and culture are housed in the museum's archives. Archival research is welcome; call the museum for an appointment. The Charleston Museum is open Mon through Sat from 9 a.m. to 5 p.m. Sun hours are from 1 to 5 p.m. Admission is $10 for adults and teens and $5 for children ages 3 to 12. The doors are closed on Easter, Thanksgiving, Christmas, and New Year's Day. (See the Charleston Museum entry in the Attractions chapter for more information.)

DRAYTON HALL, 3380 Ashley River Rd.; (843) 769-2600, (888) 349-0588; draytonhall.org. This colonial-era plantation house is shown to the public today as an architectural museum. It is considered to be the finest and earliest example of Palladian architecture in America. Built between 1738 and 1742, the

Drayton Hall

structure serves as a monument to 18th-century European and African-American artisans, who displayed highly sophisticated building skills at a remarkably early time. Now a property of the National Trust for Historic Preservation, Drayton Hall's research and education departments are in the vanguard of the nation's effort to document and acknowledge the contribution of African Americans to the colonial South. Special events and educational programs at Drayton Hall offer insight into this culture and its modern legacy. The "Connections: From Africa to America" programs are offered at 10:45, 12:45, and 2:45 p.m. Mon through Sat, and 12:45 and 2:45 p.m. on Sun. One of our most treasured exponents of African-American heritage is the Lowcountry gospel spiritual. For a little slice of heaven, attend one of the special holiday candlelight concerts performed by local African-American choirs at Drayton Hall during the Christmas season. See the Festivals & Annual Events chapter, or call the number listed for more information. Drayton Hall is open daily, except Thanksgiving, Christmas Eve, Christmas, and New Year's Day. Admission is $20 for adults, $10 for students ages 12 to 18, and $6 for children ages 6 to 11. Admission to the grounds only is $10. Admission is free to card-holding members of the National Trust for Historic Preservation. (See the Drayton Hall entry in the Attractions chapter.)

ELIZA'S HOUSE AT MIDDLETON PLACE, 4300 Ashley River Rd.; (843) 556-6020, (800) 782-3608; middletonplace.org. After the Civil War, a number of freed slaves chose to remain living and working on the huge rice plantation that was Middleton Place. They were most likely responsible for constructing in the 1870s the building that was later named "Eliza's House." It was named in memory of Eliza Leach, a South Carolina African American born in 1891 and the last person to live in the building. For 40 years or so, she worked at Middleton Place performing a variety of duties from working in the gardens to greeting visitors. She died in 1986 at age 94, and almost to the end of her life, she lived in the house in much the same way her predecessors did. The building has been restored and is now shown along with the other former plantation outbuildings that house demonstrations of weaving, spinning, blacksmithing, candle making, carpentry, and pottery making—all tasks of the plantation slaves. Eliza's House was originally built to house two families: Half of the building now depicts typical living quarters; "Beyond the Fields" is the permanent exhibit of rare images, artifacts, and documents about Middleton Place slaves. Eliza's House is open daily from 9 a.m. to 5 p.m. Middleton Place house tours are Mon through Sun from 10 a.m. to 4:30 p.m. Admission is $28 for adults to see the plantation gardens and stableyards (including Eliza's House), $15 for students, and $10 for youngsters ages 6 to 15. There is an additional $15 charge (for adults and children alike) for a guided tour of the plantation house and an additional $18 for a carriage tour around the property's woodlands and an abandoned rice field. (See more about Middleton Place in the Attractions chapter.)

MAGNOLIA PLANTATION, 3550 Ashley River Rd.; (843) 571-1266, (800) 367-3517; magnoliaplantation.com. The Magnolia Cabin Project has preserved 5 former slave dwellings that date back to 1850. "From Slavery to Freedom" is the 45-minute tour interpreting the importance of the role that the Gullah people and their culture played in Lowcountry history. The cabins were occupied from the 1850s to the 1990s, and each one depicts a different era from these times. Visitors may take a shuttle to the cabins where an interactive discussion of the tumultuous history of African Americans from slavery to segregation to civil rights is presented. Afterward, there is time to explore each of the cabins individually. The cost, in addition to paid garden admission, is $8. Children under 6 are free. Magnolia Plantation is open daily from 8 a.m. to 5:30 p.m. (Nov through Feb hours are 9 a.m. to 4 p.m.) For more on Magnolia Plantation see the Attractions and Kids chapters.

MCLEOD PLANTATION, 325 Country Club Dr., James Island; (843) 795-4386; ccprc.com. McLeod Plantation dates back to the late 17th century, when it was one of the first profitable farms to be established along the Ashley River system. Its fine collection of antebellum buildings is considered to be among the best preserved in the American South. In addition to the main house (ca. 1854), there are barns, stables, a gin house, kitchen, and a dairy plus a street of several slave cabins. According to a census taken in 1860, there were 74 slaves living in 26 dwellings on the plantation whose work was the cultivation of Sea Island cotton. McLeod was occupied by both Confederate and Union forces during the Civil War. The main house served as a field hospital, and it housed officers from the famous 54th and 55th Massachusetts Volunteers. It also became the main office for the Freedman's Bureau serving the James Island area during Reconstruction years. In 1993 the still privately owned McLeod Plantation was acquired by the Historic Charleston Foundation and held in trust while experts assessed how best to use this historic site. The foundation currently is working with the Charleston County Park and Recreation Commission to preserve and maintain this important historical site. Plans are in place to reopen McLeod again in late 2014.

Heritage Passport

For the connoisseur intending to become immersed in Charleston's history and culture, there's a way to save nearly 40 percent on regular admission to nine of the most popular attractions. Purchase a **Heritage Passport** (sold only at the visitor center at 375 Meeting St., Mount Pleasant Visitor Center at 99 Harry Hallman, Jr. Blvd., and the North Charleston Visitor Center at 4975-B Centre Point Dr.) and see the Gibbes Museum of Art, Charleston Museum, Heyward-Washington House, Joseph Manigault House, Nathaniel Russell House, Edmondston-Alston House, Aiken-Rhett House, Drayton Hall, and Middleton Place (gardens and stableyards only) at what is a very considerable savings. Ask for details at any of the visitor center information desks or visit charleston cvb.com.

OLD SLAVE MART MUSEUM, 6 Chalmers St.; (843) 958-6467; old slavemart.org. The one longtime local outlet for black cultural information in Charleston was the Old Slave Mart at 6 Chalmers St. At this site, reproduction slave-made wares and crafts were sold, and actual slave era artifacts were displayed. Unfortunately, the museum failed as a privately owned tourist attraction, and it closed in 1987. A year later, the City of Charleston bought the building and later reopened it as a museum depicting the slave trading that went on here between 1856 and 1863. Among the self-guided solemn visual materials is a firsthand audio account by former slave Elijah Green. He was born in 1843 and told his life's story in 1937 to a Works Progress Administration (WPA) writer working to preserve these memories for American history. The building encloses part of the rear yard of a now-gone tenement building known to have been used for slave auctions. First called "Ryan's Mart" (after city alderman and slave profiteer, Thomas Ryan) and later, the "Mart in Chalmer's Street," this was one of several sites in this neighborhood where African Americans were sold into slavery. It is South Carolina's only remaining slave auction house site. Museum hours are Mon through Sat from 9 a.m. to 5 p.m. Adult admission is $7; $5 for seniors 60+ and youth 6–17; free for children 5 and under. The museum is closed Thanksgiving, Christmas, and New Year's Day.

SNEE FARM (CHARLES PINCKNEY NATIONAL HISTORIC SITE), 1254 Longpoint Rd., Mount Pleasant; (843) 881-5516, (843) 883-3123; nps .gov/chpi. The interpretation of African-American history at Snee Farm centers on the influence of enslaved people of West African origin on the development of Charles Pinckney's colonial farm. This National Historic Site was established in 1988 to highlight the contributions of Pinckney, a famous statesman, politician, and signer of the US Constitution. The contribution of people of African descent is shown through exhibits, park handouts, archaeology displays, and a video program. These contributions were in the form of language, food, agricultural skills, and craftsmanship. The site has a small gift shop where various publications are sold that help illuminate the African-American story. Sometimes even a maker of sweetgrass baskets is on hand to demonstrate that distinctive local art form. Park hours are from 9 a.m. to 5 p.m. daily but closed Thanksgiving, Christmas, and New Year's Day. There is no admission charge for this site.

ETHNIC TOURS

GULLAH TOURS INC., 9 Trachelle Ln.; (843) 763-7551; gullahtours.com. This group offers Charleston folktales told in Gullah, the distinctive language spoken by Lowcountry blacks that's a separate and unique cross between English and various African dialects. Your guide is Alphonso Brown, licensed guide, lecturer, and author of *A Guide to Gullah Charleston*. The 2-hour bus tour will visit many of the important local African-American sites such as the Old Slave Mart, Denmark Vesey's house, and Catfish Row. All tours leave from the bus shed at the visitor center at 375 Meeting St. Weekday tours are at 11 a.m. and 1 p.m. Sat tours are at 11 a.m. and 1 and 3 p.m. No tours are given on Sun.

Tours are $18 per person. Reservations may be made online or by calling the number above.

SITES AND INSIGHTS TOURS, PO Box 21346, Charleston, SC 29413; (843) 762-0051, (843) 552-9995; sitesandinsightstours.com. Visit little-known black history sites, and gain a knowledge of Charleston's past from an African-American perspective. Hear stories of slavery, free blacks, the Denmark Vesey Slave Uprising, the Stono Rebellion, Catfish Row, and Charleston's colorful Sea Islands. These are 1-, 2-, and 2.5-hour motor tours that depart from the visitor center. Rates are $13 for adults of any age for the 1-hour tour and $10 for children. The 2-hour program is $18 for adults and $13 for children. A 2-hour island tour (of James, Johns, Angel Oak, and Civil War sites) is available upon request. Rates are $23 for adults, $18 for children. The 2.5-hour Plantation Tour is $40 per person with a 4-person minimum. Call or visit the website for schedules.

TOURIFIC TOURS AFRICAN AMERICAN HISTORY, 25 8th Ave.; (843) 813-8168. This company, owned by a native Charlestonian and civic leader, offers two privately guided tours of African-American history departing from the visitor center. Tour 1 lasts 1.5 hours and takes visitors on a stroll through the streets of Charleston to the boundaries of the original walled city. You'll see typical Charleston "single houses" and antebellum mansions, historic churches, the Dock Street Theatre, cobblestone streets, and the famous Four Corners of Law. Tour 2 is by car and takes visitors through the picturesque College of Charleston campus, where free people of color lived prior to the Civil War. Hear about the early contributions of African Americans to the city's history and see on-site examples of work by Charleston's famous wrought-iron worker Philip Simmons. Learn about slave uprising leader Denmark Vesey, and visit African-American churches. Reservations are required for these tours, and all require a minimum of 2 people to begin. The walking tour is $25 per person. The auto tour is $100 up to 2 people or $125 for 3.

OTHER GUIDED TOURS

Bus & Van Tours

Bus and van tours are very comfortable, if for no other reason than the fact that these tour vehicles are air-conditioned. In the summer months, that certainly counts for a lot. Most of these vehicles have small PA systems, so hearing the driver and tour guide is no problem. Be advised, however, that only certain streets are approved for larger tour vehicles, so you'll miss some of the tiny side streets and alleys that give Charleston so much of its charm. Here are some of the best of the motor tours offered:

ADVENTURE SIGHTSEEING, 1090 Ft. Sumter Dr.; (843) 762-0088, (800) 722-5394; touringcharleston.com. This company offers a variety of tours of the historic district. You may choose one of the bus or van tours with special features such as the Citadel Dress Parade (Friday only), a tour through the Old Exchange, or one of Charleston's house museums. There are also Plantation and Garden tours and a city bus tour with a boat ride to Fort Sumter. Adventure Sightseeing offers free pick-up service from the visitor center or a $2 round-trip fee from downtown hotels, the City Market, and the City Marina. Reservations are accepted 24 hours daily. Fares for 2-hour tours are $30 for adults and teens, $17 for children under 12. For Adventure's 90-minute city tour, adult fares are $23, $12 for children under 12. The plantation tours are $64 for adults and $30 for children; All Adventure tours include a complete history of the city; 2-hour tours include one house museum.

CHARLESTON TOURS INC., PO Box 31716, Charleston, SC 29417; (843) 571-0049; charleston-tours.com. These guides say they're "the Southern specialists for city or plantation tours." Tour A is a 90-minute city tour that includes the French Quarter and the Slave Market plus a stop at the Battery. The fare for adults and teens is $22. Tours D and E go out to the plantations and last about five hours. They include a visit to Magnolia Plantation and Gardens or Middleton Place. Fares are $52 (Magnolia) and $62 (Middleton). Tour C includes the city tour plus a stop at the Heyward-Washington House. Adults and teens go for $22. Tours G and H are billed as an "all-day adventure" that includes the city tour (you do lunch on your own) in the Market area, then continues on to Magnolia or Middleton Place. Fares are $63 (Magnolia) and $73 (Middleton). Ages 4 to 11 are half price for all tours and under 4 are free. Tours run Mon through Sat and depart from the visitor center, with free pick-up service from most downtown locations. Visit the website for more tour options and information.

CHARLESTON'S FINEST HISTORIC TOURS, PO Box 263, Ridgeville, SC 29472; (843) 577-3311; historictoursofcharleston.com. This company offers three daily scheduled tours—all in a luxury touring coach. Tour A begins daily at 10:30 a.m. and is a city-centered adventure, including seeing and hearing about noteworthy mansions and churches, Civil War forts, the Battery, and Slave Mart (allow 110 minutes). Adult fare is $21; youths ages 4 to 12, half

The Pest Houses on Sullivan's Island

Today there's just a bronze plaque, and even that plaque is a very recent addition to the history being interpreted for the public at Fort Moultrie on Sullivan's Island. But it is a beginning. The plaque commemorates a grim chapter in Charleston's history—the advent of the **"pest houses"** on Sullivan's Island during the city's booming slave trade in the 18th and 19th centuries.

In 1707 the local government was in fear of the diseases carried by slave ships arriving at the colony from West Africa. As a remedy for this, a law was passed requiring all slave ships to dock at Sullivan's Island and unload their human cargo for a period of quarantine—usually 10 days or so. The place for holding these unfortunate people was called a "pest house," in reference to the pestilence hopefully kept inside its primitive walls. After a period of time, during which the "cargo" was inspected for disease, the captives were moved across the harbor and sold at public auction into slavery. An estimated 40 percent of black Americans have ancestors who came through the pest houses of Sullivan's Island.

There are no surviving eyewitness accounts of what actually went on in these long-vanished structures, but in 1759 a Charleston physician, Dr. Alexander Garden (for whom the gardenia plant was named), left this description of the slave ships:

"I have often gone to visit those Vessels on their first Arrival," he writes. "But I have never yet been on board one that did not smell most offensive and noisome, what for Filth, putrid Air, putrid Dysenteries. . . . [I]t is a wonder any [people] escape with Life."

price. Tour E combines the city tour plus a visit to the Joseph Manigault House for $31. Tour B begins in the afternoon at 12:30 p.m. and lasts 4.5 hours. It includes an extended visit to Magnolia Plantation. Adult rates are $51; ages 4 to 12 half price. Tour C is an all-day combination tour for $61 for adults and $29.50 for children 4 to 12. Pick-up from downtown hotels is free.

GRAY LINE BUS TOURS, PO Box 219, Charleston, SC 29402; (843) 722-4444; graylineofcharleston.com. Gray Line offers three tours of Charleston in various configurations—all in minivans with air-conditioning and large windows. The Historic Charleston Tour 1 (allow 90 minutes) includes a stop at the Battery and points out dozens of historic sites. Adult rates are $21, children ages 4 to 11, $12. Tour 2 is called Historic Charleston and Historic Home (allow 2 hours). This tour includes a stop at the Battery and one of Charleston's house museums (which one will vary according to season and availability). Adults and teens are charged $29, children 4 to 11, $17. Tour 3 is a combination Bus and Boat Tour. This is a special pricing of Tour 1 along with a boat tour of Charleston Harbor or Fort Sumter. Adult and teen rates are $34, and children 4 to 11 pay $19 (not available in Jan and Feb). Tours depart the visitor center every 30 minutes between 9:30 a.m. and 3 p.m. (on the hour and half hour).

TALK OF THE TOWNE, 2166 St. James Dr.; (843) 795-8199; talkofthe towne.com. Enjoy panoramic views of the Battery, Rainbow Row, and all the major downtown landmarks from a minibus designed especially for touring Charleston. The 2-hour tours, leaving from the visitor center Mon through Sat, include a 35-minute guided tour of the Nathaniel Russell House or Edmondston-Alston House. Pickup from all major downtown hotels is available. The rate for adults and teens is $30; for children 12 and younger, it's $17. The 75-minute version, leaving from the visitor center at 9:15 and 11:45 a.m. and 2:45 p.m., is a nonstop, 7-mile ride through Charleston that includes the Battery, Rainbow Row, and the Four Corners of Law. Adult and teen fare is $21; for children ages 12 and younger, it's $13.

Rainbow Row

Walking Tours

Walking tours are great if you're up to the exercise. The pace is slow, the interpretation is personal, and the detail you'll see and hear is incredible. These tours—by definition—have the excitement and feel of a treasure hunt, and treasure is always found. Every one of these tours bears the stamp of your particular tour guide, and this seems to make the experience more intimate and fun. On the other hand, you cover a relatively small part of the historic Peninsula and see only a fraction of all there is to see. Here are some of our favorites:

Culinary Tours of Charleston

Believe it or not, there's even a tour of the Carolina Lowcountry's unique culinary history for those seeking insights and instruction on the secrets and traditions of Southern cooking. **Culinary Tours of Charleston** offers 2.5-hour walking tours with the inside scoop on many of the foods that have made Charleston famous. You meet chefs, bakers, food growers, and special artisans as you visit restaurants, markets, kitchens, and food shops throughout the city. The **Savor the Flavors of Charleston Tour** is offered Mon through Sat at 9:30 a.m. and 2 p.m. The **Chef's Kitchen Tour** is Fri only from 9:30 a.m. until noon. The cost for each is $42 per person and includes numerous tasting stops along the way. Reservations are required; call (843) 722-TOUR (8687), (800) 918-0701, or visit culinarytoursofcharleston.com.

ARCHITECTURAL WALKING TOURS, 1034 Tuten Rd., Round O, SC 29474; (843) 893-2327, (800) 931-7761; architecturalwalkingtoursof charleston.com. These are 2-hour tours of Charleston's remarkable architectural heritage. Your guide through 7 local public buildings is Fern Williams Tuten, a local art historian and licensed city guide. The tour of 18th-century buildings begins at 10 a.m.; the tour of 19th-century buildings is at 2 p.m. Both tours depart from the Meeting Street Inn, 173 Meeting St. (tours depart 10 minutes earlier from Doubletree Hotel). No tours are offered on Tues or Sun. The charge is $20 a person. Reservations are recommended. Special theme tours and group tours are available with advance notice. These include a house museum along with public buildings.

CHARLESTON STROLLS WALK WITH HISTORY, 40 North Market St.; (843) 722-8687; charlestonstrolls.com. This is the walking tour recommended by the *New York Times* and *Southern Living*. It operates daily all year long, leaving from outside the Palmetto Cafe in Charleston Place at 9:30 a.m., 9:40 a.m. from the Days Inn, and from the Mills House Hotel at 10 a.m. A personal guide brings to life Charleston's history from colonial days through the Civil War to the present. You'll stroll cobblestone streets, find hidden gardens, walk in famous footsteps, and much more. Rates are $20 for adults and teens, and $10 for children 7 to 12; under 7 are admitted free. Reservations are accepted, but not required.

> **i** Try spending an afternoon at one of the weekly docent-led tours given at the Gibbes Museum of Art at 2:30 p.m. on Fridays. Visitors get an in-depth view of an exhibit and often find they want to stick around and explore some more of the collection on their own. The tours are free with paid admission.

CHARLESTON'S ORIGINAL GHOST HUNT WALKING TOUR, (843) 813-5055; charlestonghosthunt.com. Here's another offering for those interested in chasing down Charleston's famous ghost stories. These "adventures" come in a number of guises these days, and this is one of the best. The tour departs from the sidewalk area in front of the US Custom House on the corner of South Market Street and East Bay at 7 and 9 p.m. (weather permitting). The tour is appropriate for adults and teens only (no children under 12), and the fare is $15. A late-night tour (at 10:45 p.m.) is offered on weekends. Reservations are required.

⭐ **CHARLESTON TEA PARTY WALKING TOUR,** (843) 722-1779; charlestonwalkingtour.wordpress.com. This 3-hour tour ends with a tea served in the private garden of your guide after a walk through the oldest section of the historic district. The tour includes colonial and 18th-century architecture, Civil War history with quotations from diaries, church history, Charleston gardens and interiors, plus insight into Charleston's preservation story. Tours begin at the King's Courtyard Inn, 198 King St., and cost $25. The 9:30 a.m. tour is offered daily except Sun. For a private 3-hour tour by van to private historic homes followed by lunch at your guide's own home, call (843) 577-5896. The fee for this special guest experience is $100 each. Reservations are required.

CIVIL WAR WALKING TOUR, 17 Archdale St.; (843) 270-2417; civilwarwalk .com. This walking tour departs from the Shops of Historic Charleston Foundation,

Gateway Walk

Looking for a way to see Charleston that's a little off the beaten path? **Gateway Walk** is a free self-guided walking tour many find unique, and it's right through the heart of the historic district.

In 1930 Mrs. Clelia Peronneau McGowan, president of the Garden Club of Charleston, came up with the idea for a walkway that would connect the city's churchyards, garden areas, and tucked-away courtyards. She was inspired by a trip to Paris, where she embraced the idea of meandering through serene gardens in the midst of a bustling cityscape. The plan was designed by noted Charleston landscape architect Loutrel Briggs and opened on April 10, 1930, to celebrate the 250th anniversary of the founding of Charleston on its peninsula site.

The walk is designated by unobtrusive plaques and foot-stone markers that lead through historic sites but depart from the sidewalk viewpoint and beckon you into the hidden core of the city blocks between Archdale Street and Philadelphia Alley. Your stroll covers 4 blocks, where you may amble through four churchyards full of fascinating old tombstones with a variety of blooming flora. It continues through the gardens of the Charleston Library Society and Gibbes Museum of Art, with its rose garden that features the Governor Aiken gates, a fountain, and sculpture. Winding your way through several centuries of Charleston history, you'll discover how Gateway Walk was named for the beautiful wrought-iron gates along the way.

An inscription on one of the plaques attributed to Mrs. McGowan reads:
"Through hand wrought gates,
alluring paths
Lead on to pleasant places,
Where ghosts of long forgotten things
Have left elusive traces."

The walk underwent its first restoration in 1953 with the continued support of Mr. Briggs. In 1992 the garden club initiated a 3-year restoration and spearheads its ongoing maintenance. The Gateway Walk is free and open 8:30 a.m. to 5 p.m. Mon through Fri. To get a map start at St. John's Church office at 5 Clifford St. usually open 9 a.m. to 2 p.m. Mon through Fri.

108 Meeting St., at 9:30 a.m. daily (except Jan and Feb). You'll hear the personal accounts and colorful anecdotes of the late Charlestonians who lived through it all. The tour includes comparisons of photos of Charleston from the 1860s with those of today. Reservations are appreciated. The adult rate is $20. Children under age 12 are free. Group rates are available, and the route is wheelchair accessible.

ED GRIMBALL WALKING TOURS, PO Box 458, Edisto Island, SC 29438; (843) 813-4447; edgrimballtours.com. Ed Grimball's walking tour of Charleston is a keeper for your memory book. He's a born-and-raised Charlestonian whose family settled on nearby Edisto Island. He knows and loves the city as only a native son can. As a registered tour guide, his entertaining insights and stories run the gamut from architecture and colonial history to the Civil War and the great earthquake of 1886. He's familiar with the stories of the heroes and statesmen, the scoundrels and bizarre characters who've helped make Charleston history what it is—endlessly fascinating. Tours last about 3 hours and depart from the Pineapple Fountain in downtown's Waterfront Park starting at 9:30 a.m., most Weds and Sats (closed Jan 1 to Feb 10 and Aug 1 to Sept 10). Call for more information or special tour arrangements. The charge is $22 for adults and $8 for children 7 to 12. Reservations are required. He goes rain or shine—even in the heat of summer.

GHOST WALK TOUR, (843) 720-TOUR (8687); ghostwalk.net. This 1.5-hour Ghost Walk tour is an eerie visit through 18th- and 19th-century historic district neighborhoods—this one with tales of ghosts, the plat-eye, voodoo, graveyards, and "Hags & Haints." Old stories and legends of paranormal experiences are interspersed with the fun and fascinating history of Charleston. These tours begin at 8 and 10 p.m. in front of 160 Church St. next to Tommy Condon's Restaurant. Adult fare is $16, children ages 4 to 12, $10; reservations are required.

THE ORIGINAL CHARLESTON WALKS, PO Box 1305, Charleston, SC 29401; (843) 408-0010; charlestonwalks.com. This company specializes in educational and group tours of 20 or more people—perfect for family reunions, small meetings, or groups of history buffs. Choose from the following seven options: the Charleston Walk, Pirates and Buccaneers, the Civil War, Patriots of Charleston, Ghost & Legends, Historic Homes, and Slavery & Freedom. One of these options is bound to please your crowd. Tours depart from Waterfront Park at the Pineapple Fountain and last for around 2 hours. They cover about a mile at a relaxed pace. Call for times, group pricing, and reservations.

The Pineapple Fountain landscape illuminated in Waterfront Park

THE STORY OF CHARLESTON, (843) 723-1670, (800) 854-1670; tour charleston.com. Reservations are required for this walking tour that claims to show visitors the Holy City "from a Charlestonian's point of view." In addition to architecture and history, this intimate, 90-minute-plus tour profiles some of the city's legendary personalities and recounts the impact of wars and disasters. Tours leave from in front of the circular fountain at Waterfront Park (at the foot of Vendue Range) at 10 a.m. and 5 p.m. Mon through Sat. Rates are $18 for adults and $12 for children 12 and younger. The same company, called Tour Charleston, offers the Ghosts of Charleston tour, which is based on the book *The Ghosts of Charleston* by Julian T. Buxton III. This 70- to 90-minute adventure is a big hit with those interested in the paranormal and departs from the fountain at Waterfront Park at 5, 7:30, and 9:30 p.m. daily. Another offering is the Ghosts of Charleston II, wherein you encounter specters on the edge of town. This tour begins at 7 and 9 p.m. leaving from the fountain at the corner of King and Calhoun Streets at Marion Square. Or if pirates intrigue you, *The Pirates of Charleston* tour can take you to the time when Blackbeard and other buccaneers terrorized the local waters. This tour is offered at 10 a.m. and 4 p.m. Mon through Sat from Waterfront Park. The same pricing applies.

TOMMY DEW'S WALKING HISTORY TOUR, (853) 853-8687; tommy dewswalkingtour.com. Tommy Dew is your host (and licensed guide) for this

Historic Market Hall was built in 1841.

historical tour that covers a timeline of events from the colonial period through the War between the States to Charleston's current renaissance. Daily tours begin at the steps of Market Hall, on Meeting Street between South Market and North Market Streets, and end along the waterfront at the Battery. They begin at 11 a.m. and last approximately 1 hour and 45 minutes. Reservations are required. Adult fare is $25; children (12 and under) pay $15.

TWO SISTERS TOURS, (843) 343-2981, (843) 270-9945; twosisters tours.com. Talk about your insiders' guides! Sisters Mary Helen Dantzler and Therese Smythe not only grew up South of Broad, but their Charleston roots go back to 1793. To say they know a thing or two about the Holy City is a given, and their lively and entertaining 2-hour tours leave you wishing for more. As licensed city guides they each lead you around 18 city blocks through Charleston's famous sites such as St. Michael's Church, Rainbow Row, and the antebellum homes along White Point Garden and the Battery. You may even venture off the beaten path a bit onto some hidden alleyways where anecdotal stories of colorful characters and events are sure to unfold. Group tours of up to 20 people are offered Mon through Sat at 10:30 a.m. and 2:30 p.m. and Sun at 2 p.m. The cost is $20 per person. Private tours may be arranged too. Reservations are required and may be made by calling either sister at the numbers above or visiting the website.

Carriage Tours

Carriage tours are an enduring Charleston tradition. There's nothing like seeing an 18th- and 19th-century city at an appropriately slow, leisurely, clip-clop pace. You'll ride through neighborhoods above and below Broad Street (ones that are approved for horse-drawn vehicle traffic) while your driver tells the Charleston story. The ambience is wonderful, but again, you're restricted to certain areas of the city for traffic management purposes, and you receive a somewhat limited view of the city's many charms. Here are the carriage tour options now available:

CAROLINA POLO & CARRIAGE COMPANY, 181 Church St.; (843) 577-6767; cpcc.com. All tour guides on these carriages are city licensed and trained by a company tour director who has been doing carriage tours since 1978. These tours depart from 16 Hayne St. and 181 Church St. (from the lobby of the Doubletree Hotel on the corner of North Market and Church Streets). Adult and teen rates are $22; children ages 4 to 11 pay $15. An advance online reservation offers a $3 discount per person. Private carriage tours are available upon request.

CLASSIC CARRIAGE TOURS INC., 10 Guignard St.; (843) 853-3747; classiccarriage.com. One of the South's best-known carriage works, Classic Carriage, specializes in the construction and restoration of 19th- and 20th-century carriages, wagons, and surreys. With Percheron draft horses and experienced, licensed tour guides as drivers, these 1-hour tours are popular with visitors and those planning special events in the Charleston area. These carriages are especially popular for traditional Charleston weddings. Reservations are strongly encouraged for the daily tours, which leave from the corner of Church and Market Streets in the City Market area from 9 a.m. to 5 p.m. daily. Adult and teen rates are $22; rates for children 5 to 11 are $14. If you book your tour in advance online, there are additional discounts.

OLD SOUTH CARRIAGE CO., 14 Anson St.; (843) 723-9712; oldsouth carriagetours.com. These are the carriage tours narrated by licensed guides wearing red sashes (Confederate uniforms, of sorts). The 60-minute tours depart from 14 Anson St., at the corner of North Market and Anson Streets, every 20 minutes beginning at 9 a.m. daily. Adult fares are $22, and fares for children ages 3 to 11 are $15. A combination ticket for the carriage tour plus a harbor tour is available Mar through Nov.

OLDE TOWNE CARRIAGE CO., 20 Anson St.; (843) 722-1315; olde townecarriage.com. These carriage tours by licensed guides leave the company barn at 20 Anson St. near the City Market starting at 9 a.m. Tours are given until dusk and run from 45 minutes to an hour. Fares for those older than 11 are $22, and fares for ages 4 to 11 are $12.

PALMETTO CARRIAGE TOURS, 8 Guignard St.; (843) 723-8145; carriage tour.com. Experienced guides narrate this 1-hour carriage tour that meanders through 25 blocks (2 miles) of antebellum neighborhoods at a clip-clop pace. Tours begin and end at the Big Red Barn at 8 Guignard St. Hours are 9 a.m. to dusk daily. Adult rates are $22, and children ages 4 to 11 are $14.

Cruise & Boat Tours

These tours offer the absolute joy of being on the breezy waters of Charleston Harbor and the wide Cooper River, both of which offer an entirely new perspective on Charleston. It's a perspective that was, after all, the one first seen by pirate scalawags and some of our country's founding fathers. This was the first view for those aboard heavily laden packet boats and cotton barges as well as those on the first ironclad warships and the crowded slave vessels out of Africa and the Caribbean. Maritime history is clearly one of Charleston's long suits, but we suggest you supplement a boat tour with another type of tour, so you don't miss the urban story. Here are some of our favorite water tours:

BARRIER ISLAND ECOTOURS, 50 41st Ave., Isle of Palms; (843) 886-5000; nature-tours.com. Here is a chance to become immersed in the ecology and natural history that make the Lowcountry a marine biologist's paradise. Young and old alike will enjoy these adventures on the barrier islands led by personable guides who skillfully teach visitors some of the most fascinating aspects about this environment. Tours depend on weather conditions and availability, but you can choose from the following adventures. Capers Island is an untouched barrier island close to Charleston with diverse wildlife to see and a breathtaking landscape to explore. The 3.5-hour tour goes Tues, Thurs, and Sat mornings year round, also Mon and Fri mornings Memorial to Labor Day. Fare is $38 for adults, $28 for children 3 to 12. The Blue Crabbing Expedition (also 3.5 hours) teaches guests how to catch, cook, clean, and consume this Lowcountry delicacy. Available only Memorial Day to Labor Day; the fare is $40

Charleston Harbor tour boat

for adults, $30 for children 3 to 12. The Dolphin Discovery Sunset Cruise (2.5 hours) is an abbreviated version of the Capers Island wildlife trip and includes a 1-hour walk on the island on Sun, Wed, and Fri evenings. Fare is $34 for adults, $24 for children 3 to 12. Call for information on the Creek Fishing Trip for adults and children and the Marine Biology Day Camp for children ages 5 to 12 during summer months. Reservations are recommended. All tours depart from Isle of Palms Marina at the end of 41st Avenue, Isle of Palms.

CHARLESTON HARBOR TOURS, 10 Wharfside Dr., Charleston Maritime Center; (843) 722-1112, (888) 224-5037; charlestonharbortours.com. These folks say they've been giving water tours of Charleston Harbor since 1908. Their current tour boat, the *Carolina Belle,* is 80 feet long and carries 300 passengers in comfort. The Harbor of History tour includes 75 points of interest including a ride past Fort Sumter and lasts approximately 90 minutes. Tour hours are 11:30 a.m. and 1:30 and 3:30 p.m. Adult fare is $21; seniors 65+, $19.50; children ages 4 to 11, $15. Tickets are sold at the boat, at the visitor center, or on the website.

SCHOONER *PRIDE,* 360 Concord St., Aquarium Wharf; (843) 722-1112, (800) 344-4483 (Zerve Ticketing); schoonerpride.com. Ah, here's a fantasy that is delightfully achievable. See Charleston from the water—as countless settlers and 19th-century immigrants saw it—from the decks of a tall ship, the Schooner *Pride*. She's 84 feet long and US Coast Guard–certified to carry 49 day passengers or 20 overnight guests. The 2-hour cruise of Charleston Harbor costs $36 for adults and children 12 and older and $28 for children under 12. Sunset sails are $46 for adults, and $33 for children under 12. Experienced sailors and quick learners may help with the ship, or you can simply sit back and enjoy the wind, sea, and unexpected pleasure of almost soundless propulsion. Call or visit the website for afternoon or evening schedules and reservations. Schooner *Pride* is moored at the Aquarium Wharf on Concord Street. All tours depart from there. Tours are offered spring, summer, and fall.

SPIRITLINE CRUISES, 360 Concord St., Ste. 201; (843) 722-2628, (800) 789-3678; spiritlinecruises.com. This is the only boat tour from Charleston that actually stops at the Fort Sumter National Monument, where the Civil War began. Tours leave daily from two locations: the National Park Service Visitor Education Center dock at Liberty Square beside the South Carolina Aquarium and Patriots Point, 40 Patriots Point Rd. in Mount Pleasant. Tour hours vary seasonally, so call for details. Adult rates are $18; seniors are $16; rates for children ages 4 to 11, $11. SpiritLine also has a nonstop Harbor Tour that departs from Liberty Square at Aquarium Wharf and from Patriots Point (Mar through Nov only). The tour lasts approximately 1.5 hours and cruises past the Battery, Patriots Point Maritime Museum, Castle Pinckney, Fort Sumter, and Fort Johnson. Adults $18; seniors 62+ are $16; rates for children (age 4 to 11), $11. The dinner cruise is aboard the *Spirit of Carolina* and departs from Patriots Point at 7 p.m. and returns at 9:30 p.m. (boarding begins at 6:30 p.m.). A sumptuous 3-course meal is served—prepared to order—with tableside service, spirits, live entertainment, and dancing. Prepaid reservations are required and are made by calling (843) 881-7337. The weekday fare is $53.53 per person; the weekend rate is $59.53, including taxes but not gratuity. Parking at Patriots Point costs $5 (cash only).

The Arts

Some people would tell you the verdict on Charleston and the arts is still out—that after an early, spectacular (even historic) colonial era start, the city fell asleep artistically and has stayed that way since . . . well, the Civil War. Others would have you believe this city, today, is a virtual mecca for experimental and traditional artists of all kinds, if only during Spoleto Festival USA. The truth probably lies somewhere in between. While there have been dormant stretches, there have also been times, such as the 1920s and early '30s, when Charleston experienced artistic stirrings that resulted in truly exciting art.

In literature, there was Charleston's own DuBose Heyward (1885–1940), whose legendary 1925 novel, *Porgy,* inspired a renaissance of artistic effort in and about the city and its people. The story, for those who may not be familiar with it, is based on the life of a poor, crippled black street vendor and his tragic love for an abused, drug-addicted woman. The novelist's playwright wife, Dorothy, cowrote the successful stage play that opened on Broadway in 1927.

In 1926 none other than George Gershwin—already famous for "Rhapsody in Blue" and bound for immortality as the composer of dozens of American musical standards—was fascinated by the story. He felt *Porgy* was just the vehicle he was looking for to create a new art form: the American folk opera.

Although it took several years to finally put it on the boards, the world-famous work known as *Porgy and Bess* was at last produced by New York's Theatre Guild in 1935. While it was never a staggering financial success (not many things were in 1935), the work was universally and artistically acclaimed. Since then, the opera has played all over the world, including in Milan's

Ornamental ironwork

prestigious La Scala. But no audience could love it more than an audience in Charleston.

But what about today? And what is all this Spoleto hoopla about? Following is an introduction to the big event. Unless otherwise noted, all addresses are in Charleston.

ORGANIZATIONS & VENUES

CITY OF CHARLESTON OFFICE OF CULTURAL AFFAIRS, 180 Meeting St., Ste. 200; (843) 724-7305; charlestonarts.org. The city of Charleston devotes this office to advocating, providing services for, and helping fund the various arts organizations that contribute to promoting the city. They provide assistance and grants to arts groups and maintain a full year-round calendar of arts events. The Office of Cultural Affairs also maintains the revolving exhibits of the City Gallery at the Waterfront Park. It produces the Charleston Farmers' Market, MOJA Arts Festival each fall, Parade of Boats and Happy New Year Charleston during the holidays, and Piccolo Spoleto in the spring.

NORTH CHARLESTON COLISEUM, 5001 Coliseum Dr., North Charleston; (843) 529-5000; coliseumpac.com. This beautiful venue has already helped put the Lowcountry on the map for many nationally known performing arts groups. Opened in 1993, the North Charleston Coliseum is the largest and most diverse indoor entertainment facility in South Carolina. Various seating configurations are possible, but, generally speaking, the Coliseum's capacity is 14,000 seats. Because of this, Greater Charleston is now a viable audience for some of the biggest traveling shows and sports attractions in America. The Coliseum has attracted the likes of Rod Stewart, Neil Diamond, the Ringling Brothers and Barnum and Bailey Circus, James Taylor, Metallica, World Cup figure skating, NHL hockey, and NCAA basketball, to name just a few. The Coliseum is also the permanent home of the South Carolina Stingrays hockey club. Tickets for all Coliseum events may be purchased at the Coliseum box office at (843) 529-5000, ext. 5113.

NORTH CHARLESTON CULTURAL ARTS PROGRAM, North Charleston City Hall, 2nd Fl., 2500 City Hall Ln., North Charleston (PO Box 190016, North Charleston, SC 29419-9016); (843) 740-5854; northcharleston.org. The Cultural Arts Program for North Charleston was created in 1979 to plan for and support artistic and cultural activities throughout the community. It provides programs and services intended to enhance the quality of life for citizens and assists in the cultural and economic development of the area. The program's offerings include the North Charleston City Gallery in the Charleston Area Convention Center Complex at 5001 Coliseum Dr. Gallery hours are daily from 9 a.m. to 5 p.m. The Dinner Theatre series in the Embassy Ballroom at the Convention Center Complex is another popular feature. By far the largest project undertaken through the program is the annual North Charleston Arts Festival, held every May. Most events and parking are free (some tickets cost up to $20) at this 9-day extravaganza mounted in the North Charleston Coliseum. The festival is a kaleidoscope of color and images with original artwork, photography, arts, and crafts plus live entertainment and food concessions.

THEATER

★ **DOCK STREET THEATRE,** 135 Church St.; (843) 720-3968, (843) 965-4032 (box office); charlestonstage.com. Much ado is made about Charleston's many firsts, not the least of which is the story about the Dock Street Theatre being the first and oldest theater in America. Let's split hairs here just for accuracy's sake. It has been academically determined that the first theater in America was erected in Williamsburg, Virginia, in the second decade of the 18th century. The second was built in New York in 1732. The third was in Charles Towne in 1736, while poor old Philadelphia didn't have a playhouse until 1749. In the early 18th century, certain buildings were called theaters, though they were no more than "long rooms"—rooms big enough to hold an audience. These places lacked a traditional stage and other theatrical facilities. The 1734 production of *The Orphan,* for instance, was actually performed in a courtroom—just such a place. Charleston's first (technical) theater was on the site of the old Planters Hotel on Church Street, which was then the only major route running the entire length of the city. It ended at White Point, which is now known as the Battery. (See more on the Battery in the Attractions chapter.) In 1736, the first building was constructed on the south side of Queen (then called Dock) Street, just a little west of heavily traveled Church Street. Records show it was less than 100 yards from the Huguenot church and St. Philip's Episcopal Church. It was said to have had a stage, pit boxes, and a gallery. Some ill fate likely soon befell this building, because no mention of it is found after 1737. Eventually, a second theater was constructed nearby, and an early hotel was built on the rear portion of the old theater lot. The year was 1800. It was called the Planters Hotel because it was popular lodging for Lowcountry planters and their families, who would traditionally leave their plantations to be in town for the winter social season and for Race Week, an exponent of Charleston's torrid 19th-century love affair with horse racing. In 1835, the Planters Hotel was remodeled and expanded. The old Planters Hotel is the structure that was still standing but in ruins when, in the 1930s, the New Deal's Works Progress Administration rebuilt it as the theater we know today. Technically, it is the oldest building still standing that was part of a colonial theatrical enterprise. On November 26, 1937, Charleston's own DuBose Heyward, already famous for *Porgy*, would write a special dedication to reopen a new facility. The reconstructed theater was called the Dock Street in honor of those early Charleston productions on the site. The reconstruction of the Dock Street auditorium recaptures the spirit of early Georgian theaters. It seats 463 people, with a pit and a parquet of 13 boxes. The walls are paneled with natural local black cypress, rubbed soft and mellow. The lighting fixtures carry out the feeling of candle brackets, and the cove ceiling has exceptional acoustic properties, as did many theaters of the time. Over the stage hangs a carved wood bas-relief of the Royal Arms of England (obligatory in all Georgian theaters), duplicated from an original that still hangs above the altar in Goose Creek's chapel of ease, built in 1711. The Dock Street's stage has a proscenium opening of 34 feet (somewhat larger than the original would have had) and features an apron forestage with "proscenium doors" on either side. This is typical of Georgian theaters. Today's Dock Street stage floor is flat, whereas the original was most likely tilted. The rebuilt Dock Street was never intended to be a museum piece or an exact reconstruction. It is, however, a modern theater capable of handling a wide variety of productions, and an integral part of Charleston's rich cultural life. After dutiful service for some 70 years, the venerable theater was due for a facelift. The Dock Street Theatre closed in 2007 for three years, reopening for the third time in 2010 after a $19 million renovation. This major renovation brought 21st-century state-of-the-art improvements to the theater to include new lighting and sound, seating, temperature control, and upfitting for seismic security and handicapped accessibility.

Acting Companies

Whether you're a confirmed theater patron, an experienced actor, or just a thespian wannabe, there's a Lowcountry theater company that will interest you. Some of these companies are long-standing members of the Greater Charleston arts community; others are embryonic or just getting off the ground. A new website for the League of Charleston Theatres, theatrecharleston.com, provides current information on most of the theater groups in the area or you may call (843) 813-8578 for more information.

The College of Charleston's multi-award-winning theater department is flourishing, with four groups currently taking bows. The work is first-rate, and these quality productions stand out as some of the best bargains in town. All college productions are mounted in various venues in the Simons Center for the Arts at 54 St. Philip St. and the Chapel Theatre at 172 Calhoun St. on campus. Thumbnail sketches of some of our local theater groups follow.

ART FORMS & THEATRE CONCEPTS, 930 Ashley Ave.; (843) 723-5399, (843) 724-7295 (box office); aftcinc.com. This exciting African-American theater group has more than a decade of successful productions behind it, including August Wilson's *Joe Turner's Come and Gone* and *Seven Guitars* and the Fats Waller musical *Ain't Misbehavin'.* The members are always busy preparing for their next MOJA production or Piccolo Spoleto performance. The director is actor, director, playwright Art Gilliard. Call for more details.

CENTER STAGE SIMONS CENTER FOR THE ARTS, 54 St. Philip St.; (843) 953-6306; cofc.edu/theatre. Center Stage is the College of Charleston student organization that, together with the school's Theater Department, produces a varied season from Oct through Apr in the Simons Center's flexible and highly creative "black box" Theatre 220. Productions are staged and directed by faculty and guest directors. Admission is free for College of Charleston students and $10 for the general public. For more information, call the number listed above.

CHARLESTON STAGE COMPANY, PO Box 356, Charleston, SC 29402; (843) 577-5967; charlestonstage.com. This group presents a full season of family-oriented plays and children's theater from July through Apr in the the historic Dock Street Theatre. It also offers various educational programs that explore stage management, scene study, projection, and creative dramatics for beginners and advanced students. Volunteers are encouraged to contact the theater to become involved. For ticket information, call (843) 577-7183.

FLOWERTOWN PLAYERS, 133 South Main St., Summerville; (843) 875-9251; flowertownplayers.org. This is a community theater in Summerville whose educational and literary objectives are to stimulate interest in the arts, music, literature, and drama in people of all ages. It has a regular season of productions and its own home facility, The James F. Dean Theatre, in downtown Summerville. Volunteers are welcome. Call the theater for more information.

THE FOOTLIGHT PLAYERS, 20 Queen St.; (843) 722-7521, (843) 722-4487 (box office); footlightplayers.net. This group enjoys strong support from Charleston's theater community for its long-standing record of exposing local audiences to interesting, instructive, and cultural plays that are in keeping with Charleston's traditional mores. Since the early 1940s, the Footlight Players have performed in a converted cotton warehouse (ca. 1840) on Queen Street, easily one of the city's most charming theatrical venues. Volunteers are welcome. Call for additional information.

MAIN STAGE, Simons Center for the Arts, 54 St. Philip St.; (843) 953-6306; cofc.edu/theatre. Main Stage is a series of several plays produced each semester that are exclusively directed and designed by faculty from the college's department of theater. Productions—often of classical or traditional works such as Shakespeare's *Macbeth* and Ibsen's *Ghosts*—are at the College of Charleston's Emmett Robinson or Chapel Theatre. For production information, call (843) 953-6306.

PURE THEATRE, 477 King St.; (843) 723-4444, (866) 811-4111 (OvationTix); puretheatre.org. PURE Theatre has quickly garnered notice in Charleston's theater community for its commitment to quality and excellence in its productions. It is a small professional theater focused on producing new plays by contemporary playwrights as well as new interpretations of established works. PURE Theatre's mission is to create theater experiences that "enliven thought, ignite dialogue, and expand consciousness," and they have received audience and critical acclaim and awards for their efforts. Call the numbers above or visit the website for the upcoming performance schedule.

ROBERT IVEY BALLET PRODUCTIONS, 1910 Savannah Hwy.; (843) 556-1343; robertiveyballet.net. Although Robert Ivey Ballet is primarily a dance company with a full-time studio, this production operation offers popular musicals on a fairly regular basis. For theater productions, open auditions are held, usually in the fall. Their performance venue is the Sottile Threatre at 44 George St., just off King.

SHAKESPEARE PROJECT AT THE COLLEGE OF CHARLESTON, College of Charleston, Simons Center for the Arts, 172 Calhoun St.; (843) 953-5604; cofc.edu/theatre. This college-sponsored Shakespeare group backs performances by student and community-based actors. The plays are presented in Aug at the Chapel Theatre, and shortened versions are performed in local schools and other venues. There's general seating, with adult tickets costing $15, student seating, $10.

WOOLFE STREET PLAYHOUSE, 34 Woolfe St.; (843) 856-1579; woolfe streetplayhouse.com. In a very short time, The Village Repertory Co. has grown into a vital performing arts organization, offering more than 150 nights of theater each season at their Woolfe Street theater location. The company brings a diverse selection of drama, comedy, and musicals, both classics and new works, to area residents and visitors. Ticket prices range from $20 to $30 for these popular productions. Call or visit the website for more details on upcoming performances.

MUSIC

CHARLESTON COMMUNITY BAND, PO Box 30274, Charleston, SC 29417; (843) 849-6121; charlestoncommunityband.com. Started in 1977, this all-volunteer concert band of around 75 members performs 15 free concerts a year throughout the greater Charleston area. Some of their regular performances are Memorial Day, Carolina Day, July 4th, The Citadel graduation, and Christmas tree lighting in Marion Square and Towne Centre in Mount Pleasant. This group of brass, woodwind, and percussion players provides a wonderful opportunity for talented local adults to continue their musical pursuits after finishing high school. Call the number listed above to speak with conductor Todd Jenkins for more information.

> **i** Opera lovers take note: The Charleston County Public Library at 68 Calhoun St. sponsors high-definition simulcasts of the Metropolitan Opera season. Shown in the library's auditorium, the productions are held on Saturdays and are free. Visit ccpl.org for dates and times.

★ **CHARLESTON CONCERT ASSOCIATION,** 131 King St.; (843) 727-1216; charlestonconcerts.org. The Charleston Concert Association (CCA) is Charleston's oldest nonprofit presenting arts organization. Founded in 1936 as a sister organization with the Charleston Symphony Orchestra (CSO), CCA's original mission was to bring internationally acclaimed musicians to Charleston as a complement to CSO. Back in 1931, the symphony's aim was to create an avenue for local musicians to develop their skills. Today, the CCA's mission is to provide local access to classical artists of international caliber throughout the year (whereas Spoleto Festival USA is a more concentrated exposure of only 2 weeks). In recent years, the CCA has expanded its vision to include all of the performing arts, including theater and film as well as dance. Among the CCA's recent presentations were the highly acclaimed Opera Verdi Europa, Venice Baroque Orchestra, the Shanghai Ballet, the Warsaw Philharmonic, Vienna Boys Choir, and the Duke Ellington Orchestra. Tickets are sold by subscription to the series, and individual prices range from $60 to $100. Call the number above for subscription rates and concert season details.

CHARLESTON SYMPHONY ORCHESTRA, 756 St. Andrews Blvd.; (843) 723-7528; charlestonsymphony.com. Charleston has a long, rich, and varied musical history. Records indicate several different orchestras were organized in the city during the years from 1819 to 1919. Today's organization, known as the Charleston Symphony Orchestra, has been in existence for more than 75 years. In December 1936, Miss Maud Winthrup Gibbon and Mrs. Martha Laurens Patterson founded what is known today as the Charleston Symphony Orchestra, and they presented a concert in Hibernian Hall on Meeting Street. The orchestra provided music for the official grand opening of the newly restored Dock Street Theatre in 1936, and the Dock Street in turn became the orchestra's official home for its first 3 years. Through the 1940s and 1950s, Memminger Auditorium was home for the group, as it brought in such famous artists as Robert Merrill, Jan Peerce, Blanche Theirbom, and Eleanor Steber. The orchestra played under the batons of conductors J. Albert Frecht, Tony Hadgi, Don Mills, and, from 1962 to 1982, Lucien DeGroote. In the late 1970s, the orchestra emerged as a fully professional organization with the employment of a core of full-time, conservatory-trained, first-chair players. The orchestra achieved "metropolitan" status in the American Symphony Orchestra League and adopted Gaillard Auditorium as its official home. In 1984 David Stahl became music director and conductor. Under his leadership, the CSO emerged as one of the leading arts organizations in the Southeast. Beginning in 2013 different guest conductors from all over the world have conducted a performance to present themselves as music director candidates. A resident orchestra of about 35 professional musicians performs a demanding concert schedule on stage and throughout the community, including special events and school programs throughout the state from Sept through Apr. The orchestra has several major concert series—Masterworks, Charleston Pops, Dock Street Theatre Chamber Concerts, and Family Concerts. In addition, the CSO performs other special concerts that cover a broad range of musical tastes. Magnetic South is a cooperative series with the College of Charleston's

Music Department to present a series of 20th-century masterpieces and works by contemporary composers. Individual ticket sales are handled through the Sottile Theatre box office at 44 George St., or by calling (843) 723-7528, ext. 110, or going to the website. Ticket prices vary according to the series, but they range from $20 to $69 for individual concerts.

> **i** Although it's mostly known in the community as sponsor of the annual Symphony Gala and the Symphony Designer Showhouse, the 300-member Charleston Symphony Orchestra League serves its namesake group in many ways. (See the Festivals & Annual Events chapter for more on the Designer Showhouse.) Through fund-raising events, the league provides major financial support to the orchestra. It annually awards scholarships to orchestra musicians for advanced study and to school-age musicians who are members of the Youth Orchestra of the Low Country. Members volunteer many hours of service in the CSO office promoting the orchestra and aiding in the sale of season tickets, and they also serve as concert ushers. The league welcomes anyone wishing to join and support the CSO. Call (843) 723-7528 or vist the website csolinc.org.

CSO CHORUS, 164 Market St., #161; (843) 723-7528; csochorus.com. First organized in 1978 as the Charleston Singers Guild, to be the choral complement of the Charleston Symphony Orchestra, this group is now called the CSO Chorus. The group performs with the CSO in major works several times a year. In addition to the large concert group of nearly 125 singers, there are two smaller performance groups that appear throughout the season. The Chamber Singers, under the direction of Robert Taylor, perform 20th-century music. Participation in CSO Chorus groups is by regularly scheduled audition. Visit the website for more details.

INTERNATIONAL PIANO SERIES, College of Charleston, 44 George St. (Sottile Theatre); (843) 953-6575; cofc.edu/music. Since 1989, the School of the Arts at the College of Charleston has had an annual International Piano

THE ARTS

Series that's also open to the general public. The series was designed to introduce students and the Charleston community to an array of fine, established performers from around the world. This is a major inspiration to music students on campus who have come from as far away as Spain, Korea, China, and Costa Rica to study in the college's piano performance program. All concerts are at 8 p.m. in the Sottile Theatre on George Street just off King, and admission is $20 at the door. Call the number above for a performance schedule and a calendar of School of the Arts events.

i The easiest ways to get the best tickets to major arts events in Charleston are to become a patron of that arts organization, participate in their annual fund-raising drive, or buy series tickets whenever possible.

MONDAY NIGHT CONCERT SERIES, College of Charleston, Simons Center for the Arts, 54 St. Philip St. (Recital Hall); (843) 953-8228; cofc .edu/music. This is one of those little gems that few people know about, and yet it's one of the best arts events going on in the city. These regularly scheduled Monday night concerts are usually presented in the Simons Center Recital Hall and feature faculty and adjunct faculty talent and advanced students from the music department. The programs vary from jazz to Renaissance music, from organ concerts to choral works from the College's Concert Choir (at the Cathedral of St. Luke and St. Paul, 126 Coming St.). The overall quality of the concerts is always quite wonderful, and the admission price of $10 (free for College of Charleston students) can't be beat. Call the School of the Arts for more information and specific concert schedules.

i Another College of Charleston musical treat is Charleston Music Fest presenting chamber music year-round. Both classical and contemporary chamber music is performed by world-class artists usually at the Simons Center Recital Hall on campus. Visit cofc.edu/ music for tickets or call (843) 953-6575.

THE ARTS

ANGLIN SMITH FINE ART, 9 Queen St.; (843) 853-0708; smithkillian .com. Treat your eyes to the bold colors and contemporary realism in Anglin Smith Fine Art. Lowcountry artist Betty Anglin Smith keeps it all in the family showcasing her work and that of her triplet children, painters Shannon Smith and Jennifer Smith Rogers and photographer Tripp Smith—all quite popular in their own right. Other works in oil are shown by Kim English and Colin Page. Expect to find subjects ranging from local to European landscapes to still life to architectural works. Bronze sculptures by Darrell Davis complete the list of dynamic offerings here. Gallery hours are Mon through Sat 10 a.m. to 5 p.m. and by appointment.

THE AUDUBON GALLERY, 190 King St.; (843) 853-1100; audubon art.com. This is one of Charleston's best galleries for the natural history and sporting art enthusiast! You'll find old and new limited-edition nature prints, Audubon prints, 19th-century city views, engravings, and antique plates. It also offers museum-quality framing and conservation services. Hours are 10 a.m. to 5 p.m. Mon through Sat.

i Don't miss the festive French Quarter Art Walks held on the first Fri in Mar, May, Oct, and Dec in the historic French Quarter area between South Market and Tradd Streets, Meeting Street and the waterfront. Stroll the gaslit alleyways and cobbled streets to stop in around 30 galleries representing more than 500 artists of all styles of work. A map is available on frenchquarterarts .com or at participating galleries.

THE ARTS

BIRDS I VIEW GALLERY, 119-A Church St.; (843) 723-1276, (843) 766-2108; anneworshamrichardson.com. Anne Worsham Richardson is a South Carolina artist and naturalist recognized across America for her wildlife paintings—especially her birds. Richardson has received many honors over the years, including induction into the South Carolina Hall of Fame at Myrtle Beach. Gallery hours are Mon through Sat from 10 a.m. to 5 p.m.

★ **CAROLINA ANTIQUE MAPS AND PRINTS, LLC,** 91 Church St.; (843) 722-4773; carolinaantiqueprints.com. This shop exclusively carries those handsome and fascinating antique maps, prints, and botanicals that make such a striking addition to an office, library, or study. Some of these maps originate from the 16th to the 19th century and depict various locations, both local and international. Of added interest is the shop's location—in Cabbage Row, which DuBose Heyward, along with George Gershwin, immortalized as "Catfish Row" in the folk opera *Porgy and Bess.* Hours are Tues through Sat, 11 a.m. to 5 p.m. or by special appointment.

★ **CAROLINA GALLERIES,** carolinagalleries.com. This gallery specializes in pre-1945 American art (including a fine selection from Charleston's own renaissance period) and what's called sporting art. Carolina Galleries has been putting artists and collectors together since 1963. You'll find a wonderful selection of works by Alfred Hutty, Alice Ravenel Huger Smith, Anna Heyward Taylor, and Elizabeth O'Neill Verner, plus antique prints, original paintings, and sculpture. The gallery carries Audubon prints and architectural drawings too. The staff is qualified to act as framing consultants. No longer located at a physical address, they can be visited "in the cloud" at the web address.

★ **CHARLESTON ARTIST GUILD GALLERY,** 160 East Bay St.; (843) 722-2425; charlestonartistguild.com. With over 70 artists' work on display, the Charleston Artist Guild Gallery has something to appeal to all artistic tastes, from traditional to contemporary. The ever-changing work on display includes original paintings in oil, pastel, and watercolor; photography; and fiber art. The Charleston Artist Guild was founded in 1953 and is dedicated to serving the arts community of Charleston. They conduct workshops for the practicing artist, offer lectures for the burgeoning collector, and provide other opportunities for arts education. The guild holds an annual Signature Show and annual Holiday Show which are juried exhibitions open to artists across the state. They also work with the City of Charleston Office of Cultural Affairs in sponsoring the Piccolo Spoleto Juried Exhibition, a display of over 100 pieces of artwork seen by thousands of residents and visitors during the Spoleto Festival. (See Festivals & Annual Events for more on the Piccolo and Spoleto Festivals.) Their Spring and Fall Sidewalk Art Shows are the longest-running art events of their kind in Charleston. Prices for original art are really good here, and even better—a portion of the proceeds goes to their community outreach programs and funding for art scholarships for talented high school students.

Philip Simmons & the Wrought-Iron Connection

The lacy wrought-iron gates, grills, and balconies seen throughout Charleston punctuate the city's eloquent architectural statement. Many of them are original 18th-century works still in situ—proud survivors of a nearly lost art. But Charleston's wrought-iron artwork, thanks to a man named Philip Simmons, is still being practiced and (perhaps more important) being taught to young artisans. Born in 1912 in the city's Mazyck-Wraggborough neighborhood, the young Philip Simmons learned the ironworking trade from his father, who learned it from his father, and so on, back through time. Indeed, Philip Simmons is an example of Charleston's rich heritage in the arts passed on through the African-American community since the days of slavery. His works have long been recognized for their fine sense of scale, balance, and craftsmanship. Simmons was a recipient of the American Folklife Award, the highest honor bestowed on folk artists in America. He is in South Carolina's Hall of Fame, and his work has been exhibited in major museums and galleries throughout the US. Today, more than 300 documented works by Philip Simmons—gates, fences, railings, and window guards—are scattered throughout Charleston. They meld handsomely with the surviving antique works and add a meaningful continuum to the city's architectural and aesthetic history.

Eighteenth century entrance gate featuring intricate ironwork in Old Town Charleston

CHARLESTON CRAFTS INC., 161 Church St.; (843) 723-2938; charleston crafts.org. This gallery, across the street from Tommy Condon's Restaurant, showcases the works of South Carolina's finest craft artists. Exhibits include works in clay, fiber, wood, jewelry, metals, glass, photography, paper, traditional crafts, basketry, leather, toys, and even soap making, with exhibitors chosen by a jury of other artists and gallery owners. Charleston Crafts offers a wide variety of gifts—from traditional to contemporary, from utilitarian to decorative, from affordable to exclusive. Demonstrations and featured craft artists change every week. Hours are 10 a.m. to 6 p.m. daily.

CHARLESTON FRAME WORKS AND GALLERY, 738 St. Andrews Blvd.; (843) 556-9373. Across the Ashley River about a mile down St. Andrews Boulevard, this gallery is making a name for itself as a source for affordable artwork. Prematted and framed prints and posters are featured here. There is a custom framing department that's well stocked and creative. Hours are usually Mon through Fri from 10 a.m. to 5:30 p.m. and Sat by appointment.

★ CHARLESTON RENAISSANCE GALLERY, 103 Church St.; (843) 723-0025; fineartsouth.com. This charming gallery is at the intersection of St. Michael's Alley and Church Street. Restructured to present a mix of old and new works, it appeals to visitors from all over the world as well as local Charlestonians. It features 19th-century Southern masterworks and the art of the Charleston renaissance period (1920s and 1930s). Among the gallery's contemporary works are paintings by William Halsey, West Fraser, and Linda Fantuzzo. For a complete list of artists represented, visit their website. Gallery hours are Mon through Fri 9:30 a.m. to 5:30 p.m. and by appointment.

CITY GALLERY AT WATERFRONT PARK, 34 Prioleau St.; (843) 958-6484; citygalleryatwaterfrontpark.com. The City Gallery at Waterfront Park is a wonderful venue for local, regional, national, and international talent with an emphasis on contemporary and innovative visual art. The city's mission here is to broaden the Charleston art outlook through a series of six to eight rotating exhibits each year. The glass-walled second and third stories of the building next to the Waterfront Park offer stunning views of the harbor to boot. The hours are Tues through Fri 10 a.m. to 6 p.m.; Sat and Sun, noon to 5 p.m.

COLEMAN FINE ART, 79 Church St.; (843) 853-7000; colemanfineart .com. This is the needle in the haystack for anyone looking for an art restoration specialist. Services include cleaning and revarnishing damaged or dirty oil paintings, plus museum and custom framing for art of all kinds. It carries children's books illustrated by Mary Whyte plus other original works and some limited-edition prints as well. Commissions are accepted for portraits. Hours are Tues through Sat 10 a.m. to 5 p.m. or by appointment.

CONE 10 STUDIOS, 1080-B Morrison Dr.; (843) 853-3345; cone10studios .com. Those with a penchant for pottery, sculpture, jewelry, handmade paper, and more will enjoy this studio featuring potters and artists from across the country. This is a working studio, as well, so even the uninitiated can enjoy watching the creative process or take part in lessons in wheelthrowing and clay sculpture. They also offer studio memberships for experienced potters. Located in the newly coined "NoMo" (North of Morrison Drive) area of Charleston, hours are Mon through Sat, 10 a.m. to 4 p.m.; Sun, 1 to 4 p.m. or by appointment.

★ **CORRIGAN GALLERY, LLC,** 62 Queen St.; (843) 722-9878; corrigan gallery.com. The Corrigan Gallery opened in 2005, presenting what artist/owner Lese Corrigan describes as "art with a future and backed by intellectual process." Located in the heart of the historic district, the gallery combines the charm of the old city of Charleston with a look to the future. Paintings, drawings, fine art prints, photography, and sculpture in a range of prices can be purchased here. Some of the artists represented include Manning Williams, Kevin Bruce Parent, John Moore, Mary Walker, Kristi Ryba, Sue Simons Wallace, Karin Olah, Richard Hagerty, and Lese Corrigan. The gallery is open Tues, Wed, Fri, Sat from 10 a.m. to 5 p.m.; Mon and Thurs 11 a.m. to 5 p.m. and also by appointment.

ELLA WALTON RICHARDSON FINE ART GALLERY, 58 Broad St.; (843) 722-3660; ellarichardson.com. Located in an architecturally impressive building on Broad Street, this gallery seems especially blessed in its convenient downtown location. Artistically, however, the gallery is far reaching in its wonderful representation of contemporary American, Dutch, and Russian artists specializing in classical realist and impressionistic art. Wildlife sculpture, jewelry, and photography join the selection of paintings by nearly a dozen artists with impressive regional and national credentials. Hours are Mon through Sat, 10 a.m. to 5 p.m., or by appointment.

GALLERY CHUMA, 188 Meeting St., #1; (843) 722-1702; gallerychuma .com. There is always a colorful and changing collection at this showcase for African and African-American art. Located in the City Market, the exhibition room features original works from local, national, and international artists. The gallery's prints and custom framing department has more than 1,500 limited-edition prints and posters. Gallery Chuma also offers a number of educational programs for schools, local community groups, and visitors. These include gallery tours, lectures, poetry readings, meet-the-artist events, classes, workshops, multimedia presentations, and more. African-American heritage tours to areas of historic importance in and around Charleston are offered in conjunction with licensed tour guides. (See the Tours chapter.) Hours are usually 9:30 a.m. to 6 p.m. Mon through Sun. Gallery Chuma features the large-format, stunning imagery of Jonathan Green, famous Gullah artist now of Naples, Florida.

GAYE SANDERS FISHER GALLERY, 124 Church St.; (843) 958-0010; gayesandersfisher.com. This is the showcase for Gaye Sanders Fisher's imaginative originals in oil and watercolor. The Carolina Lowcountry, its unique architecture, nature, and color have been Fisher's subjects for over 30 years. She also accepts commissions for a painting of your favorite house. Her work is included in many private and corporate collections throughout the country. Gallery hours are Mon through Sat from 10 a.m. to 5 p.m. and Sun from 1 to 4 p.m.

GORDON WHEELER GALLERY, 180 East Bay St.; (843) 722-2546; gordonwheeler.net. The gallery of local artist Gordon Wheeler offers original acrylic paintings of Charleston and other Lowcountry scenes as well as European, tropical, and Western works. He's mostly known for his commission work, but the shop has limited-edition prints and some very popular golf art. Gallery hours are 10 a.m. to 5 p.m. Mon through Thurs, until 6 p.m. Fri and Sat; 11 a.m. to 5 p.m. Sun.

HALSEY INSTITUTE OF CONTEMPORARY ART, College of Charleston School of the Arts, 161 Calhoun St.; (843) 953-4422; halsey.cofc.edu. The Halsey Gallery, located in the Marion and Wayland H. Cato, Jr. Center for the Arts, is administered by the School of the Arts at the College of Charleston. It exists to advocate, exhibit, and interpret visual art with an emphasis on contemporary art. In addition to housing seven major exhibitions each year, the gallery serves as an extension of the undergraduate art curricula and sponsors interpretive programs such as accompanying lectures and seminars. While the primary audiences served include the college's students, faculty, and staff, the gallery is open to the public, and participation in its programs is encouraged. Gallery hours vary according to the building's use for performances and school-related functions, but are generally 11 a.m. to 4 p.m. Mon through Sat. Call for more specific details.

HORTON HAYES FINE ART, 30 State St.; (843) 958-0014; hortonhayes .com. Here you'll find fascinating marshscapes and Lowcountry images of shrimpers, crabbers, clammers, and oyster harvesters done in oils, pastels, watercolor, and acrylics. Architectural depictions and still-life paintings are other popular subjects displayed here. The works of Mark Horton are also featured. Gallery hours are Mon through Sat 10:30 a.m. to 5:30 p.m. and Sun 12:30 to 5 p.m.

JOHN CARROLL DOYLE ART GALLERY, 125 Church St.; (843) 577-7344; johncdoyle.com. Visitors to the Market area who stop in at A. W. Shucks for lunch or for oysters and beer are totally surrounded by the unique work of popular Charleston artist John Doyle. His bold colors and striking figures are filled with life, drama, and his very special treatment of light. Doyle is nationally known for his energetic painting of blues musicians, blue marlins, and blue hydrangeas. John Doyle fine art prints of his work are for sale here too. His gallery also features the work of fellow native Charleston artist Margaret Petterson whose Lowcountry scenes blend old and new, traditional and contemporary. You're invited to visit with the artist as she paints in her studio within the gallery. Gallery hours are Mon through Sat from 10 a.m. to 5 p.m.

LOWCOUNTRY ARTISTS LTD., 148 East Bay St.; (843) 577-9295; lowcountryartists.com. A number of local artists operate this gallery on East Bay Street's busy gallery row. The quaint shop has a fine selection of original watercolors, woodcuts, pottery, oils, and prints. The specialty here is Charleston and Lowcountry scenes. You'll also find collages, handpainted tiles, colored-pencil drawings, linocuts, monoprints, etchings, and other graphics. Portrait, fine art, and commercial art commissions are welcomed. Every month, one of the participating artists has a show of new works. Hours are Mon through Sat from 11 a.m. to 5 p.m., Sun 1 to 5 p.m., or by appointment.

MARTIN GALLERY, 18 Broad St.; (843) 723-7378; martingallerycharleston .com. Located in the Grand Salon of the People's Building, here's a showcase for contemporary works by nationally acclaimed artists working in oils and acrylics—including landscape-oriented paintings by William Crosby; bronzes by wildlife sculptor Leo Osborne; marble, bronze, and terracotta sculpture by Claire McCardle, and photography by Michael Kahn. Hours are Mon through Sat 10 a.m. to 6 p.m., Sun 11 a.m. to 5 p.m., and by appointment.

NINA LIU AND FRIENDS, 24 State St.; (843) 722-2724. Nina calls this "a gallery of contemporary art objects." We call it fun. This quaint gallery is quite possibly the heartbeat of Charleston's French Quarter art scene. Her gallery makes bold and changing statements with very distinctive collections of glass, porcelain, jewelry, decorative ceramics, and fiber art. Solo shows by nationally

Historic French Quarter District

known artists are featured periodically, and you'll find paintings, photography, and sculpture as well. Her gallery/salon, which attracts an international clientele of shoppers and art patrons, is in a 19th-century town house on State Street. Hours are Mon through Sat from 10 a.m. to 5 p.m. and Sun noon to 5 p.m. or by appointment.

PINK HOUSE GALLERY, 17 Chalmers St.; (843) 723-3608; pinkhouse gallery.tripod.com. In one of the city's most picturesque buildings (first used in 1694 as a tavern), this quaint gallery features architecturals, wildlife, and florals. Look here for original works by Alice Stewart Grimsley, Nancy Wycoff Rushing, Audrey Price, Bruce Krucke, and Alexandria H. Bennington. Ravenel Gaillard's remarkable Lowcountry plantation scenes are featured here, as well. Works are shown on all three floors, and special exhibits are held in the courtyard just off the cobblestone street. Hours are Mon through Sat 10 a.m. to 5 p.m. and Sun afternoon in the spring and fall.

SPENCER ART GALLERIES, 55 & 57 Broad St.; (843) 722-6854, (843) 723-4482; spencerartgallery.com. Spencer Art Galleries I & II in two side-by-side galleries on Broad Street show work by more than 35 local, regional, national, and international artists. You'll find a broad range of contemporary fine art—everything from paintings, prints, and photography to sculpture. The friendly atmosphere offers a relaxed setting to view the art and meet and chat with some of the featured artists. Collectors enjoy the opportunity to purchase from a range of prices among their master, mid-career, and emerging artists. The galleries' hours are Mon through Sat 10 a.m. to 5 p.m. or by appointment by calling (843) 886-6617.

STUDIO 151 FINE ARTS, 175 Church St.; (843) 577-6909; studio151fine arts.com. One of Charleston's newer fine art galleries, Studio 151 Fine Arts represents a group of 12 artists to include some well-known names such as Darryl Knox, Amelia Whaley, Dixie Dugan, and Bob Graham. The broad range of works encompass traditional realism, impressionism, collage, wildlife subjects, and abstracts. Each artist executes these styles through their individual focus of pastels, watercolors, oils, monotypes, or mixed media—a veritable feast for the eyes. Hours are Mon through Thurs 10 a.m. to 6 p.m., until 8 p.m. on Fri and Sat, and Sun 11 a.m. to 5 p.m.

THE SYLVAN GALLERY, 171 King St.; (843) 722-2172; thesylvangallery .com. Located in the heart of the antique and art district of historic Charleston, The Sylvan Gallery focuses on 20th- and 21st-century traditional art. Their award-winning artists are nationally and internationally recognized. Some names here are Rhett Thurman, Scott Burdick, Ted Ellis, Karol Mack, and Guido Petruzzi. Among the notable sculptors are Glenna Goodacre, Richard Loffler, and Frank DiVita. Owners Joe and Janie Sylvan together have more than 30 years of gallery experience making this a warm and inviting gallery stop. Hours are Mon through Sat from 10 a.m. to 5 p.m. or by appointment.

UTOPIA, 27 Broad St.; (843) 853-9510; utopiacharleston.com. This small fashion boutique/art gallery on Charleston's very traditional Broad Street seems like an anomaly, but it's a welcome and refreshing break. It also displays alternative and avant-garde fashions and art, which is attracting a dedicated following. Hours are Mon through Sat from 11 a.m. to 6 p.m., and Sun noon to 5 p.m.

WELLS GALLERY, 1 Sanctuary Beach Dr., Kiawah Island; (843) 576-1290; wellsgallery.com. The Wells Gallery at the Sanctuary Resort on Kiawah Island presents a diverse palette of original work from artists who enjoy regional, national, and international success. Works range from contemporary realism to abstract expressionism, from landscape to figure, from full color to somber neutrals as well as hand blown glass. Regular gallery artists include Mark Bailey, Tina Mayland, Evan Harrington, Rick Reinert, Gary Gowans, Russell Gordon, George Pate, Wendy Whitson, Karen Larson Turner, and Curt Butler. Gallery hours are 10 a.m. to 5 p.m. daily.

THE ARTS

Festivals & Annual Events

Tradition is of utmost importance to Lowcountry residents, and successful annual events always fall into that category. Events in the Trident area run the gamut from the Lowcountry Oyster Festival—where salty oyster juice stains and face-painting masterpieces serve as souvenirs—to the sophisticated and comprehensive arts festival that is Spoleto Festival USA. Charlestonians and visitors alike turn out in big numbers for all the events listed in this chapter, so we strongly suggest you make your reservations early.

For information about any of the activities, we recommend contacting the Visitor Information Center of the Charleston Metro Chamber of Commerce (part of the area's convention and visitors bureau) at (843) 853-8000 or (800) 774-0006, or visit the website at charlestoncvb.com. The City of Charleston Office of Cultural Affairs (180 Meeting St., Ste. 200; (843) 724-7305; charleston -sc.gov) and the automated ticketing service Ticketmaster (866-448-7849; ticketmaster.com) are other good sources for information. The following listings will serve as good starting points in your efforts to dive into the traditions of the Trident. Unless otherwise noted, all events take place in Charleston proper.

JANUARY

🌟 THE CITADEL DRESS PARADE, The Citadel, 171 Moultrie St.; (843) 225-3294; citadel.edu. Almost every Friday during the school year, the nearly 2,000-member Corps of Cadets at The Citadel marches in retreat parade or review on Summerall Field to close out each week. In addition to the family and friends turnout, the Dress Parades are a long-standing local and visitor favorite due to the impressive precision of the Corps. Spectators are welcomed (for free)—just be sure to take your seat before 3:45 p.m. when the action commences. Call or visit the website for a schedule.

LOWCOUNTRY OYSTER FESTIVAL, Boone Hall Plantation, 1235 Long Point Rd., Mount Pleasant; (843) 577-4030, (843) 452-6088; boonehallplantation .com, charlestonrestaurantassociation.com. This festival, organized by the Greater Charleston Restaurant Association, is built around the mighty oyster but is geared to the whole family's appetite for fun. The gates of beautiful Boone Hall Plantation open at 10:30 a.m., and ticket holders are welcomed until the gates close at 5 p.m. An oyster-eating contest as well as other competitions are held, all in the name of fun and for the support of local children's charities. Barbecue and chili fill the void for non-oyster eaters, and if the winter temps aren't enough, there are plenty of chilled beverages—beer being the most popular—to keep things cool. Held the Sunday prior to Super Bowl Sunday in Jan. Festival admission is $20 in advance and $25 at the gate. Children under 10 are free with an adult.

FEBRUARY

⭐ **SOUTHEASTERN WILDLIFE EXPOSITION,** Various downtown locations; PO Box 20635, Charleston, SC 29413; (843) 723-1748; sewe.com. This exposition is said to be the largest celebration of wildlife art anywhere. Incredible displays of paintings, prints, sculpture, carvings, photography, collectibles, and crafts are all inspired by the boundless wonders of nature. More than 40,000 ticket-holding guests crisscross between the dozen or so exhibition sites on the Peninsula during the Presidents' Day weekend event. Tickets for the 2014 event, were $20 Fri or Sat, $10 for Sun, or $40 for a 3-day pass (children 10 and under are free with a paying adult). VIP packages start at $150 and provide opportunities to preview and purchase original artwork, attend special receptions and parties, and enter exhibits through separate entrances, and move to the front of lengthy lines. Contact SEWE for more information on the next annual exposition or advance ticket purchases.

MARCH

⭐ **CHARLESTON ANTIQUES SHOW,** Memminger Auditorium; 56 Beaufain St.; (843) 722-3405; historiccharleston.org. Supporting the programs of Historic Charleston Foundation, the Charleston Antiques Show weekend kicks off the foundation's Annual Festival of Houses and Gardens ever-popular tours with world-class exhibitors showcasing a full spectrum of period furnishings, decorative pieces, and fine art from the late-17th to the early-20th century. American, Asian, and European antiques are presented by some of the most recognized names from around the country. In addition to the exhibits, special events such as a preview party and guided group tours as well as luncheon lectures provide even more opportunities to learn and to enjoy the display. The show runs from Fri through Sun in mid-Mar. Daily passes are $15. The special events range from $25 for the behind-the-scenes tour to

$200 for the preview party. A combination ticket to the show plus a Festival of Houses and Gardens tour ticket is $60.

★ **THE CHARLESTON ART & ANTIQUES FORUM,** PO Box 22322, Charleston, SC 29413; (800) 926-2520; charlestonantiquesforum .org. Another not-to-be-missed event on Charleston's spring cultural scene is the premier lecture series, the Charleston Art & Antiques Forum, held during "Antiques Week" in mid-Mar. Nationally and internationally recognized scholars cover architecture, furniture, paintings, silver, and ceramics as they relate to the annual theme such as "By George! Celebrating 300 years of Georgian Art and Design." Benefiting arts education and preservation initiatives, the Forum presents outstanding lectures in small-scale sessions, informal chats with the speakers, and elegant receptions. A Connoisseur ticket starts at $595. Single lecture tickets are available if the packages have not sold out and go on sale Mar 1.

CHARLESTON SYMPHONY ORCHESTRA LEAGUE ASID DESIGNER SHOWHOUSE, Location varies, PO Box 22613, Charleston, SC 29413; (843) 723-0020; csolinc.org. Each year, a private historic dwelling is placed in the capable hands of volunteers from the Charleston Symphony Orchestra League to be presented in all its dazzling glory to the public in a one-house tour. The annual showhouse event, which opens in mid-Mar, continues for a month and features each room decorated by an ASID designer. It provides a great opportunity to tour an attractive home, shop the in-house boutique, and have lunch at the same residence in the tearoom (usually set up in the garden). Tickets are $15 in advance or $20 at the door, and proceeds benefit our outstanding orchestra. Hence, it's a win–win situation and another opportunity to experience the inside of Charleston.

CHARLESTON WINE + FOOD FESTIVAL, PO Box 22823, Charleston, SC 29413; (843) 727-9998; charlestonwineandfood.com. Held in early Mar, the Charleston Wine + Food Festival delights foodies with the opportunity to indulge in the unique flavors of Lowcountry cuisine. Patrons will choose from a wide variety of epicurean events presented by the country's best chefs, authors, and wine experts. The festival kicks off with a "Salute to Charleston Chefs" on Thurs and ends with a "Rigs, Pigs + Swigs" finale on Sun afternoon. Marion Square is also the site of the Culinary Village's Grand Tasting Tent, which features food, wine, and interactive events from more than 40 vendors. Other special events at local restaurants and various venues include seminars, excursions, and dining like "Spirit of Charleston: An Exploration of Rum," and "Two Cultures, One Kitchen: Latin Cuisine Using Southern Staples." Many events sell out quicky so reserve your tickets early and get ready for a weekend of culinary treats.

FOLLY BEACH SEA & SAND FESTIVAL, 32-A Center St., Folly Beach; (843) 408-6439; follybeachfestivals.com. What could be better than enjoying the beach before the crowds descend for the season? The Sea & Sand Festival at Folly Beach lets fun-loving beachgoers do just that by celebrating all things "beachy" the last weekend in Mar. The city closes down the beachfront street for leisurely strolling and browsing during this event, so break out the shorts and flip-flops. The festival is full of vendors serving up local seafood delicacies, an arts and crafts show, a surfing competition, and live music. An auction, children's games, and a hula-hoop contest add to the entertainment, and the sandcastle competition gets more creative and spectacular every year. Admission is free.

★ **HISTORIC CHARLESTON FOUNDATION'S FESTIVAL OF HOUSES AND GARDENS**, Various downtown locations, PO Box 1120, Charleston, SC 29402; (843) 723-1623, (843) 722-3405 (festival info); historiccharleston.org. Those who want to move beyond a passive, coffee-table-book enjoyment of Charleston's private homes and gardens wait for this event each year. For a month's time in Mar and Apr, more than 700 volunteers make it possible to tour more than 150 private houses and gardens. Every day the itinerary changes, with the focus on historically and architecturally distinct dwellings and gardens. To broaden the experience further, the foundation also hosts oyster roasts and musical concerts (everything from Beethoven to Bluegrass) at various historic sites. The Charleston Antiques Show is held simultaneously during the first weekend of the festival. Tickets start at $30 for special events and $50 for House and Garden Tours and are available from The Shops of Historic Charleston Foundation at 108 Meeting St. or by calling the number above after Nov 1.

KIDS FAIR, Burke High School, 244 President St.; (843) 571-6565, ext. 1017; charlestonjcc.org. Since 1988, the Charleston Jewish Community Center in partnership with the City of Charleston has sponsored this indoor fair for children ages 3 to 12. We like the safety precaution of not allowing any adult to enter if not accompanied by a child, and we appreciate the wide range of age-appropriate entertainment—from face painting, arts and crafts, and school group performances, to health-issue booths, all free of charge. In a nice change of pace, parents are admitted free with children, whose tickets are $1. Parking is free, too. The hours are 10 a.m. to 4 p.m. on a Sun in Mar.

BLESSING OF THE FLEET AND SEAFOOD FESTIVAL, Mount Pleasant Memorial Waterfront Park, 99 Harry Hallman Jr. Blvd.; (843) 884-8517; tompsc.com. The town of Mount Pleasant and the shrimping industry pull out their finest when they invite the public to celebrate the Blessing of the Fleet. Along with prayers for a successful shrimping season and a parade of shrimp boats, organizers offer a wide range of entertainment and culinary delights. From shrimp-eating and shagging contests to an art show and face painting, the formula is for fun, and the setting—beautiful. With its gorgeous view of Charleston, Memorial Waterfront Park can't be beat. The festival is held the last Sun in Apr. Drawing more than 10,000 people each year, the Blessing of the Fleet is Mount Pleasant's largest tourism event. Admission is free, but food from a variety of East Cooper restaurants ranges from about $2 to $5.

> **i** Try to be especially patient in Charleston traffic during April, May, and June. That's when Charleston's spring flowers are in bloom (bringing thousands of visitors), and Spoleto Festival USA is going full tilt. Traffic can be especially heavy during these months, and the city's narrow streets are easily overwhelmed by the volume.

BLUES BY THE SEA, Freshfields Village Green, Kiawah Island, SC, PO Box 13525, Charleston, SC 29422; (843) 762-9125; bluesbash.com/kiawah. Bring your blanket or lawn chairs to stake out your spot for kicking back and listening to the blues at Freshfields Village, a dining, shopping, and entertainment venue located at the traffic circle between Kiawah and Seabrook Islands. Musicians such as Shelley Waters, Billy Flynn, Billy Boy Arnold, Professor Bottleneck & Harmonica Frank, and Frankie's Blues Mission have played to enthusiastic crowds since this festival began in 2004. It is held in mid-April, and admission is free. Festival promoter, musician, and radio personality Gary Erwin runs the show, and you can call him for more information about Blues by the Sea and other blues happenings around town at (843) 762-9125 from 10 a.m. to 6 p.m. Mon through Sat. A Blues by the Sea brochure is available by sending a self-addressed, stamped envelope to the above address.

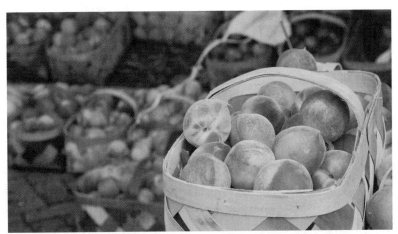

Peaches for sale at market

★ **CHARLESTON FARMERS' MARKET**, Marion Square (between King and Meeting at Calhoun); (843) 724-7309; charlestonfarmersmarket.com. Held every Sat from Apr through Dec at Marion Square (King, Meeting, and Calhoun Streets), the Charleston Farmers' Market gives you a chance to pick out fresh fruit and veggies from our best local growers. Other vendors offer light fare such as crepes, omelets, bakery goods, and barbecue for sustenance during a leisurely stroll. Each week brings a variety of special activities, and the food and family fun are offered from 8 a.m. until 2 p.m. (or often later during Spoleto and other special event weekends). Music, arts and crafts, and "Ask a Master Gardener" are just a few of the attractions. On the December Saturdays be sure to gather loads of fresh greenery and goodies to "deck the halls." We know lots of folks who are regulars at the Farmers' Market—hooked on that fresh-harvested produce and free fun.

COOPER RIVER BRIDGE RUN AND WALK, PO Box 22089, Charleston, SC 29413; (843) 856-1949; bridgerun.com. The Bridge Run, as the natives call it, is a social event as much as it is a run. Bumper stickers dare us with slogans like "Keep Calm and Run the CRBR," and banners fly around the city for weeks ahead of time—we can't say we just forgot. Still, a 10-kilometer (6.2-mile) run or walk is a bit much for some of us, if not too great a challenge for the 30,000 or so participants who pound the pavement each year (usually in early Apr). The race begins in Mount Pleasant, continues across the Cooper River over the Arthur Ravenel Jr. Bridge, and finishes downtown. The early entry fee for the run/walk is $35. All entrants receive a T-shirt and other goodies. A 1-mile Kid's

Race takes place at Hampton Park for an early entry fee of $8. For more information and an application, write to the address above or register online.

EAST COAST PADDLESPORTS & OUTDOOR FESTIVAL, James Island County Park, 871 Riverland Dr.; (843) 795-4386; ccprc.com. Since 1991, the Charleston County Park and Recreation Commission has sponsored the popular East Coast Paddlesports & Outdoor Festival (formerly known as the East Coast Canoe & Kayak Festival) at James Island County Park. The event is a full weekend of canoeing, kayaking, and stand-up paddleboarding history, technique, and hands-on experience appropriate for the beginner as well as the experienced paddler. Outdoor enthusiasts will enjoy the slack lining, archery, disc golf, mountain biking, and climbing actitvities. In addition to classes and boat demonstrations, lectures, workshops, and ACA instructor courses are held. There are commercial exhibits by equipment designers and manufacturers so you can try out new boats, paddles, and accessories at the festival site; or shop the used equipment at bargain prices. Family activities and a kids' camp round out the weekend of fun. Festival attendees are encouraged to stay on-site at the 640-acre park which features a 16-acre freshwater lake, tidal creek access, tent and RV camping, and miles of nature and bike trails. Package fees range from $15 per day up to $105 for the full weekend of events.

FAMILY CIRCLE CUP, Daniel Island Tennis Centre, 161 Seven Farms Dr., Daniel Island; (843) 856-7900, (800) 677-2293; familycirclecup.com. Take in some tennis at the $9 million Daniel Island Tennis Centre, the home of the Family Circle Cup. The 9-day Women's Tennis Association Tier I event attracts many of the top seeds in women's tennis. Some of the past competitors were Serena Williams, Steffi Graf, Monica Seles, Jennifer Capriati, Martina Hingis, and Caroline Wozniacki. Held in early Apr, the Family Circle Cup is another highlight in Charleston's spring events lineup. Ticket prices range from $10 for qualifying matches up to $80 for the finals.

FLOWERTOWN FESTIVAL, 140 South Cedar St., Summerville; (843) 871-9622; summervilleymca.org/flowertown. Summerville, a 20-mile drive from Charleston, is the setting for this wonderful small-town festival each spring. If the winter has been kind, the city—affectionately called Flowertown—will be ablaze with color on the first weekend in Apr, and the events are nonstop. Sponsored by the Summerville Family YMCA, the festival is a 3-day affair that includes arts and crafts displays with more than 200 vendors, a youth festival, sports tournaments, the Taste of Summerville food festival, and much more. There is no admission or parking fee, but there are charges from individual vendors for food and activities.

★ THE GARDEN CLUB OF CHARLESTON'S ANNUAL HOUSE AND GARDEN TOURS, Various downtown locations; PO Box 20828, Charleston, SC 29413; (843) 406-7626; thegardenclubofcharleston.org. Some of Charleston's finest historic district homes and gardens are showcased on The Garden Club of Charleston's self-guided walking tours on a Fri and Sat afternoon in mid-Apr. The members have organized this event for more than 75 years and continue to delight tourists and locals alike with the selection of private homes, breathtaking gardens, and their own flower arrangements that enhance the homes' interiors. Tickets are in the $45 range for each day and can be purchased by visiting the website or writing to the address above. If not sold out, they also may be purchased the day of the tour at the visitor center at 375 Meeting Street.

LOWCOUNTRY CAJUN FESTIVAL, James Island County Park, 871 Riverland Dr.; (843) 795-4386; ccprc.com. Crawfish-crazed connoisseurs, take heart. Here's a chance for you to get your fill this side of New Orleans at the annual Lowcountry Cajun Festival. Set in early Apr, it's a stompin' good time at the James Island County Park, where more than 5 tons of crawfish, eating contests, crawfish races, and genuine Louisiana Cajun bands make up the mix for family fun. Sponsored by the Charleston County Park and Recreation Commission, tickets for the festival are $10 for adults and free for children 12 and under with a paying adult.

MAY

DINING WITH FRIENDS LOWCOUNTRY AIDS SERVICES, 3547 Meeting Street Rd.; (843) 747-2273, (877) 874-0230; aids-services.com. Hundreds of volunteers host private dinner parties for friends in their homes in a joint fund-raising effort supporting Lowcountry AIDS Services one Sat in May. The kinds of parties run the spectrum from barbecue to black tie. Guests make a tax-deductible donation and enjoy a pleasant evening with old and new friends topped off with a Champagne and Dessert Grand Finale at 9 p.m. at the Charleston Maritime Center.

★ GRACE EPISCOPAL CHURCH TEA ROOM, 98 Wentworth St.; (843) 723-4575; gracechurchcharleston.org. Another of Charleston's special spring tearooms is the one put on by the volunteers of Grace Episcopal Church, near the College of Charleston. Lowcountry specialties are the fare here, and who can pass up an opportunity to sample a few of these: crab and okra soup, ham biscuits, and shrimp remoulade with an assortment of freshly baked desserts. Prices run from $3 to $8 an item, and you may find yourself returning several times during the 2 weeks the tearoom is open. The dates correspond with the Spoleto Festival, the last week of May and first week of June. Lunch is served Mon through Sat from 11:30 a.m. to 2 p.m., and takeout is available for your own Spoleto picnic. Proceeds benefit church outreach programs.

GREEK FESTIVAL, Greek Orthodox Church of The Holy Trinity, 30 Race St.; (843) 577-2063; charlestongreekfestival.com. Another in Charleston's delectable ethnic festivals is the Greek Festival held in mid-May at the Greek Orthodox Church. Greek food, dancing, jewelry, crafts, and cooking demonstrations are some of the highlights of the weekend-long family fun. Dine in or take out the gyros, Greek chicken dinners, spanakopita, and pastries. Check out the bazaar, and take in a tour of the beautiful church. You're bound to be speaking a little Greek by the time you leave. Hours are 11 a.m. to 10 p.m. Fri and Sat, noon to 5 p.m. on Sun. Admission is $5 at the gate, $3 for seniors and students (cash only). Children 12 and under and active military are free and so are mothers on Mother's Day Sun.

NORTH CHARLESTON ARTS FESTIVAL, Performing Arts Center of the Charleston Area Convention Center Complex, 5001 Coliseum Dr., North Charleston; (843) 740-5854; northcharleston.org. Bring the family and spend some time at the North Charleston Arts Festival. The indoor/outdoor entertainment at this weeklong festival encompasses everything from juried adult and youth art exhibits, a photography competition, and a local arts and crafts show and sale, to puppet and magic shows, live theater, and dance performances. Just listening to the variety of musical entertainment (including reggae, school choral groups, classical music, and contemporary gospel) is reason enough to check it out. Event hours begin at 9 a.m. and run into the evening hours daily. Some events are free, and others are ticketed events in the $5 to $20 range. The festival wraps up with a grand finale with performances, children's events, and fireworks at the Riverfront Park. Ample parking is available for free.

PICCOLO SPOLETO FESTIVAL, Various locations; (843) 724-7305; piccolo spoleto.com. We are particularly proud of Piccolo Spoleto, the city of Charleston's creative companion to Spoleto Festival USA. Piccolo events—including jazz cruises, a children's festival, a juried art exhibit, cabaret, and "brown bag and ballet"—are held in unusual places (anywhere from boats to parks to churches) and showcase local as well as national talent. The calendar is booked, and the ticket prices are very reasonable, ranging from free events to others that are almost always less than $30. For a more comprehensive schedule of events, write the City of

Charleston Office of Cultural Affairs, 180 Meeting St., Ste. 200, Charleston, SC 29401 or visit the website.

SPOLETO FESTIVAL USA, Various locations; (843) 722-2764, (843) 579-3100 (box office); spoletousa.org. Since 1977, Spoleto Festival USA has continued as a bright star on Charleston's arts calendar. Already accustomed to an unusually strong year-round arts agenda, the city becomes blissfully hyperactive during Spoleto with world-class theater, music, dance, opera, and visual and literary presentations. It begins on Memorial Day weekend and lasts 17 days or so. Highlights of the 2014 festival included the operas *El Niño* and *Kát'a Kabanová* and performances by Laurie Anderson and Ireland's Gate Theatre, as well as the ever-popular chamber music series and Westminster Choir. Tickets for individual Spoleto events range from about $15 to $85. For an up-to-date schedule, contact the event box office at 14 George St., Charleston, SC 29401.

JUNE

BOHICKET MARINA INVITATIONAL BILLFISH TOURNAMENT, 1880 Andell Bluff Blvd., Johns Island; (843) 768-1280; govcup.dnr.sc.gov, bohicket.com. One of the five tourneys in the South Carolina Governor's Cup Billfishing Series, the Bohicket Invitational is one of the major tournaments in the area. Held in early June, this one brings in the big boys competing for serious money; first prize for the largest marlin garners $10,000. Placing here can lead to even bigger prizes in the Governor's Cup competition. This tag-and-release tourney also awards $1,500 for the largest wahoo, dolphin, and tuna and the best female and youth angler. Get your crew, sportfishing yacht, and checkbook ready for an entry fee of $2,000 and a sportin' good time. It's called an invitational, but anyone can join in the fun.

CAROLINA DAY, 1214 Middle St., Sullivan's Island; (843) 723-3225, (843) 883-3123; nps.gov/fosu. Sullivan's Island in the summer is cause for celebration in itself. Add to the natural charm of the venue an event like Carolina Day, and you're in for some serious fun. No admission is charged for this annual reenactment program at Fort Moultrie, and it is a wonderful opportunity to learn about the history of the patriots' Revolutionary War victory over the British Navy on June 28, 1776. Other Carolina Day events include a special church service and the ringing of church bells in Charleston, Mount Pleasant, Sullivan's Island, Isle of Palms, and North Charleston. An open house at the South Carolina Historical Society and a South Carolina Art Tour at the Gibbes Museum of Art (see the section on Museums & Other Sites in the Attractions chapter) are both free of charge. A procession takes place in the afternoon. It is composed of historical and lineal groups that make up the Palmetto Society of Charleston, the group that sponsors Carolina Day. The parade moves from Washington Park downtown to White Point Garden at the Battery, where a wreath-laying ceremony and band concert wrap up the procession. The program runs from 9 a.m. to 8 p.m. (See the Attractions chapter for more information on Fort Moultrie.)

RICE PLANTERS AMATEUR GOLF TOURNAMENT, Snee Farm Country Club, 1200 Club Dr., Mount Pleasant; (843) 884-2600; thericeplanters .com. Since 1973, Snee Farm Country Club has hosted the Rice Planters Amateur Golf Championship. This tournament attracts top collegiate golfers, seasoned talent from across the US, and terrific international amateur players. Past champions and competitors have included current pros Tom Lehman, Davis Love III, Scott Hoch, Stewart Cink, Andy Bean, Hal Sutton, and Mark O'Meara. Held in mid-June, this event is open to the public at no charge. Call Snee Farm for more information.

JULY

PATRIOTS POINT 4TH OF JULY BLAST, Patriots Point Naval and Maritime Museum, 40 Patriots Point Rd., Mount Pleasant; (843) 884-2727; patriotspoint.org. With one of the biggest Fourth of July fireworks displays in the Palmetto State, the festivities at Patriots Point Naval and Maritime Museum on Charleston Harbor are a blast. It all begins at 4:30 p.m. with free admission to the ships of the museum, including the aircraft carrier USS *Yorktown.* Food and arts and crafts vendors add to the fun atmosphere, and the kids will enjoy a jump castle, climbing rock wall, and more in the Kids Zone. Popular area bands perform live before and after the fireworks for dancing the night away. The fireworks light up the sky usually just after 9:30 p.m. More than 10,000 people have celebrated our nation's birthday here in earlier years, so allow time for traffic and parking. (For more on Patriots Point Naval and Maritime Museum, see our Attractions chapter.)

AUGUST

FISHING FOR MIRACLES KING MACKEREL TOURNAMENT, PO Box 21199, Charleston, SC 29422; (843) 214-1408; fishingformiracles.org. This king mackerel fishing tournament, held in mid-Aug, is one of the largest saltwater fishing tournaments in South Carolina. Based out of Ripley Light Yacht Club, the tournament awards cash prizes for the biggest catch as well as other categories. The tournament proceeds benefit the Medical University of South Carolina Children's Hospital and the Coastal Conservation Association of South Carolina. The entry fee is $300 before Aug 1 and $350 thereafter.

SEPTEMBER

CHARLESTON SCOTTISH GAMES AND HIGHLAND GATHERING, Boone Hall Plantation, 1235 Long Point Rd., Mount Pleasant; (843) 529-1020; charlestonscots.org. The tartan-clad clans gather, and traditions abound when the Scottish Games and Highland Gathering, sponsored by the Scottish Society of Charleston, is held at Boone Hall Plantation. All ages are incorporated into the festivities, which range from highland and country dancing and bagpipe music to tossing the caber. Those interested in finding out more about their Scottish roots enjoy talking to clan members at various booths, and everyone has a chance to sample Scottish culinary delights such as meat pies, scones, and shortbread. Boone Hall Plantation is a lovely setting for all of this, and Sept is usually a very temperate month in the Lowcountry. Advance tickets for the 9 a.m. to 9 p.m. Sat gathering are $17 for adults and teens and $4 for children ages 6 to 12. Gate prices are $20 and $5, respectively. Parking is $5 per car, which includes a program. For more information, contact the Scottish Society at PO Box 31951, Charleston, SC 29417–1951.

MOJA ARTS FESTIVAL, Office of Cultural Affairs, 180 Meeting St., Ste. 200; (843) 724-7305; mojafestival.com. Running for 10 days in Sept and Oct, MOJA—a Swahili word for "source" or "beginning"—celebrates the long and fascinating African-American and Caribbean traditions and contributions to western cultures. Charleston becomes a stage for lectures, theater, and dance performances, art exhibits, concerts, and general festivities. Activities for the young and old provide the opportunity for sharing good times and harmony among people. Expect broad strokes of color, graceful movement, and beauty and revelry in abundance. Check *The Post and Courier* for special features and a listing of specific events with admission prices (many events are free), or call the above number for more information. (See the Tours chapter for more about MOJA and Charleston's African-American tradition.)

SOUTHERN LIVING TASTE OF CHARLESTON, Boone Hall Plantation, 1235 Long Point Rd., Mount Pleasant; (843) 577-4030; charlestonrestaurantassociation.com. If you have ever dreamed of sampling just a bite here and a bite there from the great restaurants all around town, this event is your dream come true. The Taste of Charleston is an all-day affair at Boone Hall Plantation, where more than 50 restaurants, all members of the Greater Charleston Restaurant Association, sell their specialties in sample proportions at bite-size prices. The fare may include shrimp and grits, beef kebabs, Greek chicken, seafood dishes, and a variety of desserts. Plan to nibble your way around the plantation grounds, then watch the Waiters Wine Race (make a bet on who'll spill) and ice-carving competition. Adults love the beer- and wine-tasting booths, and children delight in the acrobatics and juggling. The event is usually scheduled for three days in Sept, and admission is $20 in advance or $25 at the gate. Food tickets are incremental and cost $2 at the event. Children 10 and under are admitted free with an adult.

OCTOBER

KOMEN LOWCOUNTRY RACE FOR THE CURE, 9300 Medical Plaza Dr., Ste. F, North Charleston, SC 29406; (843) 556-8011; komenlowcountry .org. Since starting out in 1994 with 900 participants in the Charleston area, the Race for the Cure has quickly grown in popularity among runners of all ages to become the largest 5K race in South Carolina. The event is held by the Susan G. Komen Breast Cancer Foundation, which sponsors the 5K Race for the Cure around the country. It is a breast cancer awareness race, in which participants are invited to wear the name of loved ones who have battled cancer. The race takes place at the Family Circle Cup Tennis Centre on Daniel Island, and early registration fees are $25 for the 5K run/walk and the 1-mile family fun run/walk. Children under 5 are free but must be registered. Late registration is $30. Proceeds benefit both local and national grants awarded for breast cancer prevention and research.

LATIN AMERICAN FESTIVAL, Wannamaker County Park, 8888 University Blvd., North Charleston; (843) 795-4386; ccprc.com. Celebrate the sights, sounds, and tastes of the Latino world at the Latin American Festival on a Saturday afternoon in early Oct. In between nachos and chicken tamales, delight in the red-hot beat of hot salsa and merengue music. The Parade of Nations and folk dances add to the colorful display of the beautiful ethnic costumes. Admission is $10 for adults; students or military ID are $5; children 12 and under are free. Food, beverages, and merchandise are purchased with tickets in $1 increments.

MOUNT PLEASANT CHILDREN'S DAY FESTIVAL, Park West Recreation Complex, Mount Pleasant; (843) 884-8517; comeonovermp.com. On an October Sunday afternoon, the town of Mount Pleasant holds the Children's Day Festival to honor the children of the community and provide them with live entertainment, games, food, and fun. The event is organized by the Mount Pleasant Recreation Department and East Cooper schools, all of which set up game and food booths at the Park West Recreation Complex. Past years' entertainment lineup delighted more than 10,000 children and families. Mandrake the Magician, Becky Becker's Box of Puppets, the Gravity Brothers Comedy Juggling Duo, the Citadel Cheerleading Squad, and the band Lunch Money have all performed here. If that's not enough to make the little ones' eyes light up, there's a climbing wall, jump castles, a petting zoo, a giant slide, and pony rides. A Halloween costume contest also puts the children in the spotlight. Parking and admission are free.

⭐ **PRESERVATION SOCIETY OF CHARLESTON'S FALL TOURS OF HOMES AND GARDENS,** Various downtown locations; (843) 722-4630; preservationsociety.org. These tours, sponsored by the Preservation Society of Charleston, are a splendid opportunity to experience some of the privately owned homes and gardens, as well as plantations and churches in Charleston. Tourists and locals alike enjoy the romantic walk along several city blocks between dwellings and appreciate the commentary on the architecture, history, and folklore of each property by the volunteer guides. The evening Charleston Architectural Overview tours run from 6 to 9 p.m. on Thurs night. The Fri, Sat, and Sun afternoon tours hours are from 2 to 5 p.m. Tickets are $50 per tour, which features a different location in the historic district each week. Wed afternoon garden tours last from 2 to 5 p.m. and cost $40. Plantation tours by private coach run $125. You can find out more about the tours by writing the Preservation Society at PO Box 521, Charleston, SC 29402. (See the Attractions chapter for more information about the society.)

THAT BIG BOOK SALE, Omar Shrine Temple Auditorium, 176 Patriots Point St., Mount Pleasant; (843) 805-6882; ccpl.org. Organized by the Friends of the Library's volunteers to raise money for Charleston County libraries, this used-book sale just gets bigger and better. Since 1983, the event, now held at the Omar Shrine Auditorium, has included categories such as fiction, nonfiction, history, cooking, and travel, just to name a few. The books all are donated by the public—paperbacks sell for $1; hardbacks are $3. A "better book" section has individually priced books. Children's hardcover books are $1 and paperbacks are 50 cents. Peruse the selection of more than 70,000 books, tapes, DVDs, and CDs during the 3-day event, which has no admission fee. Event hours are Fri from 9 a.m. to 7 p.m., Sat from 9 a.m. to 5 p.m., and Sun from 10 a.m. to 3 p.m.

NOVEMBER

THE BATTLE OF SECESSIONVILLE, Boone Hall Plantation, 1235 Long Point Rd., Mount Pleasant; (843) 884-4371; boonehallplantation.com. Sponsored by the Confederate Heritage Trust, the Battle of Secessionville is reenacted right before your eyes with all the splendor and tragedy of the Civil War. Some of the activities to witness on this mid-November weekend include cavalry and artillery performances, battle aftermath reenactments, uniform demonstrations, and tours of the Boone Hall Plantation house and slave village. (For more on Boone Hall, see the Attractions and Tours chapters.) Camps open at 9 a.m., and the battle commences at 2 p.m. Admission prices are $20 for adults, $18 for seniors 65+, and $10 for children ages 6 to 12. (To learn more about the Battle of Secessionville, see "Battery Wagner" in the Forts section of the Attractions chapter.)

CHARLESTON FINE ART ANNUAL, Charleston Fine Art Dealers' Association, PO Box 942, Charleston, SC 29402; (843) 819-8006; cfada.com. Immerse yourself in the visual arts when the Charleston Fine Art Dealers' Association holds its annual event weekend in early Nov. There are 8 of Charleston's finest galleries that sponsor receptions, painting demonstrations, a high school art competition, and special exhibit openings with extended hours over the 2 days. The plein air painting demonstrations by CFADA gallery artists take place under the live oaks in Washington Park on Sat morning. Completed paintings are sold by bidding at the CFADA galleries or online, with proceeds benefiting local schools' art programs. What better remembrance of your experience could you take home than an original work by one of Charleston's leading artists? Most events are free. CFADA also sponsors their popular Palette & Palate Stroll, an evening of fine art, cuisine, and wine in mid-July. Visit the website for more details.

HOLIDAY FESTIVAL OF LIGHTS, James Island County Park, 871 Riverland Dr.; (843) 795-4386; holidayfestivaloflights.com. Young and old delight in the more than 700 magical lighting displays set up in the James Island County Park from mid-Nov through New Year's Eve. Set your own pace as you take the 3-mile driving tour, winding through the park and enjoying the spectacle. The lights burn from 5:30 to 10 p.m. Sun through Thurs and until 11 p.m. on Fri and Sat. Admission is $15 a car (or $10 with nonperishable food item Mon through Thurs) and $40 for 16-passenger vans. A Holiday Festival of Lights Fun Run and Walk the day before opening gives participants a preview of the 2,000,000 glittering lights. The 5K Fun Run or the 2-mile walk is a $12 advance entry fee for ages 3 and up. Start a new family tradition of viewing the dazzling display every year.

THE JUNIOR LEAGUE OF CHARLESTON "WHALE OF A SALE," Omar Shrine Temple Auditorium, 176 Patriots Point St., Mount Pleasant; (843) 763-5284; jlcharleston.org. This is the rummage sale to end all rummage sales. If you don't believe it, ask the dozens who camp out the night before in the parking lot to be the first ones through the door. Everything from large appliances, furniture, and computers to toys, sports equipment, clothing, and "you name it" is donated by the Junior League's membership, and there is new merchandise from area merchants. Of course, it's all available at rock-bottom prices. This event is a treasure hunter's paradise, so come prepared to search for loads of bargains. The doors open at 8 a.m. and close at 1 p.m., usually on the second Sat in Nov.

★ PLANTATION DAYS AT MIDDLETON PLACE, 4300 Ashley River Rd.; (843) 556-6020, (800) 782-3608; middletonplace.org. Consider getting a feel for plantation life at Middleton Place's Plantation Days. On one weekend in mid-Nov, visitors can observe craft workers in action as they showcase the tasks necessary for existence on an 18th- or 19th-century plantation. It's not hard to imagine the harvest season in full swing as you watch demonstrations of actual cane pressing, spinning, brick making, leather tanning, and cider making. Sweetgrass baskets, like those sold downtown at the City Market (see the Close-up in the Shopping chapter), are fashioned before your eyes as you immerse yourself in a different era. Regular gate admission to see the stableyards and gardens during Plantation Days is $28 for adults, $15 for students, and $10 for children ages 6 to 13. An additional $15 is charged to see the house. (For more on Middleton Place, see our Attractions chapter.)

DECEMBER

★ ANNUAL SPIRITUALS CONCERT AT DRAYTON HALL, 3380 Ashley River Rd., Charleston, SC 29414; (843) 769-2638; draytonhall.org. African-American spirituals, rooted in the work songs of West Africa and developed during the days of slavery, are incredibly moving. A cappella voices and rhythmic double-clapping are characteristic of the songs. The opportunity to hear them performed is rare. This early-December event begins with an informal candlelight house tour and refreshments on Sat evening at 4:30 p.m. followed by the hourlong concert around 5:30 p.m. A matinee performance is offered on Sun from 3 to 5 p.m. To order tickets at $35 per person ($30 for Friends of Drayton Hall), write to the address or call the number above. Seating is limited in Drayton Hall, so advance reservations are required. (For more on Drayton Hall, see the Attractions chapter.)

FAMILY YULETIDE, 4300 Ashley River Rd., Middleton Place; (843) 556-6020, (800) 782-3608; middletonplace.org. There's a fire for chestnut roasting, Jack Frost could very well be nipping at your nose, and you can bet that yuletide carols are going to be sung by a choir. It's all part of Family Yuletide at Middleton Place's Stableyards, which is usually held on the second Sat in Dec. There will be holiday storytelling by the bonfire, and crafters will be working by torchlight in their shops to get the venerable plantation ready for Christmas. The children can create peanut butter pinecone bird feeders, rag quilt ornaments and popcorn and cranberry strings. Reservations are recommended for this family event. Admission is about $15 per adult and $5 for children ages 4 to 13.

Christmas in Charleston

If you're thinking of spending the holidays in history, look into the **"Christmas in Charleston"** festival. Plan to celebrate during November and December with a variety of special events such as Christmas carriage rides, gallery art walks, holiday shopping excursions, and tree lightings complete with visits from Santa. The music of the season can be experienced through children's choir performances and plantation concerts, and the tastes can be enjoyed at Victorian teas, oyster roasts, and progressive dinners in historic Charleston. Homes, churches, storefronts, boats, and parks are all decked out for the holidays, and Christmas walking tours as well as holiday tours of homes and gardens provide an up-close view of the finery. For a complete schedule of events, call the CACVB at (800) 853-8000, or visit christmasincharleston.com.

HAPPY NEW YEAR, CHARLESTON!, Various downtown locations; (843) 724-7305; charleston-sc.gov. Happy New Year, Charleston! marks the passage of one year into the next with a broad selection of arts and cultural performances in the downtown historic district. The slant is a family-oriented, affordable, nonalcoholic, entertaining way to ring in the New Year. The 30- to

Palm trees lit with Christmas lights and garland

45-minute offerings include ballet, theater, improvisational comedy, puppetry, and an array of music from choral, chamber, and ethnic to folk and big band. Much of King Street is blocked off for pedestrian-only traffic, allowing a festive atmosphere at every turn with roving musicians and actors, jugglers, face painters, and dancing. All the events are within walking distance. Children's programming begins at 4 p.m.; the major events begin at 7 and last until 10:30 p.m. with free admission.

HOLIDAY PARADE OF BOATS, Various downtown locations; (843) 724-7305; charleston-sc.gov. For more than 30 years the Holiday Parade of Boats has been a popular spectacle for participants and spectators in Charleston. Usually the first Saturday evening in Dec, festively decorated boats of all descriptions leave from Mount Pleasant around 5 p.m. (depending on weather, current, or other conditions) crossing the Cooper River and Charleston Harbor to the Ashley River. These boats and skippers often get quite creative, and prizes are awarded for the top displays. Many viewers vie for a prime location along the Cooper River from the Aquarium to Waterfront Park to the Battery to watch this fun, nautical parade.

Kids

For starters, know that Greater Charleston is a fabulous vacation destination. Over 4 million people come to the Lowcountry every year, and a majority of those visitors arrive in the form of families.

A quick glance through the Attractions chapter might give you the impression that Charleston primarily serves up nothing but history—forts, house museums, plantations, and historic sites. While this wouldn't seem to be very kid-friendly, we've found that, almost without exception, Charleston's major annual events and attractions have been designed (at least partially) with children in mind.

And don't forget that children love to learn. Greater Charleston is a living, breathing, three-dimensional, full-color, interactive classroom for learning about America (which is really learning about ourselves). Here's the best part: It's a classroom with a beautiful ocean nearby, and that means beaches! Are we talkin' fun, or what?

Let's take stock. What have we got here? Interesting (new and old) places to go with really neat stuff to see; places where people used to live and work (and play) hundreds of years ago; ships of all types and all sizes that you can actually climb around on; and beaches close by with plenty of sand and sunburn to go around. We've got ballparks, game parks, and parks where you can swim. There are places to camp, rivers to explore, even new foods to taste. Ever eat a crawfish? We've got farms where you can pick your own strawberries and blueberries when the season is right. We've got something for every kid out there.

Walking along the Battery

This chapter is dedicated to fun activities that children and parents can do together. Let's get started.

Price Code

The following price code table is provided to give you an idea of the price of admission to those establishments that charge an admission fee. Please note that prices, means of payment, and hours change often and may vary seasonally, so call ahead for details. If no price code is designated, there is no charge to enter, but there may be other fees.

$	Less than $5
$$	$5 to $10
$$$	$10 to $20
$$$$	More than $20

OUTDOOR EXPLORATIONS

There are many public parks in the area. We have found that some are particularly appealing to children, and we describe those in more detail below. Whatever outdoor plans you make, be sure to bring plenty of sunscreen during the warm months and bug repellent for those pesky no-see-ums (gnats) present most of the year.

BOONE HALL FARMS, US 17 N., Mount Pleasant; (843) 884-4371, (843) 856-8154; boonehallfarms.com. During the spring and summer months, area farms offer you-pick-it produce, and one of our favorite spots is Boone Hall Farms, the working farm of Boone Hall Plantation in Mount Pleasant. Children carry buckets out into the fields and delight in gathering and eating seasonal berries right off the vine. Strawberries (as well as other seasonal produce such as tomatoes, pumpkins, and peaches) are carried home by the pound and can stimulate some creative pie and ice-cream making later. This can be a pleasant morning or afternoon that teaches kids that food doesn't just come from the grocery store or drive-through. The fields are open 9 a.m. to 7 p.m. Mon through Sat and 10 a.m. to 6 p.m. on Sun in season; call the number listed for directions and produce selections. Also check out the wonderful Boone Hall Farms Market at 2521 US 17 N., where produce and more are available. (See the Tours and Attractions chapters for more on Boone Hall Plantation.)

★ **CHARLES TOWNE LANDING STATE HISTORIC SITE,** 1500 Old Towne Rd., between I-26 and SR 171; (843) 852-4200; southcarolinaparks .com; $$. This state park is many things to many people, and it really is a terrific introduction to a hands-on history lesson. Founded in 1970, Charles Towne Landing State Historic Site is 663 acres of walking, bicycling, and in-line skating paths; an animal forest; an area dedicated to the depiction of the lives of settlers; and more. Children can expect to see native animals such as wolves, alligators, pumas, otters, bison, and maybe even a bear or two in a natural habitat setting. They can also enjoy the craft-making demonstrations and appreciate the period clothing worn by the park staff. Recent archaeological digs are centered on uncovering information about the original settlement of Charles Towne prior to its relocation across the Ashley River on the peninsular site. These excavations are bound to stir some excitement among visitors of all ages. We recommend strolling or biking through the park passing by the Legare-Waring historic home and down to Old Towne Creek, where a reproduction of a 17th-century trading vessel named *Adventure* is ready for exploring. Wonderful special events throughout the year as well as summer and holiday day camps attract a steady flow of young people. The park is open daily (except Christmas Eve and Christmas) all year. Hours are 9 a.m. to 5 p.m. Children younger than 5 get in free. (See the History and Attractions chapters for more information.)

Mysterious Charleston

Take the kids to help solve the mystery of the *H. L. Hunley*—the world's first submarine to sink an enemy ship in combat. After attacking and sinking the USS *Housatonic* 4 miles off Sullivan's Island in February 1864, the Confederate sub disappeared with its brave crew. For 136 years it remained on the ocean's floor until its raising in August 2000. Archaeology and conservation are under way at the **Warren Lasch Conservation Center** on Charleston's old Naval Base, but visitors are allowed every Sat from 10 a.m. to 5 p.m. and Sun from noon to 5 p.m. Advance tickets are $12 plus a service charge (a limited number are available on a walk-up basis), and proceeds support the conservation work. They may be purchased by calling (877) 448-6539 or visiting hunley.org.

DANIEL ISLAND WATERFRONT PARK & TRAILS, 101 River Landing Dr., Daniel Island; (843) 724-7327; charlestonparksconservancy.org. Among the many green spaces on Daniel Island, this is a favorite one because of its access to the scenic beauty of the Wando River. Walking, biking, and boardwalk trails provide access to the gorgeous vistas. There is a children's park with ample playground equipment. There are benches and picnic tables under the moss-draped live oaks for Mom and Dad to relax while keeping a close eye on the kids' climbing, swinging, and romping. There is no admission charge.

FORT SUMTER NATIONAL MONUMENT, Charleston Harbor; (843) 722-2628, (800) 789-3678, (843) 883-3123 (National Park Service); fortsumtertours.com; $$$. What could be a more awe-inspiring setting and thrilling experience for a young person than arrival by tour boat at Fort Sumter, the fort where the Civil War began? In the middle of Charleston Harbor, Fort Sumter looks much like it did over a century ago and affords an incredible view of the city and surrounding islands. We recommend careful supervision of children, as the fort is surrounded by water, and there are many precarious climbs. The gift shop has an array of interesting items (a kit of historically accurate paper dolls or replica buttons, for example) and Civil War books, and it is air-conditioned—a major plus after a hot day scouring the fort. National Park Service rangers are on-site to answer questions, and there is a museum. Tour boats depart from the National Park Service dock and visitor education facility at Liberty Square next to the South Carolina Aquarium in downtown Charleston and also Patriots Point in Mount Pleasant. Call for schedules and ticket prices; the fort is open year-round. (For more on Fort Sumter, see the Forts section of the Attractions chapter and the Tours chapter.)

HAMPTON PARK, 30 Mary Murray Dr.; (843) 724-7327; charlestonparks conservancy.org. As children, we came to Hampton Park to play around the 60 inner-city acres, so it's a particular treat to experience the park these days with the next generation. Children delight at the same simple pleasures we remember: feeding ducks and geese in the pond, smelling the gorgeous roses, and just frolicking in the wide-open spaces. The parcourse exercise trail is a favorite of older children and adults. The Piccolo Spoleto finale, a Teddy Bear Picnic, and in-line skating night during warm weather are great reasons to plan a Hampton Park visit. The park is free, but keep in mind the midtown location and possible safety concerns if you're venturing to Hampton Park at night.

⭐ **JAMES ISLAND COUNTY PARK,** 871 Riverland Dr.; (843) 795-4386; ccprc.com; $–$$$. This beautiful, 643-acre park offers biking, keowees (junior-size kayaks), skating, fishing or crabbing, a climbing wall, a super playground, and much more. Splash Zone, however, is the James Island park's great water attraction. With two 200-foot tube slides, a 500-foot lazy river is enlivened by a spray-filled, waterfall-peppered "adventure channel." There's a leisure pool perfect for kiddies and a Caribbean play structure with interactive elements. Splash Zone is simply awesome. Showers, concessions, lockers, and restrooms are available. The annual Holiday Festival of Lights will dazzle young and old alike with more than 700 lighting displays on view mid-Nov through New Year's. (See Festivals & Annual Events for more on this festival.) Park hours vary, so call for details. Gate admission is $1 per person (2 years and under are free), but Splash Zone will run you an additional fee. (For more, see the Boating & Water Sports chapter.)

MAGNOLIA PLANTATION AND GARDENS, 3550 Ashley River Rd.; (843) 571-1266, (800) 367-3517; magnoliaplantation.com; $$$–$$$$. While the horticultural maze and antebellum cabin (an original, dating back to around 1840) are first stops for the little ones, the petting zoo with African pygmy goats, deer, and other friendly animals is the real calling card for toddlers and elementary school kids visiting Magnolia. They can buy handfuls of grain to feed the gentle creatures but should expect an occasional nibble on the posterior from a pushy goat or two. Older children can rent canoes or bikes (or you can bring your own), and everyone enjoys the 45-minute, 4-mile tram ride through the property. Leashed pets are welcome too. Magnolia is open 365 days a year from 8 a.m. to 5:30 p.m. (Winter hours may vary slightly.) A basic admission price is charged, with additional fees for the Plantation House, Nature Train/Boat, Slavery to Freedom tours, and Audubon Swamp. Kids under 6 are admitted free. (See the Attractions chapter for more on Magnolia Plantation and Gardens.)

MIDDLETON PLACE, 4300 Ashley River Rd.; (843) 556-6020, (800) 782-3608; middletonplace.org; $$$–$$$$. In addition to being lots of fun for the kids, the incredible beauty of the gardens and forest trails of Middleton Place tends to leave parents lingering, trying to drag out the good times a little bit longer. A shady picnic area near the greensward is a delightful place to enjoy the vistas. And here's the chance for everyone to milk a cow, card wool, or grind corn. Middleton is a working plantation. Free-range farm animals mill about, and craftspeople are hard at work so that visitors can observe or even take part in the reenactment of history. Plantation Days and Family Yuletide are fun, educational events on one Sat in Nov and one in Dec when demonstrations of plantation harvesting, candle dipping, syrup making, shepherding, and more take place (see the Festivals & Annual Events chapter). Gates are open daily from 9 a.m. until 5 p.m. Middleton Place is open year-round. Children younger than 6 are admitted free. An additional $15 is charged for the house

Middleton Place Plantation

tour, and a carriage tour is offered for $18. (For more on Middleton Place, see the Plantations & Gardens section of the Attractions chapter.)

PALMETTO ISLANDS COUNTY PARK, 444 Needlerush Pkwy., Mount Pleasant; (843) 884-0832; ccprc.com; $–$$. This nature-oriented park is on more than 900 acres of typical Lowcountry terrain and features a mile-long wilderness trail along a boardwalk through the marsh. Little children enjoy playing at the Big Toy, a play area with lots of wooden equipment such as towers, slides, and swings; their older siblings enjoy the tunnel, slide, and view associated with the observation tower. Pedal boats and canoes are for rent, and many visitors enjoy exploring on bicycles—rent one or bring your own. Splash Island is the hot attraction here for warm-weather patrons. A 200-foot slide, a 16-foot otter slide (no otters, just a fun name), sprays, waterfalls, geysers, and a delightful sand play area await. In addition to the park admission of $1 per person, there are fees for Splash Island with a small break for Charleston County residents. Hours vary by season, so call or visit the website for specifics. (See the Boating & Water Sports chapter for more information on this park.) Plan to bring swimsuits, but leave the coolers at home for your day at Splash Island. Proper swimming attire is required, and no outside food or beverages are allowed.

SULLIVAN'S ISLAND PARK, 1610 Middle St. (Station 21 and Middle Street), Sullivan's Island; (843) 883-3198; sullivansisland-sc.com. Involved parents and other residents of Sullivan's Island have worked hard to make this park the little gem that it is. With two sections of play equipment, lots of wooden things to crawl in and on, and sliding-friendly apparatuses, children are fairly contained and easily occupied. There is even a fence around one area for additional safety for younger children. The man-made mound, leftover from World War II, was built as a mortar battery to store ammunition. It is referred to by locals as "The Hill" and is the place to go if your kids are into sliding. Dress appropriately, bring a big piece of cardboard and your steady nerves, then climb to the top and slide down . . . over and over and over again. At least, that's the way it works with kids. While this is the same good, clean fun we had here as children, be forewarned that there is danger in the shape of a huge pit in the mound's center that is not particularly well marked. Keep children away from the edges, and also avoid letting the kids make solo treks into the bamboo groves or other isolated areas. Although Sullivan's is an island of good neighborhoods, there is safety in numbers where children are concerned. There is no admission charge.

★ **WATERFRONT PARK,** 1 Vendue, Cumberland Street to North Adgers Wharf; (843) 724-7327; charlestonparksconservancy.org. Just off East Bay Street in downtown Charleston, the lovely Waterfront Park is another nice picnic and cool-your-heels spot. Sea breezes keep the tables under the covered pier area perfect for just these pursuits. Children have fun splashing around in the pineapple-shaped fountain or getting soaked in the circular spray fountain. We've seen pictures of half a kindergarten class in one of the large swings that line the pier, a 400-foot extension into Charleston Harbor. No admission is charged.

WHITE POINT GARDEN AT THE BATTERY, 2 Murray Dr., South tip of East Bay and King Streets; (843) 724-7327; charlestonparksconservancy .org. Frisbee throwers and cannon climbers love White Point Garden. Children can run free beneath the canopy of trees and pretend to lift the immensely heavy and immovable cannonballs. Lots of photo ops here! There is usually a pleasant breeze off the water (the harbor circles around the point), and this open space is a much-loved haven of respite in the city. We used to search through the oyster-shell fill along the walks to find ancient shark teeth or other treasures. Don't expect any more luck than we had decades ago, but do plan to enjoy the leisurely pace of an old-fashioned park. Of course, no admission is charged. (For more info, see the History and Attractions chapters.)

KID-FRIENDLY BEACHES

Though there are many great beach destinations in a coastal area like this one, one of our favorite swimming areas for children is on Folly Beach at the Folly Beach County Park, (843) 588-2426. Unlike some other area beaches, this one has its own parking, lifeguards, and facilities. Take a right off Folly Road onto Center Street, and follow it to its end. Young surfers will want to head for the midsection of the island, where waves are best. Admission is $7 a car ($10 Sat and Sun May through Labor Day).

Kiawah, most of which is a private resort community, does offer public access at Beachwalker Park, (843) 768-2395, on the west end. Lifeguards, parking, restrooms, and equipment rentals are available from May through Sept. Turn just before the gates to Kiawah to find the park. The ocean frontage is somewhat off-the-beaten-path, thus allowing for 11 miles of unspoiled sand and surf. A $7 fee is required per car ($10 Sat and Sun May through Labor Day).

We can cautiously recommend the beaches on Sullivan's Island and the Isle of Palms, but urge parents to keep several general cautions in mind before you send the children skipping to the surf. Note that strong, tricky currents are prevalent at each end of Sullivan's Island as well as the south end of the Isle of Palms. Convenient parking can be tough to find on both islands, but the Isle of Palms County Park, (843) 886-3863, located mid-island, offers lots of parking and lifeguards on duty during the summer months for a $7 per car entrance fee ($10 Sat and Sun May through Labor Day). Walk-ins and bicycles are admitted at the three beach parks at no charge. Showers and picnic areas are other nice amenities at each of these beach parks.

CULTURAL FUN

★ THE CHARLESTON MUSEUM, 360 Meeting St.; (843) 722-2996; charlestonmuseum.org; $$. In addition to being the oldest history, art, and science museum in the country (founded in 1773), the Charleston Museum is one of the best resources for children in the city. We love to try to keep pace with the kids as they scamper through the modern complex (the facility is well designed and very kid-older-than-4-friendly). There are special kids' tours and interesting programs throughout the year—such as "Mad Science Saturdays," "Charleston Critters," and "Historic Crafts"—that usually last one afternoon session and are included in admission. We've found that starting off on a rainy day in the Kidstory room, with its "touch-me" exhibits, is the best way for little ones to unwind and connect with the museum. The museum is across the street from the visitor center. It is open 9 a.m. to 5 p.m. Mon through Sat and 1 to 5 p.m. on Sun but closed on major holidays. Free parking is available in a small lot behind the museum off John Street. (For more information, see the Attractions chapter.)

CHARLESTON STAGE COMPANY THEATRE SCHOOL, 629 Johnnie Dodds Blvd., Mount Pleasant; (843) 856-3822; charlestonstage.com. "All the world's a stage" . . . and maybe your youngster would like a chance to learn more about it. Charleston Stage is a prime creative outlet for that dramatist in the family. The Theatre School offers a variety of acting and theatre education opportunities for children in grades K–12. The program introduces theatrical skills in classes designed to enhance acting skills, bolster self-confidence, and encourage self-expression. Advanced students may participate in Performance Troupe, the performing troupe for middle school students, and TheatreWings, the apprentice program for high school students. The Theatre School students are encouraged also to audition for roles in the Charleston Stage's MainStage and Family Series productions each season. Classes are offered year-round in 2-week summer sessions to weekly afternoon classes throughout the school year at the rehearsal studios at The Plaza at East Cooper in Mount Pleasant.

CHILDREN'S MUSEUM OF THE LOWCOUNTRY, 25 Ann St.; (843) 853-8962; explorecml.org; $$. The newest museum on the scene with a focus on kids is the Children's Museum of the Lowcountry. Located near the visitor center in the Camden Tower Sheds, this popular concept is to inspire a love of learning in children through interactive, interdisciplinary, hands-on environments and experiences in the arts, sciences, and humanities. The fun exhibits include climbing a tower in the Castle, sliding into the art room, painting on a mural wall, playing with water in WaterWise, exploring an antique fire truck, and searching for buried treasure about the CML Pirate Ship. This immersion environment for children and their families leads to creative thinking, problem-solving skills, and confidence. Who knows what a visit here may spark? Children under age 1 are admitted free. Hours are Tues through Sat 9 a.m. to 5 p.m. and Sun noon to 5 p.m.

GIBBES MUSEUM OF ART, 135 Meeting St.; (843) 722-2706; gibbes museum.org; $$. The Gibbes is a source of pride for many Charlestonians. Not only are the collections impressive, but the facility itself and the enthusiasm of the membership also spark creativity in the young and old alike. Studio art classes at the Gibbes are very popular with Charleston children. From drawing to working with clay to watercolor art or photography, the offerings appeal to many levels of artistic interest and skill. Classes cost between $40 and $180. A variety of special events and activities are held for children throughout the year, so call for a calendar with all the details. With exhibits ranging from the contemporary to the abstract, a simple visit to the museum any time can be a visual thrill. Hours are 10 a.m. to 5 p.m. Tues through Sat and 1 to 5 p.m. on Sun. The museum is closed Mon. Annual family memberships are $100, and they include a 10 percent discount on museum shop purchases and classes. (For more on the Gibbes, see the Attractions chapter.)

OLD EXCHANGE AND PROVOST DUNGEON, 122 East Bay St. (at Broad Street); (843) 727-2165, (888) 763-0448; oldexchange.org; $$. Make history really come to life for your child. The period-costumed docents at the Old Exchange and Provost Dungeon tell the stories of the extraordinary events of Old Charles Towne at this site, including the imprisonment of the notorious pirate, Stede Bonnet, seizure and storage of British tea, ratification of the US Constitution, and George Washington's visit. Animatronic storytellers in the Provost Dungeon entertain all ages with wonderful tales of pirates and patriots

The Old Exchange and Provost Dungeon was built between 1769 and 1772.

held captive within these eerie confines. Remnants of the 1698 fortification wall surrounding Charles Towne are here too. The Old Exchange is open daily from 9 a.m. to 5 p.m. Children 6 and under are admitted free. (For more about the Old Exchange and Provost Dungeon, see the Attractions chapter.)

> **i** For even more ideas about things to do with kids while in Charleston, visit the Charleston Area Convention and Vistors Bureau website dedicated to family fun. It's charlestonfamilyfun.com and has categories for attractions, tours, beaches, recreation, and dining—many arranged by areas of town. It even has money-saving coupons from lots of the area sights and restaurants to get you started on your way to a memorable family vacation.

INDOOR FUN & GAMES

CAROLINA ICE PALACE, 7665 Northwoods Blvd., North Charleston; (843) 572-2717; carolinaicepalace.com; $$. Charleston's coolest place for family fun is the Carolina Ice Palace with 2 NHL-size ice rinks for recreational skating, instruction, hockey teams and leagues, and birthday parties. Open 7 days a week for you to perfect that double axel, the Ice Palace has hours designated for public skating, after-school skating, and Family Night specials. Other on-site attractions are the video arcade, virtual reality center, and giant pro shop for skate rental and sharpening. Burgers and pizza can take care of the hungries, and a lounge with satellite TV provides a little relaxation while watching your future Olympic star. Call the number listed for a seasonal schedule of times and fees. Of course, birthday parties are a popular option here for ages 3 to 18. Skating and hockey classes, conducted by professional instructors, are available on a group or individual basis.

CHARLESTON COUNTY LIBRARY STORYTIMES, 68 Calhoun St.; (843) 805-6930; ccpl.org. "Tell me a story, please." Charleston County Libraries have the answer. They offer a series of storytimes for young children ages 12 months to 5 years old. "Wee Reads" is a 20-minute weekly morning program for ages 12 to 24 months. "Time for Twos" is another weekly morning program lasting 30 minutes for ages 24 to 36 months. All toddlers must be accompanied by a parent or caregiver. There is a preschool storytime for ages 3 to 5 that includes 30 minutes of interactive storytelling, sometimes with videos and crafts. Family Storytime welcomes all ages. Call the number above or your branch library to register.

FRANKIE'S FUN PARK, 5000 Ashley Phosphate Rd., North Charleston; (843) 767-1376; frankiesfunpark.com; $–$$$$. This is Charleston's answer to the kiddies' cry for an amusement park. Children can spend money on a variety of activities—from bumper boats and a batting cage to go-karts and fun slides. A rock-climbing wall offers another challenge. Three miniature golf courses and a lighted, 90-position driving range offer a slower-paced experience. There is no general admission, but park activities cost between $2 and $10 each. A family with two kids can expect to spend $20 to $30 at Frankie's if Mom and Dad don't participate; it'll likely be $40 or more if everyone joins in. There are picnic tables, a snack bar, and clean restrooms. Frankie's is open daily but hours vary seasonally. It's closed on Thanksgiving, Christmas Eve, Christmas, and New Year's Day.

⭐ **SOUTH CAROLINA AQUARIUM,** 100 Aquarium Wharf (near Calhoun and Concord Streets); (843) 577-FISH (3474), (800) 722-6455; scaquarium.org; $$$$. The South Carolina Aquarium is located at the edge of historic Charleston Harbor. Two-thirds of the building projects over the water, and multiple decks complete the views of the Cooper River, both the bustling activity of the shipping industry and the serene natural landscape. The 93,000-square-foot facility displays more than 60 exhibits featuring otters, birds, turtles, fish, reptiles, aquatic invertebrates, and insects from the diverse habitats here in South Carolina. Visitors will experience five major regions of the Southeast Watershed of South Carolina: the Mountain Forest, the Piedmont, the Coastal Plain, the Coast, and the Ocean. Their education master plan encompasses interactive displays, special toddler exhibits, an education center, a discovery lab, and several education stations. "Mini-gascar" within the "Madagascar Journey" exhibit is a dedicated space just for toddlers, and the touch tank is a hit with all ages. The

> **i** If you need a stroller when in town, just call at least 24 hours ahead to Tots Around Town, (843) 442-3118, to rent one. For a complete list of the baby equipment available for rent, visit totsaround town.com.

KIDS

4-D Theater incorporates special sensory effects such as wind gusts, seat vibrations, and water spray. As a part of their sea turtle rescue program, sea turtle hospital tours are a chance to see the current patients and the care provided to them. These populars tours are offered at noon and 2 p.m. daily for an additional fee. Open daily, hours are generally 9 a.m. to 5 p.m. The aquarium is closed Thanksgiving and Christmas Day and a half day on Christmas Eve. (See the Attractions chapter for more on the South Carolina Aquarium.)

DAY CAMPS

Many community centers, schools, and churches operate day camps around the Trident. Extended-day programs are available for many working parents and run from the end of the school day until 6 or 6:30 p.m. at most schools and centers. Like camps, some offer enrichment courses such as karate, piano, foreign language study, drama, and arts and crafts.

CHARLESTON COUNTY AFTER SCHOOL, Charleston County Community Education Program; 75 Calhoun St.; (843) 937-7910; charlestoncoce .org. Working parents of school-age children will be glad to take advantage of the extended-day programs available in many of the local public elementary and middle schools. These programs provide a safe, supervised, and educational environment at your child's own school. This affordable after-school alternative offers organized activities, snacks, and time to complete homework assignments, and many have a selection of enrichment courses. The average cost is $55 a week, but it varies by school and activity. The following community school directors' offices can provide additional information: Downtown, (843) 579-4828; Mount Pleasant, (843) 881-8272; North Charleston, (843) 529-3926 or (843) 746-6372; James Island, (843) 762-2793; Johns Island, (843) 559-6208; West Ashley, (843) 573-1212; McClellanville, (843) 577-0970; Hollywood, (843) 889-6852. Charleston County Community Education also offers summer day camps with arts and crafts, reading, science, field trips, and sports.

SUMMER CAMPS

It has an all-too-familiar ring: "Mom, Dad, I'm bored."

Once school is out, you better have a plan to keep the kids occupied and happy on those never-ending, lazy summer days. Fortunately, several of the recreation departments, county parks, private schools, arts organizations, churches, and scout groups around the Trident area offer a plethora of summer day-camp adventures. Lots of fun stuff is organized to pique your child's interest in something new or improve skills in a favorite pastime. A brief sampling of some of the day camps with a mix of activities are listed below, plus a few sports- and arts-oriented camps. Prices may vary slightly.

> **i** Three hundred thousand and counting: That's the number of kids who have enjoyed a unique overnight camping experience aboard the aircraft carrier USS *Yorktown* at Patriots Point in Mount Pleasant. Campers (in groups of at least 10 plus a chaperone) sleep in the bunks once occupied by the crew, dine in the ship's galley, and hop in the cockpit of a real fighter jet. Fun-filled excursions are an option, too. Call (800) 248-3508, or visit patriotspoint.org for more information.

THE CITADEL BASKETBALL CAMP, McAlister Field House, The Citadel, 17 Moultrie St.; (843) 953-5070, (843) 606-2737; driesellbball.com, citadelsports.com. Citadel head basketball coach Chuck Driesell serves as camp director of this popular basketball program for boys and girls ages 7 to 16. The staff includes Citadel basketball coaches, area high school coaches, and collegiate players. The instruction takes place in McAlister Field House, where the big Bulldogs play their college games, and also at Porter-Gaud school in West Ashley. The 1-week sessions run from 9 a.m. to 4 p.m. on Mon through Thur and 9 a.m. to noon Fri. Fees are $200 for the week. The Citadel also offers baseball, soccer, football, track & field, volleyball, and wrestling camps. Contact the school's athletic department for more information.

CITY OF CHARLESTON JUNIOR TENNIS SUMMER CAMP, Maybank Tennis Center, 1880 Houghton Dr.; (843) 406-8814; charleston-sc.gov/recreation. The city's Junior Tennis Summer Camp has an excellent program for your budding tennis enthusiast. The camp is for beginners to advanced intermediate students ages 4 to 18. It meets from 9 a.m. to noon Mon through Fri. Daily instruction includes working on fundamental strokes, video analysis, and personal attention. Games and prizes add to the positive, fun environment. Fees are $100 per week. This camp is also offered at the Charleston Tennis Center at 19 Farmfield Avenue, (843) 769-8258. The City of Charleston offers many more summer camps with a range of activities from athletics to crafts. Visit the website for more details.

CREATIVE SPARK, 757 Long Point Rd., Mount Pleasant; (843) 881-3780; creativespark.org. Let your child's creativity and imagination be sparked. Creative Spark Center for the Arts presents a wonderful variety of summer camps in the performing and visual arts to do just that. Art, an improvisational drama workshop, and musical theater camps, along with creative writing, dance, and private music instruction, are among the choices for ages 4 and older. Call the above number for a complete brochure with details on sessions and fees. Birthday parties with an art, music, or dance theme are fun options here. A cake, favors, activities, supervision, and cleanup are provided for up to 12 for $275 on Saturday.

STONO RIVER RIDING ACADEMY SUMMER RIDING CAMP, 2962 Hut Rd. (at 3000 River Rd.), Johns Island; (843) 559-0773. Learn about the splendor of the horse! Stono River Riding Academy is the equestrian facility at the former Stono River Stable. It provides professional instruction under the direction of Michelle Folden who has an extensive background in training and competing on the national level. The emphasis here is on safety and fun. One-week sessions are offered throughout the summer months for ages 5 to 16. The classes last from 9 a.m. to 1 p.m. daily and cover grooming and tacking up, riding lessons, and horse care. The last hour changes each day from bareback riding to games on horseback to trail rides and more. Classes are limited to 12 students per day and the 1-week fee is $375.

SUMMER ART CAMP, Gibbes Museum of Art, 135 Meeting St.; (843) 722-2706, ext. 41; gibbesmuseum.org. Hands-on art and imaginary travels await your 4- to 7-year-old or 8- to 12-year-old at the Summer Art Camp held at the Circular Congregational Church directly across from the Gibbes. Each of the three 1-week sessions encourages creativity, helps develop fine motor skills, and builds confidence. The Summer Art Camp focuses on art-inspired adventures through different eras and cultures. Past offerings have included "Modern Art of the Gibbes Museum," where students learn to paint in an abstract style or make collages inspired by works in the Gibbes collection and "Charleston and the Sea" using the visual arts and history to create landscape or nautical paintings. The Summer Art Camps meet Mon through Fri from 9 a.m. to noon. Tuition is $175 per week for Gibbes members, $200 a week for nonmembers. (See the Attractions chapter for more about the Gibbes Museum of Art.)

SUMMER FUN ON THE ISLAND DAY CAMP, James Island Recreation Complex, 1088 Quail Dr.; (843) 795-5678; charleston-sc.gov. Sponsored by the City of Charleston Department of Recreation, Summer Fun on the Island is a camp for youths between the ages of 6 and 12 years old. Mon through Fri from 7 a.m. to 6 p.m., campers are engaged in arts and crafts, swimming, storytelling, movies, music, aerobics, and sports divided by age groups. Once a week, campers venture out on field trips to great spots such as James Island and Folly Beach County Parks, Middleton Place, Riverbanks Zoo, and Splash Zone. Four sessions are offered from June to Aug, with fees for city residents set at $150 per 2-week session. Nonresidents of the city pay $175 per 2-week session. The City of Charleston offers many other summer camps at area parks, playgrounds, and community centers around the city. Visit the website for more details.

SUMMER PROGRAMS AT ASHLEY HALL, Ashley Hall, 172 Rutledge Ave.; (843) 965-8452, (843) 722-4088; ashleyhall.org. Ashley Hall's campus provides a perfect in-town setting for summer programs designed to entertain, educate, and challenge your children (girls only except the co-ed Early Childhood Summer Program for ages 3 to 6). Day camps, athletics, enrichment adventures, and academic skills let you sign 'em up for a variety of sessions throughout those long summer months. The day camps keep campers on the go with tennis, gymnastics, group games, and arts and crafts. Athletic challenges sap some of that boundless energy with archery, basketball, volleyball, lacrosse, and swimming. The enrichment adventures allow students to explore and develop new interests in areas such as guitar and piano lessons, jewelry making, fiction writing, and French. Computer skills and study and reading skills workshops are some of the academic offerings. Contact the school for a complete brochure outlining sessions and fees.

Golf

Greater Charleston can take justifiable pride in the variety of golf challenges available to the area's visitors and residents.

If you're a serious tournament player with world-class experience, or if you're just one of those relatively harmless twice-a-year duffers, Charleston has you well covered when it comes to golf. After all, this is the site of America's very first golf course—among the city's many claims to fame. The actual site of the first course, laid out in 1786 and known as "Harleston Green," has long ago been overtaken by subsequent urbanization, but golf is always proudly mentioned when the list of Charleston's "famous firsts" comes up.

Today, Lowcountry golf is a wealth of opportunity. From the world-ranked resort courses to the ever-popular public tracks, from the private courses to the semiprivate offerings, it's possible to golf every day for nearly a month and play a different 18-hole course each day.

Clearly, the great drawing card for Lowcountry golf is the weather. Here the winter chill hardly ever discourages the stouthearted player, and the summer's sweltering heat only adds another challenge to the dedicated would-be pro. Indeed, for the vast majority of the year, Charleston area golf courses sing the siren's call to golfers from (literally) all over the world.

We'll start with some of the famous designer names that are associated with Lowcountry golf courses. Then, we'll take you on a brief tour of some of our infamous signature holes, where even the best players are tested to make birdie.

We'll give you a tour of the area's public courses, and then go out to the island resorts where an array of designer courses await the serious golfer determined to be tested by the very best.

BETTER BY DESIGN

Every area course is different in some way. Each has its own charm and individual characteristics, not to mention frustrations. That, in part, may be because most of the world's best golf architects have designed courses here in the Lowcountry. You'll find the work of Pete Dye, Tom Fazio, Arthur Hills, Jack Nicklaus, Gary Player, Arnold Palmer, Robert Trent Jones Sr., and Rees Jones, among them.

Pete Dye's name is one of the biggest in the industry. His most famous courses include Harbour Town on Hilton Head Island and the Stadium Course at PGA West in La Quinta, California. A more recent Dye offering is the Ocean Course at Kiawah Island, which hosted the 1991 Ryder Cup matches, the prestigious World Cup of Golf in 1997, UBS Warburg Cup 2001, the 2003 World Golf Championships World Cup, plus the 2007 Senior PGA Championship. The most recent major event at the Ocean Course was the PGA Championship in 2012.

The Ocean Course rivals Tom Fazio's Lowcountry masterpiece, the Links Course at Wild Dunes Resort, which is ranked among the world's best by *Golf* magazine. Fazio's golf courses are possibly the best known here in the Lowcountry, because he designed both courses on Wild Dunes (the Links and Harbor Course), and he also laid out Kiawah's popular Osprey Point.

Whereas Pete Dye frequently uses railroad ties (a signature of his work), Arthur Hills prefers to use more of a site's natural elements in his designs. Hills did the newest course at Dunes West, which opened in 1991 and showcased the 1992 Amoco Centel Championship. Hills's other famous golf course designs include Eagle Trace, a TPC course in Coral Springs, Florida, cited in *Golf Digest*'s "100 Best Courses in America."

Another name to note among the Charleston area's most popular golf designers is Willard Byrd, who gave us Patriots Point in Mount Pleasant back in 1981. He's also responsible for the Ocean Winds course on Seabrook Island.

Dr. Michael Hurdzan is another of the "name" designers to provide Charleston-area golfers with a challenge to their skills. His contribution is the 27-hole Golf Club at Wescott Plantation in North Charleston. Dr. Hurdzan's design allows players to enjoy the natural elements on the course and "play in various directions and lengths" around them.

And Arnold Palmer's signature course at RiverTowne Country Club in Mount Pleasant is drawing plenty of accolades with its 5 sets of tees, multi-tiered greens, and spectacular views.

SIGNATURE HOLES

Here's a sampling of the flavor of Lowcountry golf—a few of the area signature holes you'll want to be prepared for.

Patriots Point has its famous No. 17, a par 3, 112-yard island green that catches the uninitiated off-guard. This hole requires the player to take into careful consideration the ever-changing winds off Charleston Harbor.

The No. 6 hole at Fairfield Ocean Ridge is another island hole that can be a spoiler. It's a tough 380-yard, par 4 challenge.

Crowfield Plantation offers its par 5, 500-yard No. 7 hole that features treacherous mounds that make players feel as if they've found a bit of old Scotland.

Rees Jones's Charleston National design, which opened in 1990, features the demanding No. 15 hole, a par 3, 183-yarder from the white tees. It plays 210 yards from the blue tees and has an innocent-looking pond on the right that attracts errant balls like a magnet.

On the Links Course at Wild Dunes, No. 9 is said to be the most difficult. It is a long, straight 451-yard par 4 that often plays even longer, because it is usually played into the wind. The green is closely guarded on the left by a hidden pond. This green is also the most unforgiving on the course—it slopes severely from back to front. All things considered, a par on No. 9 is an excellent score.

The signature hole at Kiawah's Turtle Point is No. 11. There's water along the entire right side from the tee past the green. According to Jack Nicklaus, its designer, "You can drive the ball as far as you want, but the farther you drive it, the greater the chance of slicing it into the water. There is a secondary landing area, or an out where those who won't want to chance it can play the shot. Then putt it or chip it or, as the Scots say, 'play a bumble' back into the green."

SCENERY

Pete Dye's Ocean Course on Kiawah and Tom Fazio's Links Course at Wild Dunes both make spectacular use of the Atlantic Ocean in their designs. Fazio's Harbor Course on Wild Dunes uses the Intracoastal Waterway as a backdrop. The Links at Stono Ferry, designed by Ron Garl in 1989, is another opportunity to play along the colorful and busy Intracoastal. But most of the Lowcountry's golf courses take full advantage of the beautiful salt marshes, signature of the area itself, in their layout designs. Gary Player's redesigned Cougar Point on Kiawah is probably the best example. A curious alligator has even been known to occasionally wander onto the course.

In fact, the area's multiple charms make the Lowcountry a favorite destination for golf widows and widowers and the assorted family members who often get swept up in a spouse's or parent's pursuit of the sport. The rationalization usually goes something like this: While golfers are challenged to play the many private, semiprivate, and public courses throughout the area, the unenlightened can always explore the beautiful Lowcountry plantations, the splendid museums, the beaches, and the interesting shops, thus staying contented and amused.

GOLF

That brings up another benefit of Charleston area golf: Because there are so many other things to do here, the area courses are relatively uncrowded. That means excellent starting times and an unhurried atmosphere.

Here we provide brief profiles of the area courses, so tee up when it suits you, and play at least 18 relaxing and scenic Lowcountry holes. You'll find descriptions of who designed the courses and when, plus who can play them, how much it costs (during high season), and where to call for more details. Greens fees quoted are in-season rates including carts (unless otherwise noted) and exclude tax.

CHARLESTON AREA GOLF COURSES

CHARLESTON NATIONAL COUNTRY CLUB, 1360 National Dr., US 17 N., Mount Pleasant; (843) 884-4653; charlestonnationalgolf.com. The idea for Charleston National Country Club was conceived more than 20 years ago, but the once-private golf community was just coming into focus when Hugo struck in 1989. Redesigned and refurbished with input from original designer Rees Jones, the par 72, 18-hole course (now semiprivate) is 7,084 yards long. Charleston National has a beautiful 8,000-square-foot clubhouse with luxury amenities including a pool and tennis center. Charleston National's pro is Chase Wells. Greens fees range from $29 to $63.

CITY OF CHARLESTON GOLF COURSE, 2110 Maybank Hwy.; (843) 795-6517; sc-charleston.civicplus.com. This public course, only 5 minutes from downtown Charleston, has been around since 1929. Although it lost some 350 mature trees in Hugo's wrath, the course was beautifully replanted and is now in very good shape. The par 72 course is 6,432 yards long from the blue tees; it's 5,200 and par 72 from the forward tees. You'll find small greens, well-tended fairways, and an on-site pro shop with a snack bar. PGA- and LPGA-trained instructors are on hand for lessons, and this is the only public course in South Carolina with a Slazenger club-fitting system available for beginners and experts alike. Individual greens fees are $22 (for walkers). The rate goes up to $24 on weekends. Add $15 per person for a golf cart. Charleston residents get a $7 discount on greens fees. Call about a week in advance for tee times.

THE CLUB AT PINE FOREST, 1000 Congressional Blvd., Summerville; (843) 851-1193; pineforestcountryclub.com. The 18 holes at The Club at Pine Forest in Dorchester County wind through the tall Summerville pines with some live oaks, dogwoods, and a lake system thrown in for good measure. Designed by architect Bob Spence in 1992, Pine Forest is noted for their well-kept golf challenges. It is one of the most talked-about USGA courses in the Lowcountry. The course is 6,905 yards long from the championship tees, with an equal representation of straightaways, doglegs, and elevation changes. It is nicely balanced, with fun in store for golfers of all abilities. Rental clubs and carts are available. The head pro is Marty Mikesell. Call for reservations. Greens fees vary by season, but weekdays are about $30. Sat and Sun fees are $40.

COOSAW CREEK COUNTRY CLUB, 4110 Club Course Dr., North Charleston; (843) 767-8988; coosawcreek.com. Coosaw Creek, a 645-acre residential community in North Charleston, offers an Arthur Hills course designed in 1993. The par 71 semiprivate course is 6,593 yards long from the middle tees. The bonus here is on accuracy instead of length; good tee shots, as well as a deft short game, are the keys to low scoring. Hills had more natural topography to work with at Coosaw Creek than most Lowcountry lay-outs offer. You'll find rolling fairways, subtle mounding, and gradual elevation changes. The best opportunity to score low is on the front nine, as the back side brings more of the water and wetlands into play. Mike Benner is the pro on hand. In-season, weekday greens fees are $65, Sat and Sun fees are $70, taxes included. South Carolina residents pay less.

CROWFIELD GOLF PLANTATION, 300 Hamlet Circle, Goose Creek; (843) 764-4618; crowfieldgolf.com. Crowfield Golf Plantation offers championship golfing on a semiprivate course designed in 1990 by Tom Jackson and Bob Spence. Their par 72, 18-hole layout is 6,590 yards long. The course is slightly Scottish in that it has a rolling terrain accompanied by acres of fairway and green-side bunkers. Shooting ability is of prime importance here. Undulating greens and imaginative pin placements test the nerves of the most skilled players. Crowfield's pro shop is well stocked, and there's a restaurant and cocktail lounge on-site. Breakfast, lunch, or dinner may be ordered from the menu. Call pro Rob Brock for lesson details. Tee times are accepted up to 1 week in advance. Mon through Fri greens fees are $41 before noon and $31 after noon; Sat through Sun fees are $46 before noon and $36 after noon. Seniors, military, and juniors receive discounts.

DUNES WEST GOLF & RIVER CLUB, 3535 Wando Plantation Way, Mount Pleasant; (843) 856-9000; duneswestgolfclub.com. Ten miles northeast of Charleston in the fast-growing East Cooper area, Dunes West is part of a 4,700-acre residential community that's been in development since the late 1980s. The highly rated course—set on a high, marshy peninsula bounded by three tidal creeks—was designed by Arthur Hills on the site of the historic Lexington Plantation house. Like its sister course on Isle of Palms, Dunes West takes full advantage of its natural setting. The par 72 championship course is 6,871 yards long. The opening holes, cut from tall pines, have fairway corridors leading to elevated and bunkered greens. The back nine has a typical Lowcountry flavor with moss-draped oaks lining the fairways and expansive views of the marsh from several of the tees and greens. There's a handsome clubhouse with every modern luxury amenity. The pro is Kevin Zemnickas. The Hills course at Dunes West was the site of the 1992 Amoco Centel Championship, and it is now a semiprivate course. High season greens fees Mon through Thurs range from $50 to $80; Fri through Sun, they are $50 to $96.

THE GOLF CLUB AT WESCOTT PLANTATION, 5000 Wescott Club Dr., North Charleston; (843) 871-2135, (866) 211-GOLF; wescottgolf.com. Opened in the fall of 2000 with the full 27 holes up and ready for play early the following year, the Club at Wescott Plantation is North Charleston's worthy answer to the trendy designer courses on the resort islands closer to the coast. Designed by Dr. Michael Hurdzan, who took full advantage of the natural elements on the course, all 27 holes are tree-lined with plenty of definition to each hole. Each hole has 5 tees so golfers can choose tees from 5,018 yards up to 7,200 yards—depending on their ability. The course winds through streams, ponds, wetlands, and key sentinel trees, with holes playing in various directions and lengths from these features. The club also features a full driving range,

GOLF

a completely outfitted pro shop, a full-service restaurant, and meeting/conference spaces. Steve Rudd is the head pro. Weekdays (except holidays), Tri-County resident fees are $40, weekend fees are $47. Nonresident fees are $89. Prices are $25 during twilight hours.

LEGEND OAKS PLANTATION, 118 Legend Oaks Way, Summerville; (843) 821-4077, (888) 821-4077; legendoaksgolf.com. Located about 30 minutes from Charleston along scenic SR 61 is Legend Oaks Plantation, a traditional-style golf layout on the site of an old rice plantation. A romantic avenue of 250-year-old live oaks leads to the Clubhouse, which is reminiscent of Augusta National. The par 72 course was designed by Scott W. Pool, an associate of Pete Dye, and savvy players say it's akin to Pinehurst No. 2 with its presentation of challenges described as being "straightforward." Spacious fairways, generous greens, and staggered tees give everyone a chance to enjoy the game, but water comes into play at half the holes, and huge live oaks stand between the golfer and the green. An ability to work the ball is required to score well here. From the blue tees, the course is 6,209 yards—a near-perfect test for the average bogey shooter. Joey Bradley is head pro, and greens fees are around $55 on weekdays and $65 on weekends with discounts for Tri-County residents.

THE LINKS AT STONO FERRY, 4812 Stono Links Dr., Hollywood; (843) 763-1817, (888) 785-1813; stonoferrygolf.com. This 18-hole, par 72 course is on SR 162, off US SR 17 S. near the little town of Hollywood, about 15 miles or a half hour from Charleston. The Links opened in 1989 and was designed by Ron Garl to accompany the exclusive Stono Ferry Plantation development. In 2003 the course was upgraded with all-new greens of championship Bermuda grass—adding luster to the Stono challenge. The course is 6,756 yards long and open to the public 7 days a week. It has three scenic holes on the Intracoastal Waterway, and it is a fair test from the back tees. You'll find a complete pro shop and a driving range, plus a full-service restaurant. Head pro Patrick Brown is on hand for tips and lessons. Rental clubs are available. Advance registration is required. Greens fees range from $77 to $89. Rates may vary in season.

PATRIOTS POINT GOLF LINKS, One Patriots Point Rd. (off US 17 Business), Mount Pleasant; (843) 881-0042; patriotspointlinks.com. This 18-hole public course is across the Cooper River Bridge in Mount Pleasant, just off US 17 N., near the towering USS *Yorktown,* anchored in Charleston Harbor. (See the Attractions chapter.) The par 72 layout, open since 1980, has had a $2.1 million upgrade with a new state-of-the-art irrigation system installed. Patriots Point affords spectacular views of the harbor, with oceangoing cargo ships frequently passing by. The course is 7,000 yards in length, with well-contoured fairways and well-bunkered greens. PGA teaching pro Brandon Ray is on hand for lessons and more information. Amenities include a complete pro shop, a driving range, rental clubs and carts. A grill and snack bar are available, too. Call ahead for tee times. Greens fees vary by season but range from $65 to $85.

THE PLANTATION COURSE AT EDISTO, 19 Fairway Dr., Edisto Beach; (843) 869-1111; theplantationcourseatedisto.com. This 18-hole championship layout, designed by Tom Jackson in 1976, was renovated and reopened in October 2006. The 6,130-yard, par 70 course features water holes, dense subtropical vegetation, and (for early risers) frequent visits by native wildlife. The Plantation Course has its share of old bull gators, but local wisdom says they prefer sunning and running to fighting. The course has dune ridges throughout. Where the Nos. 2 and 3 tees are now situated was once a Confederate stronghold. The overall feel of the course is natural, as it was primarily carved from tidal marsh and jungle-thick Lowcountry vegetation. The No. 1 green provides a spectacular view of the Atlantic. You'll find a fully stocked pro shop opened in May 2007 with club and cart rentals available. Clinics and private instruction are offered. Tee-time reservations are required. Daily rates are $59 for 18 holes.

RIVERTOWNE COUNTRY CLUB, 1700 RiverTowne Country Club Dr., Mount Pleasant; (843) 849-2400; rivertownecountryclub.com. RiverTowne Country Club, just off SR 41 in Mount Pleasant, is Arnold Palmer's first signature course in the greater Charleston area. Palmer is quoted as saying, "We wanted to create a golfing experience as distinctive and memorable as the city itself." His 7,188-yard championship layout features beautiful tree-lined fairways, spectacular views of the Lowcountry marsh, and 13 holes positioned along the Wando River and Horlbeck Creek. RiverTowne was the site of the LPGA Championship hosted by Annika Sörenstam in 2007 and 2008. Club amenities include GPS-equipped golf carts with full-color graphics of each hole and tournament leader boards. There's also a driving range, chipping and putting greens, and a fully stocked golf shop with apparel, clubs, shoes, and accessories. Head pro is Pete Dunham. Tee times for the public may be reserved by phone or on the website. Greens fees range from $60 to $100 with discounts for Tri-County residents.

SHADOWMOSS PLANTATION GOLF AND COUNTRY CLUB, 20 Dunvegan Dr. (off SR 61); (843) 556-8251, (877) 897-1016; shadowmossgolf .com. Public play is welcome at this scenic course, designed by Russell Breeden

GOLF

and opened in 1973 along SR 61, the old Ashley River Road. In 1986, the 18-hole par 72 course was extensively renovated, and several water hazards were added to increase the challenge. Other modifications were made after Hurricane Hugo. The course is 6,701 yards long and cuts through pines, oaks, and hickories. A mosaic of ponds and streams comes into play in an area once dotted with early 18th- and 19th-century plantations. You'll find a well-stocked pro shop, a snack bar, a grill with a lounge, and locker rooms. There's also a putting green as well as a chipping green and driving range. The golf pro at Shadowmoss is J. P. Ringer. Tee times can be arranged through a number of local hotels and inns or by calling Shadowmoss. Mon through Fri greens fees start at $36, Sat and Sun fees are $39 to $55.

COURSES AT LOWCOUNTRY RESORTS

Wild Dunes
Only 15 miles from Charleston is Wild Dunes, which offers a total of 36 holes of Tom Fazio golf among its many upscale amenities.

THE HARBOR COURSE, 5881 Palmetto Dr., Isle of Palms; (843) 886-2004, (800) 845-8880; wilddunes.com. The Harbor Course, which opened in 1985, has four holes set directly along the Intracoastal Waterway. The course is a par 70, with a 6,359-yard layout that really challenges players. Two holes play from one island to another across the Yacht Harbor, where the wind can be a major factor. Frequent players say to beware the challenging 17th hole. The pro is Jeff Minton, and instruction is available through the fully stocked pro shop. From Mon through Sun (Mar through May), the greens fees range from $85 to $110.

★ WILD DUNES LINKS COURSE, 10001 Back Bay Dr., Isle of Palms; (843) 886-2002, (800) 845-8880; wilddunes.com. The Links opened in 1980, with a 6,709-yard par 72 layout from the black tees. Because two of the finishing holes (a par 4 and a par 5) are right on the Atlantic, you'll want to pray for a nonwindy day. Indeed, wind can make the course different every day, but the scenery compensates for its fickle nature. The course is in great condition from tee to green, with rolling fairways and oak and palm trees in abundance. The Links (and Wild Dunes's other offering, Harbor Course) have a high-tech yardage system for golf guests. Using a golf cart–mounted display screen linked to a GPS system, players can determine the distance to a target with pinpoint accuracy. The pro shop is first rate, with Jeff Minton riding herd on the whole golf program. *Golf* magazine included Wild Dunes Links among its Top 100 courses in the country. The daily greens fees are $120 to $155.

Kiawah Island Resort

Internationally famous Kiawah Island offers no fewer than six separate, distinct golf layouts for the adventurous Lowcountry golfer. Popular Brian Gerard heads Kiawah's golf program. The River Course is exclusively reserved for property owners on the island, but Kiawah golf is so famous and popular there's still great opportunity for the tour elite, low handicappers, and the average player, too. Oak Point, on Johns Island, is the newest acquisition. Four Kiawah courses—Cougar Point, Turtle Point, Osprey Point, and the Ocean Course—are semiprivate and open to homeowners, guests visiting the island, and Lowcountry vacationers who call specifically for reservations at least 24 hours in advance. Visit each on the website listed below for a hole-by-hole course tour. Check with each course individually for tee times. Note that summer greens fees are slightly lower.

COUGAR POINT WEST BEACH VILLAGE, 12 Kiawah Beach Dr., Kiawah Island; (843) 266-4020, (800) 654-2924; kiawahresort.com. Cougar Point, formerly called Marsh Point, reopened in 1996 after a complete year-long makeover by original (1981) course designer Gary Player. Now, this par 72 course has a 6,875-yard layout from the championship tees. Ric Ferguson is the resident pro, with a topflight shop to boot. There's even a halfway house on the 10th hole. Sometimes, four-footed furry creatures, along with alligators, ospreys, hawks, and a few snakes, have been known to be in the gallery here. Daily greens fees in season are $228.

> **i** When you're playing on one of the Lowcountry's many marsh-front golf courses like Cougar Point on Kiawah or the Harbor Course at Wild Dunes, don't be surprised if you find yourself sharing the green with a curious alligator. The unofficial rule is: Let the gator keep the ball; no penalty stroke incurred.

OAK POINT, 4694 Hope Plantation Dr., Johns Island; (843) 266-4100, (800) 654-2924; kiawahresort.com. Part of Kiawah Island Golf's comprehensive golf package, Oak Point is tucked away within Hope Plantation adjacent to Kiawah and Seabrook Islands. It was designed by Clyde Johnson and built in 1989. The par 72, 6,701-yard-long course is challenging to both the novice golfer and the experienced professional. Wide areas of windswept fairways stretch along salt marshes and heavily foliaged woodlands. There are numerous vistas of freshwater ponds and winding creeks. Word is that some area golfers prefer this course to Kiawah's Turtle Point, and it's a great choice for 36-hole-a-day players seeking a variety of challenges in the Kiawah-Seabrook area. The pro shop was recently renovated, and pro Scott Ammon provides instruction for golfers at all levels of play. Hours can vary seasonally; call for tee times and more information. Daily greens fees in season are around $151.

★ **THE OCEAN COURSE,** 1000 Ocean Course Dr., Kiawah Island; (843) 266-4670, (800) 654-2924; kiawahresort.com. The Ocean Course was designed by Pete Dye and completed just in time for the Ryder Cup matches in 1991. That year, *Golf Digest* named the Ocean Course "best new resort course of the year." Now the magazine calls it America's Toughest Resort Course, and a $2.5 million overhaul finished in the fall of 2002 means the challenge is even greater. More recently this was the site of the 2007 Senior PGA Championship, and hosted the PGA Championship in 2012. In fact this course is one of only four in the country to host every major PGA event held in the US. The cliffhanger finish of the 1991 Ryder Cup put the course on the must-play list of pros and amateurs everywhere. Dye's beautiful design gives you a par 72, 7,356-yard challenge from the championship tees. All 18 holes of the Ocean Course offer panoramic views of the Atlantic Ocean, and 10 holes play directly along the pristine, windswept beach. The clubhouse includes a restaurant, bar, pro shop, and locker rooms. The head pro at the Ocean Course is Stephen Youngner. Daily greens fees are $370. Note that the Ocean Course is a walking-only course until noon and additional caddy fees apply.

OSPREY POINT, Vanderhorst Plantation, 1000 Governors Dr., Kiawah Island; (843) 266-4640, (800) 654-2924; kiawahresort.com. Tom Fazio designed Osprey Point in 1986. The par 72 course is 6,932 yards from the middle tees and has four large, natural lakes. At Osprey Point, Fazio used this superb natural canvas to create a golf challenge of amazing playability and variety. In addition to the natural lakes, there are fingers of saltwater marsh and dense forests of live oaks, pines, palmettos, and magnolias. Jim Kelechi is the head pro here, and the club has a restaurant, bar, lounge, and locker rooms. Daily greens fees in season are $228. Please note that Osprey Point will undergo a major renovation during the summer of 2014 and is scheduled to reopen in late Oct.

TURTLE POINT, East Beach Village, 1 Turtle Point Ln., Kiawah Island; (843) 266-4050, (800) 654-2924; kiawahresort.com. Turtle Point, designed by Jack Nicklaus, is an 18-hole, par 72 course that's 7,061 yards long from the middle tees. It opened in 1981. Turtle Point is a low-profile design with fairway and green settings blended into the existing landscape. Nowhere is this more evident than along the spectacular 3-hole stretch woven through rolling sand dunes directly along the Atlantic Ocean. Head pro at Turtle Point is Mark Schaffer. Turtle Point has been the site of the Carolina Amateur and the 1990 PGA Cup Matches. Daily greens fees in season are $228.

Seabrook Island

Golf on Seabrook Island is limited to island residents, friends of club members, and visiting resort guests. There are two distinctly different golf challenges on the island: Crooked Oaks, designed by Robert Trent Jones Sr., and Ocean Winds, designed by Willard Byrd. Both courses have been executed in beautiful, undisturbed surroundings for challenging championship play. Seabrook's golf courses were the first in South Carolina to earn full certification in the Audubon Cooperative Sanctuary Program.

CROOKED OAKS, 1002 Landfall Way, Seabrook Island; (843) 768-2529, (866) 650-7918; discoverseabrook.com. Crooked Oaks is an 18-hole, 6,780-yard, par 72 course that meanders through the lush maritime forest and around several blackwater lagoons. When Jones designed it back in 1979, he described it as his "hard par–easy bogey" course. After its $2.3 million renovation, most of the greens are elevated or well-bunkered; there are no lucky shots to the bent-grass greens. It has rolling fairways weaving through stately live oaks, Spanish moss, sea marsh, and thick forest. Private and group instruction is offered by PGA pro Brian Thelan. The fully stocked pro shop has sports fashions as well as equipment. Peak season greens fees are $170. Nine-hole rates are available.

OCEAN WINDS, 1002 Landfall Way, Seabrook Island; (843) 768-2529, (866) 650-7918; discoverseabrook.com. Ocean Winds, designed by Willard Byrd, is slightly older (1973) and is a 6,765-yard, par 72 course from the middle tees. It plays a bit closer to the ocean. As a result, the Atlantic breezes can be a real test for even the best golfer. Ocean Winds golfers enjoy the benefits of a full-service clubhouse facility and a large pro shop, plus clinics and private instruction offered by an excellent teaching staff. Tournament coordination is available from PGA pro Brian Thelan. Daily greens fees are $170 and nine-hole rates are available.

Boating & Water Sports

Boating is an integral part of the Lowcountry lifestyle. State figures reveal that Charleston County is home to the most boats in South Carolina. The Trident area represents around 14 percent of the South Carolina total. There seems to be no end in sight for the boating frenzy, as newcomers and old salts alike discover and rediscover the pleasures of spending time on the water. From moonlight sails and family picnics on barrier islands to morning hunts in the back creeks and deep-sea fishing adventures, many are the occasions when "by boat" is the only way to go.

You can bring your own, or you can buy, rent, or charter a boat while you are here. Whatever the case, make certain to acquire, in navigational terms, "local knowledge" before you leave shore. We recommend contacting the US Coast Guard about its Auxiliary Public Education Courses. These cover information about navigational rules, aids to navigation, legal requirements, safety equipment, trailering, and coping with emergencies. State law requires that any person younger than 16 operating a boat or personal watercraft with an engine of 15 horsepower or greater without adult supervision must complete the boating safety training. The courses are held several times a year or may be completed by self-study online at dnr.sc.gov/education. For a schedule visit the website or call (800) 277-4301.

The local Marine Resources Division is at 217 Fort Johnson Rd. and can be reached at (843) 953-9300. We suggest you request the department's pamphlet on equipment requirements, rules, and regulations. To find out specifically about licensing, boat titles, and registration, call (843) 953-9301.

Those who want to launch their boat in the Lowcountry will be happy to know that there are a number of landings for public use. On weekends they are generally crowded, and early risers will find it easier to park a car and trailer. The parks department provides public access to 19 area boat ramps. For more information about the area landings, contact the Charleston County Park and Recreation Commission at (843) 795-4386 or visit ccprc.com.

MARINAS

If you are interested in docking your boat at a Lowcountry marina, consider the following options. We offer several choices, scattered throughout the Trident area and listed alphabetically.

★ **BOHICKET MARINA & MARKET,** 1880 Andell Bluff Blvd., Seabrook Island; (843) 768-1280; bohicket.com. Next to Kiawah and Seabrook resorts, Bohicket is 12 miles south of Charleston but just 6 miles from the Intracoastal Waterway. Within minutes, boaters are in the open sea. Bohicket's 200 wet slips and floating docks are on deep water, and dry storage is available. The marina reserves wet slips for long- and short-term rentals. Shower and bathroom facilities, a laundry, shops, and restaurants make this marina a first-class destination. There's also a 1-bedroom villa for nightly/weekly rental. Boat charters, parasailing, and water tours are offered, and fuel is available at the ship's store.

THE BRISTOL MARINA, 145 Lockwood Blvd.; (843) 723-6600; thebristol marina.com. One of Charleston's newest marinas, The Bristol is located on the Peninsula's Ashley River side just north of the Ashley River bridges. It offers 148 wet slips (for boats less than 70 feet) and 38 drive-on docks (for boats 12–20 feet). Cable, water, and 30- and 50-amp service is at every slip. There are shower and bathroom facilities and a nice gazebo for gatherings before or after your boating. No transient traffic is served here. A short drive from the marina brings you into the historic district for shopping, dining, and cultural events.

★ **CHARLESTON HARBOR RESORT & MARINA,** 24 Patriots Point Rd., Mount Pleasant; (843) 284-7062, (888) 856-0028; charlestonharbor marina.com. This full-service marina offers convenient ocean access with its location at the southwestern tip of Patriots Point in Mount Pleasant. (See more about Patriots Point Naval and Maritime Museum under the Museums & Other Sites section in the Attractions chapter.) The deepwater marina with 459 permanent and transient slips features state-of-the-art design with wide floating docks and protective breakwaters. Amenities include gasoline and diesel fuel, a laundry, restrooms, and showers, electric and manual courtesy carts, a ship's store, and potable dockside water. Other special services are a shuttle service to downtown Charleston and the Charleston International Airport; rentals of power boats, sailboats, and windsurfers; and inshore and offshore fishing and sailing charters. Adjacent to the Charleston Harbor Resort (see the Accommodations chapter) and the Patriots Point Links (see the Golf chapter), this resort complex provides endless opportunities for dining, entertainment, and recreation.

CHARLESTON MARITIME CENTER, 10 Wharfside St.; (843) 853-DOCK (3625); charleston-sc.gov. The Charleston Maritime Center has an all-season, deepwater marina with floating docks for 30 wet slips that can accommodate boats up to 180 feet in length. Located on the Peninsula's Cooper River side, this facility is near the city market with loads of shops and restaurants for exploring and a major grocery store, Harris Teeter. The Maritime Center is part of Charleston's waterfront area development that includes the South Carolina Aquarium and Liberty Square complex nearby. (For more on these sites see the Attractions and Kids chapters.) On-site there are showers, a dock shop, pump-out stations, gas and diesel fuel, ice, and 30- and 50-amp power. Transient boaters are a specialty here.

★ CITY MARINA, 17 Lockwood Dr.; (843) 723-5098; charlestoncitymarina .com. This marina is close to all the action around the Peninsula. There are 400 slips and transient dockage, and there is a convenient downtown shuttle service. This marina can accommodate vessels as large as 300 feet at its new megadock. Electric 30-, 50-, and 100-amp power as well as gas and diesel fuel are available. The Marina Variety Store restaurant and Salty Mike's Deck Bar are adjacent for a little land-side dining and recreation. A 5-year expansion and improvement project at the marina added more slips and facilities such as the ship's store, the reception center, the MegaDock, and state-of-the-art control room.

COOPER RIVER MARINA, 1010 Juneau Ave., North Charleston; (843) 554-0790; ccprc.com. Your fastest tack to Charleston Harbor may be the Cooper River Marina, located 2 miles north of the Cooper River bridges at the former Charleston Naval Base. This deepwater marina is operated by the Charleston County Park and Recreation Commission and has floating, concrete docks with electric hookups and plenty of free parking. Boat yard storage, security, laundry, fax, and Wi-Fi service, restroom facilities with a shower, a marina store, and ice are available. Charleston County residents receive a discount on slip fees.

DANIEL ISLAND MARINA & BOAT CLUB, 669 Marina Dr.; (843) 884-1000; danielislandmarina.com. This marina has 54 wet storage slips and 400 in dry stack storage. With the development of Daniel Island, the marina is seeing more traffic, and it now has a ship's store and deck bar, a shower, and restrooms. Fuel, ice, and live bait are available. No ramp is here, but work racks, a fish cleaning station, and a boat washing area are offered. Members in the boat club enjoy boating programs and social activities.

DOLPHIN COVE MARINA, 2079 Austin Ave., North Charleston; (843) 744-2562; dolphincovemarina.net. Dolphin Cove is on very deep water on the Ashley between the Ashley River Bridge and the North Bridge. The marina offers 125 wet slips with an additional 350 in dry stack storage. Gas is available here, along with complete on-site engine, hull, and accessory service. Short-term dockage is available, and the facility is equipped with showers, a laundry, picnic area, lounge, and restaurant.

THE HARBORAGE AT ASHLEY MARINA, 33 Lockwood Dr.; (843) 722-1996; ashleymarina.com. This 230-slip marina, at intracoastal marker 470 on the Ashley River, is on the Peninsula and convenient to all areas of the city. A courtesy shuttle takes transient boaters to downtown's popular attractions. Diesel and gasoline are available at the fuel dock, and there is room for 880 feet of boat docking. In addition to a captain's lounge, ship's store, showers, and a laundry, there is a fax machine, cable TV, and Wi-Fi. Marina managers can supply names and phone numbers of charter boats that leave from their marina.

Manatee Watch

Boaters, keep your eyes out for manatees in area waters during the summer months. The gentle, huge, seal-like mammals migrate northward from Florida by ocean, estuaries, and creeks, often swimming along the edges of waterways and in shallow water near marsh grass. Be sure to slow to no-wake speeds, and stay in deeper channels where manatees can dive to avoid collisions. If you see a manatee in South Carolina, call the state's Department of Natural Resources at (800) 922-5431 or visit dnr.sc.gov/marine/manatee. The department is tracking and recording sightings of this endangered species.

ISLE OF PALMS MARINA, 50 41st Ave., Isle of Palms; (843) 886-0209; iopmarina.net. This marina, on the Intracoastal Waterway marker 116 at Wild Dunes Resort, is a full-service facility with 50 wet slips, floating docks, a restaurant, bathrooms, showers, a laundry, Wi-Fi, cable TV, and a ship's store with supplies for boating. Isle of Palms Marina also offers inshore- and offshore-chartered trips, ecotours, and Jet Ski and boat rentals. Limo service is also available here.

MARINER'S CAY MARINA, 3-A Mariner's Cay Dr., Folly Beach; (843) 607-4254; marinerscay.net. Mariner's Cay is part of Mariner's Cay Resort and is on the Folly River across from the Folly boat ramp. Just 2 miles from the ocean and 9 miles from the Intracoastal Waterway, this 83-slip marina is one of Charleston's closest facilities to the Atlantic. Their services include gas and diesel fuel, ice, and 24-hour security. A laundry room, restrooms with showers, cable TV hookups, and a ship's store complete the amenities. Two-bedroom condos are available to rent on a short-term basis.

RIPLEY LIGHT YACHT CLUB, 95 Ripley Pointe Dr.; (843) 766-0908; ripleylightyc.com. Just west of the Ashley, in the shadow of California Dreaming (see the Dining chapter), you'll find Ripley Light. This private marina accommodates transients, short-, and long-term dockage in their 83 wet slips. Their 6,500-foot pier is nice for a stroll or to watch the boats returning from a day's fishing. Fuel, bait, and ice are available as well. The nearby dry stack marina has 220 dry stack units (accommodating boats up to 40 feet) for rent on a monthly basis and can be reached at (843) 766-2100.

RIVER'S EDGE MARINA, 4354 Bridge View Dr., North Charleston; (843) 554-8901; riversedgemarina.com. River's Edge, on the Ashley River in North Charleston, is both a wet and dry storage marina. It has 50 wet slips, 486 inside dry stack spaces, and a Captain's lounge, ship's store, fish cleaning station, picnic, and grill area, plus restrooms and showers. A mechanic is on-site too.

ST. JOHN'S YACHT HARBOR, 2408 Maybank Hwy.; (843) 557-1027; stjohnsyachtharbor.com. Near Intracoastal Waterway marker 11, is a deepwater marina that's just minutes from the city's municipal golf course. New owners bought the former Buzzard's Roost and Stono marinas to create this facility. There are 176 wet slips along with dockage for transients up to 130 feet in length. A laundry, shower, and gas and diesel fuel are available, and free in-slip pump out. You will find a Captain's retreat, ship's store, outdoor kitchen, and pool and cabanas here.

SEABREEZE MARINA, 50 Immigration St.; (843) 853-0932. One of the newer marinas on Charleston's Peninsula is the dry stack storage facility called Seabreeze Marina. Conveniently located near the Ravenel Bridge on the Cooper River, this site is unobstructed with deepwater access to Charleston Harbor. The experienced marina staff is ready to make your day on the water hassle-free and fun. Call ahead to have your boat launched and fueled, and the cooler packed with your favorite refreshments and snacks from the ship's store. When you return, they are ready to wash down the boat inside and out, flush the engine, drain the bilge, and return her to her storage berth. All this service practically guarantees an enjoyable boating experience. A fish cleaning station, maintenance work racks, air-conditioned restrooms and showers, and plenty of floating dock space and parking are other amenities featured here.

SHEM CREEK MARINA, 526 Mill St., Mount Pleasant; (843) 884-3211; shemcreekmarina.com. Shem Creek offers 200 dry stacks for boat storage. Convenient for East Cooper residents, Shem Creek is often filled to capacity and offers some basic amenities like outdoor showers, restrooms, fuel, and ice. A new deck area with umbrella tables and chairs, fans, and misters overlooks the creek. Adjacent to the Shem Creek boat ramp, this marina bills itself as "Mount Pleasant's neighborhood marina."

> **i** Note that laws governing boating under the influence are strictly enforced on South Carolina waters. Boat operators will be tested for blood-alcohol content in the event of accidents. For more information, call the Boating Safety Division of the South Carolina Department of Natural Resources at (843) 953-9301.

TOLER'S COVE MARINA, 1610 Ben Sawyer Blvd., SR 703 at Intracoastal Waterway, Mount Pleasant; (843) 881-0325; tolerscovemarina.com. East of the Cooper, Toler's Cove—surrounded by the Marsh Harbor development—is across the harbor from Charleston and across the Intracoastal Waterway from Sullivan's Island and the Isle of Palms. Toler's Cove can accommodate vessels up to 100 feet in length. The marina has showers and a laundry as well as gas, bait, ice, and other necessities. This is a good source for charters and boat rentals as well.

BOAT SALES & REPAIRS

If you are in the market for a new boat, shop the retail stores in the Trident area for reliable sales and service. Beware of fly-by-night operations selling boats out of cow pastures, however, as they are sometimes fronts for liquidation operations and may not be there to help mediate with the manufacturer when your new boat springs a leak.

From the city out to North Charleston, here's a sampling of some of the older establishments. These are also good places to start if you find yourself in need of a boat mechanic while visiting the Lowcountry. If you require a boatyard for more extensive repairs and maintenance contact one of the following: Charleston City Boatyard at (843) 884-3000; Detyens Boatyard, (843) 308-8000; Pierside Boatworks at (843) 554-7775; Rockville Marine, (843) 559-1124; or Ross Marine at (843) 559-0379.

CHARLESTON YACHT SALES, 3 Lockwood Dr., Ste. 201; (843) 577-5050, (866) 429-0958; charlestonyachtsales.com. These knowledgeable yacht brokers handle both sail and powerboats with a large selection to choose from. They also offer service, repairs, appraisals, delivery, and surveys. They're next to the municipal marina and are a longtime fixture (since 1965) on the Peninsula.

HALL MARINE CHARLESTON, 142 Sportsman's Island Dr.; (843) 747-1889; hallmarine.com. This store is the area's exclusive Scout Boats dealer, selling sport boats, cruisers, and yachts as long as 61 feet. Sea Ray, Boston Whaler, Yamaha Jet Boats, Nautique, Bennington Pontoons, and Harris FloteBote are other brand names here, and service and accessories are also offered.

LONGSHORE BOATS, 2650 Clements Ferry Rd., Wando; (843) 216-4700; longshoreboats.com. Located on Daniel Island at the entrance to Daniel Island Marina Village, Longshore Boats is a Mercury and Yamaha Outboards as well as Volvo Penta and MerCruiser stern drives dealer. The staff continues to work on all models with parts, service, and accessories available. Some of the popular lines of new boats are Edgewater, Chaparral, and Robalo.

> i Remember that Charleston Harbor is a busy "highway" for large ships coming in and out of the Port of Charleston daily. Recreational boaters (both power and sail) must stay clear by avoiding the ship channels, where possible, or crossing them quickly at right angles. Always be alert, and watch for ship or tugboat traffic.

ST. BARTS YACHTS, 3 Lockwood Dr., Ste. 301; (843) 577-7377; st-barts .com. In recent years, Beneteau USA moved its North American corporate headquarters to Charleston, and St. Barts is the local dealer for Beneteau Yachts. Beneteau's factory in Marion, South Carolina, builds sailboats from 30 to 46 feet long as well as custom lengths. St. Barts also represents the Barracuda and Sense lines and handles brokerage of all types of sailboats.

SEEL'S OUTBOARD, 1937 US 17 S.; (843) 556-2742; seelsoutboard.com. Seel's carries Evinrude and Yamaha motors, and Grady White boats as well as Alumacraft, Hurricane, Sundance, and Sea Hunt. With two locations, on Savannah Highway in West Ashley and the bypass in Mount Pleasant, Seel's is an established boat dealership that has been in operation since the 1960s. The second location is at 2910 US 17 N., Mount Pleasant (843-849-8788).

SAILBOAT RACING

With the popularity of the Around Alone (formerly the BOC Challenge), the solo sailor around-the-world yacht race, hosted by Charleston in 1994–95 and 1998–99, sailboat racing events have sprung up in this area. The Charleston Ocean Racing Association, established in 1967, holds 35 to 40 sailing events year-round in Charleston Harbor and offshore waters, promoting sailing and assisting members in obtaining competent crews and desirable berths. Also, a Charleston to Bermuda Race sails its 12th competition from Charleston Harbor in May 2015.

Local regattas are popular events too, particularly in the warmer months. From the Carolina Yacht Club and Charleston Yacht Club regattas to those hosted by the Hobcaw, James Island, and Sea Island clubs, there are races throughout the summer. A schedule is set in Jan and posted in the area yacht clubs. Spectators enjoy watching these races, free of charge, from the Battery or from the grounds of the club hosting the event. Children are welcome and may even start asking about those Charleston Yacht Club Summer Junior Sail Program lessons (see sidebar in this chapter). Call the sailing department at the College of Charleston (which, by the way, traditionally has a fine sailing team) at (843) 953-8252, or visit cofc.edu/sailing for more information about non-credit community sailing classes or sailing association memberships.

CHARLESTON RACE WEEK, 4208 Pace St., Unit B, North Charleston; (843) 628-5900; charlestonraceweek.com, charlestonoceanracing.org. Sperry Top-Sider in association with the Charleston Ocean Racing Association (CORA) presents the annual Charleston Race Week during the month of April. Race Week comprises an inshore competition for sailboats from 20 to 80 feet, selected one-design regattas, and an offshore race. The Charleston Race Week Cup and overall Race Week winners are determined based on cumulative scoring results. Race Headquarters and the Race Village are located at the Charleston Harbor Resort & Marina in Mount Pleasant. More than 275 boats competed in 2014, and a good time was had by all.

CHARLESTON TO BERMUDA RACE, (843) 278-8659; charlestonbermuda race.com. Alternating years with the Daytona to Bermuda Race, the Charleston to Bermuda Race, also known simply as "C2B," leaves our city in May 2015. The 777-nautical-mile race is hosted on the receiving end by the Royal Bermuda Yacht Club (formed in 1844), and the finish line is off the St. David's Lighthouse in Bermuda. The 30-foot and larger sailboats are entered in either a double-handed class (two crew) or the fully crewed class with a minimum of four. Hundreds of spectators lined the Waterfront Park and the Battery and also watched from more than 100 spectator boats as the sailors set out on this challenge in May 2013.

Set Sail!

For more than 25 years, children have learned to sail in the Charleston Yacht Club Summer Junior Sail Program. If you have kids ages 8 to 17, this may be just what you're looking for to add a little excitement to their lives. Five 3-week sessions are offered each summer. Beginner sessions are $325 and intermediate are $150. For more information, call (843) 722-4968, visit charlestoncommunity sailing.org, or write to the Summer Youth Sailing Program, Charleston Yacht Club, PO Box 20474, Charleston, SC 29413.

SAILING INSTRUCTION

Sailors or aspiring sailors will find plenty of company in the Lowcountry. If you are interested in learning more about the sport or the local regatta schedule, talk to the enthusiasts at the College of Charleston Sailing Association. They are based at the Charleston Harbor Marina and can be reached at (843) 953-8252. (See listing.) Another good source for information as well as sails, rigging, and repairs is UK-Halsey Sailmakers at (843) 722-0823.

The following listings will steer your ship in the right direction when it comes to sailing instruction and service.

COLLEGE OF CHARLESTON SAILING ASSOCIATION, Charleston Harbor Marina, 24 Patriots Point Rd., Mount Pleasant; (843) 216-8450, (843) 953-8252; sailing.cofc.edu. The College of Charleston offers adult noncredit sailing classes that meet at the Charleston Harbor Marina. Equipment is furnished, and no advanced skills are required. Basic and intermediate classes are offered Apr through Aug. The cost is $455 for 15 hours of sailing instruction on J/22 boats and 2 hours of classroom instruction. Call the association for details.

OCEAN SAILING ACADEMY, Charleston Harbor Marina, 24 Patriots Point Rd., Mount Pleasant; (843) 971-0700; charlestonsailingacademy.com. The Ocean Sailing Academy offers US Sailing Certification courses from the Learn to Sail level on up through Open Ocean Passage Making. Instructors even guarantee skippering ability at the conclusion of any of their courses. Completion of just one course will give you the freedom and certification to rent a boat and head out for a day of sailing. Instruction is given on a range of boats, including Colegate 26, and Beneteau 323 and 473s. Classes may be customized to fit your needs, or you may participate in one of the regularly scheduled courses. The academy operates Charleston's only public charter sailing club. For more information about classes, the sailing club, team-building programs, and prices, call the number above, or visit the website.

CHARTERS

If you are dreaming of gliding across Charleston Harbor at sunset or entertaining your friends on a weekend outing, several area power and sailboat charter companies have all types and sizes of yachts to match your fantasy.

AQUASAFARIS, Charleston Harbor Marina, 24 Patriots Point Rd., A-Dock, 2nd Fl. Marina Building, Ste. 1, Mount Pleasant; (843) 886-8133, (800) 524-3444; aqua-safaris.com. AquaSafaris is a water sport facility at Charleston Harbor Marina, Isle of Palms, Shem Creek, and Bohicket Marinas (see previous listings). Bareboat rentals of 17- to 21-foot skiffs are available by the hour or half-day and full-day. Prices range from $200 for 2 hours up to $645 for the full day. Other adventures here are private sailing charters, including day sails, harbor cruises, sunset sails, or island beach excursions. The fleet of inshore and offshore fishing boats consists of all types—flats boats, sportfishing yachts, island hoppers, and head boats. Charters are arranged for 1 to 100 people by the hour, or half or full day. Group charters are offered for parties and special events, and catering with customized menus is available. AquaSafaris, Inc., also handles charters worldwide. Call for reservations and more details on pricing.

BOHICKET BOAT ADVENTURE AND TOUR CO., 2789 Cherry Point Rd., Wadmalaw Island; (843) 559-3525; bohicketboat.com. Bohicket Boat provides all kinds of boating fun for visitors and locals alike. They offer

Charleston Harbor at sunset

powerboat rentals, sailing charters, river and kayaking tours, and sunset cruises. Bohicket Boat even customizes tours geared to your special interest, be it dolphin watching, crabbing, shrimping, shelling, or fishing around the barrier islands in the Lowcountry. Prices range from $60 per hour (2-hour minimum) for a 16-foot jon boat to $330 per day for a 23-foot deck boat. The custom tours cost $240 to $475 for 2 to 4 hours with up to 6 passengers. Call for a monthly calendar of activities and reservations.

SCHOONER *PRIDE,* 360 Concord St.; (843) 722-1112, (800) 979-3370; schoonerpride.com. Sit back, relax, and take a 2-hour harbor or sunset cruise on a 3-masted, gaff topsail schooner (class C tall ship). What better way to enjoy the vistas of Charleston's historic waterfront? Reservations are recommended, and the fee is $36 for adults and children 12 and older and $28 for children ages 11 and younger. The sunset sail is $46 for adults and $33 for children. A moonlight sail, sunset wine-tasting, and ghost tour are other special cruises offered seasonally. The Schooner *Pride* is also available for private parties of up to 49 people. Call for group rates. The *Pride* departs from the Aquarium Wharf (near the South Carolina Aquarium). (See the Cruise & Boat Tours section of the Tours chapter for more on the *Pride.*)

CANOEING/KAYAKING/STAND-UP PADDLEBOARDING

With the amazing system of waterways in the Lowcountry, there are many great opportunities for canoeing, kayaking, and paddleboarding. The Charleston County Park and Recreation Commission, (843) 795-4386, can help with a list of community school courses in paddling. Also, each spring, it cosponsors the East Coast Paddlesports & Outdoor Festival with the Trade Association of Paddlesports (TAPS). The event is held at James Island County Park. The symposium regularly attracts more than 1,000 paddling enthusiasts of all skill levels for a weekend of lectures, on-water demos, and classes. Reflecting the growing national interest in paddling, local support has made this one of the top events of its kind in the country. See the Festivals & Annual Events chapter for more on this event.

Boating News

Old salts (and new ones too) will want to pick up a copy of *Tideline* for the latest scoop on all the area's boating and water sports info. The monthly tabloid, published by *The Post and Courier* is distributed along the Lowcountry waterfront. With stories about regattas, boat shows, boatyards, marinas, fishing, and other maritime pursuits, this is a lively read. The free paper can be found at marinas, boating supply stores, and nautical shops, or call (843) 937-5568 or visit tidelinemagazine.com to subscribe.

COASTAL EXPEDITIONS TOURS, 514-B Mill St., Mount Pleasant; (843) 884-7684; coastalexpeditions.com. Coastal Expeditions rents kayaks and paddleboards and offers tours all over the Lowcountry from marsh creeks to secluded beaches. Naturalists and instructors certified by the American Canoe Association and British Canoe Union run this operation and take groups of 2 to 40 on nature tours. A quality operation, Coastal Expeditions welcomes beginners and experienced kayakers/paddleboarders and also sells new and used equipment. It offers private and group lessons as well. The half-day tours are $58 per person and $88 per person for a full day. Single kayaks and stand-up paddleboards rent for $38 for a half day and $48 for a full day; double kayaks are $48 for a half day and $58 for a full day. Overnight expeditions for 4 or more people are a fun option too.

JAMES ISLAND COUNTY PARK, 871 Riverland Dr.; (843) 795-7275; ccprc.com. James Island County Park offers lots of classes and clinics; and day, after-work, and overnight tours are offered in sea kayaking, canoeing, and stand-up paddleboard (SUP). Canoe lessons range from $15 to $50 for Charleston County residents and $18 to $60 for nonresidents. Kayak classes and tours range from $40 for county residents and $48 for nonresidents for a basic course, up to $70 for residents and $84 for nonresidents for more advanced offerings. SUP classes start at $15 for residents and $18 for non-county residents. Trips are around $30, resident, and $36, nonresident. Contact the park for the quarterly program guide to check out the variety of paddler offerings.

LOWCOUNTRY PADDLERS, PO Box 13242, Charleston, SC 29422; (843) 556-5865; lowcountrypaddlers.net. Regular meetings are open to any-one interested. Guest speakers talk about their experiences as well as conservation issues and upcoming trips. Meetings are held the third Mon of each month at Providence Baptist Church on Daniel Island. Paddling trips are organized by skill level, distance, and pace. This family-oriented group publishes a monthly newsletter and has about 150 members. The annual membership (which includes membership in the American Canoe Association) is $45 for an individual or $61 for a family. Call the Charleston County Park and Recreation Commission for contact information about this group.

★ **MIDDLETON PLACE KAYAKING,** 4290 Ashley River Rd.; (843) 628-2879, (800) 543-4774; charlestonkayakcompany.com, theinnatmiddleton place.com. The Inn at Middleton Place offers nature-based kayaking on the Ashley River year-round and in the blackwater cypress swamp seasonally from Feb through Apr. Learn to roll and rescue while perfecting your paddle techniques, then follow your guide on a Lowcountry adventure. The basic kayak instruction with guided 2-hour tour costs $45 per person. The blackwater cypress swamp tour is available on a limited basis for $65 per person. Kayak rentals are also available for $20 to $30 per person for up to 3 hours.

PALMETTO ISLANDS COUNTY PARK, 444 Needlerush Pkwy., Mount Pleasant; (843) 884-0832; ccprc.com. This 943-acre nature facility is in a heavily wooded area, with a 2-acre pond and 1-mile canoe trail. It is a perfect place to canoe, paddleboard, or kayak (rentals are no longer available, but you can bring your own), and a nominal admission fee of $1 a person is charged. They also have a storage rack with slips for rent on a space available basis. (See the Kids chapter for more on this exciting park.)

Other water recreation opportunities abound in our area and don't necessarily involve owning or chartering a boat. Local waters offer lots of spots that are waiting to be explored on personal watercraft or investigated by scuba diving. Surfing, windsurfing, and waterskiing provide ways to catch a wave or a breeze or jump a wake while demonstrating your finesse. Or maybe just plunging into a pool for a refreshing swim is your answer to the oft-daunting Lowcountry heat. A list of the folks who can help you get started follows.

PERSONAL WATERCRAFT & OTHER WET TOYS

To jump on your own Jet Ski and zip around the endless waterways, inlets, and creeks in the Lowcountry for the day, contact one of the following for rental or purchase of personal watercraft.

CAROLINA WATERSPORTS AT TROPHY LAKES, 3050 Marlin Rd., Johns Island; (843) 559-2520; carolinawaterskischool.com, trophylakes.com. Trophy Lakes is the place for waterskiing, kneeboard, and wakeboard lessons taught by instructors who are nationally ranked on the pro tours. The lessons are taught on two private lakes on Johns Island and are scheduled by appointment. The rates are $55 for approximately 25 minutes. Water-ski and wakeboard pulls are $45 for 25 minutes. A kids' camp, birthday parties, and rental of the lake for your private event are other options here. Waterskiing competitions are held here as well, so call Carolina Watersports for a schedule of events. Their 4wake.com website shows the full range of gear available at their shop. A disc golf course is another attraction for those who prefer to keep their feet on the ground.

CHARLESTON POWER SPORTS, 3571 West Montague Ave., North Charleston; (843) 552-7900; charlestonps.com. Representing the Sea-Doo, Yamaha, and Kawasaki lines, Charleston Power Sports has the largest selection in the area of personal watercraft and jet-powered boats for sale. They run from 85 to 310 horsepower, with lengths up to 20 feet. These boats are good for touring, skiing, and all-around family fun.

TIDAL WAVE WATERSPORTS, 69 41st Ave., Isle of Palms; (843) 886-8456; tidalwavewatersports.com. Tidal Wave Watersports' locations have personal watercraft rentals, parasailing, and waterskiing. The Jet Ski rental rates are $99 an hour for a single, $119 double, or $139 triple. A special safari tour from Wild Dunes (that's the Isle of Palms address) is a very popular, 90-minute guided excursion by WaveRunner. You venture out into the ocean, up to Capers or Bulls Island (with a stop for beachcombing), and return on the Intracoastal Waterway. The 30-mile round-trip starts at $119. Parasailing choices are offered with flights costing $60 (at Isle of Palms or Kiawah Island beach or at Charleston Harbor) for the 600-foot pull and $80 for the 800-foot thrill (it's a 1.5-hour trip). What a way to check out the beach from a bird's-eye view. Believe it or not, takeoff and landing are dry, and anyone age 2 and older may try it. (The minimum weight requirement is 80 pounds, or you fly with someone else.) Tidal Wave Watersports also offers waterskiing and wakeboarding for two hours up to a half day. For 2 hours it's $320 plus $120 for each additional hour for up to 6 people and includes a boat, captain, and equipment. Call ahead for more information and reservations.

The Lowcountry Splash

Are you ready to take the plunge? The annual Lowcountry Splash, a 2.4-mile and 5-mile open-water swim organized by Logan Rutledge Children's Foundation, is attracting more and more participants who are up to the challenge. The race through Charleston Harbor starts at Hobcaw Yacht Club (2.4-mile course) or the Daniel Island Pier (5-mile course) on the Wando River in Mount Pleasant and continues under the Cooper River Bridge past the USS *Yorktown*, finishing at the Patriots Point Naval and Maritime Center. The Splash is held in late May or early June so that the water temperature has usually warmed up a bit, and, depending upon the tide and weather, swimmers may experience varying conditions—all part of the event. The cost to enter is $65 ($55 in advance), and more information can be found at lowcountrysplash.com or by calling (843) 884-7880.

SCUBA DIVING

There are many scuba enthusiasts in this area. Diving the numerous wrecks under Charleston's waters is a real kick. For information about dive trips and activities, our listings give you some good places to start. The College of Charleston also offers a scuba class from time to time. Call (843) 953-5960 to find out about the next scheduled class.

CHARLESTON SCUBA, 335 Savannah Hwy.; (843) 763-DIVE (3483); charlestonscuba.com. This conveniently located store is a center for diving enthusiasts. It provides retail sales, gear rentals, on-site repairs, scuba charter trips, and classes—from open-water certification to dive master. The PADI skin diver course is $145 for the one 2-hour class plus one 2-hour pool session with two dives for certification for an extra fee. The Free Diving Instructors International course is $395 plus gear and dives. Charleston Scuba is adjacent to the Holiday Inn Riverview west of the Ashley.

LOWCOUNTRY SCUBA, 4-C Seafood Dr., Mount Pleasant; (843) 884-1500; lowcountryscuba.com. Lowcountry Scuba on Shem Creek offers beginning dive classes and certification. The open-water beginner weekend class is $840. Lowcountry Scuba also organizes trips to many locations, including the Caribbean, the Bahamas, and Florida. To dive local waters, call to schedule offshore dive charters. Ask about the Charleston Dive Club here too.

SURFING

The surfing craze has been reborn among the young crowd, much to the delight of all those baby-boomer surfer dudes. The Lowcountry's most popular spots for wave action are on Folly Beach and the Isle of Palms. The Washout at East Ashley Avenue, a designated surfing area on Folly Beach, attracts all ages in search of the perfect wave. Other good surf can be found near the Folly Pier at East Atlantic Avenue, 10th Street on Folly Beach, and near the pier and the county park on the Isle of Palms. (Keep in mind that it is illegal to surf closer than 200 feet to a pier.) Bert's Break, at Station 22 on Sullivan's Island, is probably the best low tide break in the area. Local surf shops are equipped with surfing and beach-going needs. A couple of options follow.

MCKEVLIN'S SURF SHOP, 8 Center St., Folly Beach; (843) 588-2247, (843) 588-2261 (Surf Line); mckevlins.com. Opened back in the '60s, McKevlin's carries a full line of surfboards, clothing, and accessories. Some of its better-known board brands are Bing, Island Inspired, Sharp Eye, Lost, Channel Islands, and Allison. McKevlin's offers rental of surf and body boards and videos seven days a week. Call the Surf Line for the latest on wind and wave conditions, tides, and water temperatures.

OCEAN SURF SHOP, 31 Center St., Folly Beach; (843) 588-9175, (843) 633-0268 (Surf Report); oceansurfshop.com. Ocean Surf Shop sells surfboards and all the accessories you can think of to catch a wave. Just getting started? No problem—this place gives lessons and rents boards, too. Some of their major brands are Perfection, Webber, Surftech, and Quiet Flight. You'll find fins, nose guards, leashes, car racks, decals, and sports watches to complete the gear. Wetsuits, tees, board shorts, sandals, and sunglasses from Billabong, Reef, Volcom, O'Neill, and Costa Del Mar outfit you wet or dry. This is the place to get "Edge of America" logo items to prove you've spent a day on the Edge. (See the Welcome to Greater Charleston chapter for more on Folly Beach.)

SWIMMING

JAMES ISLAND RECREATIONAL COMPLEX, 1088 Quail Dr.; (843) 795-5678; charleston-sc.gov. Operated by the city's Department of Recreation Aquatics Division, this 25-yard, outdoor pool with lifeguards is open June through Aug. Water fitness classes and swimming lessons are planned for the mornings, and open swimming is the norm in the afternoon. Adult city residents can swim for $2, nonresidents for $4; residents 17 and younger pay $1.50; nonresidents, $3. City residents pay $20 for youth swimming lessons and $25 for adult lessons; parent and tot swims are $15. Nonresidents pay $30 for youth lessons, $35 for adults, and $25 for parent and tot swimming.

PALMETTO ISLANDS COUNTY PARK, 444 Needlerush Pkwy., Mount Pleasant; (843) 884-0832; ccprc.com. The outdoor water playground at Palmetto Islands County Park is open 10 a.m. to 6 p.m. on weekends in May and mid-Aug through Labor Day, and every day from Memorial Day until mid-Aug. Charges for county residents are $6.99 for an adult and $5.99 for a child under 42 inches tall; nonresidents pay $7.99. Children younger than 2 can swim for free. Swimming fees are in addition to a $1 per person park admission. (For more on this and other Charleston County parks, see the Kids chapter.)

i Practice Plus-One Boating, meaning what you take out on your boating trip be sure to bring back plus one—one piece of litter or debris, every time. If it floats, net it. If it blows out, go back and get it. Act ethically and responsibly to keep our waterways clean for the enjoyment of all.

RICHARD L. JONES RECREATION CENTER POOL, 391 Egypt Rd., Mount Pleasant; (843) 884-2528; mtpleasantrec.com. There is a 6-lane, indoor swimming pool at the Richard L. Jones complex. Swimming lessons, aquatic exercise classes, lap and recreational swimming are some of the many options. Membership is open to anyone. Mount Pleasant residents pay only $25 for a 1-year membership plus $2 each time they swim. Children 4 and younger swim free. Nonresidents pay $175 for annual memberships plus the $2 swim fee. Swimming lessons range from $28 to $45 for residents and from $35 to $60 for nonresidents. A similar schedule of lessons is also offered at the Park West Complex Pool. Call (843) 856-2536 for more information.

W. L. STEPHENS AQUATIC CENTER, 780 West Oak Forest Dr.; (843) 769-8261; charleston-sc.gov. This is a good place to start your exploration of swimming pools in the Greater Charleston area, as the City of Charleston Aquatics Division has an office here. Open year-round, this indoor pool has 6 lanes and is 25 yards long. It is a popular winter birthday-party venue—nothing like a warm swim when there's frost on the windows—and draws its share of regular lap swimmers. There are full showers. The fees are the same as the James Island pool listed above.

APPENDIX:
Living Here

In this section we feature specific information for residents or those planning to relocate here. Topics include retirement, relocation, media, and much more.

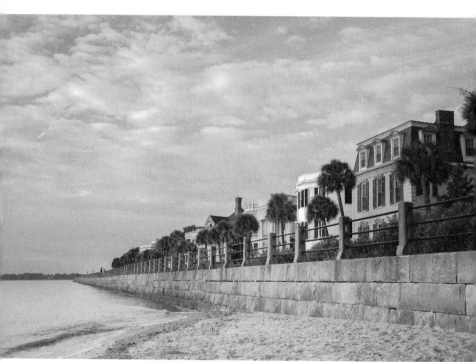

Sunrise along the Battery

Relocation

If you're among those thinking seriously about moving to the Lowcountry and making Charleston your permanent or part-time home, we have a news flash for you: This idea is not entirely original. It has occurred to others, with some frequency. Starting with the influx of military retirees who fell in love with the area during their World War II Navy days spent here, the concept of retiring to Charleston has only grown more popular with each passing year. And why not? The Lowcountry really has it all—sun, sea, golf, history, culture, plus educational and entertainment opportunities galore. Young people are similarly attracted to the area. Employment opportunities, especially for professionals, are getting more plentiful as the population surges upward. Therefore, a Relocation chapter is in order—as a helpful service to the next generation of insiders who will soon be calling Charleston and its environs "home."

We've thrown in some practical information, such as where to get your new driver's license, how to register to vote, what are the utility hookup contacts, and even some recycling information for our new neighbors who, we hope, will be ecology-minded citizens here in the Lowcountry.

MOTOR VEHICLE INFORMATION

New South Carolina residents may use a valid out-of-state driver's license for up to 90 days. Military personnel may use their home state license as long as it is valid. Licensed newcomers must take a vision test and bring their birth certificates or other proof of citizenship, proof of South Carolina residency, liability insurance information, and proof of Social Security number. New drivers must meet the same requirements and take the road, written, and vision tests. A quick review of the rules of the road booklet available in the South Carolina Department of Public Safety Division of Motor Vehicles offices or online may be beneficial prior to taking the written test. Drivers should apply at the SCDMV offices listed below.

New residents have 45 days to purchase South Carolina license tags for their vehicles. Before getting a tag, property taxes on the vehicle must be paid at your local county tax office. Then, new residents may apply by filling out Form 400 at any of the SCDMV locations below. General information on driver's licenses and tags/registration and their fees is available at (803) 896-5000 or scdmvonline.com.

180 Lockwood Blvd., Charleston

3790 Leeds Ave., North Charleston

135 Wimberly Dr., Ladson

445 . Hwy. 52 N., Moncks Corner

1189 Sweetgrass Basket Pkwy., Ste. 500, Mount Pleasant

Express Office (no road tests or tags/registration): 1119 Wappoo Rd., Unit G, Charleston

VOTER REGISTRATION

To register to vote, a new resident must be a US citizen, 18 years old by the date of the election, mentally competent, and not under conviction of a felony or, if previously convicted, have served the entire sentence, including probation or parole. Proof of residency is required. Registration must take place at least 30 days prior to an election to vote in that election, and a photo ID is now required to vote. Newcomers may register at the local county voter registration office, driver's license offices, or by mail. Visit charlestoncounty.org, berkeley countysc.gov, or dorchestervotes.org for more information, or call the following numbers:

Berkeley County: (843) 719-4056, Moncks Corner line; (843) 723-3800, ext. 4056, Charleston line; (843) 567-3136, ext. 4056, St. Stephen line

Charleston County: (843) 744-8683

Dorchester County: (843) 563-0132, St. George line; (843) 832-0071, Summerville line

UTILITIES

For natural gas, electricity, water, and telephone services in Greater Charleston, call one of the following:

Natural Gas & Electricity

Berkeley Electric Cooperative, (843) 572-5454; becsc.com.

Santee Cooper (South Carolina Public Service Authority), (843) 761-8000; santeecooper.com.

South Carolina Electric and Gas (SCE&G), (800) 251-7234; sceg.com

Water

Berkeley County Water and Sanitation Authority, (843) 572-4400 (Charleston line); (843) 761-8817 (Moncks Corner line); (843) 567-3597 (St. Stephen line); bcwsa.com.

Charleston Water Systems—Water & Sewer, (843) 727-6800; charleston water.com.

Dorchester County Water & Sewer Department, (843) 832-0075 (Summerville line), (843) 563-0075 (St. George line); dorchestercounty.net.

Dorchester County Water Authority, (843) 875-0140; dcwaonline.com.

Mount Pleasant Waterworks, (843) 884-9626; mountpleasantwaterworks .com. Many other municipalities have their own water and sewer commissions such as Isle of Palms, Kiawah Island, Folly Beach, Summerville, Goose Creek, Moncks Corner, and North Charleston. If you are relocating to one of these areas, consult the telephone directory for their individual numbers.

Telephone

AT&T provides telephone services for the majority of the area. For residential services, call (800) 288-2020; for business services, call (877) 253-0009. You may also visit the website at att.com.

RECYCLING

Curbside recycling in blue bins is offered in most of the urban areas of Charleston County on an every-other-week basis. Drop-off sites are located throughout the county. Materials currently recycled include plastic containers (nos. 1 through 7), steel food cans, aluminum and aerosol cans, and glass jars and bottles. Newspapers, magazines, office paper, and mail are recyclable as well, and corrugated cardboard, motor oil, paint, batteries, lightbulbs, and electronics can be brought to the drop sites. (Visit recycle.charlestoncounty.org for a complete listing of sites and what they accept.) For more information about recycling in Charleston County, call (843) 720-7111; in Berkeley County, (843) 572-4400; and in Dorchester County, (843) 832-0070.

RELOCATION

Retirement

With its mild climate and natural beauty, the Trident area is an attractive retirement destination. The mature market represents over 30 percent of the adult population here, and that number is growing every year. There are numerous residential communities, geared to different levels of independence, and a growing array of services in the business sector that are tailored to the needs of those enjoying their golden years. Many stores such as Rite-Aid, Harris Teeter, Publix, Lowe's, Belk, SteinMart, Ross, and Waccamaw Home Superstore even run regular discounts for shoppers 60 or older. A 1 percent sales tax discount is given to seniors age 85 and over.

The Charleston County Public Library system maintains a community information database that provides detailed listings of organizations and resources, many geared toward senior citizens. It is updated on a continual basis and can be accessed by contacting any of the 15 county libraries. A listing of the county libraries can be found in the blue pages of the phone book or on their website, ccpl.org. For more information about this useful resource, contact the Main Library at 68 Calhoun St., (843) 805-6930.

Walkway lined with live oaks, azalea, and Spanish moss

ADVANTAGE/SENIOR SERVICES, Roper Hospital, 1st Fl., 316 Calhoun St.; (843) 724-2489; rsfh.com/advantage. A senior services department at Roper St. Francis Healthcare is set up to deal with age-specific health issues. The Advantage program is a membership program for South Carolina residents of all ages but offers many senior-focused health and wellness classes. Membership also provides discounts on selected hospital services. Monthly meetings are held for an Alzheimer's support group, Mall Walkers, and an AARP chapter with locations in Roper Downtown, Roper North, and Bon Secours–St. Francis hospitals. Other community programs are offered throughout the year on topics such as healthy aging, memory and vascular health screenings, and strength training. Additional benefits include a no-cost discount prescription card, eyewear discounts, and insurance assistance. Advantage Gold membership costs a nominal fee per year. Basic membership offers fewer benefits but keeps South Carolina residents informed and is free.

CENTER FOR CREATIVE RETIREMENT, College of Charleston North Campus, 5300 International Blvd., North Charleston; (843) 216-6640; cofc .edu/academics. There is ample opportunity for seniors to join umbrella service organizations such as the Center for Creative Retirement at the College of Charleston, which is an affiliate of the Elder-hostel Institute Network. Classes are held at the St. Joseph's Family Center, 1695 Wallenberg Blvd. in the West Ashley area, during fall, winter, and spring. Noncredit courses comprise educational seminars, tours, lectures, and discussion groups. Some past topics have included "Bottlenose Dolphins and Human Health," "MUSC Study of Age-Related Hearing Loss," "Future of Print Media," "Middleton Barbados Connection," and "The Nostalgia of Model Trains." The annual membership fee is $50.

CHARLESTON AREA SENIOR CITIZENS SERVICES INC., 259 Meeting St.; (843) 722-4127; charlestonareaseniors.org. This nonprofit agency serves older adults in the Tri-County area. Its information and assistance line operates from 8 a.m. to 4 p.m. Mon through Fri. The senior center offers a noon meal, programs, activities, and health education. For the homebound, home-delivered meals and transportation on the Peninsula are provided. The agency's major focuses, which are making a difference in our community, are sponsorship of the Foster Grandparent Program and a job-training program with subsidized employment for people 55 and older. The agency also operates a 77-unit housing complex, Ansonborough House, for seniors.

RETIREMENT

CHARLESTON COUNTY COMMUNITY EDUCATION, Charleston County School District, 75 Calhoun St.; (843) 937-7910; charlestoncoce .org. For those who are ready to plunge into creative stimulation, an interesting option is the moderately priced Adult and Community Education Programs, sponsored jointly by the Charleston County School District and the Charleston County Park and Recreation Commission. Categories of classes encompass arts and crafts, business and vocational concerns, computers, culinary arts, fitness and health, language arts, sports, and special interests. The 10 community schools across Charleston County are the sites of the classroom instruction. Offerings run the gamut from 1-night, free sessions to 6-week classes with fees of up to $150. Charleston County residents age 60+ may request a Gold Card by calling the number above which allows a 20 percent discount off of class fees. Pick up information on the quarterly programs from the county school district offices on Calhoun Street or at Charleston County libraries. Please note that the district does not mail out class schedules.

COLLEGE OF CHARLESTON, 65 George St.; (843) 953-5620; cofc.edu; **THE CITADEL,** 171 Moultrie St.; (843) 225-3294; citadel.edu. South Carolina resident seniors 60 or older who are not employed full-time and are eager for an intellectual challenge can take any of the wide array of courses offered (on a space-available basis) at these two outstanding Charleston colleges. The cost is just $25 a semester at the College of Charleston. The costs are a $15 registration fee plus a $25 technology fee, and a one-time application fee of $30 at The Citadel (parking is $40).

LOWCOUNTRY SENIOR CENTER, 865 Riverland Dr.; (843) 762-9555; lowcountryseniorcenter.org. After more than 5 years of fund-raising and planning, the new 10,500-square-foot Lowcountry Senior Center opened in the spring of 2002. The concept behind the center was to build a place for active seniors who want more out of life than "sitting in front of the tube all day." The center, managed by Roper St. Francis Healthcare, serves adults age 50 and older with a wide variety of programs and coordinated activities focused on wellness, education, fitness, recreation, and volunteer services. It also serves as a resource for senior-oriented information and houses a computer lab, fitness and arts and crafts rooms, and a main room for social activities like dancing, movies, and wine tastings. The Lowcountry Senior Center is located near the entrance to the James Island County Park on Riverland Drive and offers ample free parking. One-year memberships are $70 for Charleston County residents and $80 for nonresidents. Gold memberships including use of the fitness room are $105 for county residents and $115 for nonresidents.

TRIDENT SENIOR HEALTH CENTER, 9302 Medical Plaza Dr., Ste. C; (843) 797-0416; tridenthealthsystem.com. Under the umbrella of the Trident Health System the Senior Health Center provides health care that meets the needs of residents age 65 and older. The center, which accepts Medicare assignments, is near Northwoods Mall. Staffed by Board-certified primary care physicians with advanced training in geriatric medicine, the center also includes nurses, a geriatrician, and other health care professionals who are experienced in the special needs of the senior population. Primary medical care is provided for chronic illnesses such as heart disease, diabetes, and Alzheimer's. Trident Senior Health Center also takes a partnership role in wellness, with monthly health education programs, health screenings, and a senior health library. Additional assistance is offered with insurance or billing questions as well as other social service needs.

RETIREMENT HOUSING

Charleston offers retirement housing options ranging from resort living to private-patio or high-rise apartments to supervised care. The choice is yours, depending on the physical wants and needs of those involved, as well as budget. Note that we do not include the resort areas (Kiawah, Seabrook, and Wild Dunes) in this chapter. The resorts are upscale choices that are popular with many retirement-age residents, but they do not offer any provisions for assisted living. See the Accommodations, Welcome to Greater Charleston, and Golf chapters for more specific information about resort properties and amenities. The following living arrangements for seniors in the Trident area are a sampling of what is available.

Retirement Apartments

CANTERBURY HOUSE, 175 and 165 Market St.; (843) 723-5553. Those interested in relocating into an apartment building for seniors will find the Canterbury House an appealing option. The Episcopal Church–sponsored complex added a new building in 2000, Canterbury House East, of 46 1-bedroom apartments to the original one of 204 apartments. The location on the Peninsula is within easy walking distance of shopping on King and Market Streets. The independent-living facility offers efficiencies, 1-bedroom efficiencies, and 1-bedroom apartments for seniors 62 years old and older whose income does not exceed certain specified levels for individuals or couples. Location and convenient parking make it handy for visitors and volunteers such as local musicians and children's choirs, who participate in special programs for residents.

There is usually a lengthy waiting list for these apartments, so get your name in early if the Canterbury House is the place for you.

Retirement & Life-Care Communities

BISHOP GADSDEN EPISCOPAL RETIREMENT COMMUNITY, 1 Bishop Gadsden Way; (843) 762-3300, (800) 373-2384; bishopgadsden.org. Affiliated with the Episcopal Church, Bishop Gadsden is on a 70-acre site on James Island. Members enjoy the benefits of group living in a lovely setting and are often entertained and enlightened with lectures or presentations by volunteers from Episcopal churches and others in the community. An assisted-living option is also available. A 1999 expansion added 215 apartments and individual homes to the existing facility, and further expansion plans are in the works. A full range of amenities includes a wellness center, pool, casual and formal dining, beauty parlor, banks, a chapel, and convenience stores on the premises. Services such as skilled nursing and dementia care make Bishop Gadsden the only nonprofit, church-sponsored life-care community in the state.

THE ELMS OF CHARLESTON, 9100 Elms Plantation Blvd., North Charleston; (843) 572-8170; theelmsofcharleston.org. The Elms is a beautifully landscaped, controlled-access, 55+ community of custom-built patio homes, duplexes, town houses, and condominiums. Next to Charleston Southern University and Trident Regional Medical Center, the amenities at the Elms are extensive and include tennis and croquet courts and an 8,000-square-foot clubhouse with a fitness center, swimming pool, exercise area, spa, and library. The Wannamaker County Park with walking trails borders the property. Shopping, dining, golf, and other cultural opportunities are minutes away. Management maintains the yard and home exteriors. Assisted living and long-term care are in nearby facilities.

FRANKE AT SEASIDE, 1885 Rifle Range Rd., Mount Pleasant; (843) 856-4713, (800) 940-7435; frankeatseaside.org. This residential-care facility, operated by Lutheran Homes of South Carolina, is located in Mount Pleasant, just 1 mile from the beach at the Isle of Palms. It offers private and companion rooms with some assistance available. A full-time staff of licensed practical nurses and certified nursing assistants provides quality medical attention. There are 158 1- and 2-bedroom apartments in 3 buildings as well as 75 patio homes for independent living options. Residents enjoy a wellness program, meals, housekeeping, and transportation. Emotional support is offered through family support groups, volunteer interaction, and a chapel program. A new 44-bed skilled nursing center was recently added to the community, and plans are under way for additional independent living cottages, patio homes, and apartments. The Burges Center is a 24,000-square-foot resident's club and wellness center.

THE PALMS OF MOUNT PLEASANT, 937 Bowman Rd., Mount Pleasant; (843) 884-6949; thepalmsofmtpleasant.com. Several options are available at The Palms, including apartments, lakefront villas, and assisted-living quarters. A 2008 $3.5 million facelift of the former Cooper Hall upgraded the full range of choices available here. Assisted-living options include studio and 1- or 2-bedroom apartments with kitchens and private bathrooms. Housekeeping services, respite care, medication management, 3 meals a day plus snacks, and a full slate of recreational activities are offered with transportation into town. Those in retirement living may choose from standard or deluxe 1- or 2-bedroom apartments with amenities such as an indoor swimming pool, piano cocktail lounge, hair salon, laundry facility, fitness center, and billiard rooms. There is a licensed nurse on call at all hours, and residents can order from the dining room menu.

> **i** For active and retired businesspeople who want to lend a helping hand to young entrepreneurs and their start-up businesses, there's the Service Corps of Retired Executives (SCORE). These counselors offer in-depth, one-on-one consulting to help their clients plan, market, manage, and package their ideas. They can be reached at (843) 727-4778, or visit score285.org.

PRESBYTERIAN COMMUNITY IN SUMMERVILLE, 201 West 9th North St., Summerville; (843) 873-2550, (866) 315-4725; preshomesc.org. The independent living options at this Presbyterian Community called The Village at Summerville include 59 outside cottages, 20 efficiency apartments, and 17 2-bedroom apartments. There are also 120 residential rooms with private baths, and residents are served 3 meals a day. Assisted living is an option here. On-site are a beauty shop, barber services, and entertainment such as field trips to the Spoleto Festival, Monday night movies, ceramics, painting, and exercise classes. Bible classes and chapel are conducted, and transportation to the doctor or shopping facilities is furnished. Licensed nurses run a 90-bed infirmary. Opened in 1958, this community gives priority to South Carolina resident Presbyterians.

SANDPIPER VILLAGE, 1224 Village Creek Ln., Mount Pleasant; (843) 884-5735; premierseniorliving.com. Sandpiper Village is an 11-acre campus-like gated community with independent living in 1- and 2-bedroom cottage-style homes. These attractive residences have front and rear entrances with convenient access to the Community Center. The Sandpiper Courtyard apartments offer assisted living. Meals, housekeeping, transportation to doctor appointments, and emergency call buttons are included. Home health care, rehab, and skilled nursing facilities are available as well. Daily activities and social events including bingo, bridge, arts and crafts, church services. Amenities offered are a beauty and barbershop, spa, gentlemen's club, heated swimming pool, exercise room, media center, and a library.

SWEETGRASS VILLAGE SENIOR LIVING COMMUNITY, 601 Mathis Ferry Rd., Mount Pleasant; (843) 881-9809; sweetgrassvillageseniorliving.com. Opened in 2000, this center offers 4 floor plans in room or suite choices. Varying levels of care are available from short-term and traditional assisted living. The 69-unit facility offers licensed nursing care on-site 24 hours a day. Amenities include activity/exercise rooms, lounges, a library, outdoor patios, a housekeeping/linen service, and a beauty and barbershop. A full-time social director is on staff. Small pets are welcome. A nearby facility for Alzheimer's and memory care patients called Sweetgrass Court is affiliated with Sweetgrass Village Senior Living.

RETIREMENT

Media

The Greater Charleston area ranks 99th among the nation's television markets. There are affiliates for all three major television networks, plus Fox Broadcasting and the Public Broadcasting System. The largest cable television provider is Comcast Cablevision, serving the Greater Charleston area. Be sure to check in your specific area, since new cable, Internet, and mobile communications providers are springing up across the Lowcountry.

TELEVISION

The major cable provider in the Greater Charleston area is Comcast Cable (comcast.com, 843-554-4100). Comcast serves Charleston, Johns Island, Folly Beach, Kiawah, Seabrook, Wadmalaw, Wild Dunes, Awendaw, Edisto Beach, and the Hollywood–Ravenel area. The satellite companies, Dish Network and DirecTV, are other options. The following is a list of local network affiliates, with the cable channel numbers.

WCBD, Channel 2 (NBC)—Comcast (Channel 3)

WCIV, Channel 4 (ABC)—Comcast (8)

WCSC, Channel 5 (CBS)—Comcast (9)

WITV, Channel 7 (PBS)—Comcast (11)

WTAT, Channel 24 (FOX)—Comcast (6)

NEWSPAPERS

Daily

The Post and Courier, 134 Columbus St.; (843) 577-7111; postand courier.com.

Weekly

Berkeley Independent, 323-B East Main St., Moncks Corner; (843) 761-6397; berkeleyind.com.

Catalyst (MUSC newspaper), 135 Cannon St.; (843) 792-4107; musc .edu/catalyst.

Charleston Chronicle, 1111 King St.; (843) 723-2785; charlestonchronicle.net.

Charleston Mercury, 193 King St., Ste. 2A.; (843) 793-3723; charleston mercury.com.

The Daniel Island News, 225 Seven Farms Dr., Ste. 108, Daniel Island; (843) 856-1999; thedanielislandnews.com.

The Gazette, 104 East Doty Ave., Summerville; (843) 572-0511; ourgazette.com.

Hanahan Goose Creek North Charleston News, 1231 Yeaman's Hall Rd., North Charleston; (843) 744-8000.

Moultrie News, 134 Columbus St., (843) 958-7482, moultrienews.com.

The Patriot, PO Box 2016, Mount Pleasant; (843) 412-5861; charlestonmilitary.com.

Summerville Journal Scene, 104 East Doty Ave., Summerville; (843) 873-9424; journalscene.com.

TABLOIDS

Charleston City Paper, 1049 B Morrison Dr.; (843) 577-5304; charleston citypaper.com.

Charleston Regional Business Journal, 1439 Stuart Engals Blvd., Ste. 200, Mount Pleasant; (843) 849-3100; charlestonbusiness.com.

Island Life, PO Box 447, John's Island, SC 29457; (843) 768-4404; islandlife.homestead.com.

Skirt!, 1 Henrietta St., 1st Fl.; (843) 958-0028; charleston.skirt.com.

MAGAZINES

Charleston Gateway, PO Box 80626, Charleston, SC 29416; (843) 224-5865; charlestongateway.com.

Charleston Magazine, PO Box 1794, Mount Pleasant; (843) 971-9811; charlestonmag.com.

Traveler of Charleston, (843) 580-9054; travelerofcharleston.com

Where Charleston, wheretraveler.com.

Index

Acknowledgments

For their input, expertise, and assistance in many forms, many thanks go to all who helped with the production of this book, including the research departments at the Charleston Area Convention and Visitors Bureau, the Avery Research Center for African-American History and Culture, the Charleston County Public Library, Historic Charleston Foundation, the South Carolina Department of Natural Resources, and the Public Affairs office of the 437th Airlift Wing at Charleston Air Force Base.

Gracious thanks go as well to the various Lowcountry attractions whose staffs provided information enhancing descriptions for this book.

Lee also extends her appreciation to her mother, Rachel Davis, for her diligent archival research and to her husband, Rhett Perry, for his encouragement and support. A nod goes to her yellow lab, Brummy, for providing several much-needed diversions involving tossing her retrieving decoy into the otherwise serene waters of Lake Murray.

With poignant memories, Lee reflects on the contributions of the late Mike McLaughlin, coauthor of previous editions, for his beautiful descriptions of the Charleston Lowcountry. His love and enthusiasm for the "Holy City" remain an inspiration for these pages.

Finally, thanks go to Amy Lyons and Lauren Brancato for working on a schedule that was career-friendly for all concerned. And thanks to Globe Pequot for recognizing the value of the Insiders' Guide series and for opting to bring it to the people in markets all over the country, where the information can be used and appreciated.

About the Author

Lee Davis Perry was raised in Charleston and returned to her beloved city in 1987 after pursuing her education and a 9-year stint away in "the urban fast lane." Lee received a journalism degree from the University of Georgia in 1976. In 1979 she began her career in Atlanta, working for several ad agencies, among them J. Walter Thompson USA, where she was a senior media planner.

The pull of the ocean and the traditions of her childhood proved too strong to abandon for long, though: "Who says you can't go home again? Being away from Charleston only sharpened my focus on the city's enduring appeal." Lee has also coauthored, with the late Michael McLaughlin, a short volume of stories relating South Carolina history, Globe Pequot's *It Happened in South Carolina* (2011) and also *South Carolina Curiosities* (2011). Another endeavor for a popular Globe series is *More than Petticoats: Remarkable South Carolina Women,* a collection of brief biographies of outstanding women from her native state.

Lee and her husband, Rhett, divide their time between the Lowcountry and the Midlands of South Carolina. Both locales provide the perfect settings to contemplate the timeless beauty, vitality, and diversity of Charleston and the Palmetto State.